E YOU.
THAT'S WHY I LIKE YOU."

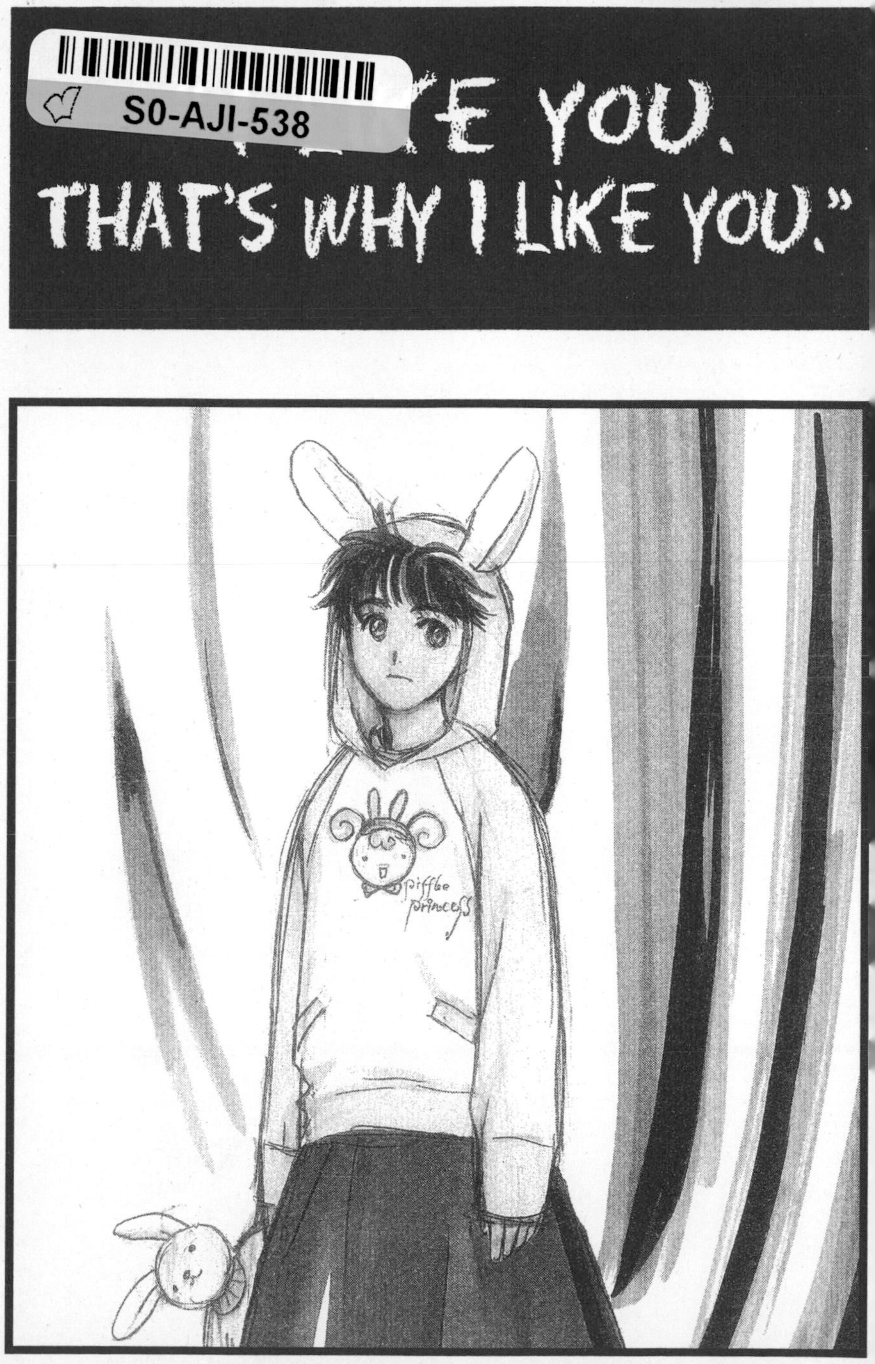
piffle
princess

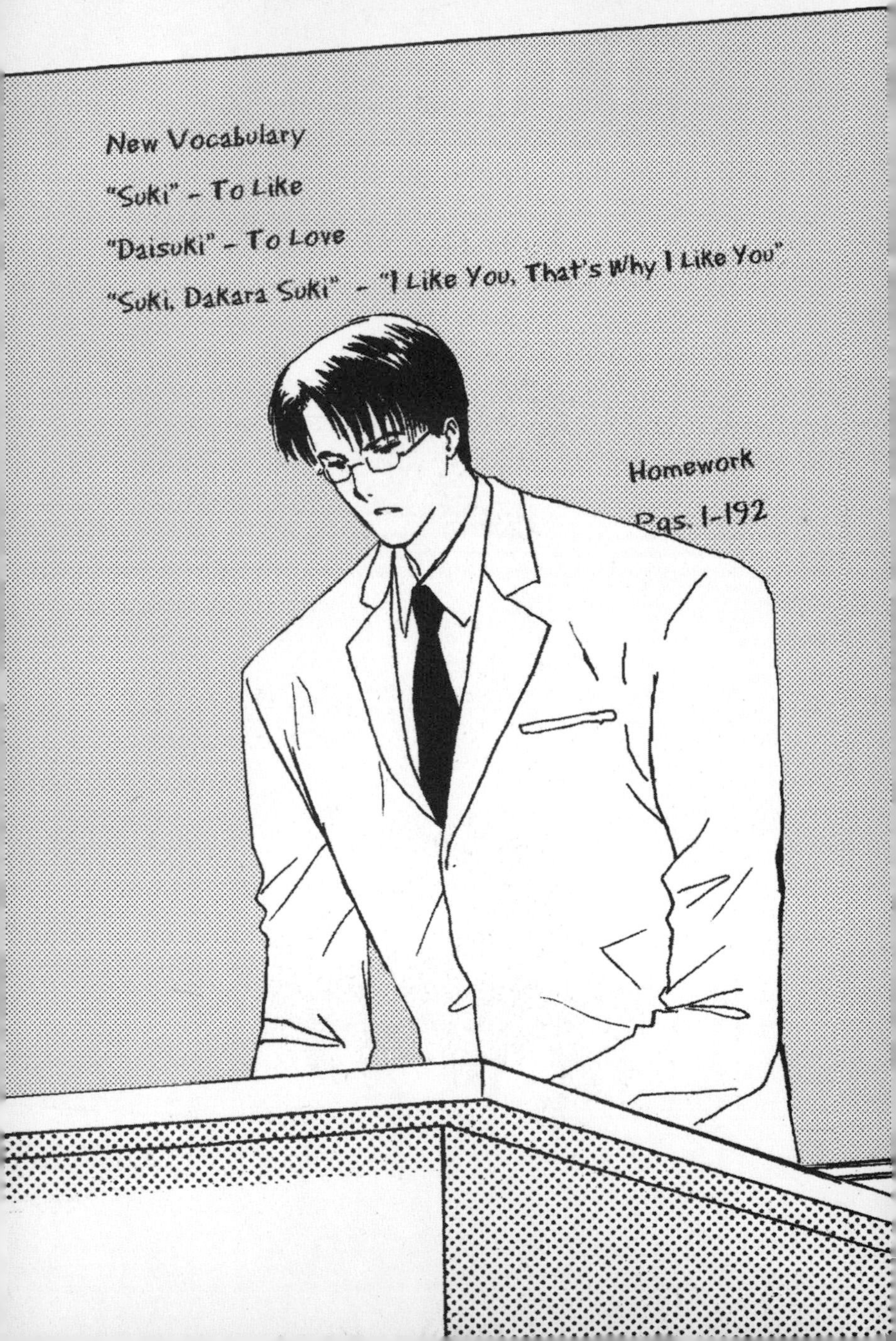
New Vocabulary
"Suki" - To Like
"Daisuki" - To Love
"Suki, Dakara Suki" - "I Like You, That's Why I Like You"
Homework
Pgs. 1-192

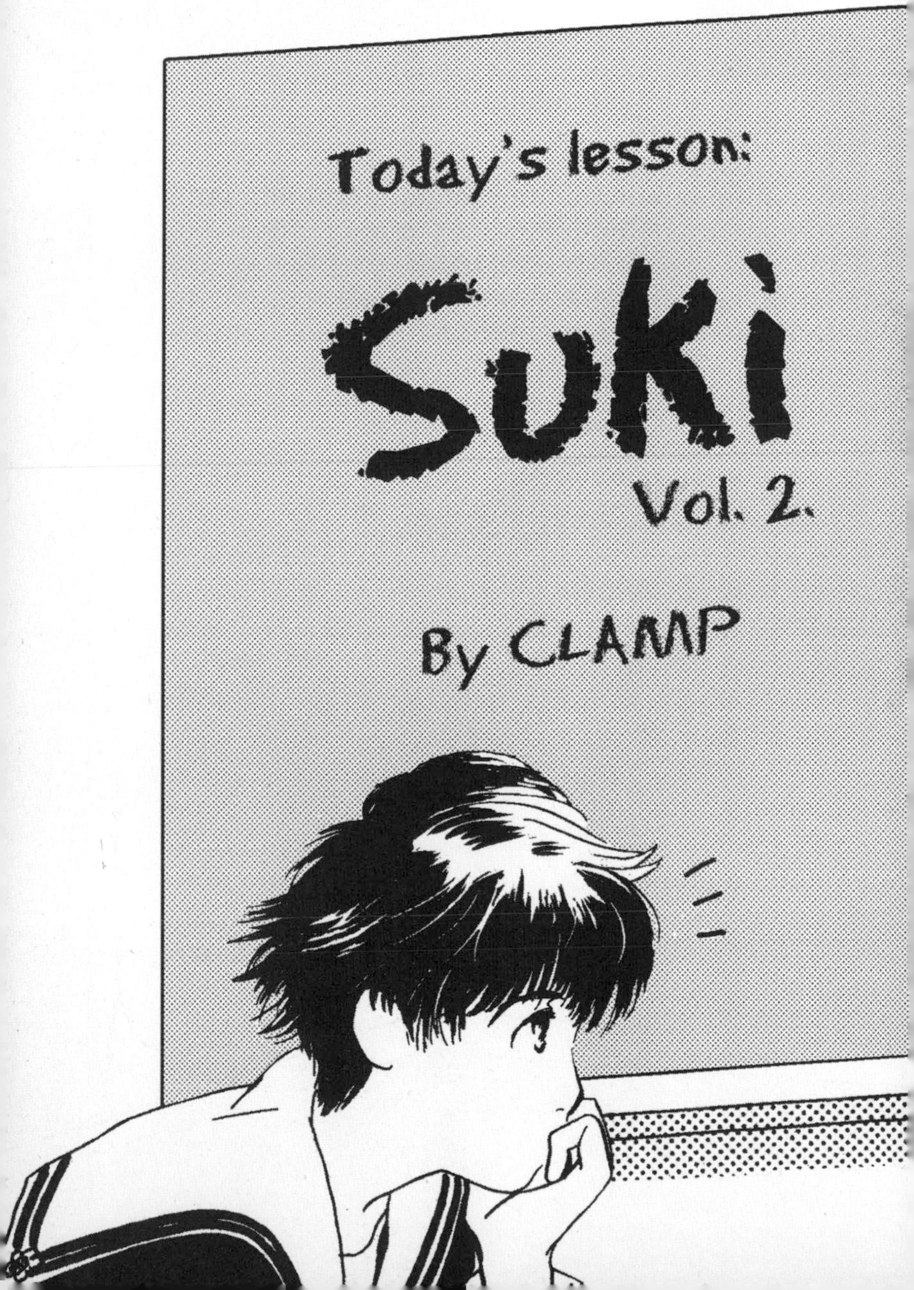
Today's lesson:
Suki
Vol. 2.
By CLAMP

Translator - Ray Yoshimoto
English Adaptation - Carol Fox
Retouch and Lettering - Abelardo Bigting
Cover Layout - Christian Lownds
Graphic Designer - Anna Kernbaum

Editor - Jake Forbes
Digital Imaging Manager - Chris Buford
Pre-Press Manager - Antonio DePietro
Production Managers - Jennifer Miller, Mutsumi Miyazaki
Art Director - Matt Alford
Managing Editor - Jill Freshney
VP of Production - Ron Klamert
President & C.O.O. - John Parker
Publisher & C.E.O. - Stuart Levy

E-mail: info@TOKYOPOP.com

Come visit us online at www.TOKYOPOP.com

A  Manga

TOKYOPOP Inc.
5900 Wilshire Blvd. Suite 2000
Los Angeles, CA 90036

Suki Vol. 2

SUKI. DAKARA SUKI volume 2 © 1999 by CLAMP
First published in Japan in 1999 by KADOKAWA SHOTEN PUBLISHING CO., LTD., Tokyo.
English translation rights arranged with KADOKAWA SHOTEN PUBLISHING CO., LTD.,
Tokyo through TUTTLE-MORI AGENCY, INC., Tokyo.

ISBN: 1-59182-761-2

First TOKYOPOP printing: April 2004

10 9 8 7 6 5 4 3 2 1

Printed in the USA

TABLE OF CONTENTS

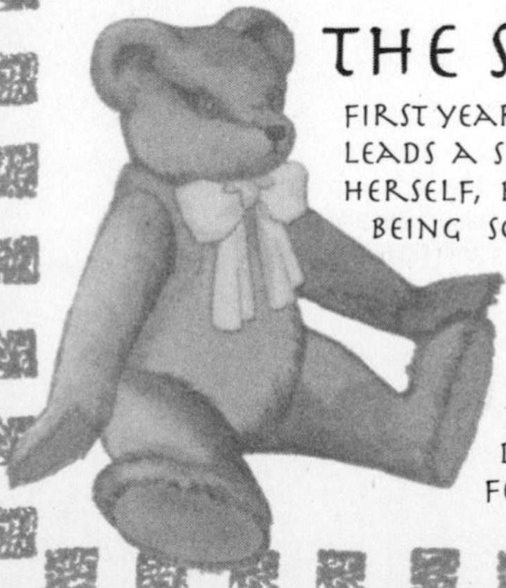

THE STORY SO FAR...

FIRST YEAR HIGH SCHOOL STUDENT HINATA ASAHI LEADS A SOLITARY LIFE. SHE NOT ONLY LIVES BY HERSELF, BUT AT SCHOOL SHE'S PICKED ON FOR BEING SO NAIVE. HER LIFE BECOMES A LOT MORE INTERESTING WHEN THE NEW HOMEROOM TEACHER, SHIRO ASOU, MOVES INTO THE HOUSE NEXT DOOR. AS HINA STARTS TO SPEND TIME WITH THIS MYSTERIOUS, OLDER MAN, SHE DISCOVERS AN EMOTION SHE'D NEVER FELT BEFORE—COULD IT BE LOVE?

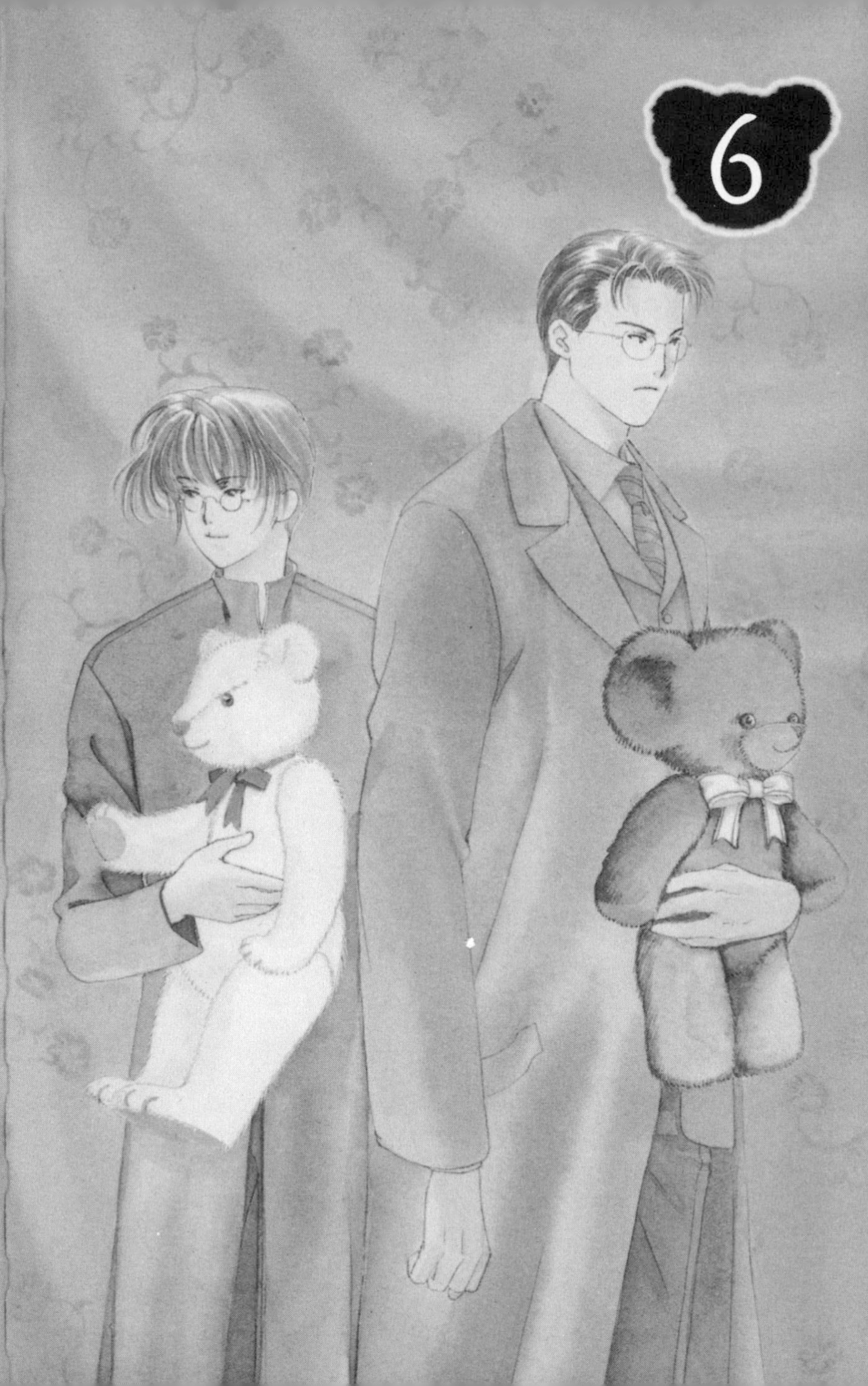
6

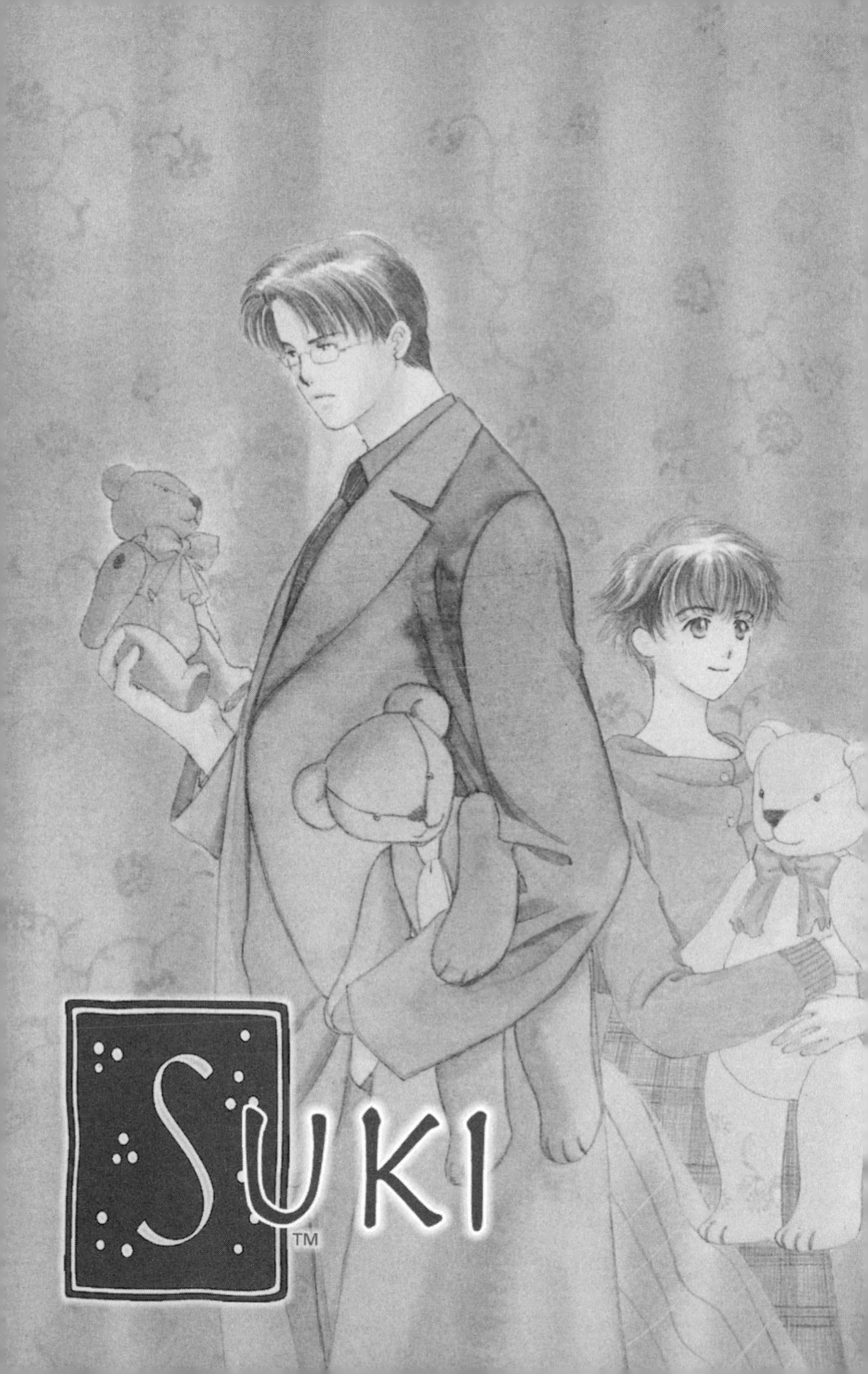
SUKI™

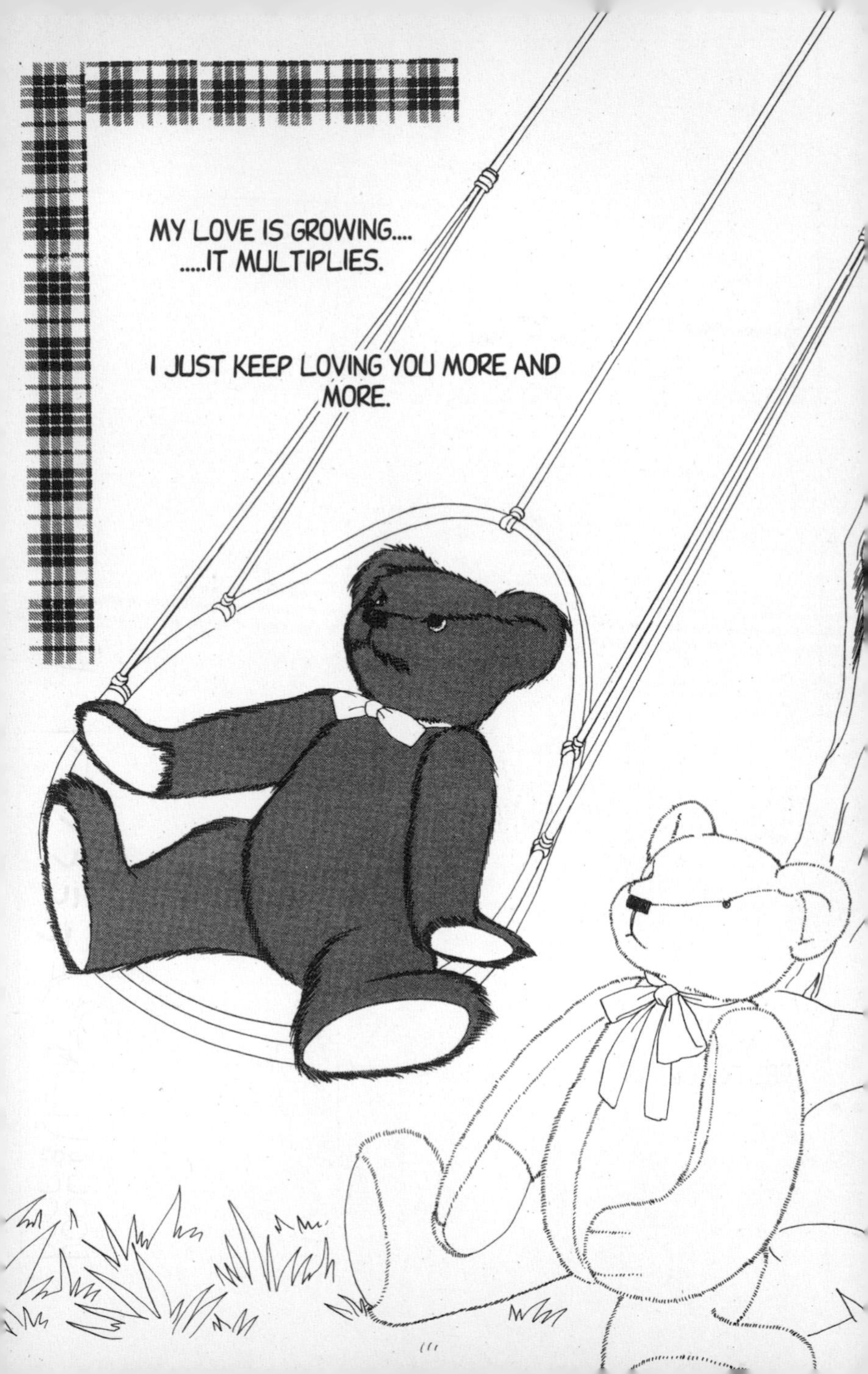
MY LOVE IS GROWING....
.....IT MULTIPLIES.
I JUST KEEP LOVING YOU MORE AND MORE.

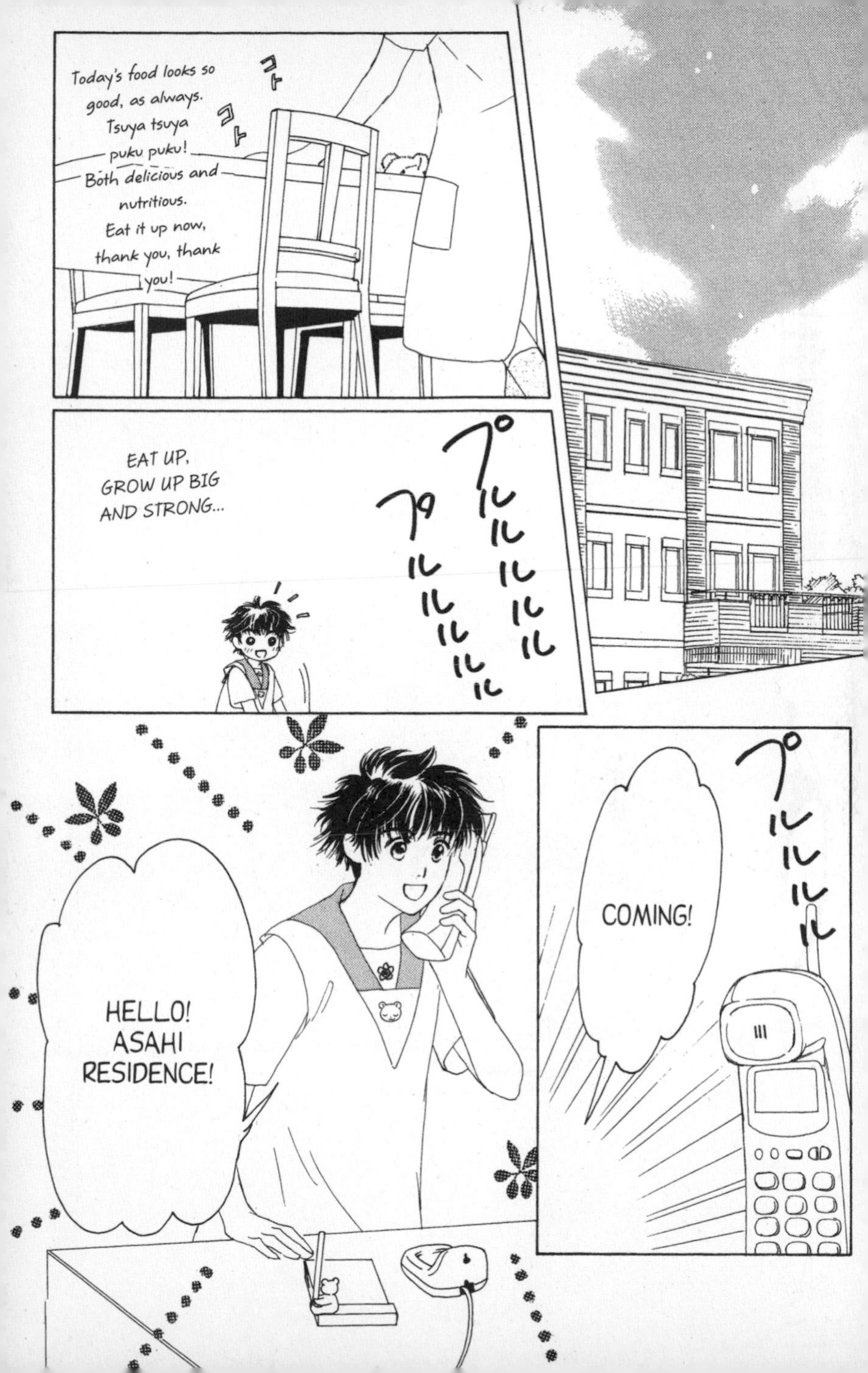

コト
コト
Today's food looks so good, as always. Tsuya tsuya puku puku! Both delicious and nutritious. Eat it up now, thank you, thank you!
プルルルル
プルルルル
EAT UP, GROW UP BIG AND STRONG...
プルルル
COMING!
HELLO! ASAHI RESIDENCE!

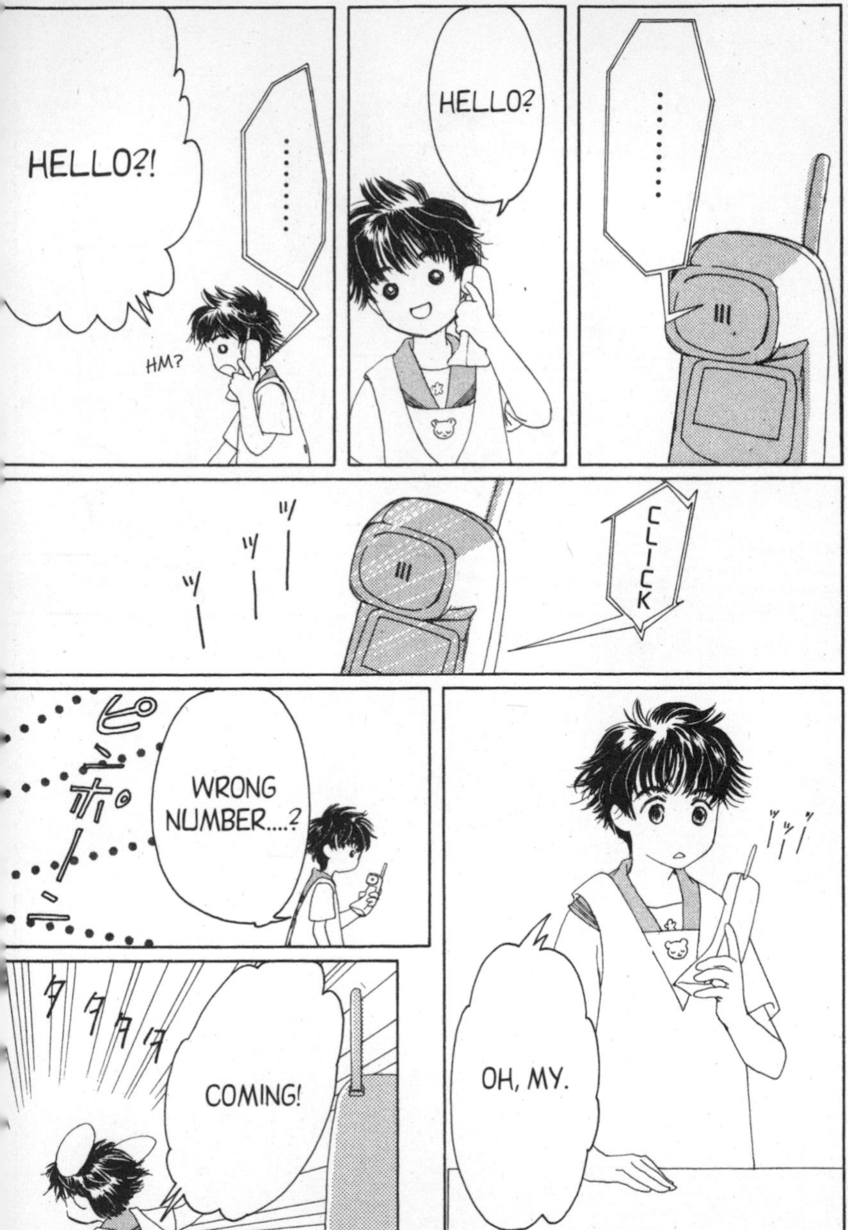
....
HELLO?
....
HELLO?!
HM?
CLICK
ツー
ツー
ツー
OH, MY.
ツツ
WRONG NUMBER....?
ピンポーン
COMING!
タタタタ

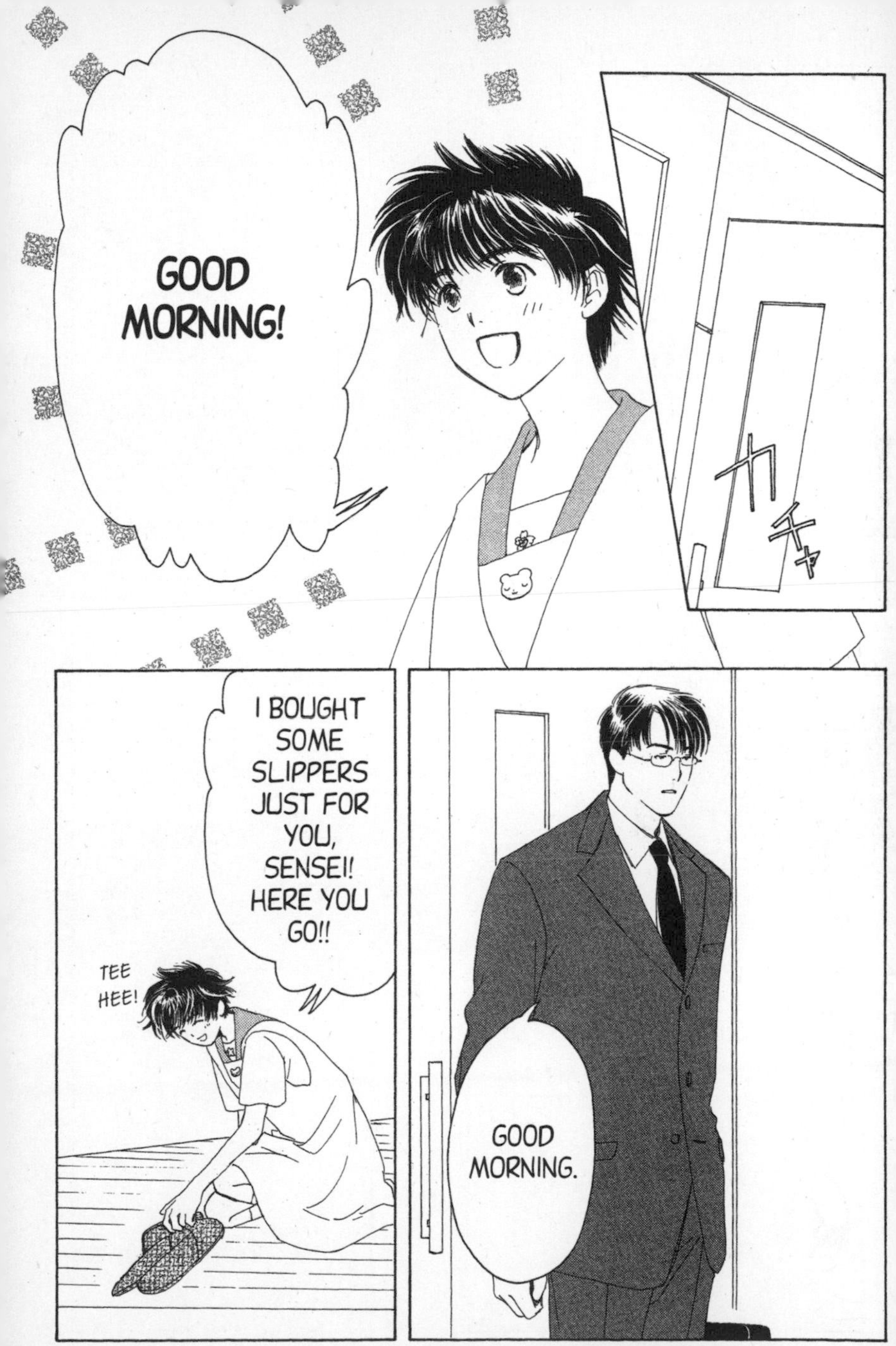
カチャ
GOOD MORNING!
GOOD MORNING.
I BOUGHT SOME SLIPPERS JUST FOR YOU, SENSEI! HERE YOU GO!!
TEE HEE!

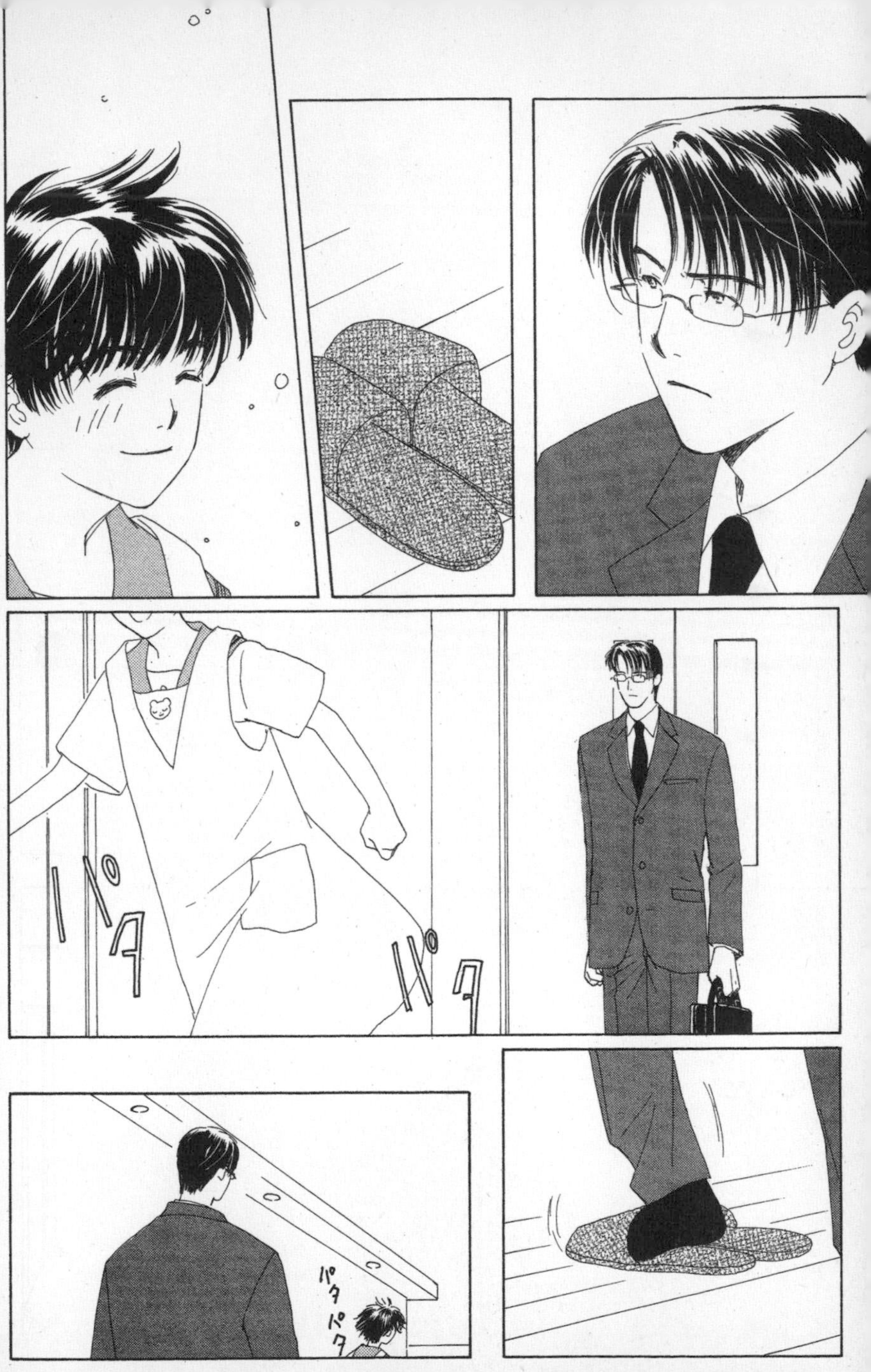
パタ
パタ
パタパタ

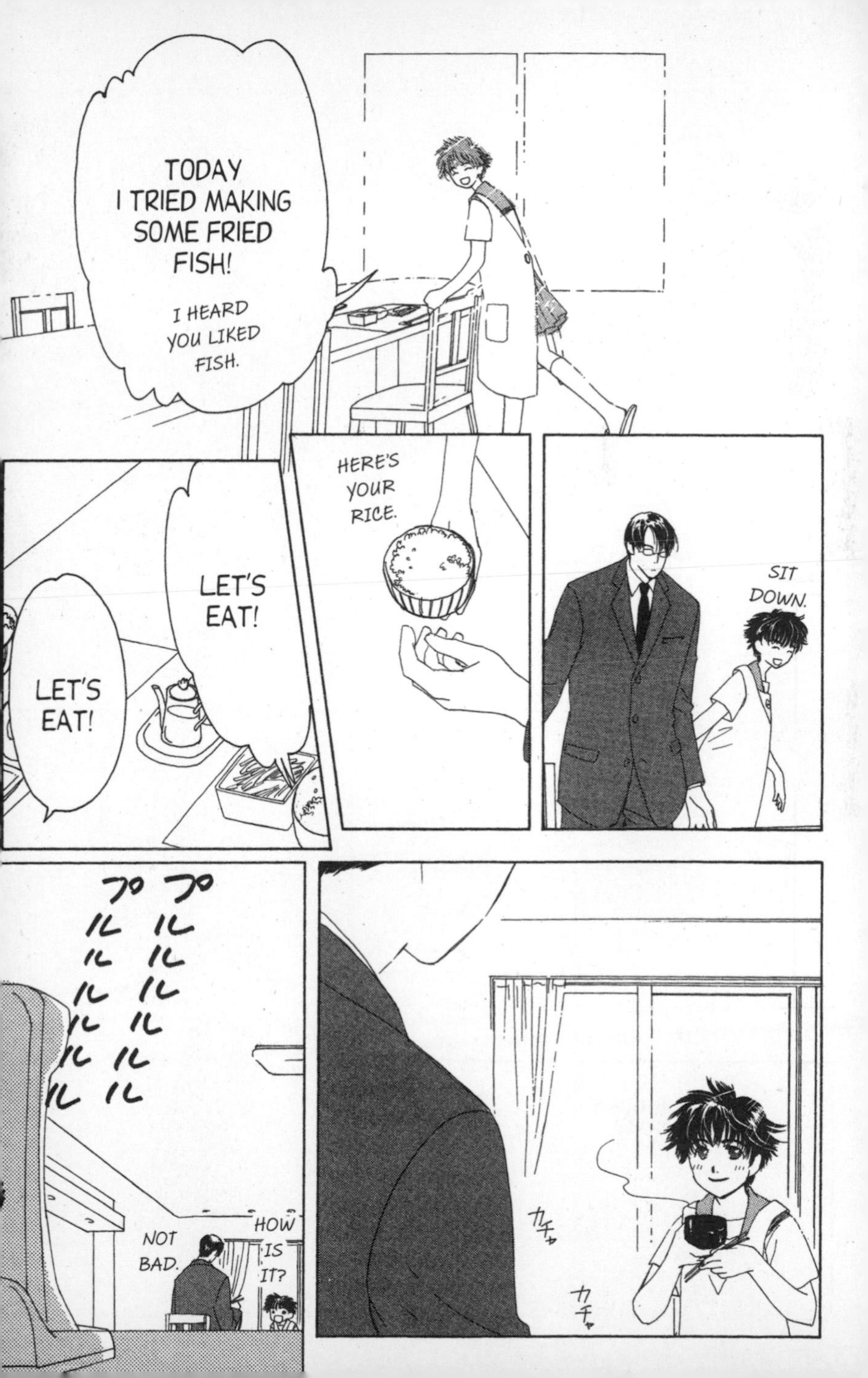
TODAY I TRIED MAKING SOME FRIED FISH!
I HEARD YOU LIKED FISH.
SIT DOWN.
HERE'S YOUR RICE.
LET'S EAT!
LET'S EAT!
カチャ
カチャ
プルルルルルル
プルルルルルル
HOW IS IT?
NOT BAD.

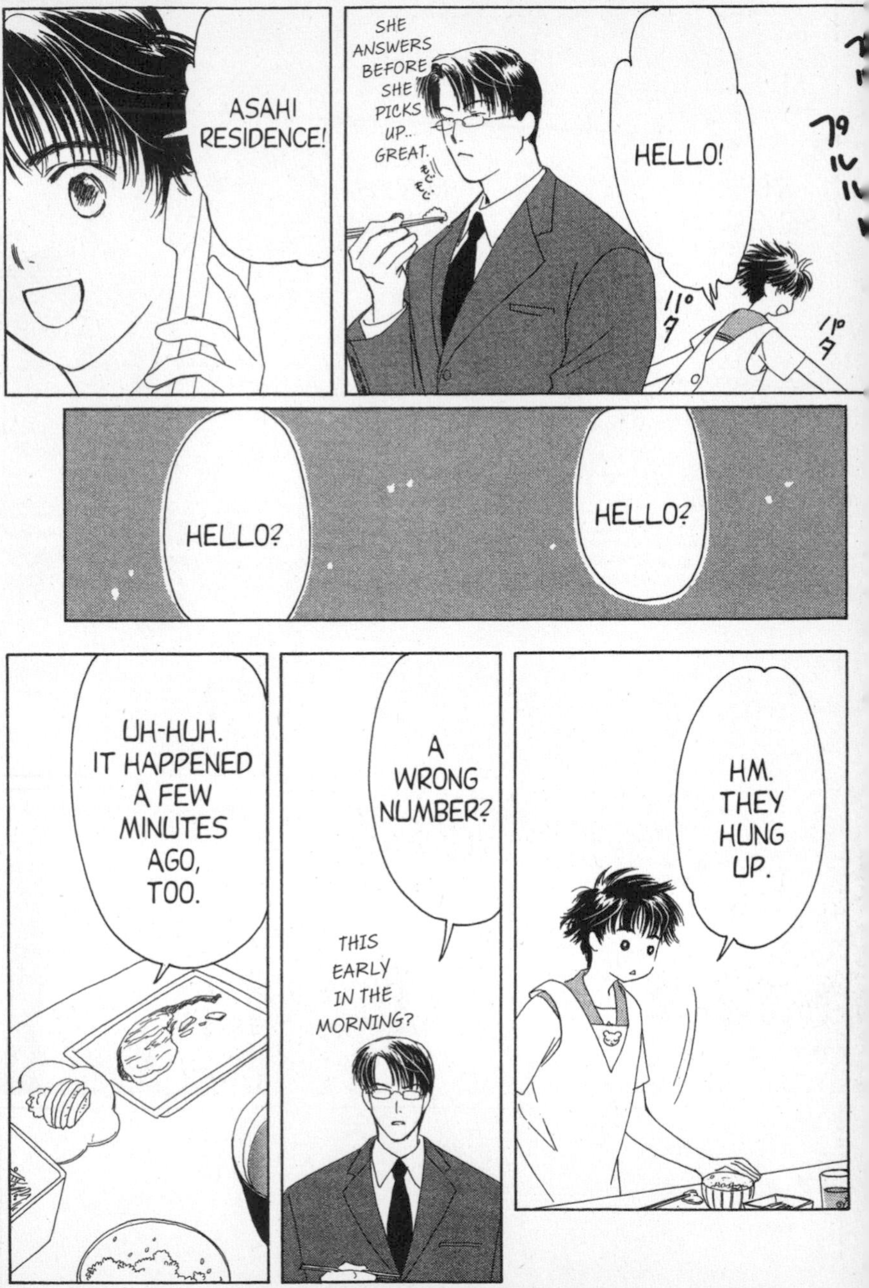
HELLO!
パタ
パタ
SHE ANSWERS BEFORE SHE PICKS UP.. GREAT.
もぐもぐ
ASAHI RESIDENCE!
HELLO?
HELLO?
HM. THEY HUNG UP.
A WRONG NUMBER?
THIS EARLY IN THE MORNING?
UH-HUH. IT HAPPENED A FEW MINUTES AGO, TOO.

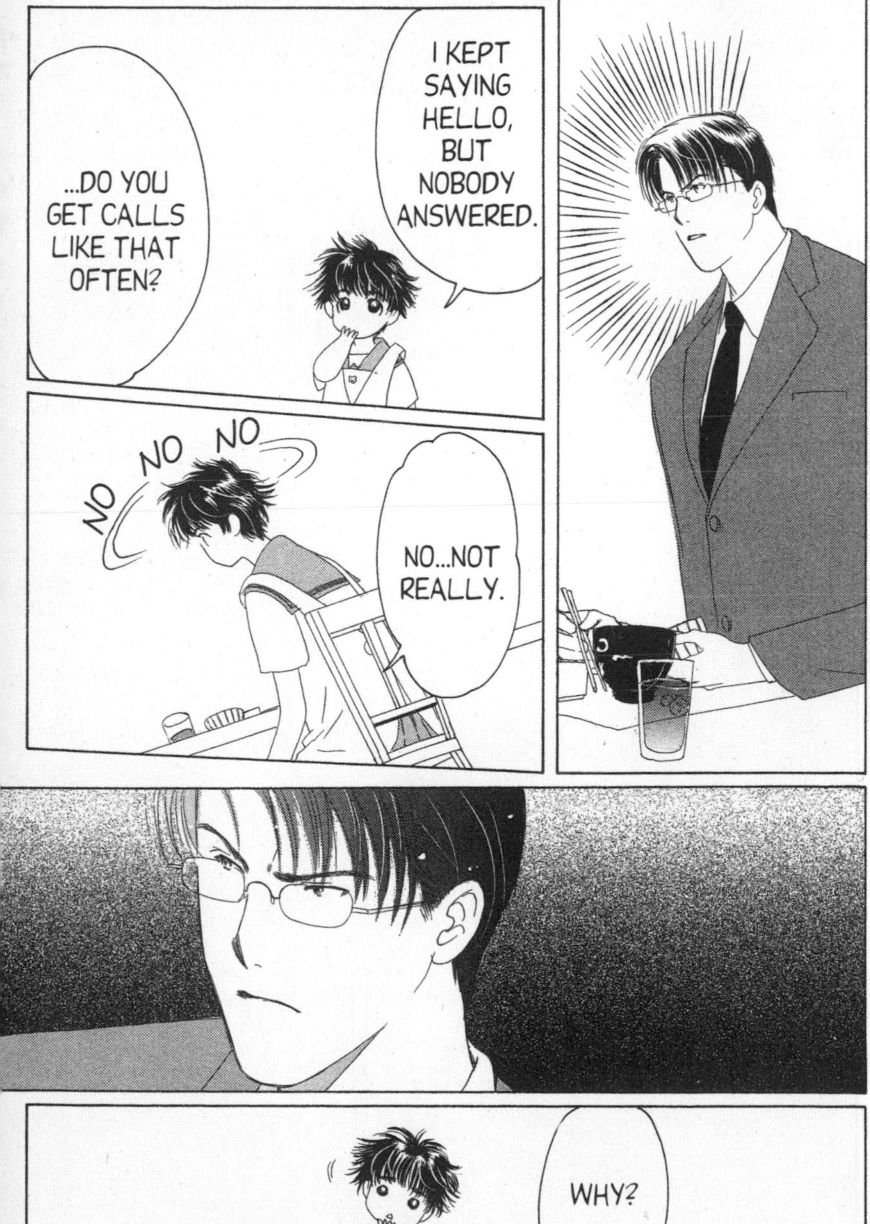
I KEPT SAYING HELLO, BUT NOBODY ANSWERED.
...DO YOU GET CALLS LIKE THAT OFTEN?
NO...NOT REALLY.
NO NO NO
WHY?

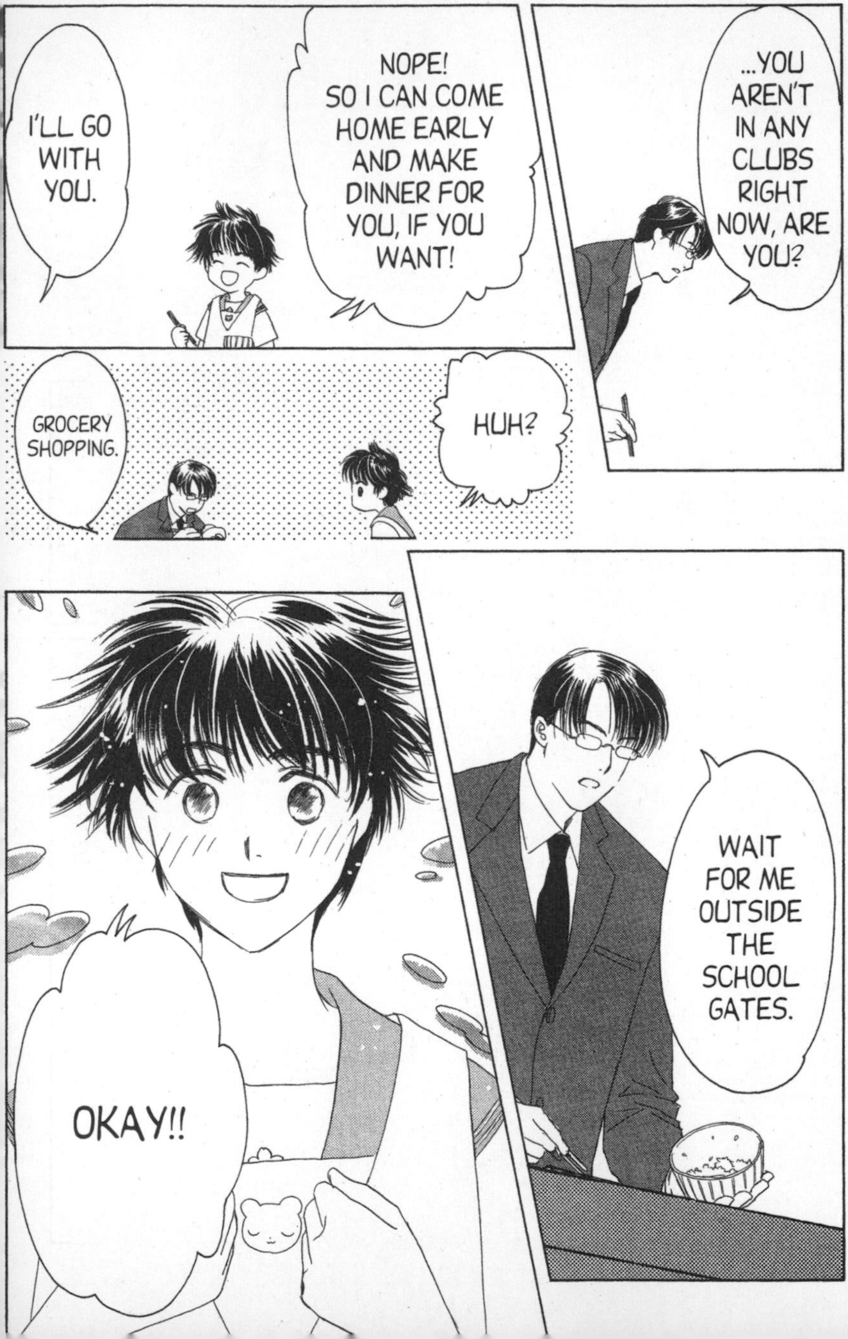
...YOU AREN'T IN ANY CLUBS RIGHT NOW, ARE YOU?
NOPE! SO I CAN COME HOME EARLY AND MAKE DINNER FOR YOU, IF YOU WANT!
I'LL GO WITH YOU.
HUH?
GROCERY SHOPPING.
WAIT FOR ME OUTSIDE THE SCHOOL GATES.
OKAY!!

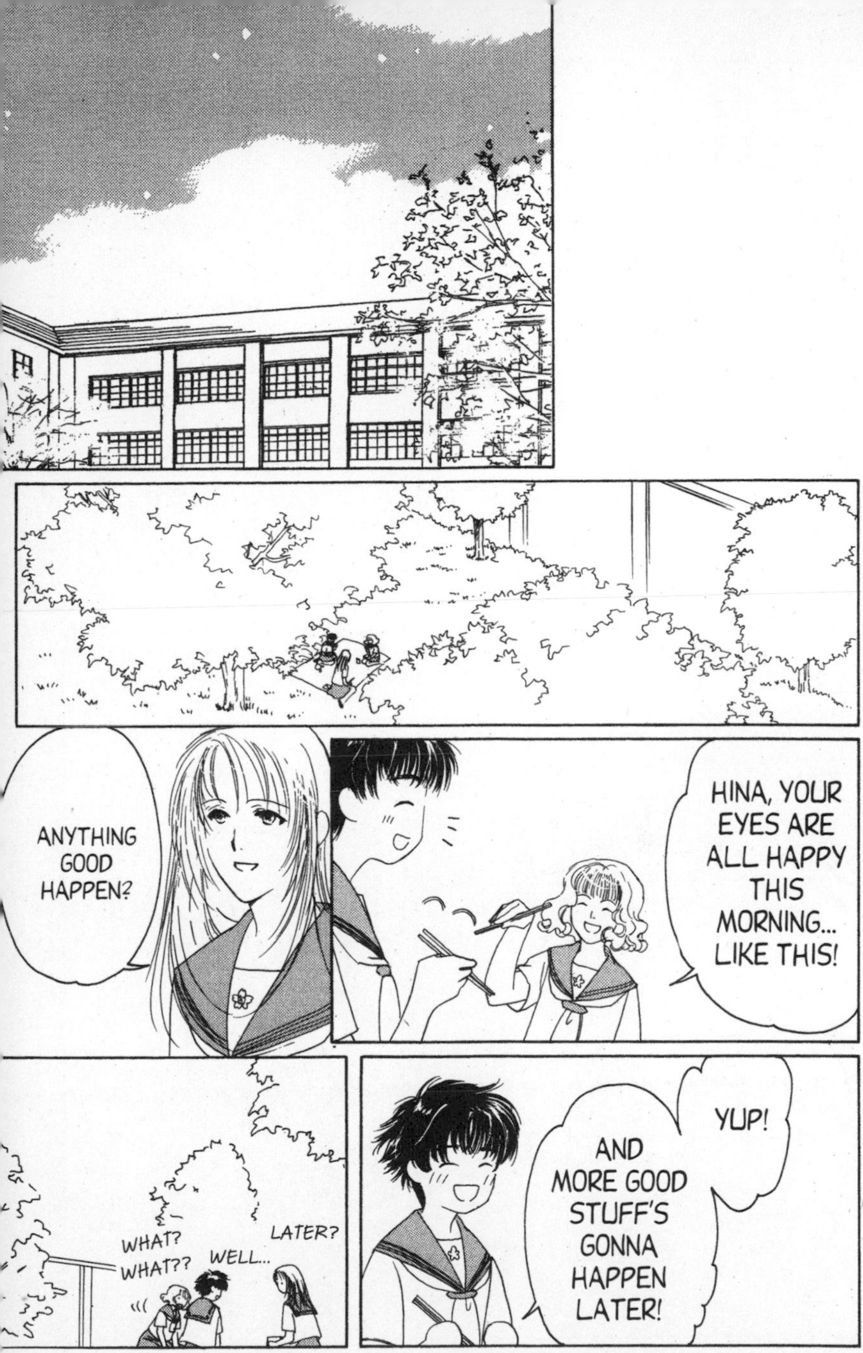
HINA, YOUR EYES ARE ALL HAPPY THIS MORNING... LIKE THIS!
ANYTHING GOOD HAPPEN?
YUP!
AND MORE GOOD STUFF'S GONNA HAPPEN LATER!
LATER?
WHAT? WHAT??
WELL...

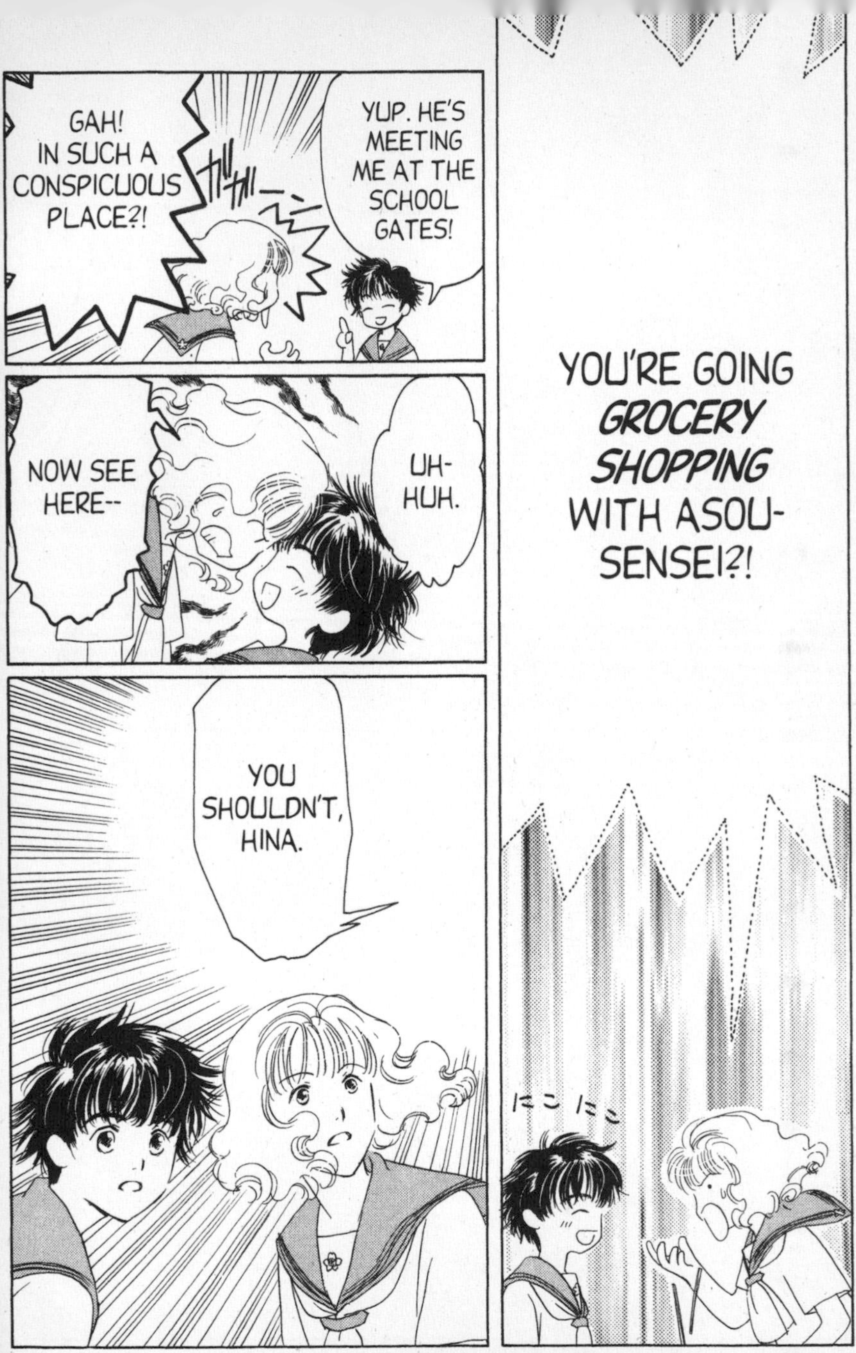
YOU'RE GOING GROCERY SHOPPING WITH ASOU-SENSEI?!
にこ にこ
YUP. HE'S MEETING ME AT THE SCHOOL GATES!
GAH! IN SUCH A CONSPICUOUS PLACE?!
UH-HUH.
NOW SEE HERE--
YOU SHOULDN'T, HINA.

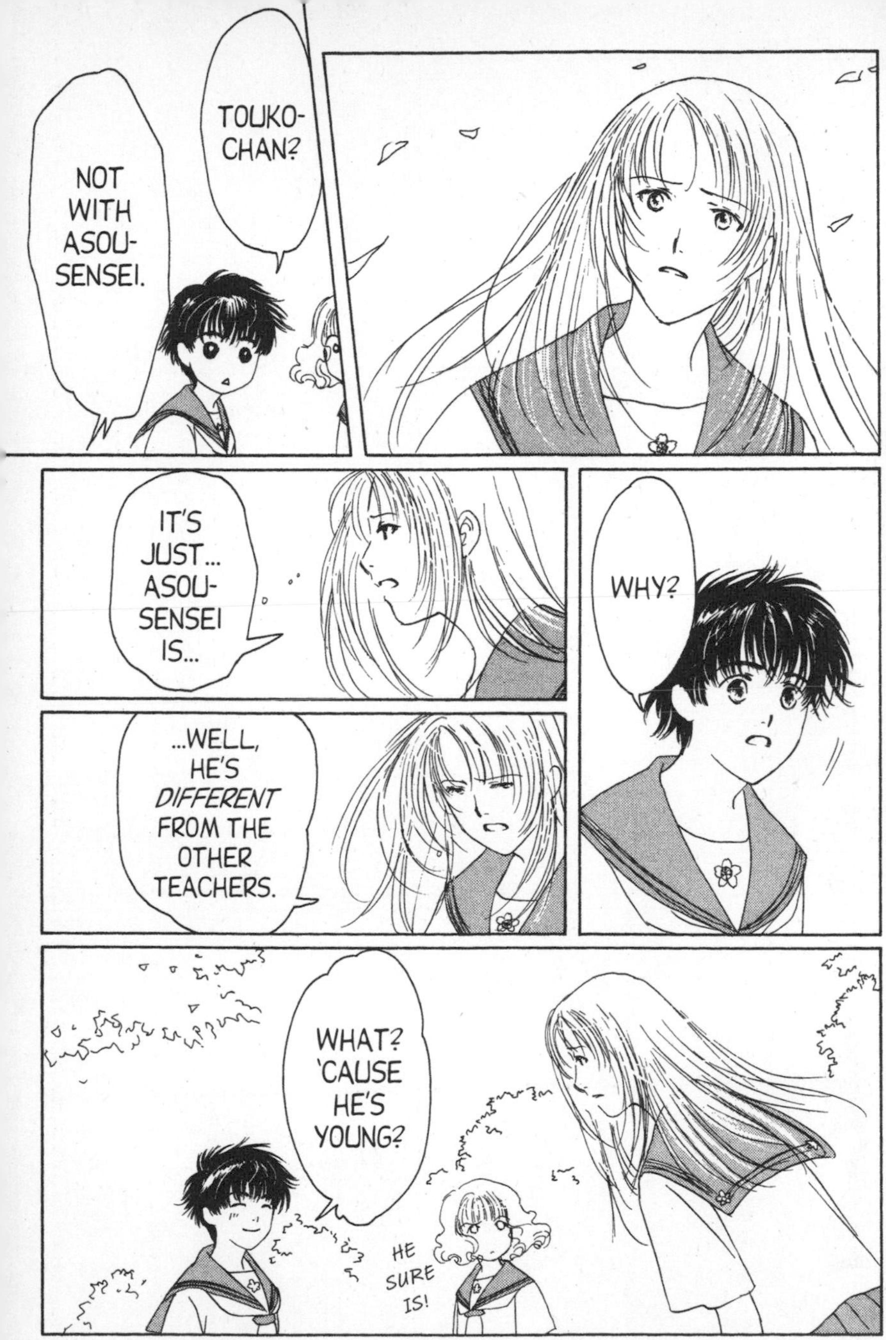
TOUKO-CHAN?
NOT WITH ASOU-SENSEI.
WHY?
IT'S JUST... ASOU-SENSEI IS...
...WELL, HE'S *DIFFERENT* FROM THE OTHER TEACHERS.
WHAT? 'CAUSE HE'S YOUNG?
HE SURE IS!

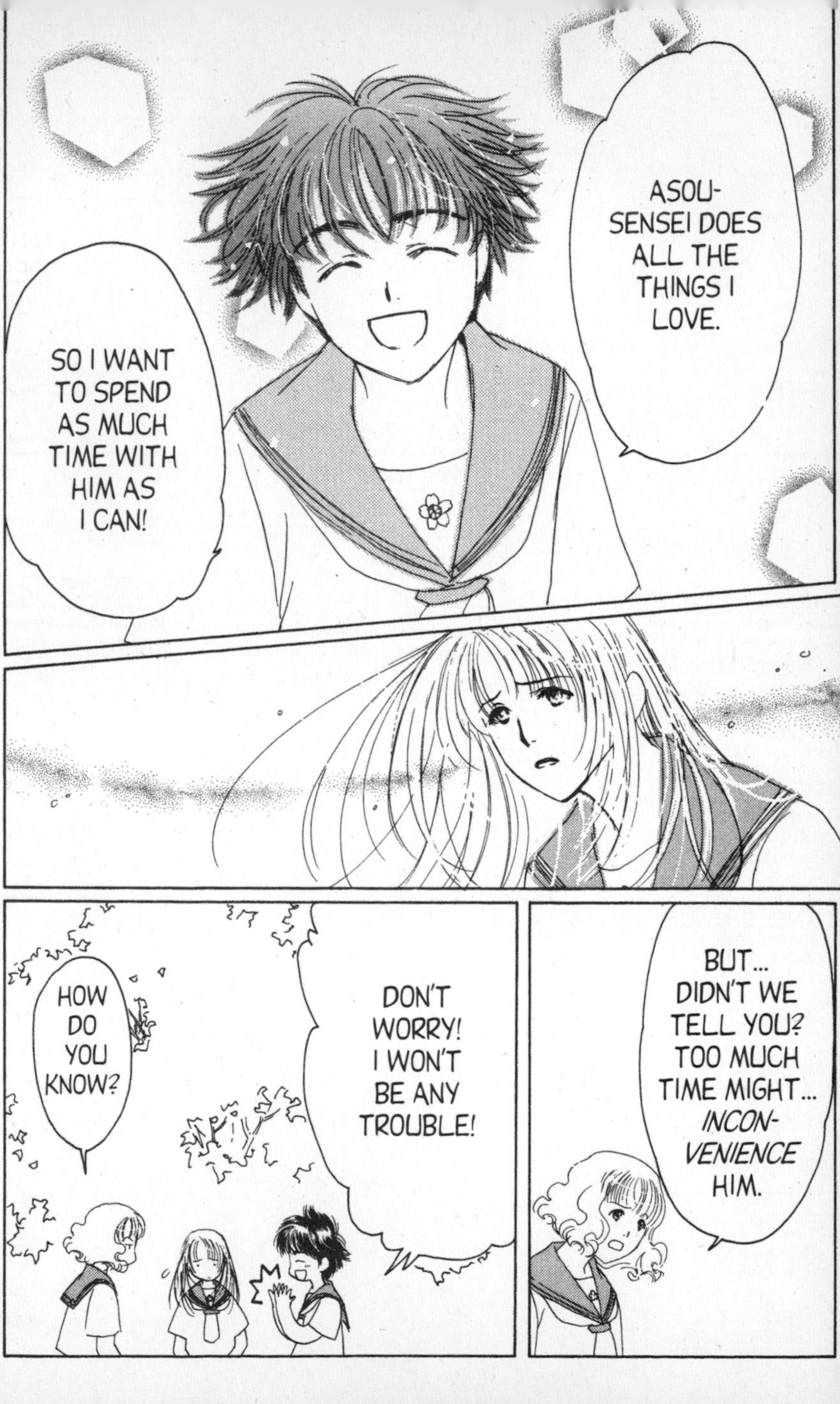
ASOU-SENSEI DOES ALL THE THINGS I LOVE.
SO I WANT TO SPEND AS MUCH TIME WITH HIM AS I CAN!
BUT... DIDN'T WE TELL YOU? TOO MUCH TIME MIGHT... *INCONVENIENCE* HIM.
DON'T WORRY! I WON'T BE ANY TROUBLE!
HOW DO YOU KNOW?

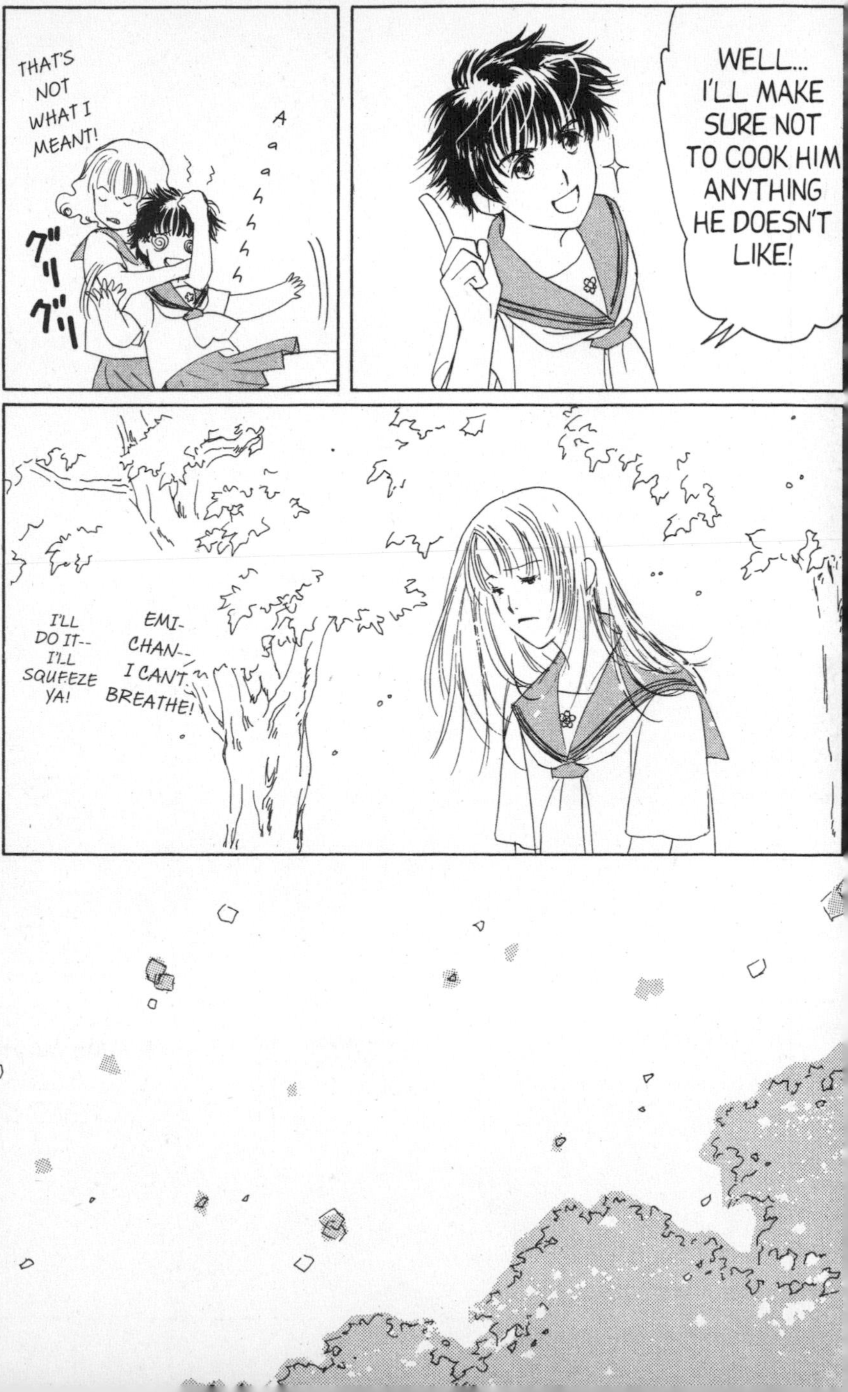
WELL... I'LL MAKE SURE NOT TO COOK HIM ANYTHING HE DOESN'T LIKE!
THAT'S NOT WHAT I MEANT!
Aaahhhhh
グリグリ
EMI-CHAN-- I CAN'T BREATHE!
I'LL DO IT-- I'LL SQUEEZE YA!

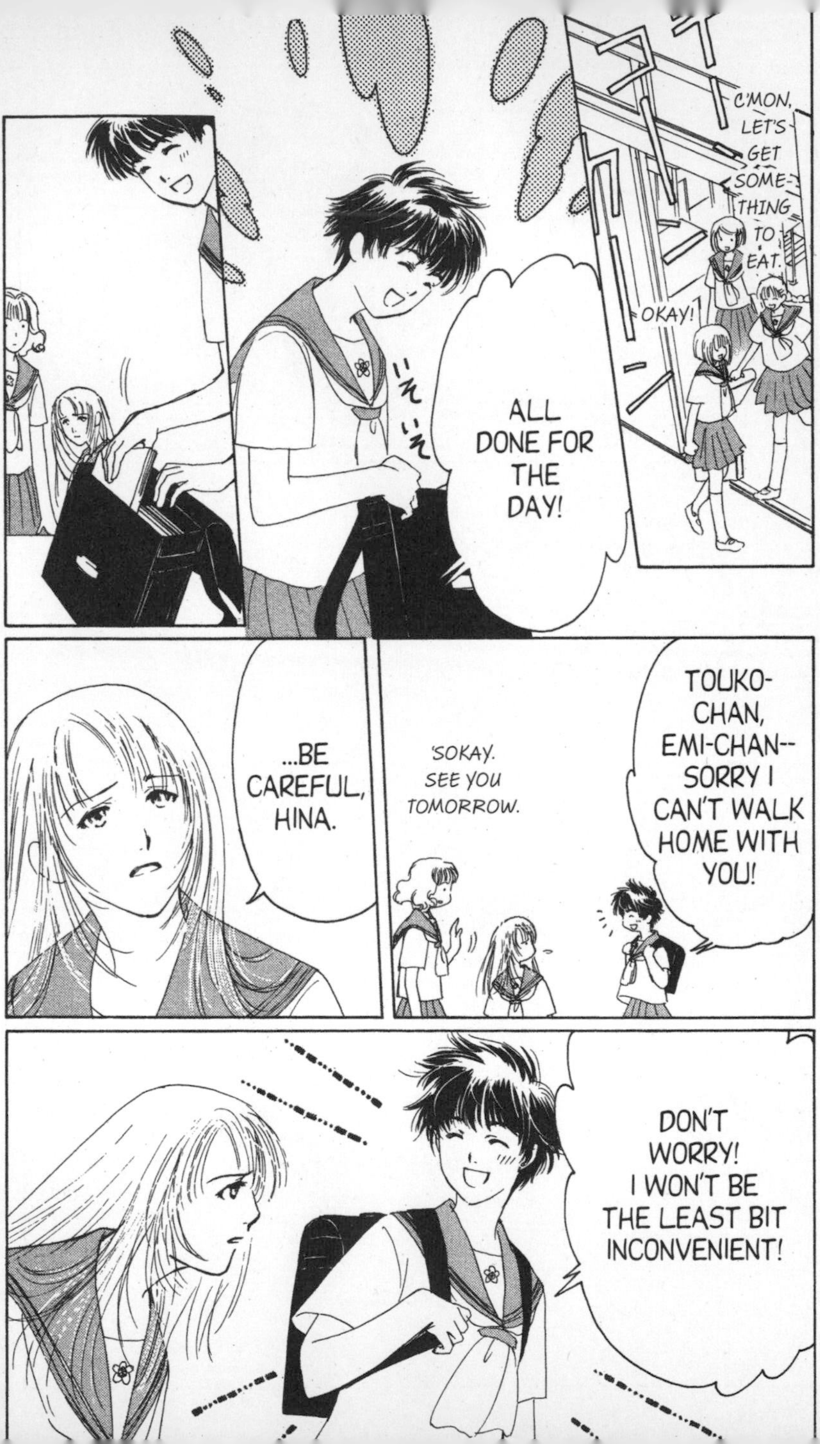
C'MON, LET'S GET SOMETHING TO EAT.
OKAY!
ALL DONE FOR THE DAY!
いそいそ
TOUKO-CHAN, EMI-CHAN-- SORRY I CAN'T WALK HOME WITH YOU!
'SOKAY. SEE YOU TOMORROW.
...BE CAREFUL, HINA.
DON'T WORRY! I WON'T BE THE LEAST BIT INCONVENIENT!

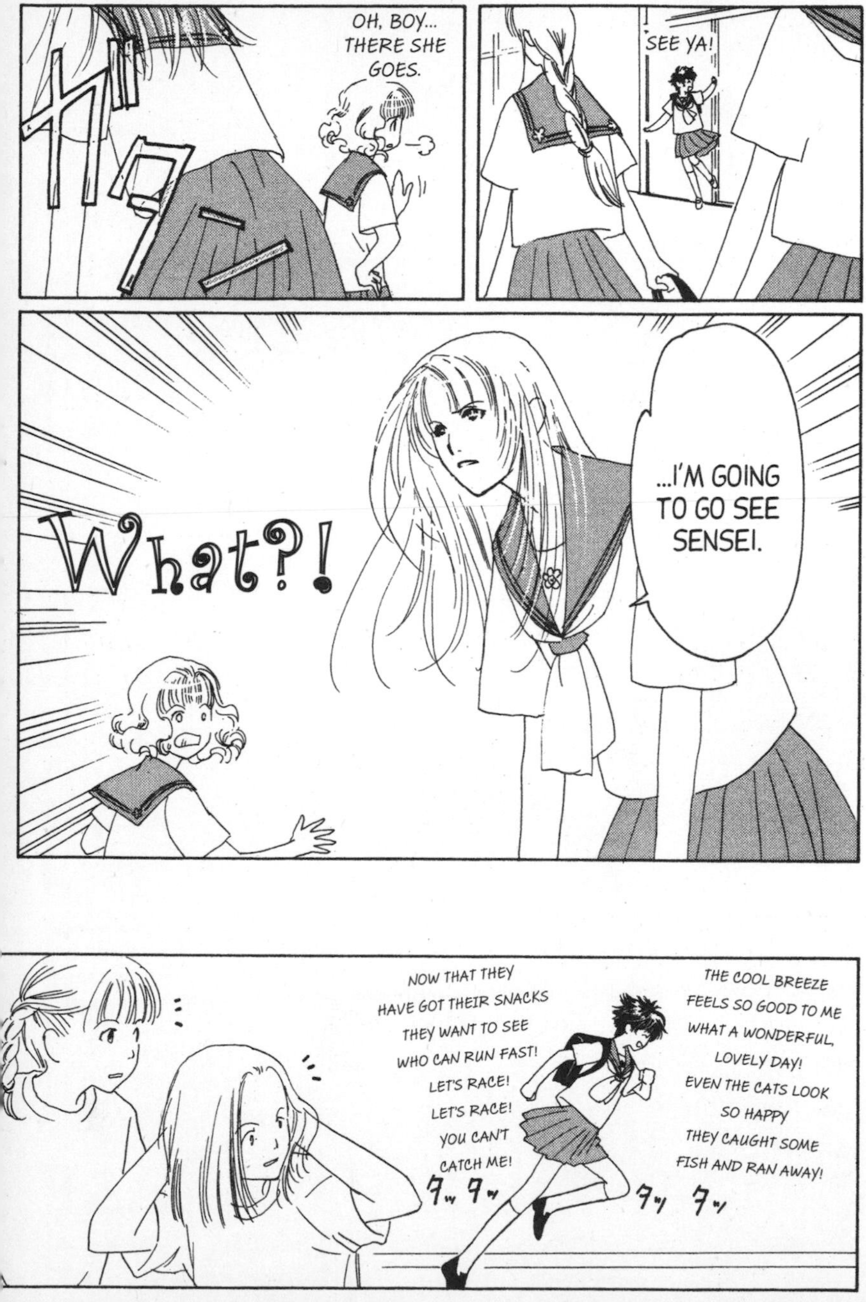
SEE YA!
OH, BOY... THERE SHE GOES.
...I'M GOING TO GO SEE SENSEI.
What?!
THE COOL BREEZE FEELS SO GOOD TO ME WHAT A WONDERFUL, LOVELY DAY! EVEN THE CATS LOOK SO HAPPY THEY CAUGHT SOME FISH AND RAN AWAY!
NOW THAT THEY HAVE GOT THEIR SNACKS THEY WANT TO SEE WHO CAN RUN FAST! LET'S RACE! LET'S RACE! YOU CAN'T CATCH ME!

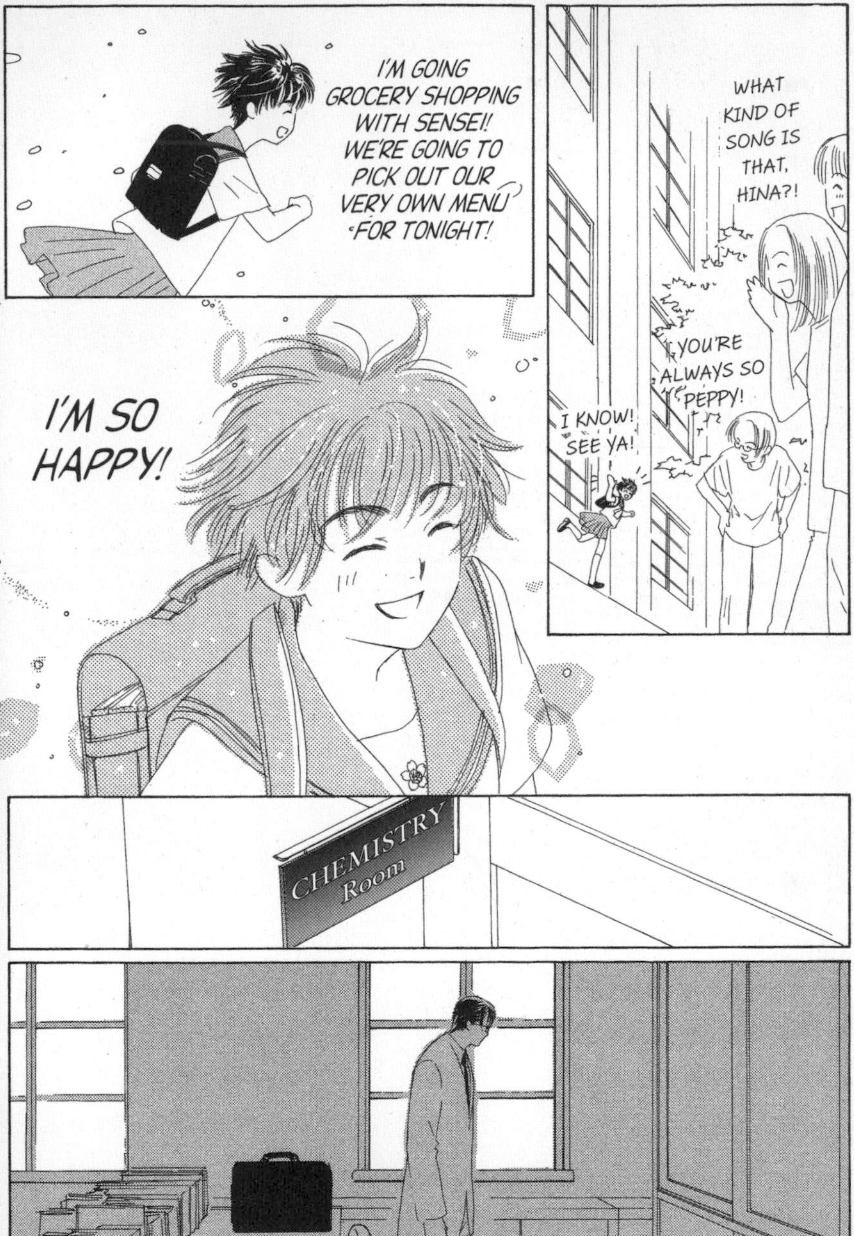
WHAT KIND OF SONG IS THAT, HINA?!
YOU'RE ALWAYS SO PEPPY!
I KNOW! SEE YA!
I'M GOING GROCERY SHOPPING WITH SENSEI! WE'RE GOING TO PICK OUT OUR VERY OWN MENU FOR TONIGHT!
I'M SO HAPPY!
CHEMISTRY Room

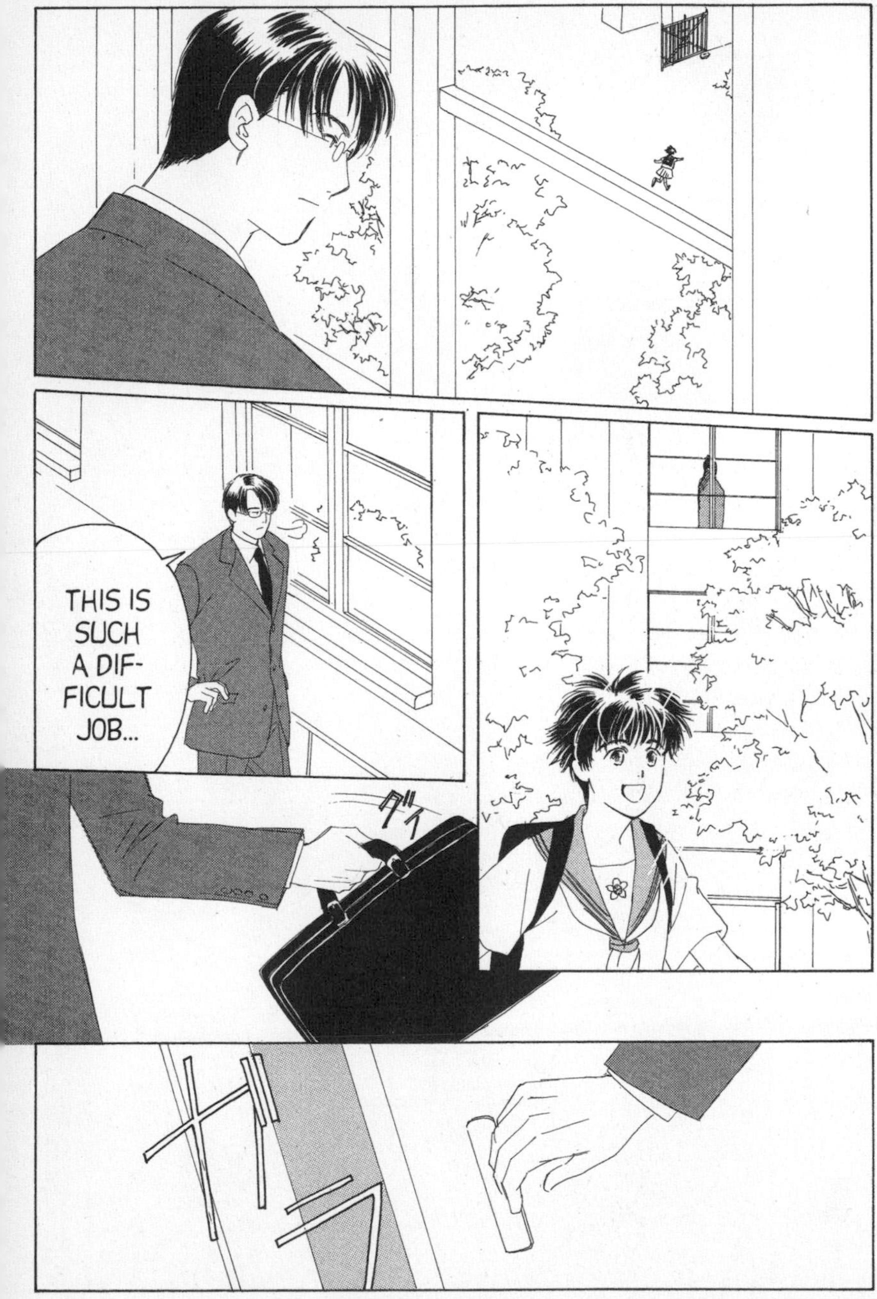
THIS IS SUCH A DIF-FICULT JOB...
グイ

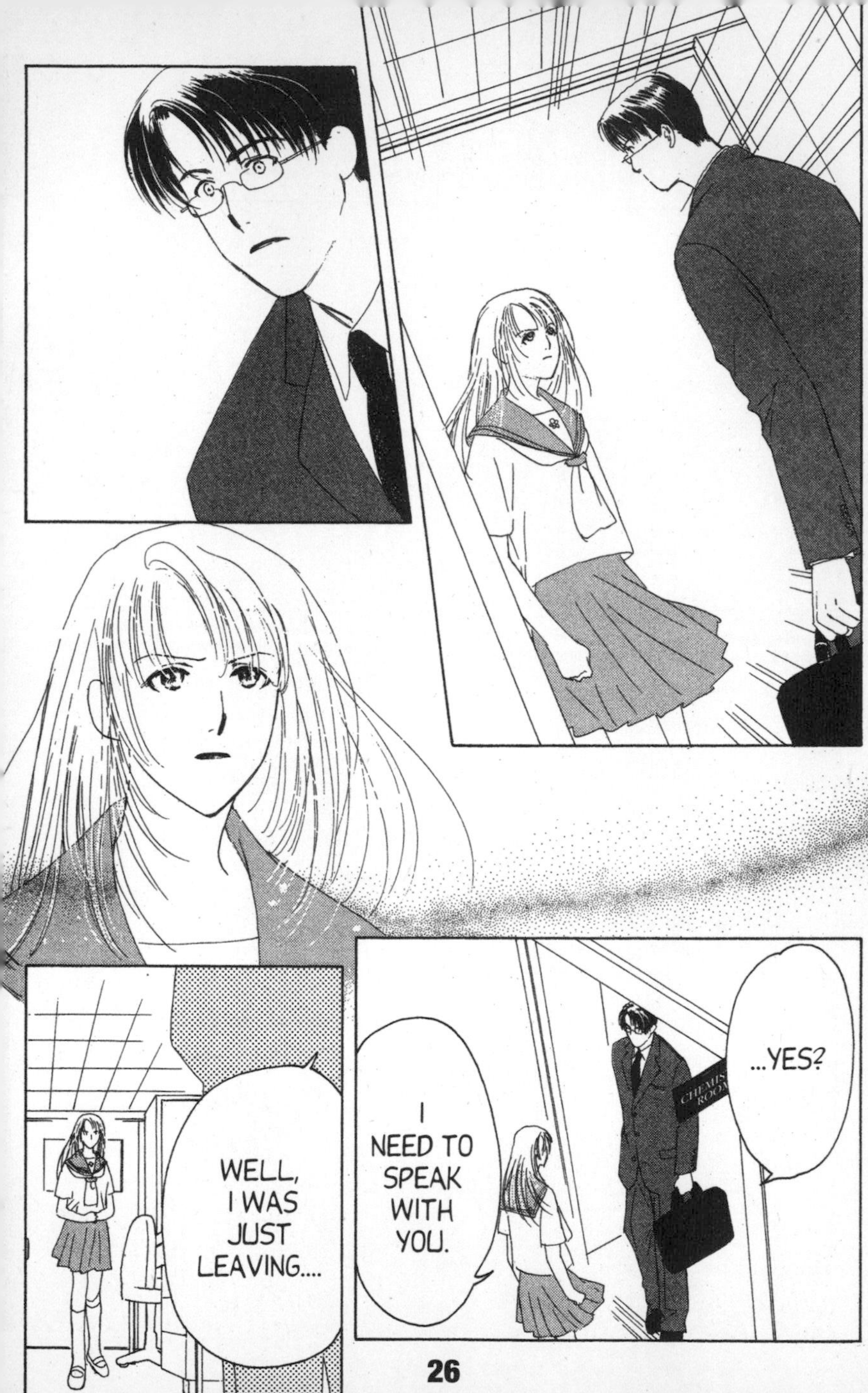
...YES?
I NEED TO SPEAK WITH YOU.
WELL, I WAS JUST LEAVING....

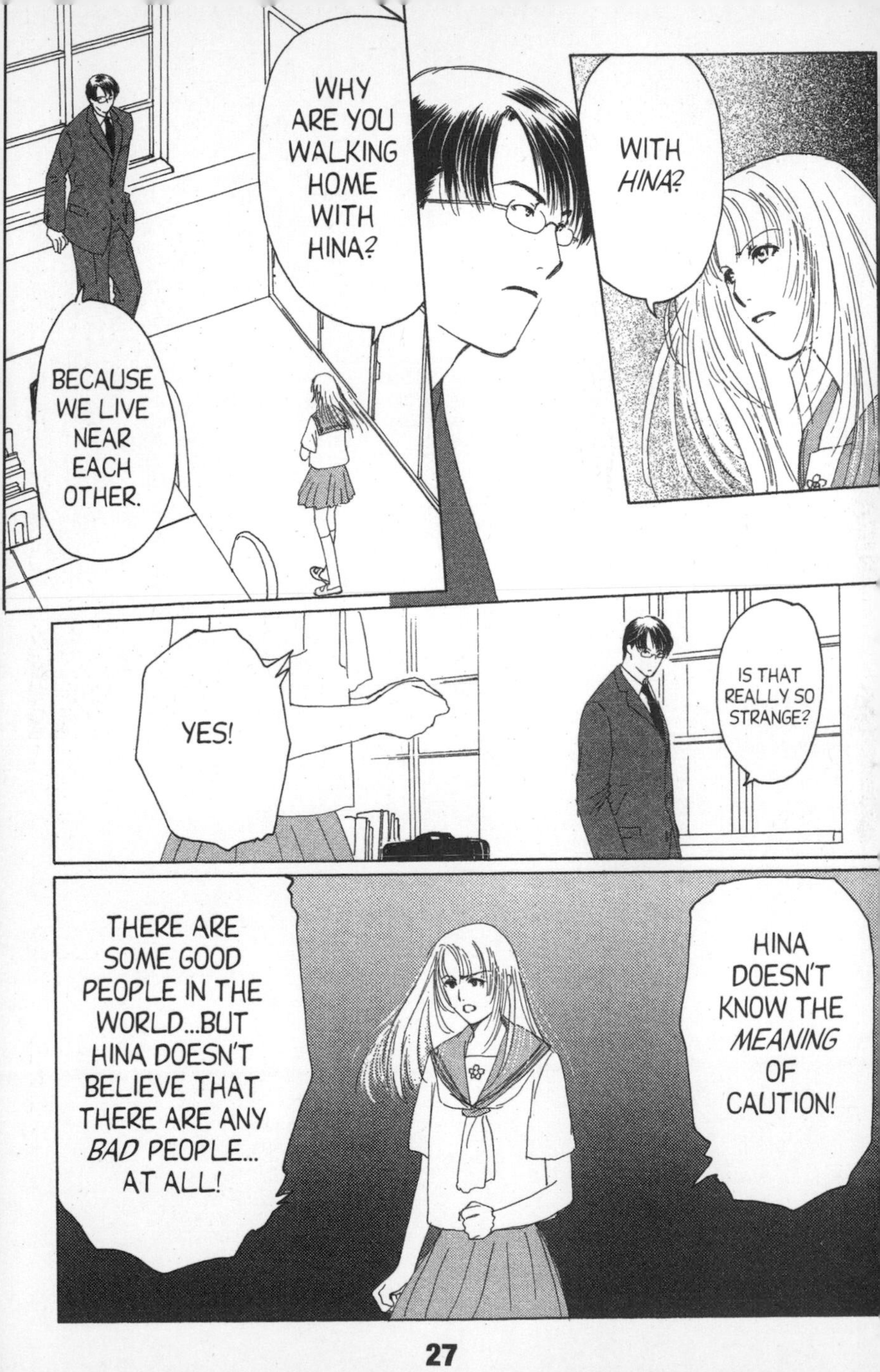
WITH *HINA*?
WHY ARE YOU WALKING HOME WITH HINA?
BECAUSE WE LIVE NEAR EACH OTHER.
IS THAT REALLY SO STRANGE?
YES!
HINA DOESN'T KNOW THE *MEANING* OF CAUTION!
THERE ARE SOME GOOD PEOPLE IN THE WORLD...BUT HINA DOESN'T BELIEVE THAT THERE ARE ANY *BAD* PEOPLE... AT ALL!

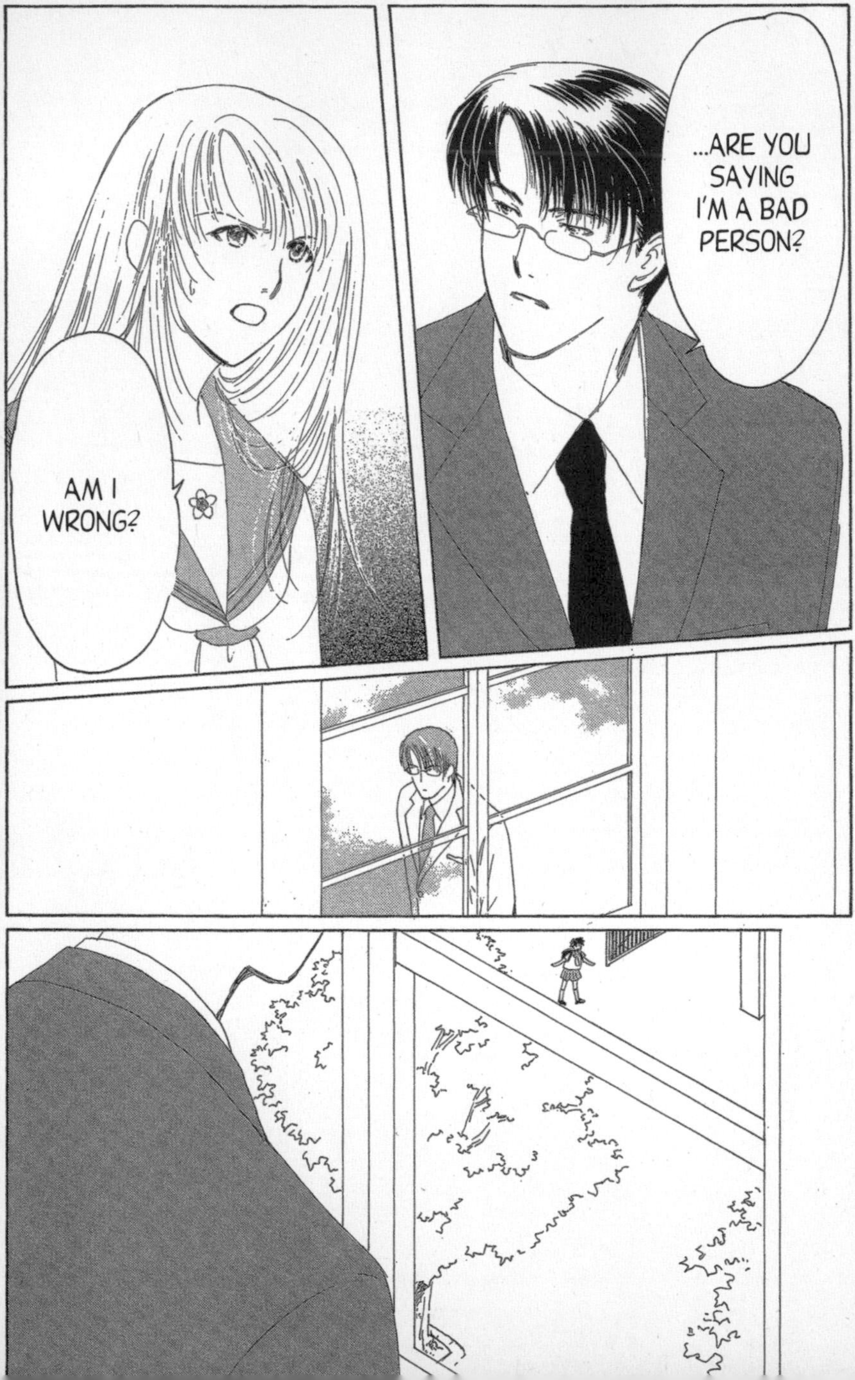
...ARE YOU SAYING I'M A BAD PERSON?
AM I WRONG?

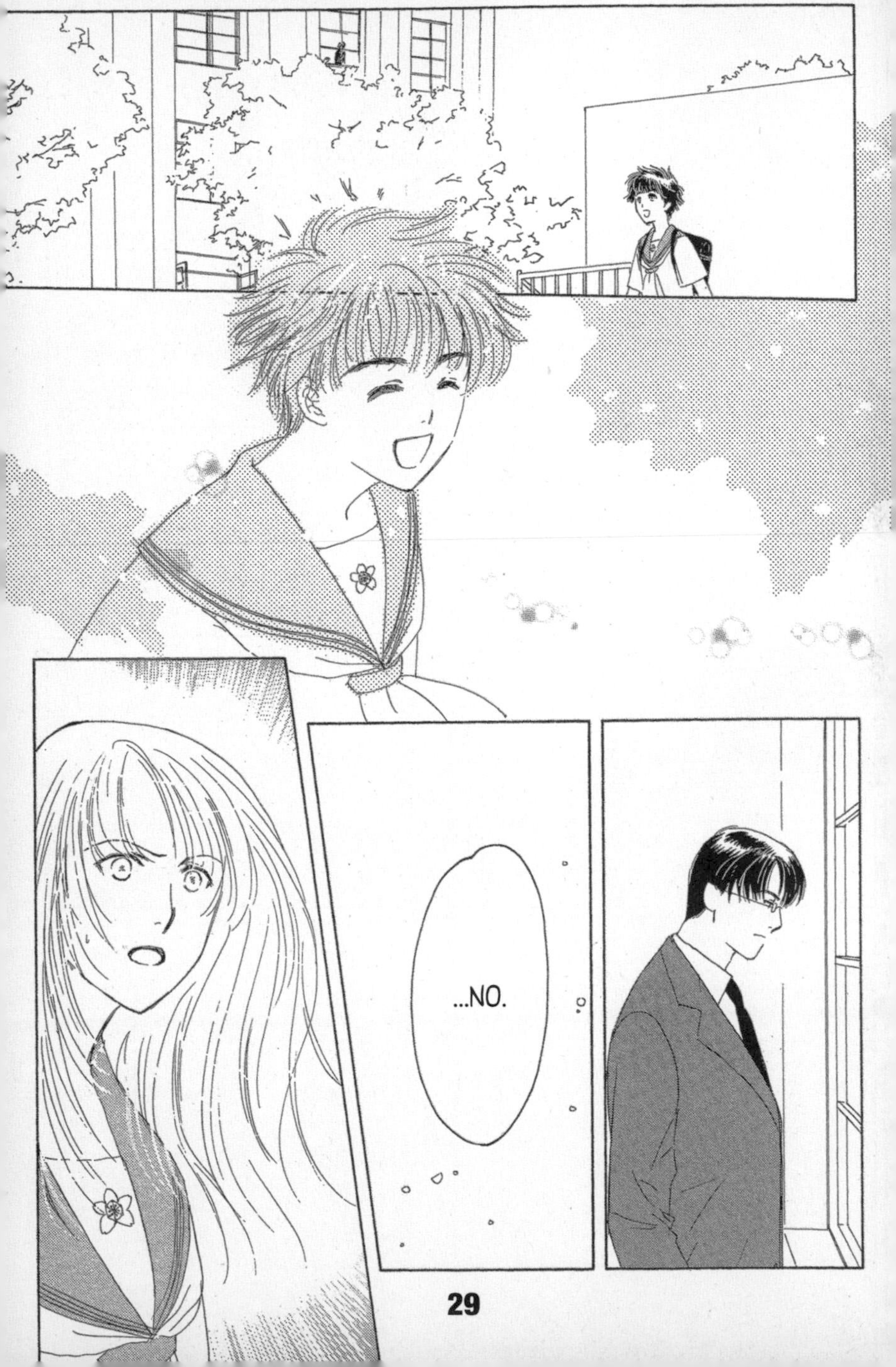
...NO.

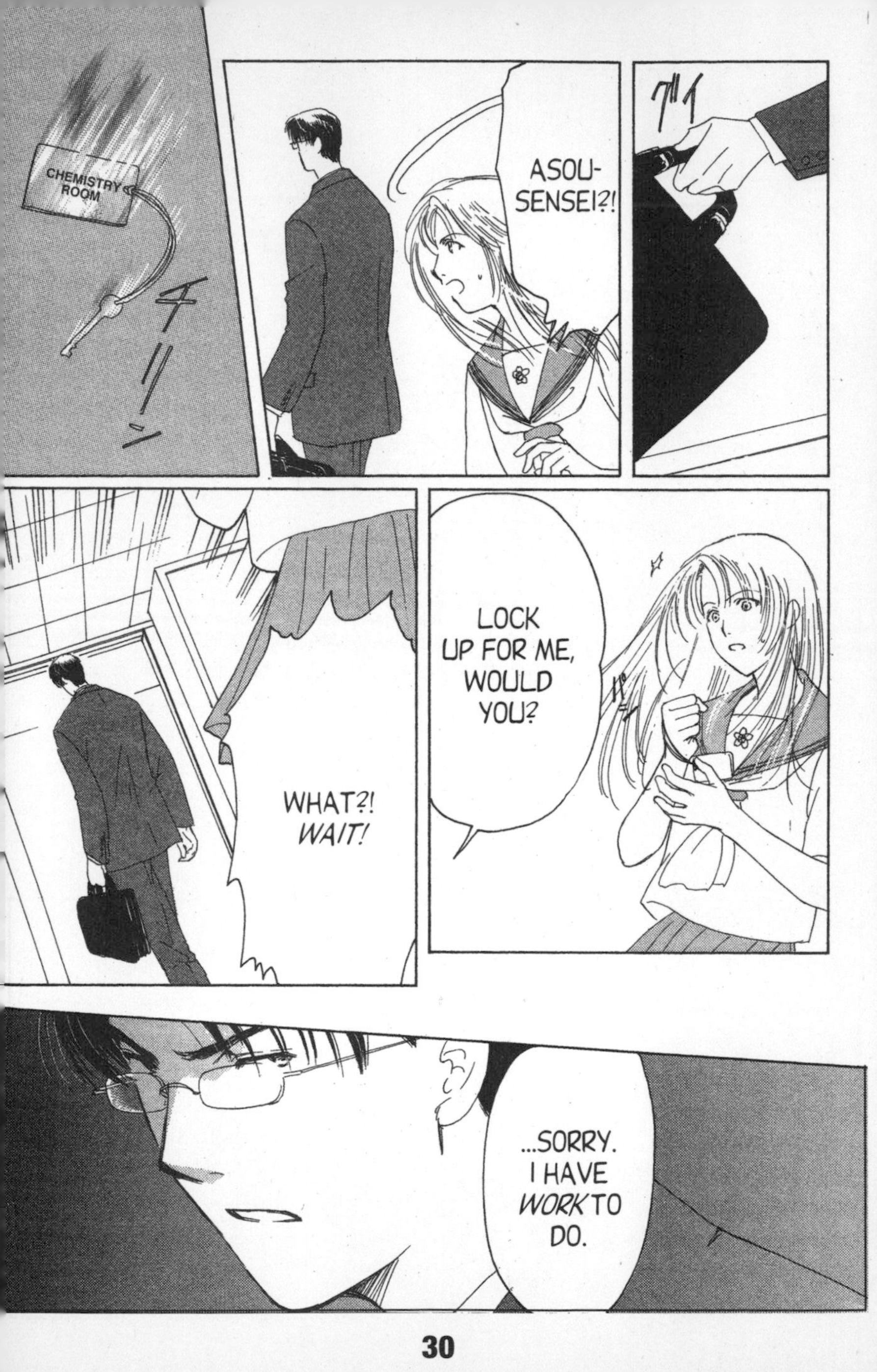
ASOU-SENSEI?!
CHEMISTRY ROOM
LOCK UP FOR ME, WOULD YOU?
WHAT?! WAIT!
...SORRY. I HAVE WORK TO DO.

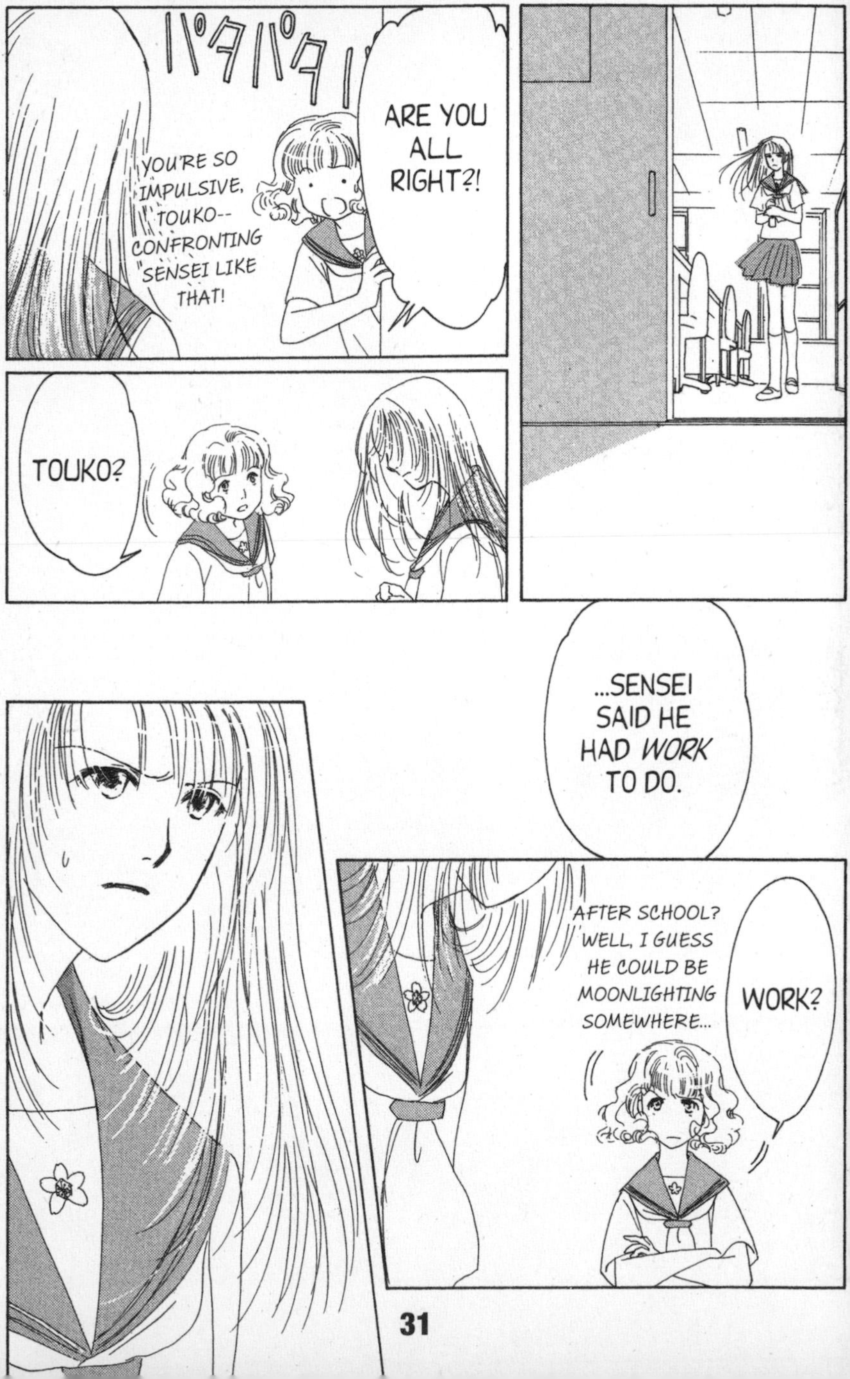
パタパタ
ARE YOU ALL RIGHT?!
YOU'RE SO IMPULSIVE, TOUKO-- CONFRONTING SENSEI LIKE THAT!
TOUKO?
...SENSEI SAID HE HAD *WORK* TO DO.
WORK?
AFTER SCHOOL? WELL, I GUESS HE COULD BE MOONLIGHTING SOMEWHERE...

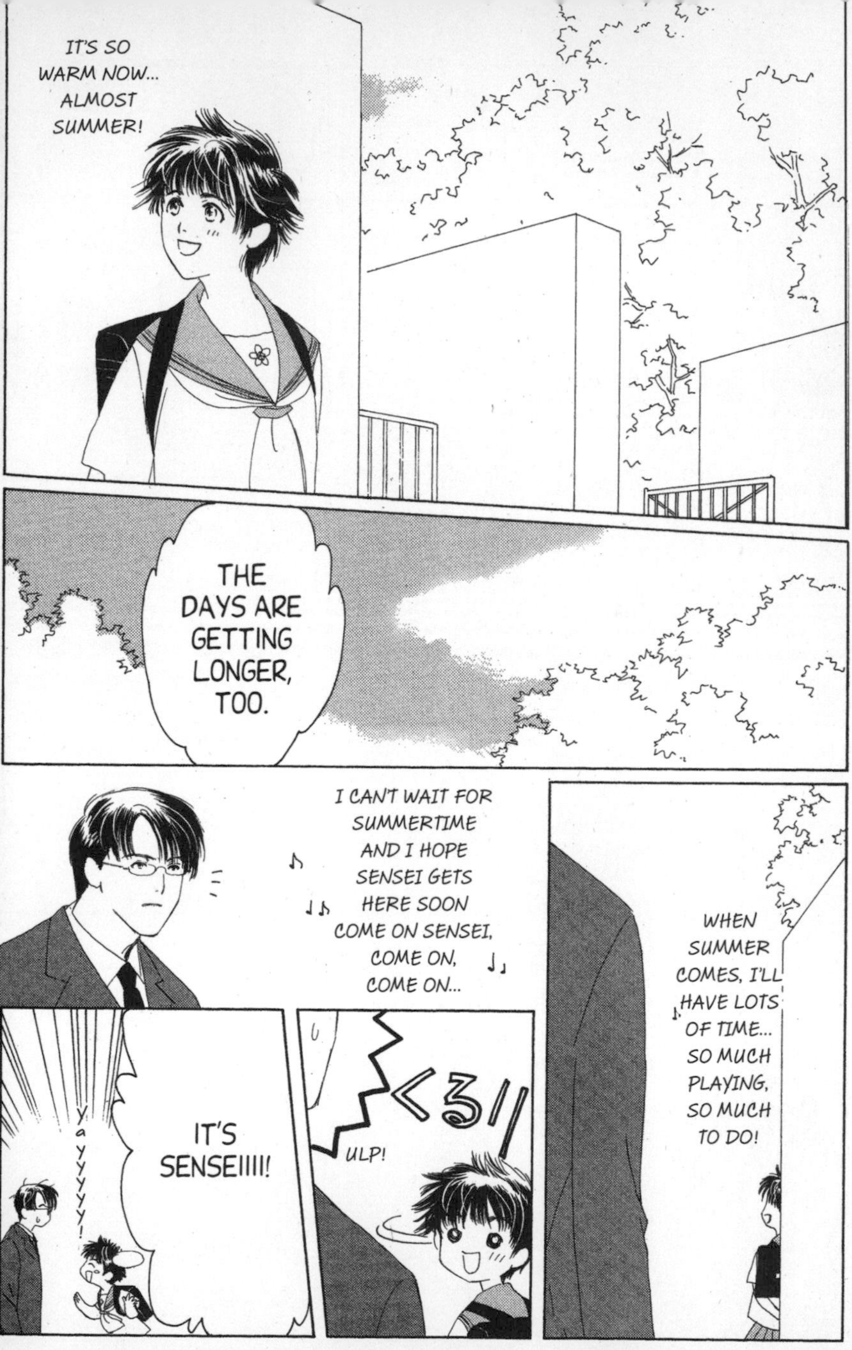
IT'S SO WARM NOW... ALMOST SUMMER!
THE DAYS ARE GETTING LONGER, TOO.
WHEN SUMMER COMES, I'LL HAVE LOTS OF TIME... SO MUCH PLAYING, SO MUCH TO DO!
I CAN'T WAIT FOR SUMMERTIME AND I HOPE SENSEI GETS HERE SOON COME ON SENSEI, COME ON, COME ON...
くる
ULP!
IT'S SENSEIIII!
YaYYYYY!

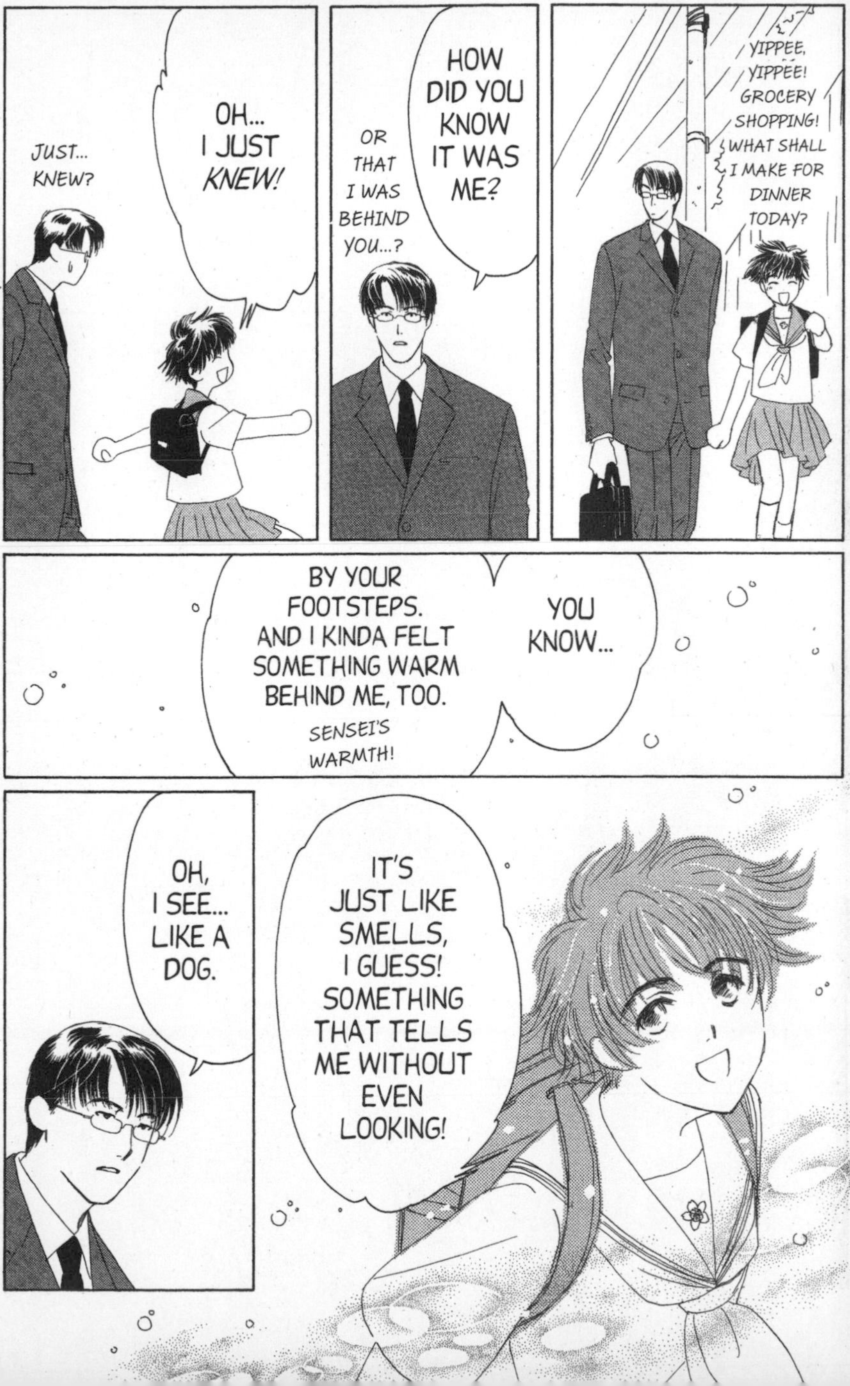
YIPPEE, YIPPEE! GROCERY SHOPPING! WHAT SHALL I MAKE FOR DINNER TODAY?
HOW DID YOU KNOW IT WAS ME?
OR THAT I WAS BEHIND YOU...?
OH... I JUST *KNEW!*
JUST... KNEW?
YOU KNOW...
BY YOUR FOOTSTEPS. AND I KINDA FELT SOMETHING WARM BEHIND ME, TOO.
SENSEI'S WARMTH!
IT'S JUST LIKE SMELLS, I GUESS! SOMETHING THAT TELLS ME WITHOUT EVEN LOOKING!
OH, I SEE... LIKE A DOG.

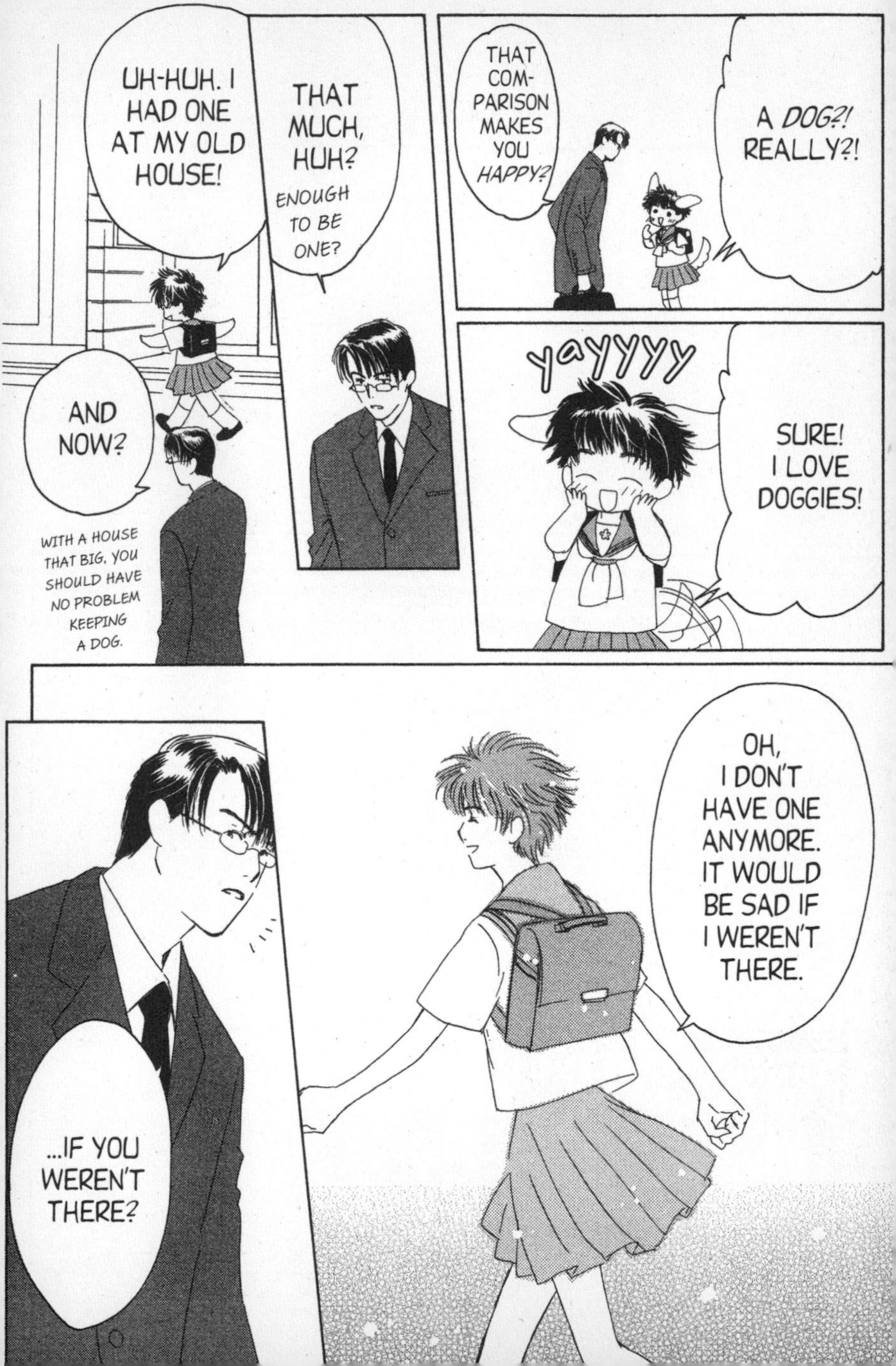
A DOG?! REALLY?!
THAT COMPARISON MAKES YOU HAPPY?
yayyyy
SURE! I LOVE DOGGIES!
THAT MUCH, HUH?
ENOUGH TO BE ONE?
UH-HUH. I HAD ONE AT MY OLD HOUSE!
AND NOW?
WITH A HOUSE THAT BIG, YOU SHOULD HAVE NO PROBLEM KEEPING A DOG.
OH, I DON'T HAVE ONE ANYMORE. IT WOULD BE SAD IF I WEREN'T THERE.
...IF YOU WEREN'T THERE?

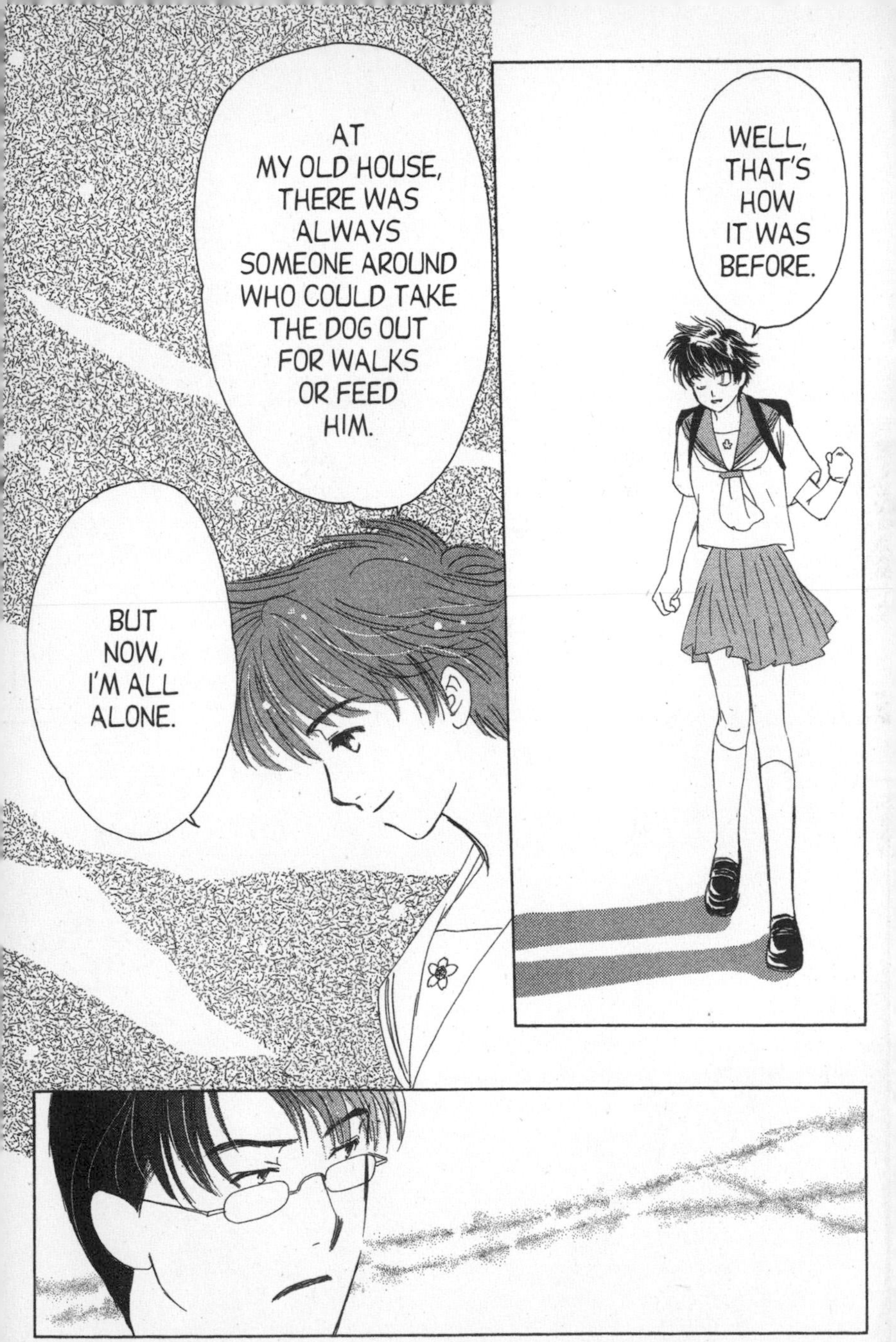
WELL, THAT'S HOW IT WAS BEFORE.
AT MY OLD HOUSE, THERE WAS ALWAYS SOMEONE AROUND WHO COULD TAKE THE DOG OUT FOR WALKS OR FEED HIM.
BUT NOW, I'M ALL ALONE.

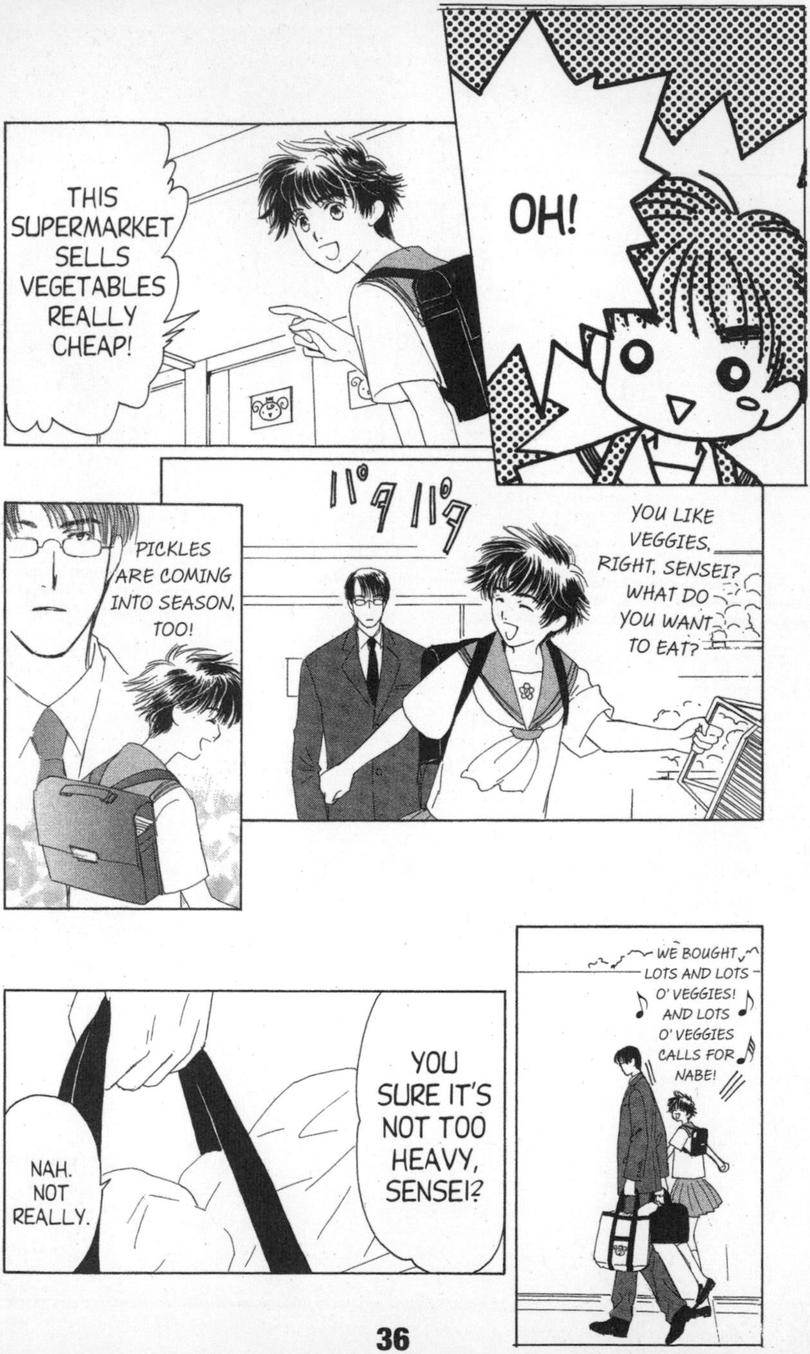
OH!
THIS SUPERMARKET SELLS VEGETABLES REALLY CHEAP!
パタパタ
YOU LIKE VEGGIES, RIGHT, SENSEI? WHAT DO YOU WANT TO EAT?
PICKLES ARE COMING INTO SEASON, TOO!
WE BOUGHT LOTS AND LOTS O' VEGGIES! AND LOTS O' VEGGIES CALLS FOR NABE!
YOU SURE IT'S NOT TOO HEAVY, SENSEI?
NAH. NOT REALLY.

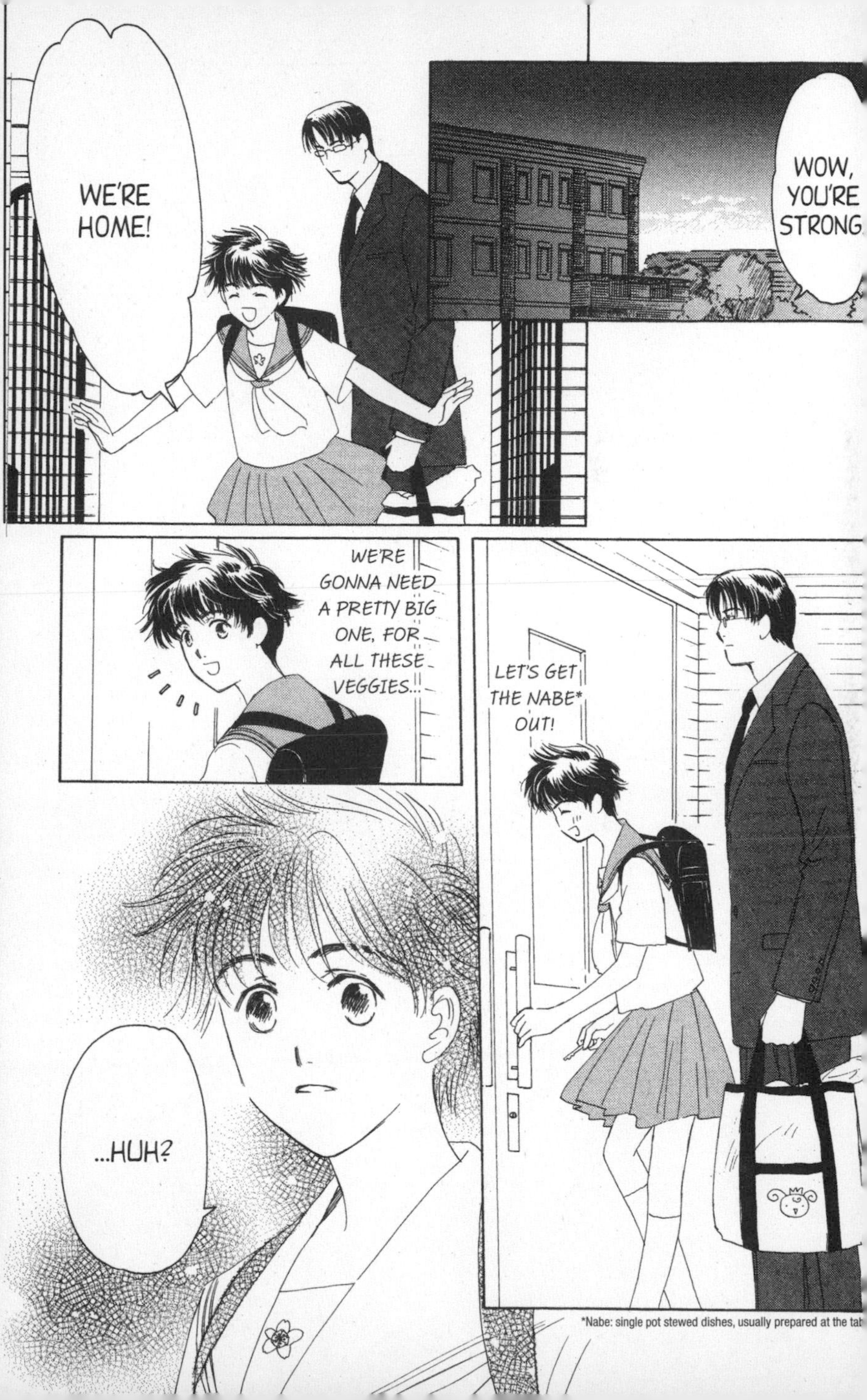
WOW, YOU'RE STRONG.
WE'RE HOME!
LET'S GET THE NABE* OUT!
WE'RE GONNA NEED A PRETTY BIG ONE, FOR ALL THESE VEGGIES...
...HUH?

*Nabe: single pot stewed dishes, usually prepared at the ta

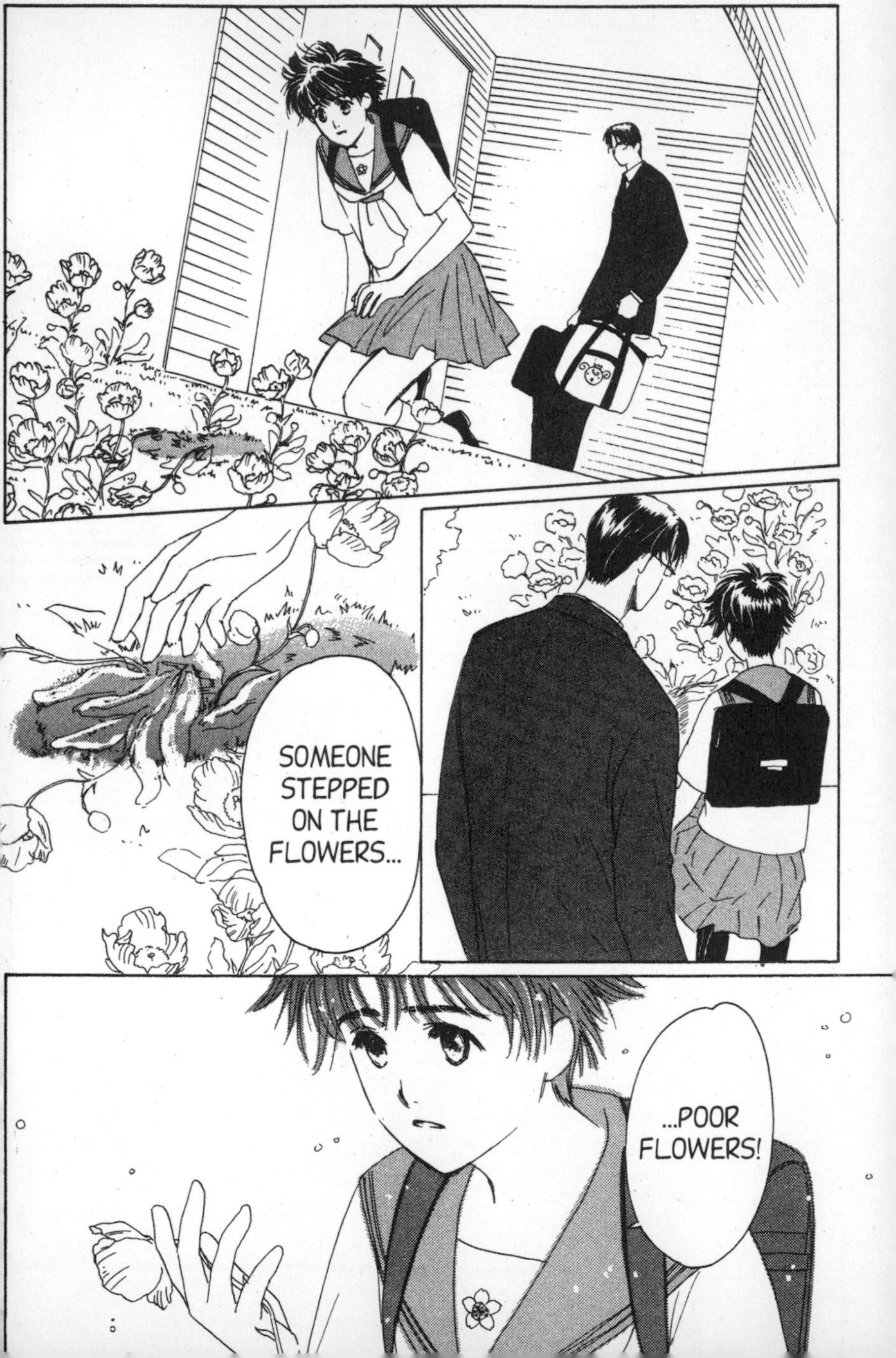
SOMEONE STEPPED ON THE FLOWERS...
...POOR FLOWERS!

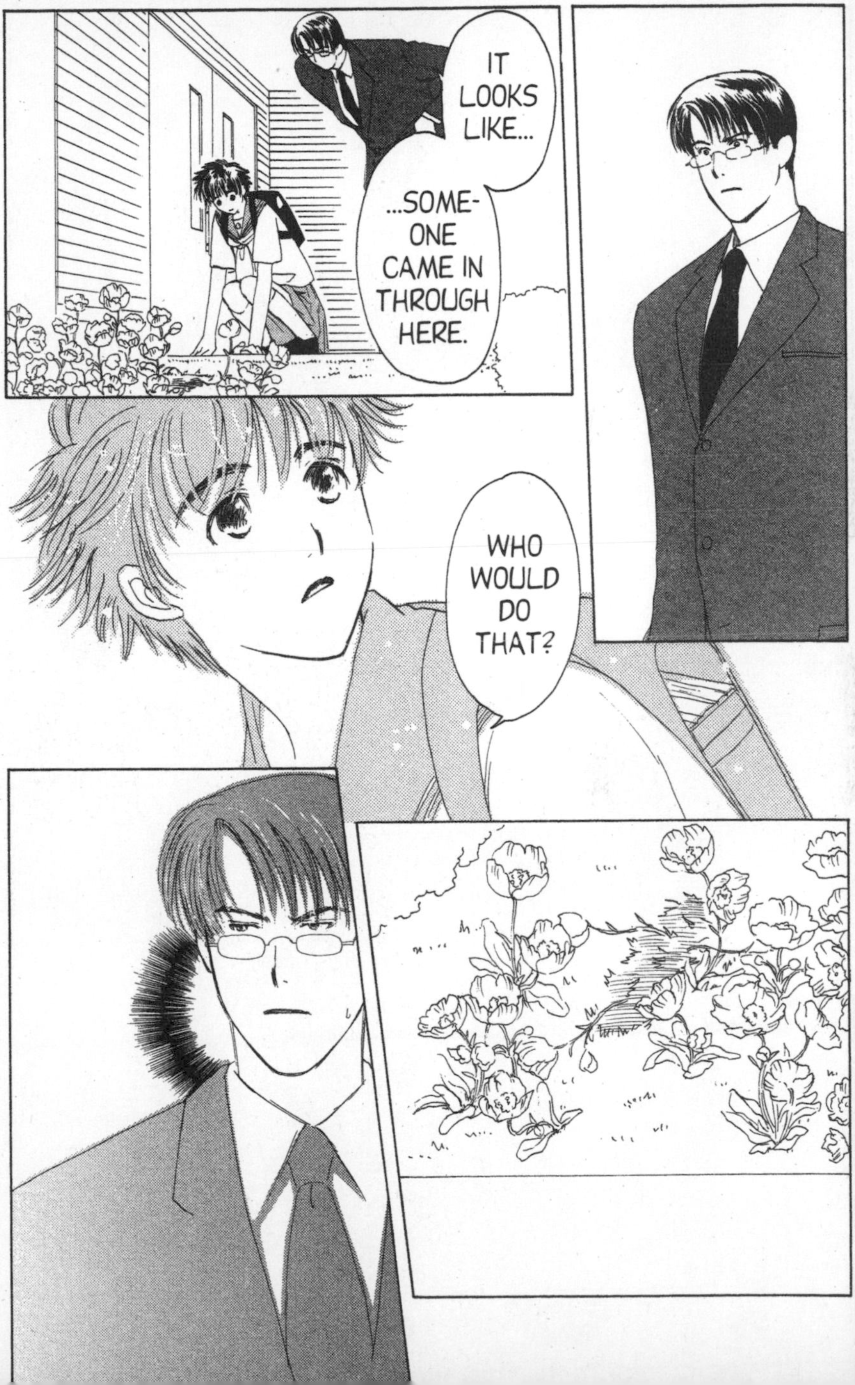
IT LOOKS LIKE...
...SOME-ONE CAME IN THROUGH HERE.
WHO WOULD DO THAT?

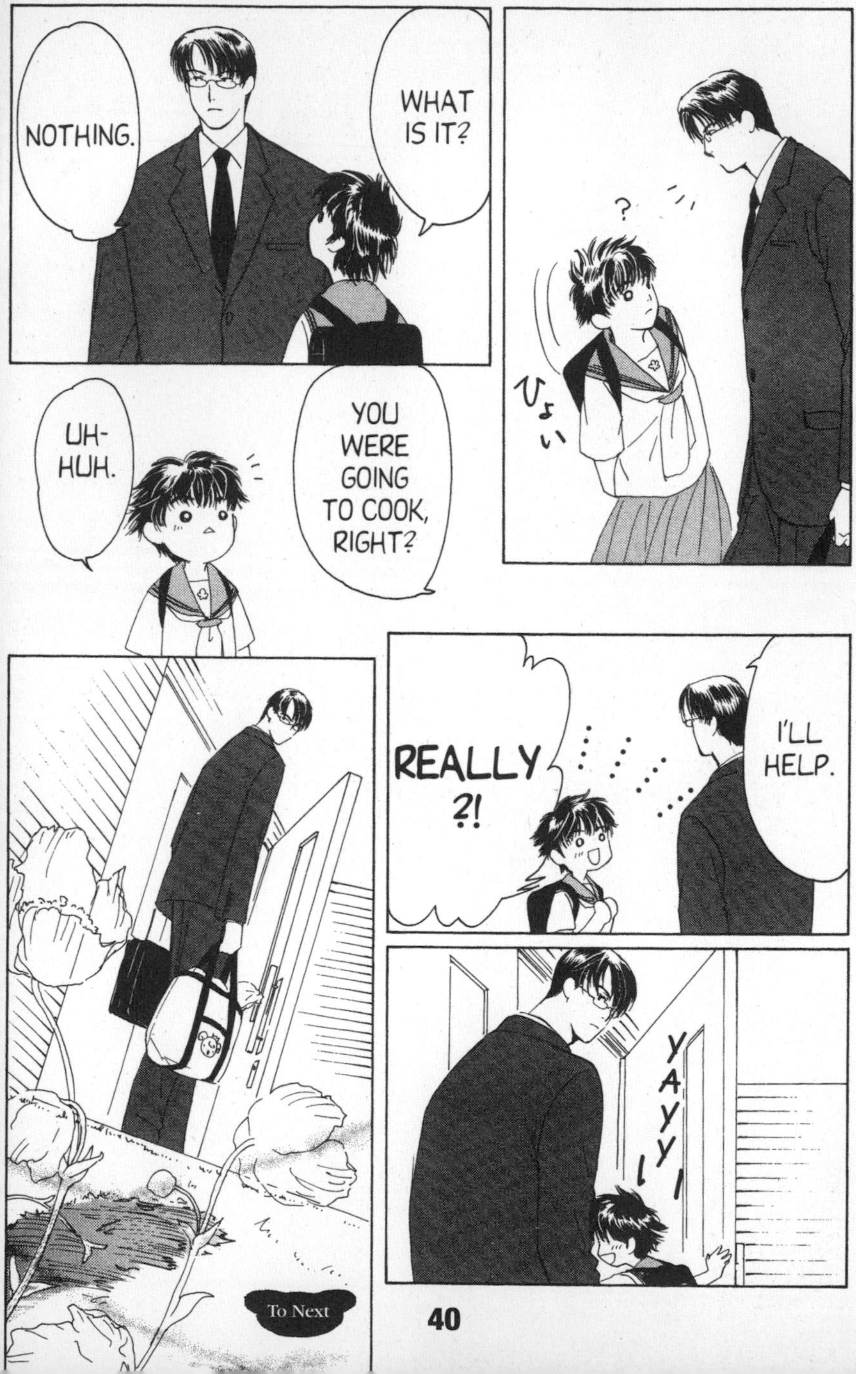
?
ひょい
WHAT IS IT?
NOTHING.
YOU WERE GOING TO COOK, RIGHT?
UH-HUH.
I'LL HELP.
REALLY?!
YAYY!
To Next

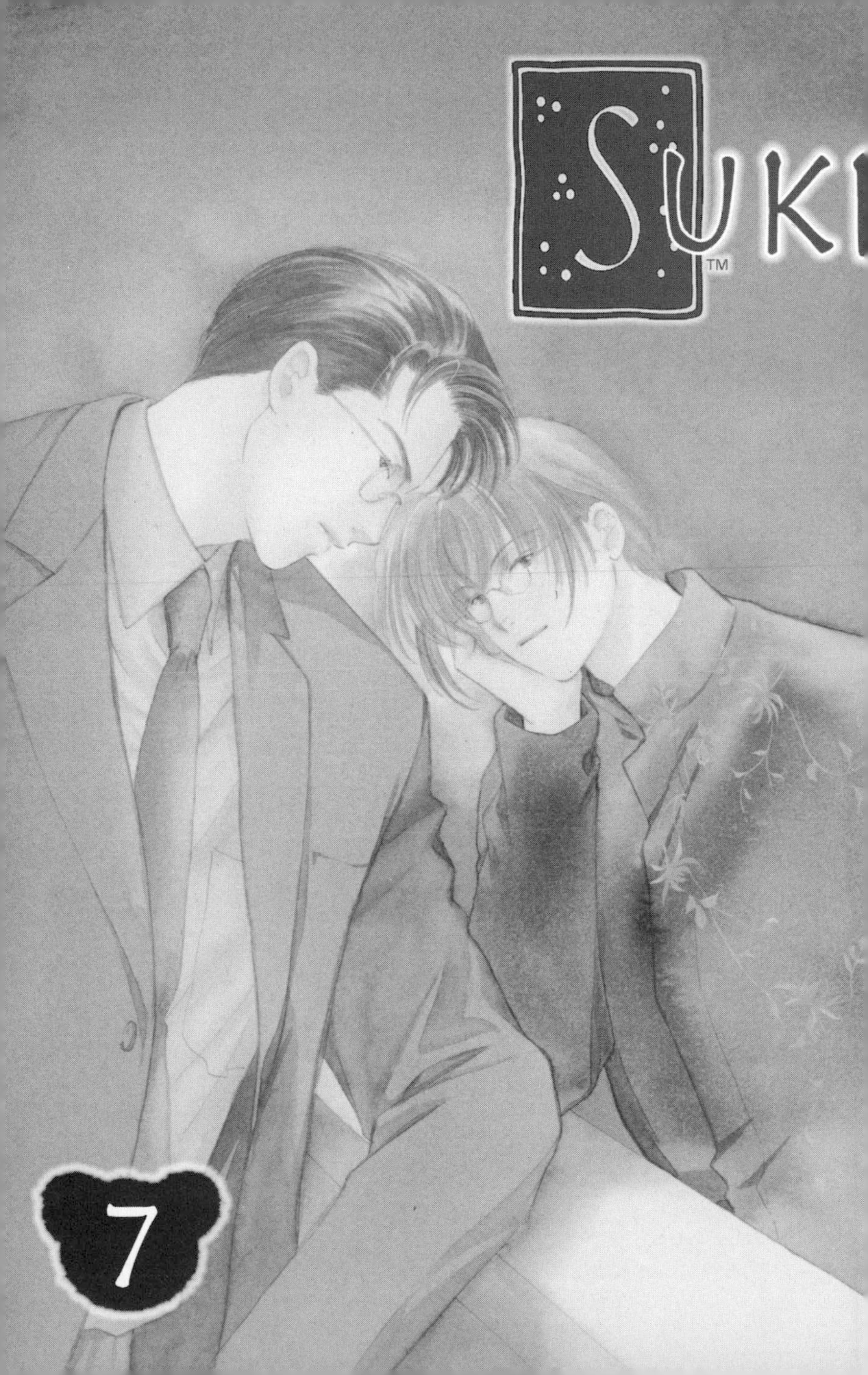
SUKI™
7

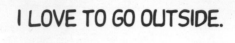

I LOVE TO GO OUTSIDE.

I LOVE TO HOLD HANDS.

I LOVE TO BE WITH YOU.

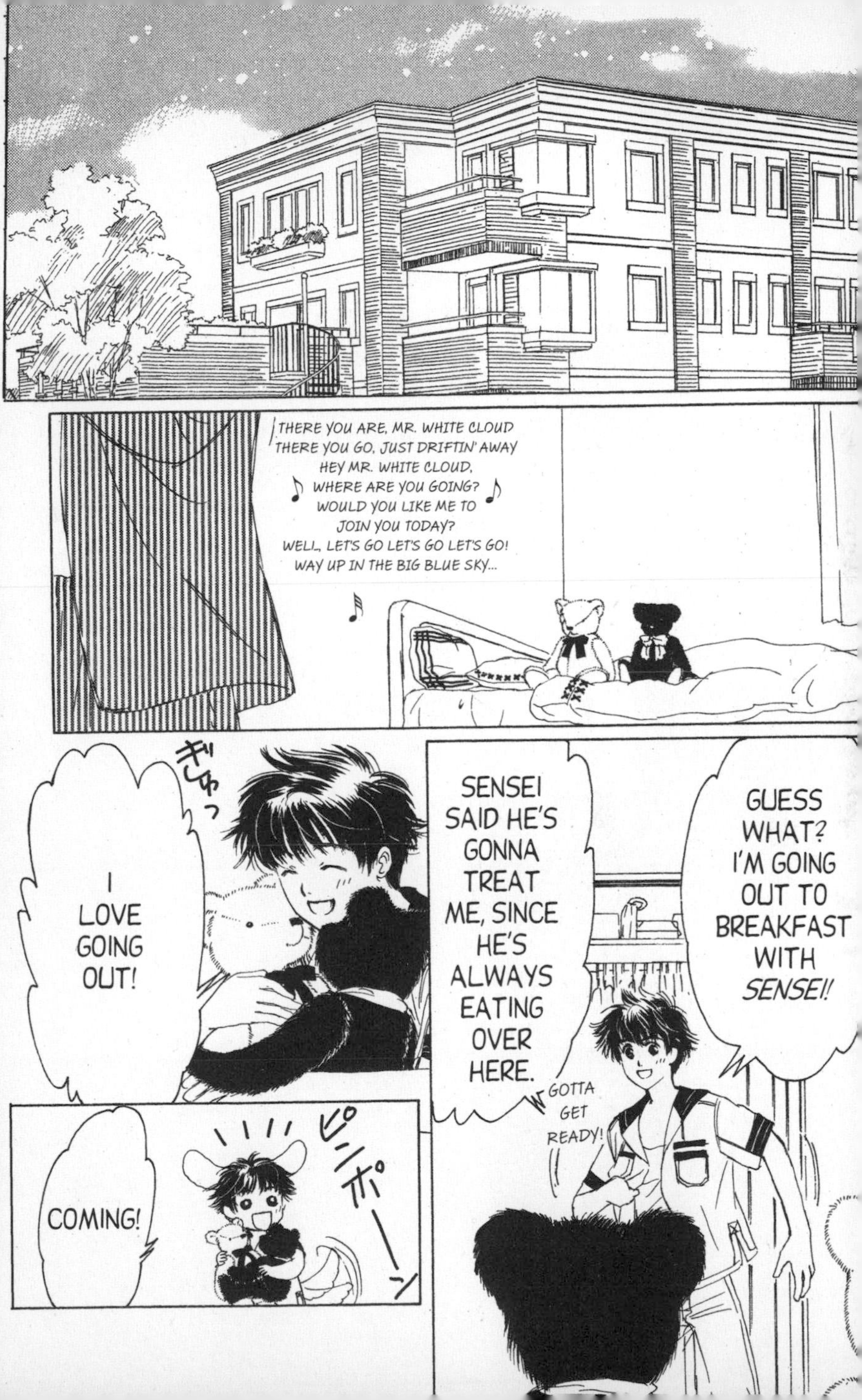
THERE YOU ARE, MR. WHITE CLOUD
THERE YOU GO, JUST DRIFTIN' AWAY
HEY MR. WHITE CLOUD,
WHERE ARE YOU GOING?
WOULD YOU LIKE ME TO
JOIN YOU TODAY?
WELL, LET'S GO LET'S GO LET'S GO!
WAY UP IN THE BIG BLUE SKY...
GUESS WHAT? I'M GOING OUT TO BREAKFAST WITH SENSEI!
SENSEI SAID HE'S GONNA TREAT ME, SINCE HE'S ALWAYS EATING OVER HERE.
GOTTA GET READY!
ぎゅっ
I LOVE GOING OUT!
ピンポーン
COMING!

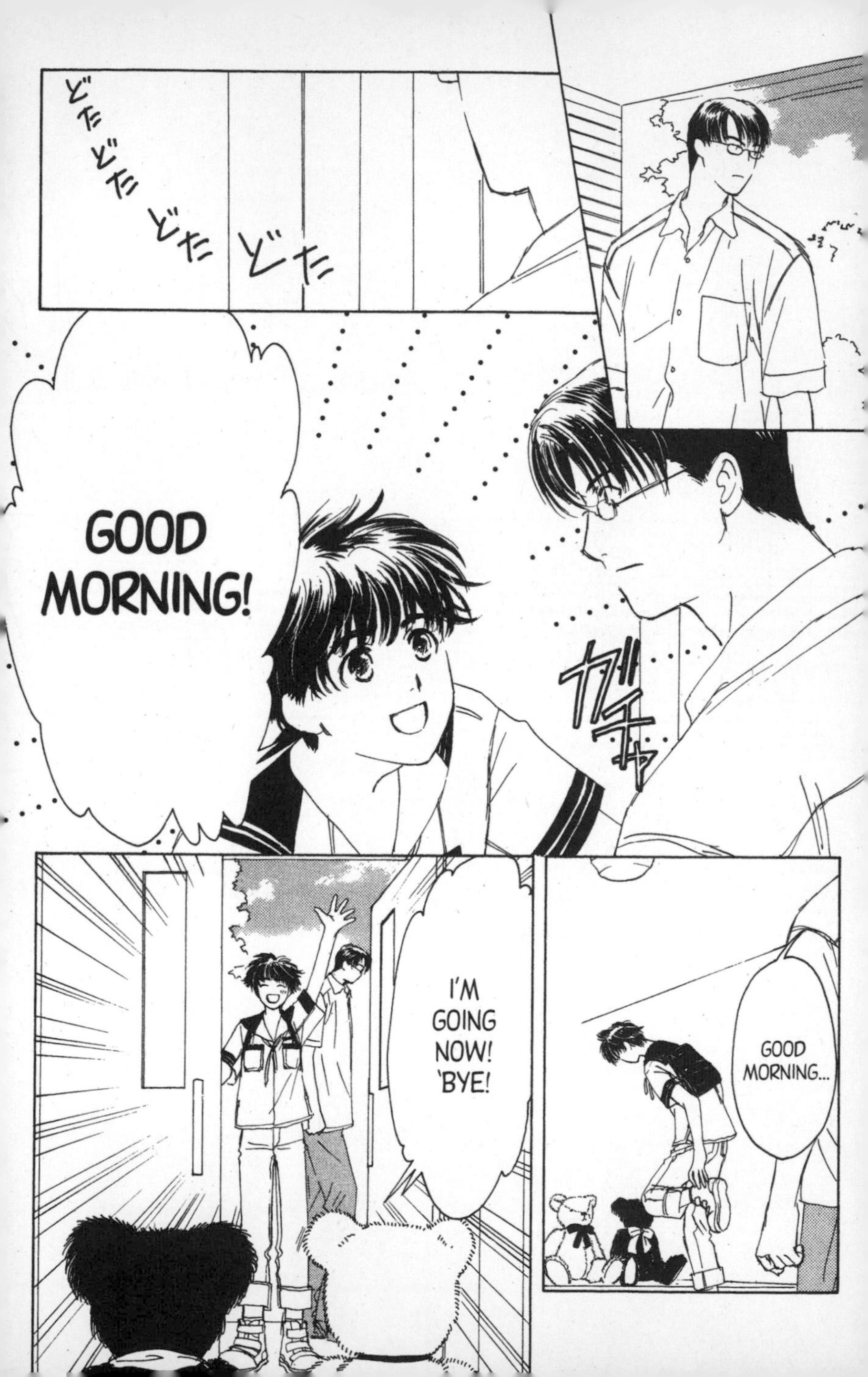
どた どた どた どた
GOOD MORNING!
ガチャ
GOOD MORNING...
I'M GOING NOW! 'BYE!

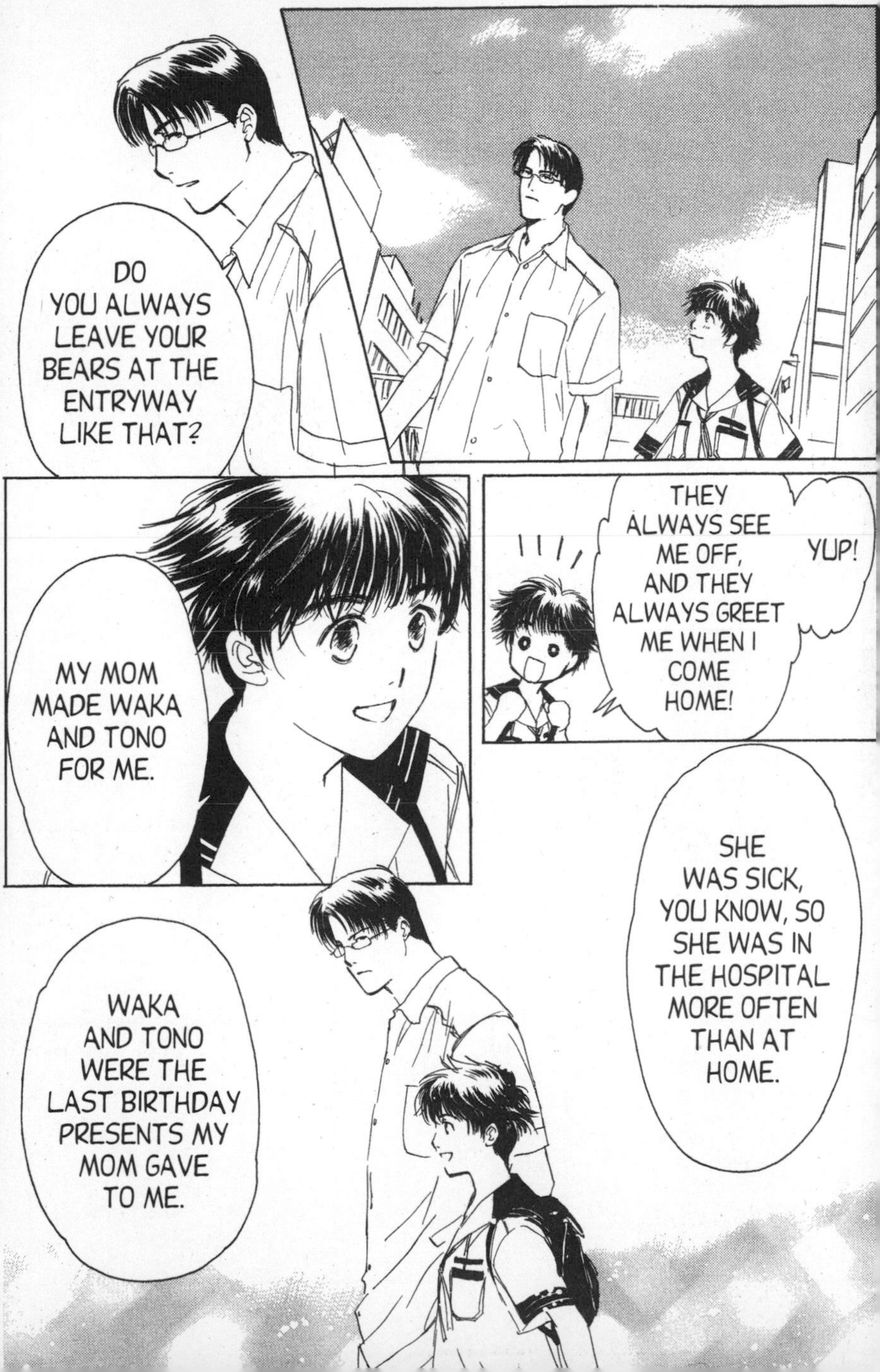
DO YOU ALWAYS LEAVE YOUR BEARS AT THE ENTRYWAY LIKE THAT?
YUP!
THEY ALWAYS SEE ME OFF, AND THEY ALWAYS GREET ME WHEN I COME HOME!
MY MOM MADE WAKA AND TONO FOR ME.
SHE WAS SICK, YOU KNOW, SO SHE WAS IN THE HOSPITAL MORE OFTEN THAN AT HOME.
WAKA AND TONO WERE THE LAST BIRTHDAY PRESENTS MY MOM GAVE TO ME.

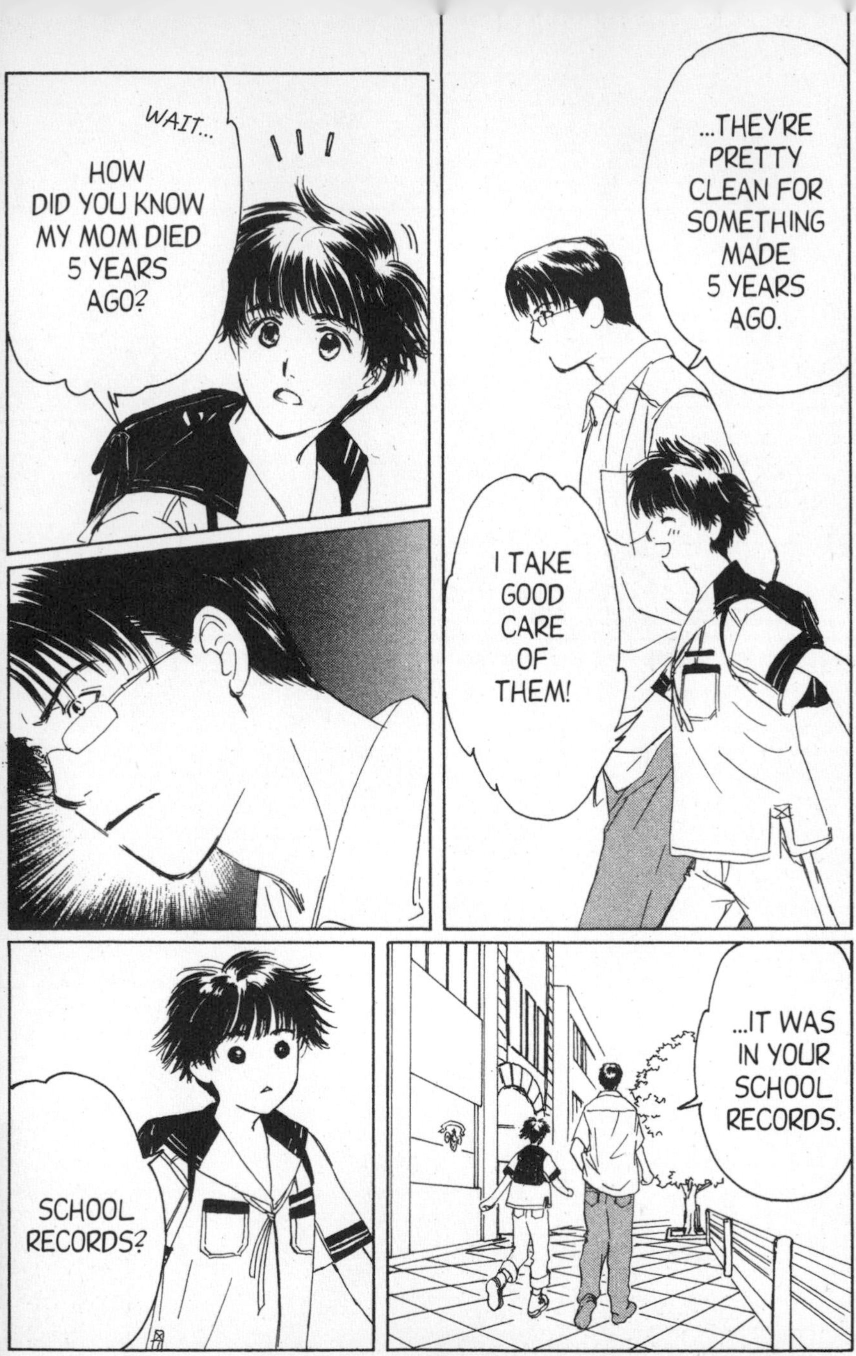
...THEY'RE PRETTY CLEAN FOR SOMETHING MADE 5 YEARS AGO.
I TAKE GOOD CARE OF THEM!
WAIT...
HOW DID YOU KNOW MY MOM DIED 5 YEARS AGO?
...IT WAS IN YOUR SCHOOL RECORDS.
SCHOOL RECORDS?

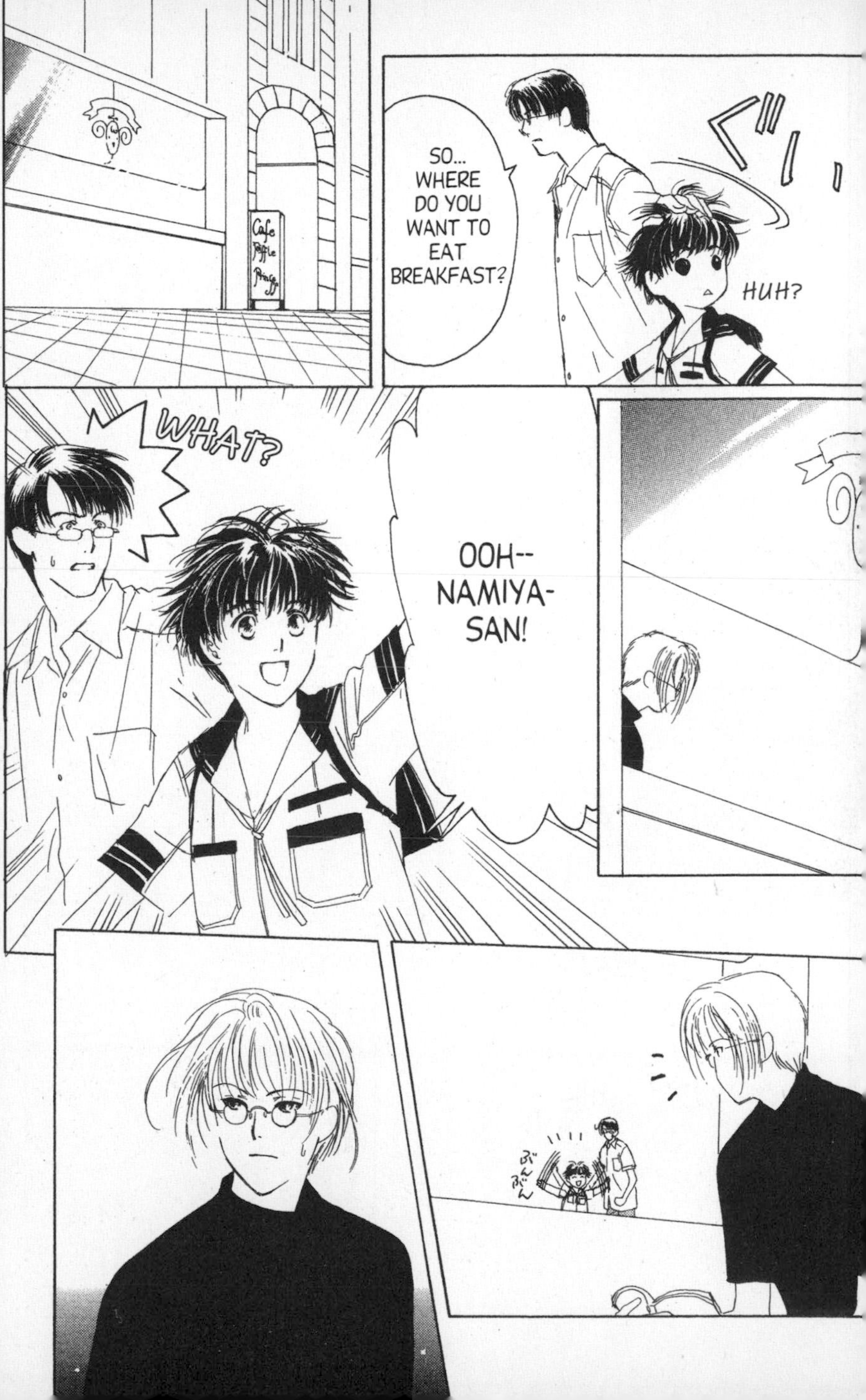
SO... WHERE DO YOU WANT TO EAT BREAKFAST?
HUH?
OOH-- NAMIYA-SAN!
WHAT?
ぶんぶん

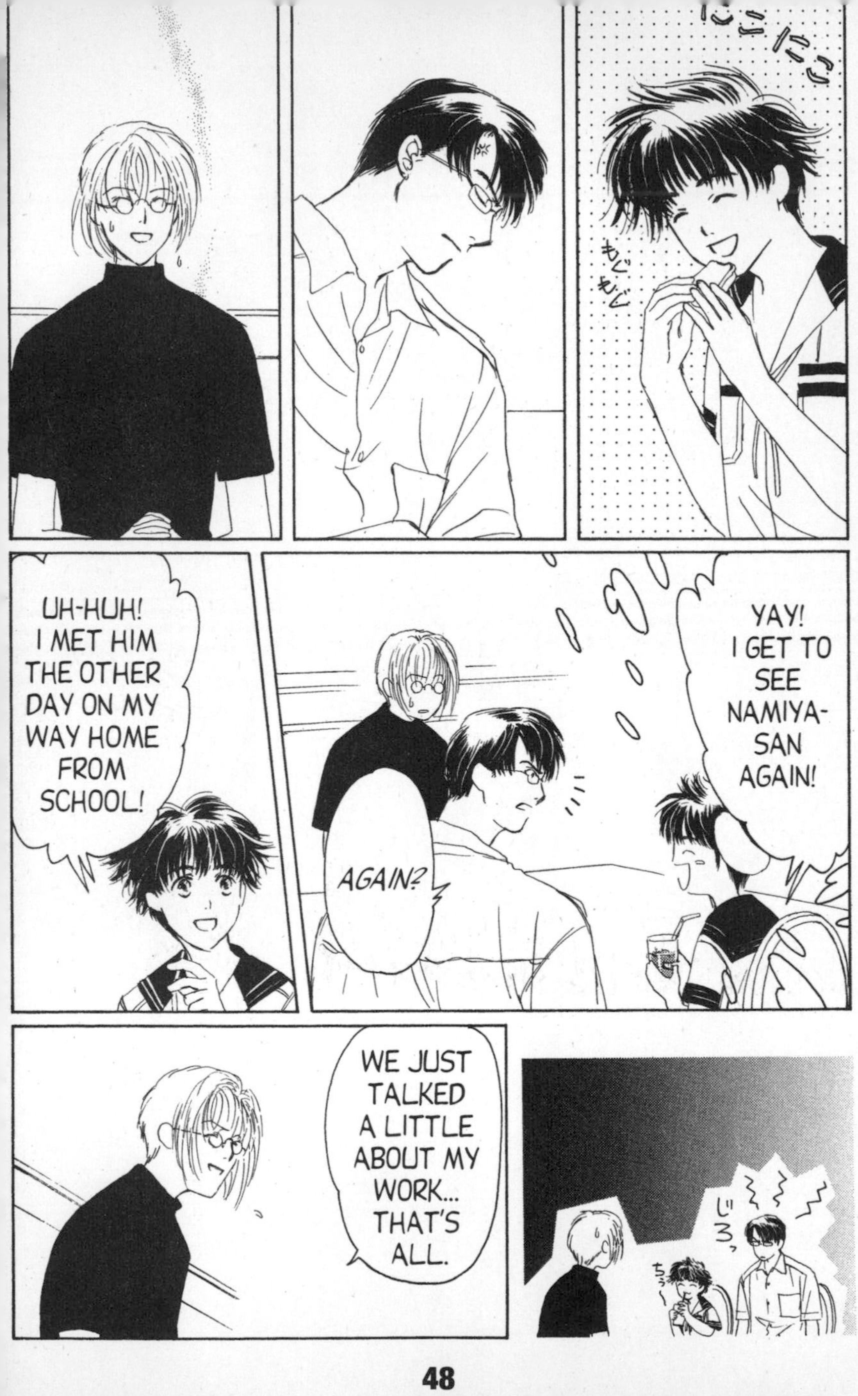
にこにこ
もぐもぐ
YAY! I GET TO SEE NAMIYA-SAN AGAIN!
AGAIN?
UH-HUH! I MET HIM THE OTHER DAY ON MY WAY HOME FROM SCHOOL!
じろっ
WE JUST TALKED A LITTLE ABOUT MY WORK... THAT'S ALL.

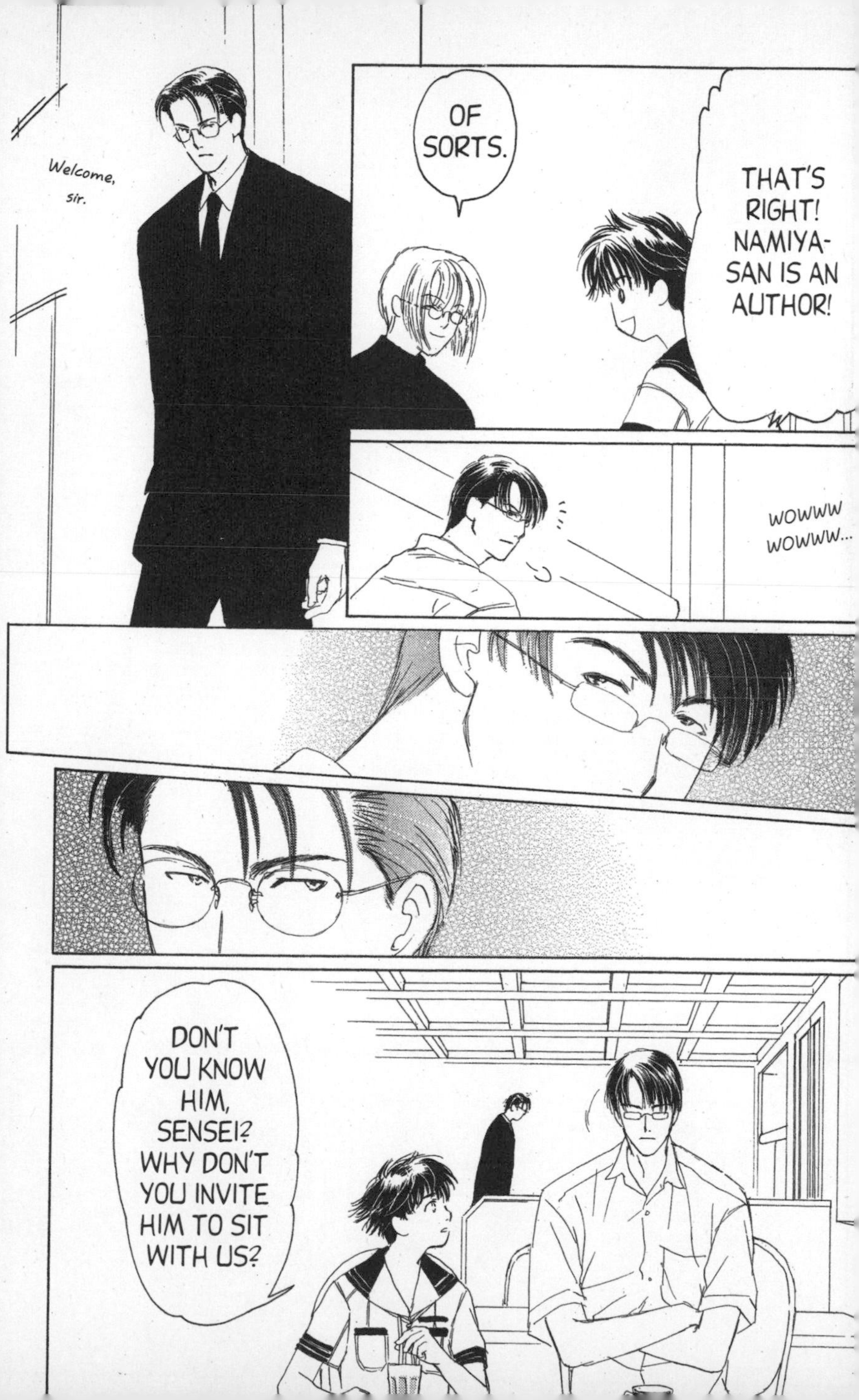
THAT'S RIGHT! NAMIYA-SAN IS AN AUTHOR!
OF SORTS.
WOWWW WOWWW...
Welcome, sir.
DON'T YOU KNOW HIM, SENSEI? WHY DON'T YOU INVITE HIM TO SIT WITH US?

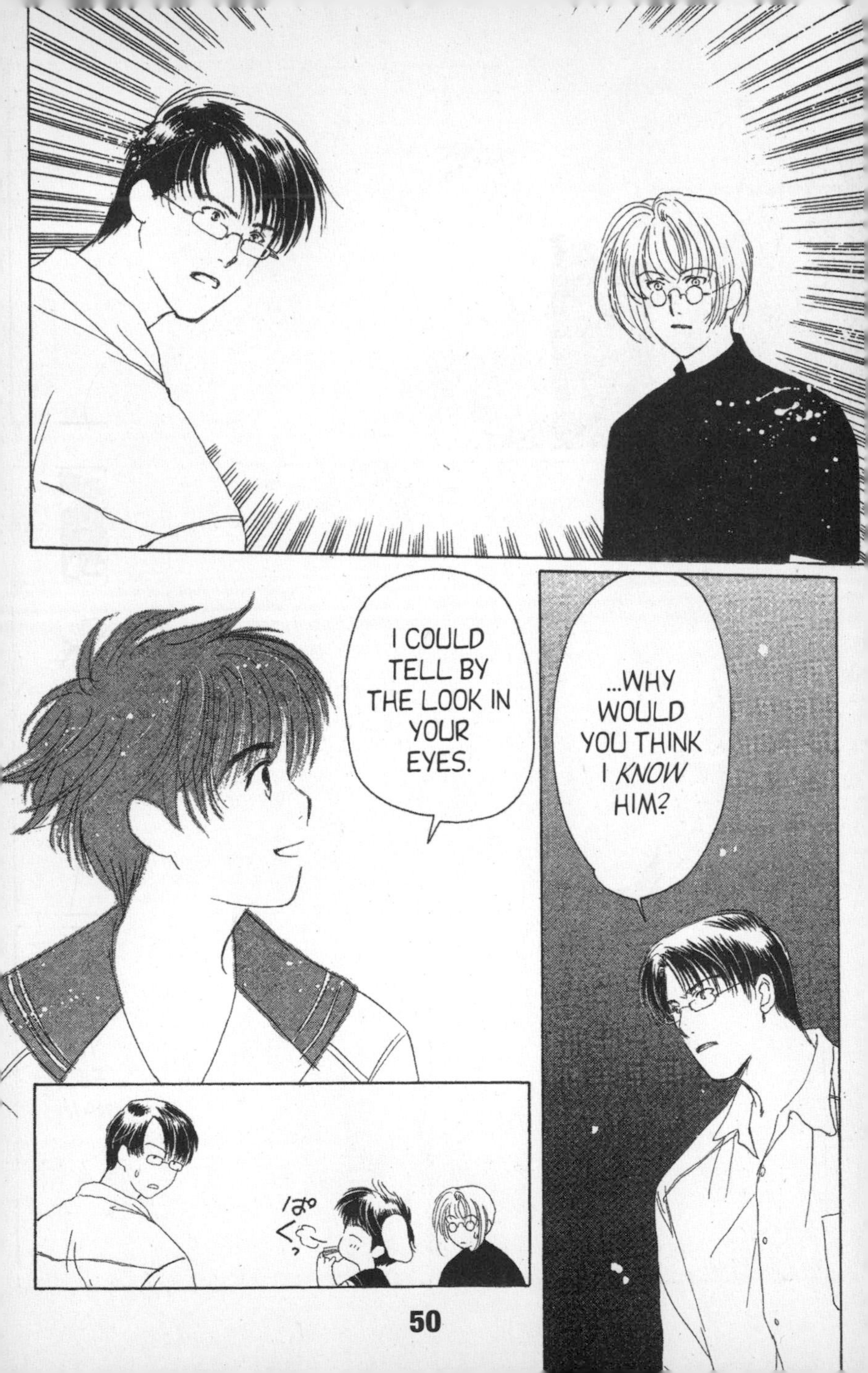
...WHY WOULD YOU THINK I *KNOW* HIM?
I COULD TELL BY THE LOOK IN YOUR EYES.
ぱくっ

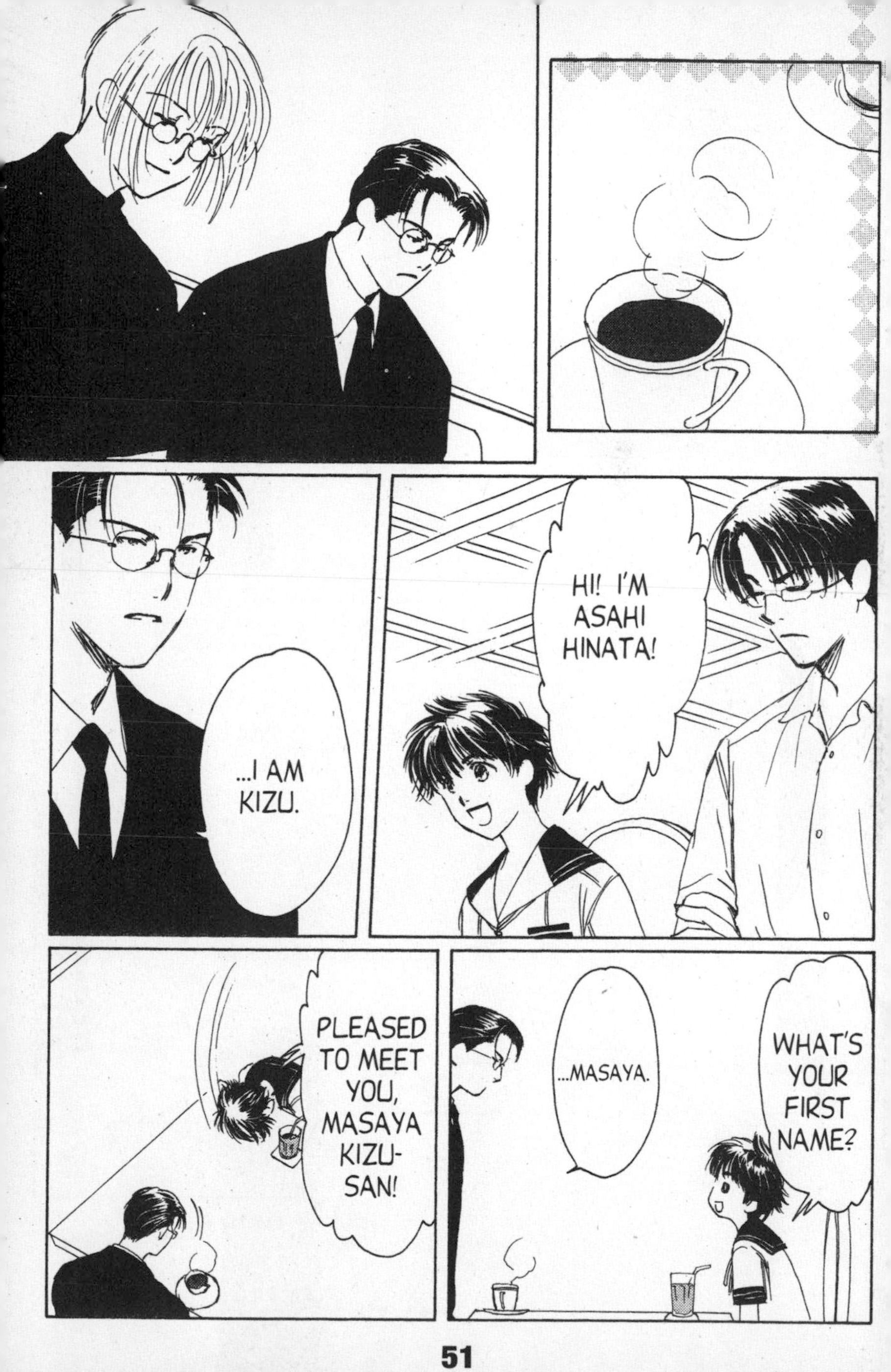
HI! I'M ASAHI HINATA!
...I AM KIZU.
WHAT'S YOUR FIRST NAME?
...MASAYA.
PLEASED TO MEET YOU, MASAYA KIZU-SAN!

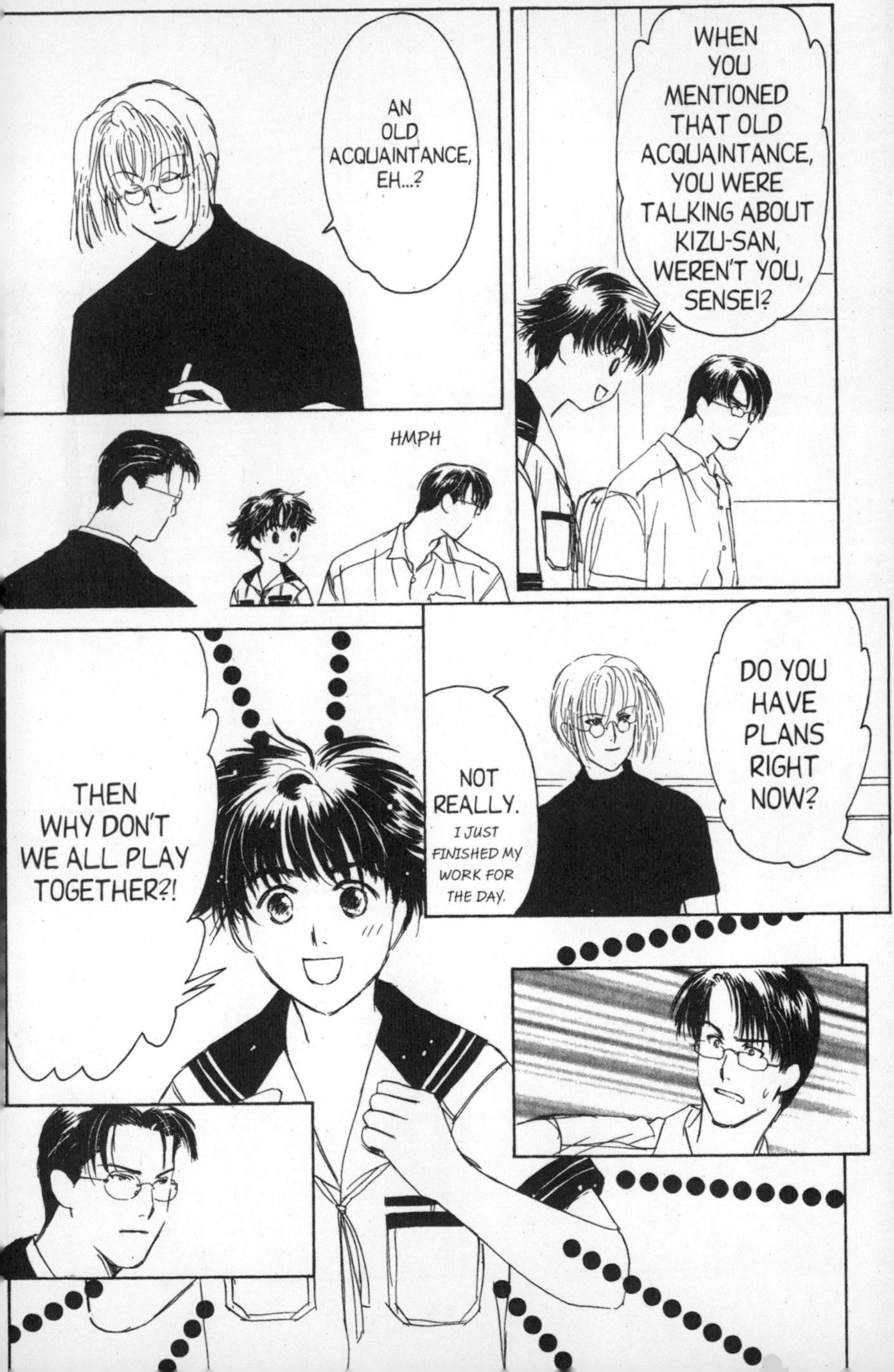
WHEN YOU MENTIONED THAT OLD ACQUAINTANCE, YOU WERE TALKING ABOUT KIZU-SAN, WEREN'T YOU, SENSEI?
AN OLD ACQUAINTANCE, EH...?
HMPH
DO YOU HAVE PLANS RIGHT NOW?
NOT REALLY.
I JUST FINISHED MY WORK FOR THE DAY.
THEN WHY DON'T WE ALL PLAY TOGETHER?!

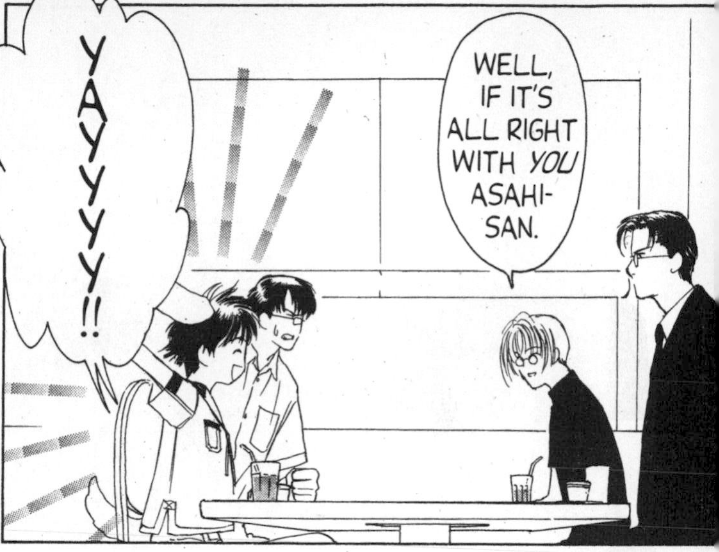
WELL, IF IT'S ALL RIGHT WITH *YOU* ASAHI-SAN.
YAYYYYY!!

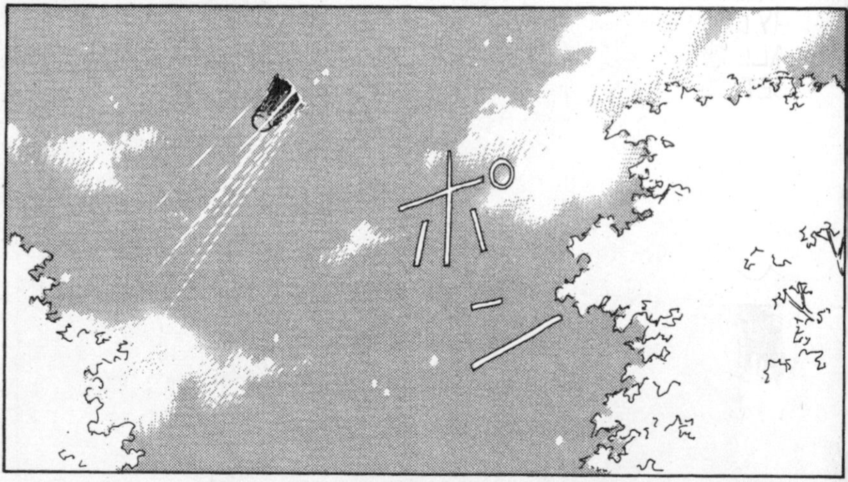
ポーン

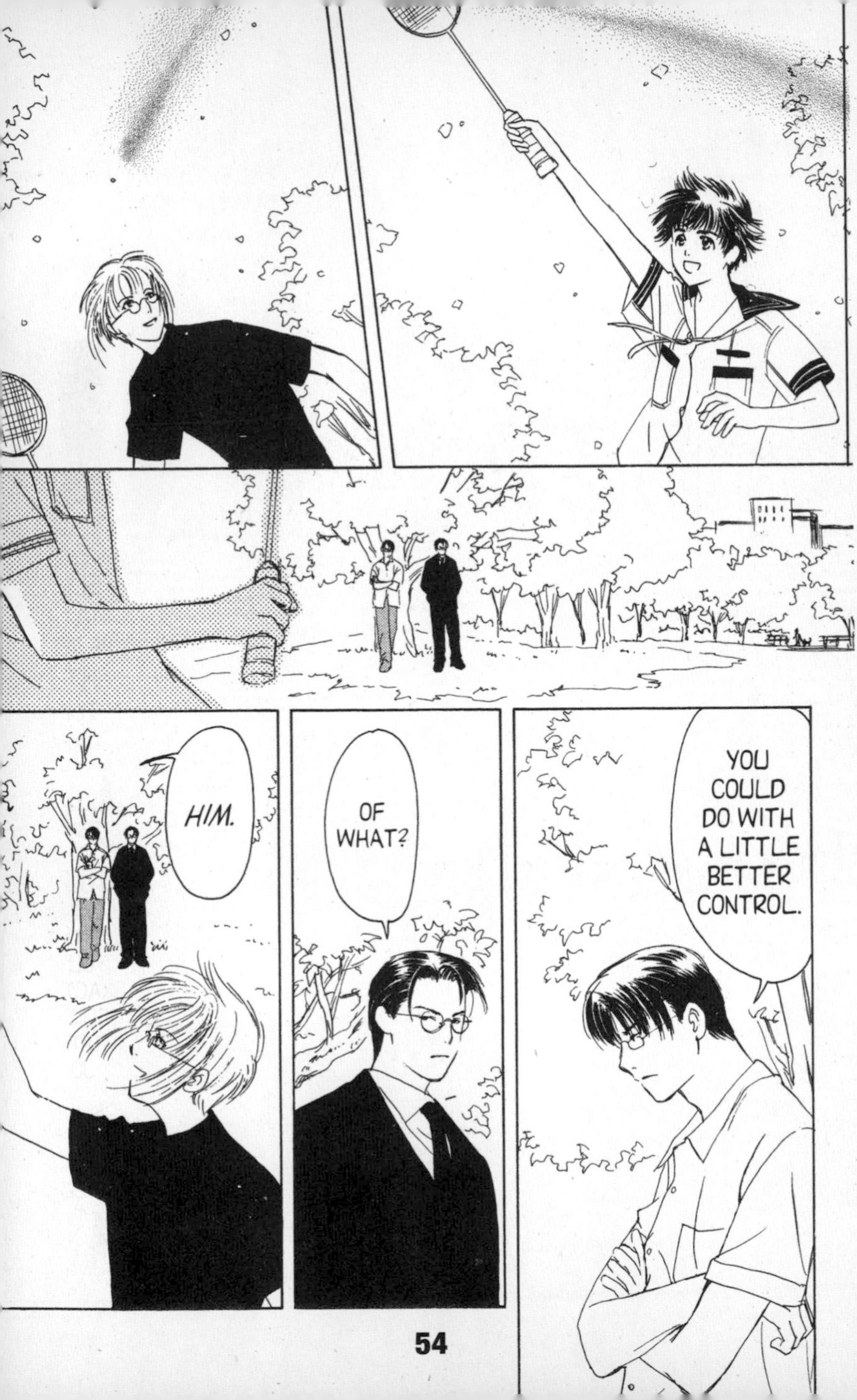
YOU COULD DO WITH A LITTLE BETTER CONTROL.
OF WHAT?
HIM.

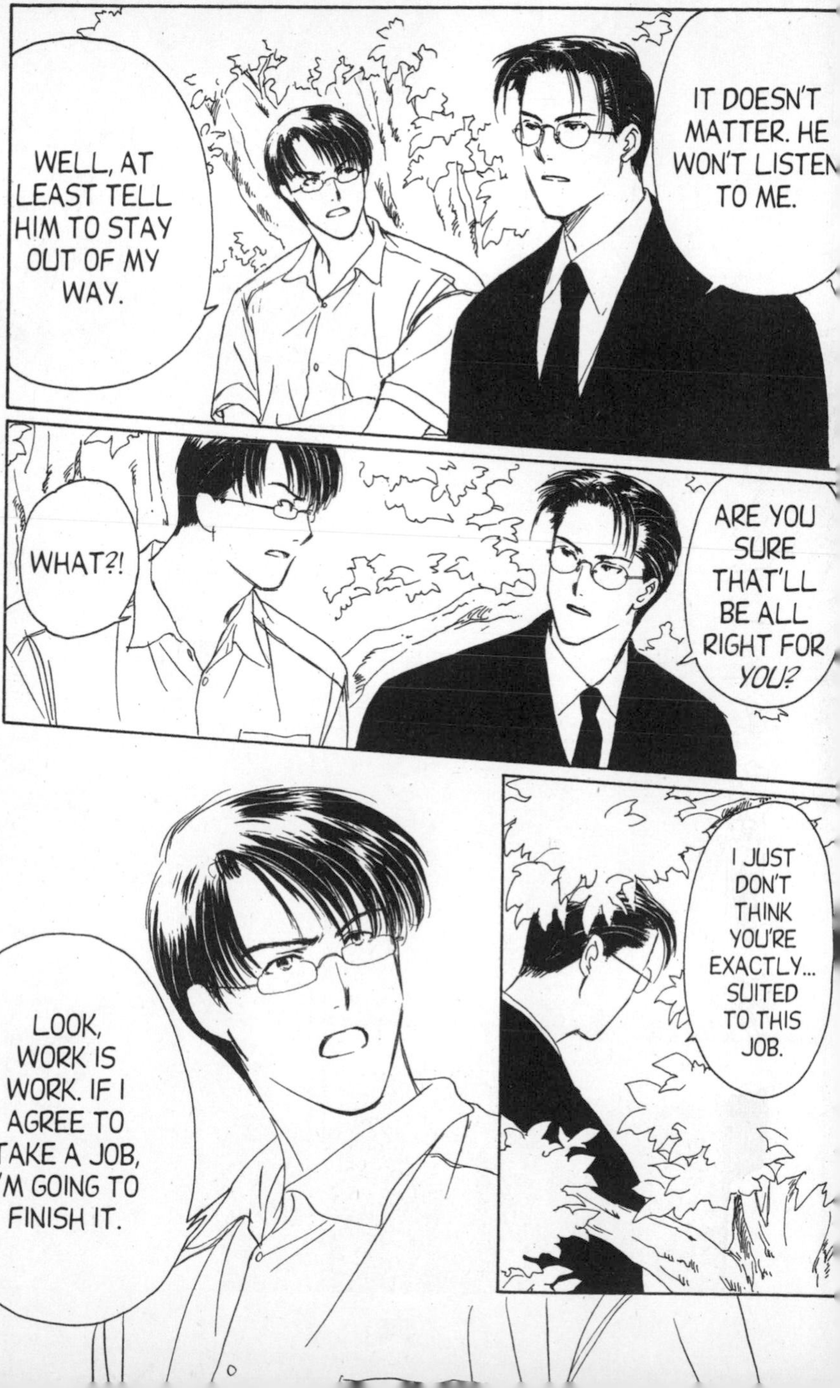
IT DOESN'T MATTER. HE WON'T LISTEN TO ME.
WELL, AT LEAST TELL HIM TO STAY OUT OF MY WAY.
ARE YOU SURE THAT'LL BE ALL RIGHT FOR *YOU?*
WHAT?!
I JUST DON'T THINK YOU'RE EXACTLY... SUITED TO THIS JOB.
LOOK, WORK IS WORK. IF I AGREE TO TAKE A JOB, I'M GOING TO FINISH IT.

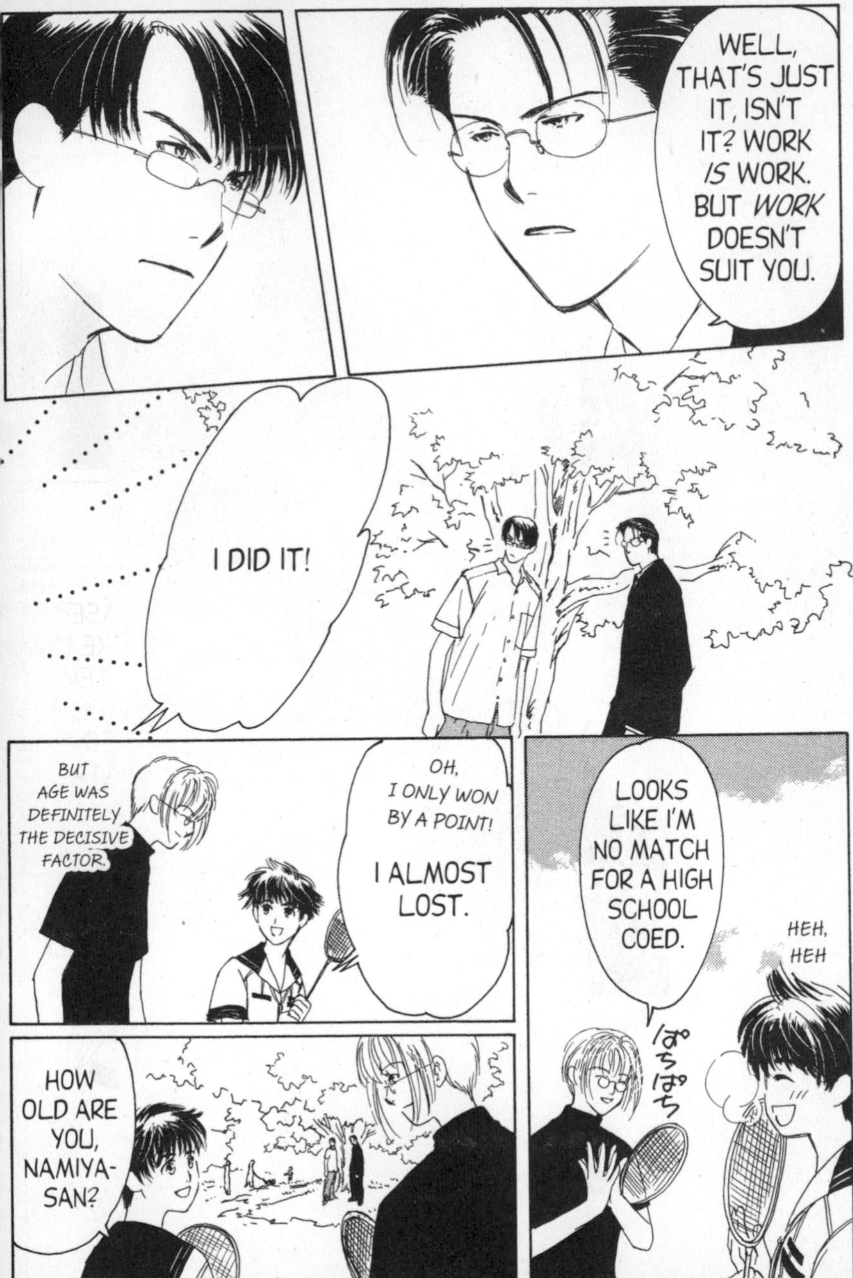
WELL, THAT'S JUST IT, ISN'T IT? WORK *IS* WORK. BUT *WORK* DOESN'T SUIT YOU.
I DID IT!
LOOKS LIKE I'M NO MATCH FOR A HIGH SCHOOL COED.
HEH, HEH
ぱちぱち
OH, I ONLY WON BY A POINT!
I ALMOST LOST.
BUT AGE WAS DEFINITELY THE DECISIVE FACTOR.
HOW OLD ARE YOU, NAMIYA-SAN?

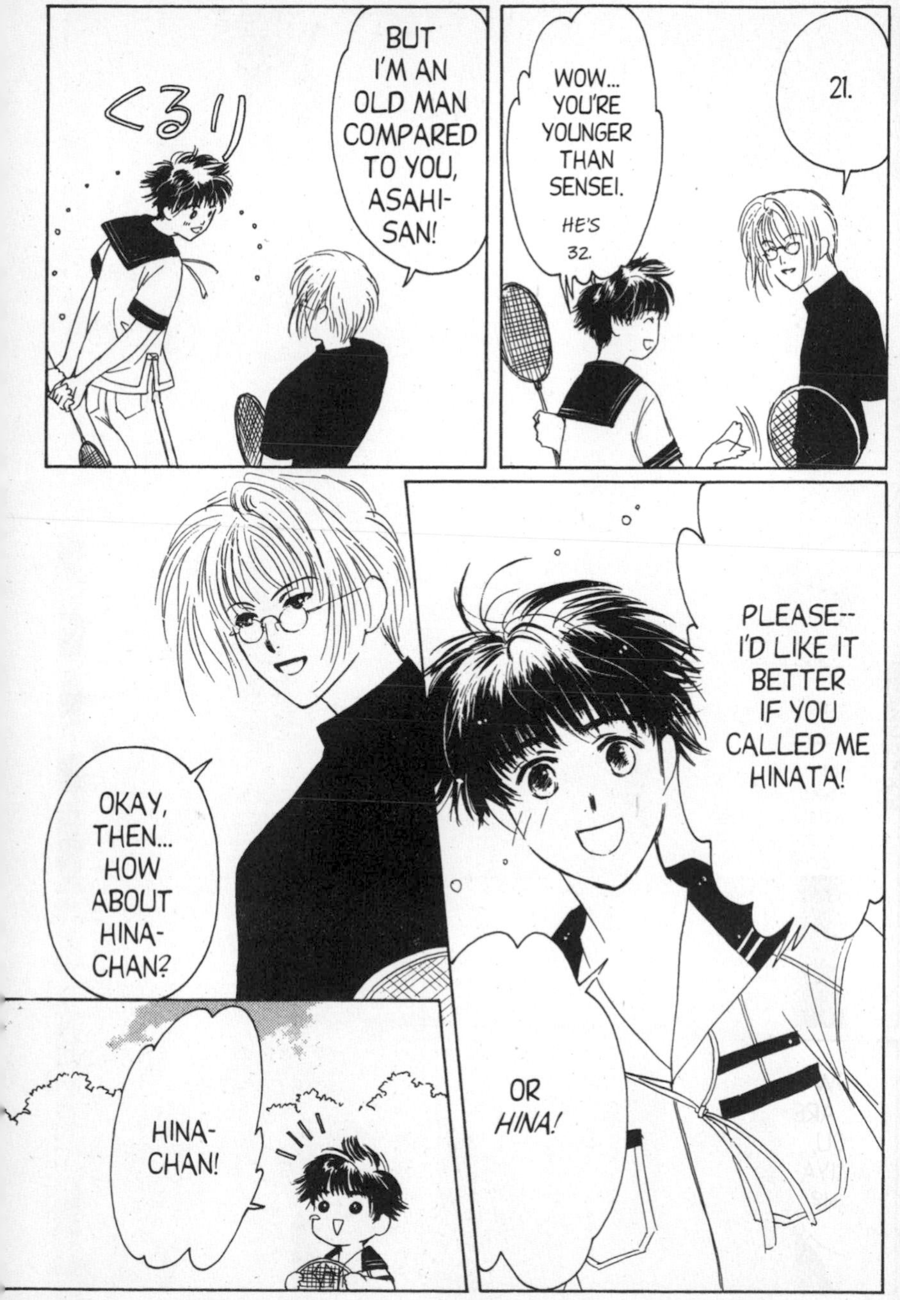
21.
WOW... YOU'RE YOUNGER THAN SENSEI.
HE'S 32.
くるり
BUT I'M AN OLD MAN COMPARED TO YOU, ASAHI-SAN!
PLEASE-- I'D LIKE IT BETTER IF YOU CALLED ME HINATA!
OR *HINA!*
OKAY, THEN... HOW ABOUT HINA-CHAN?
HINA-CHAN!

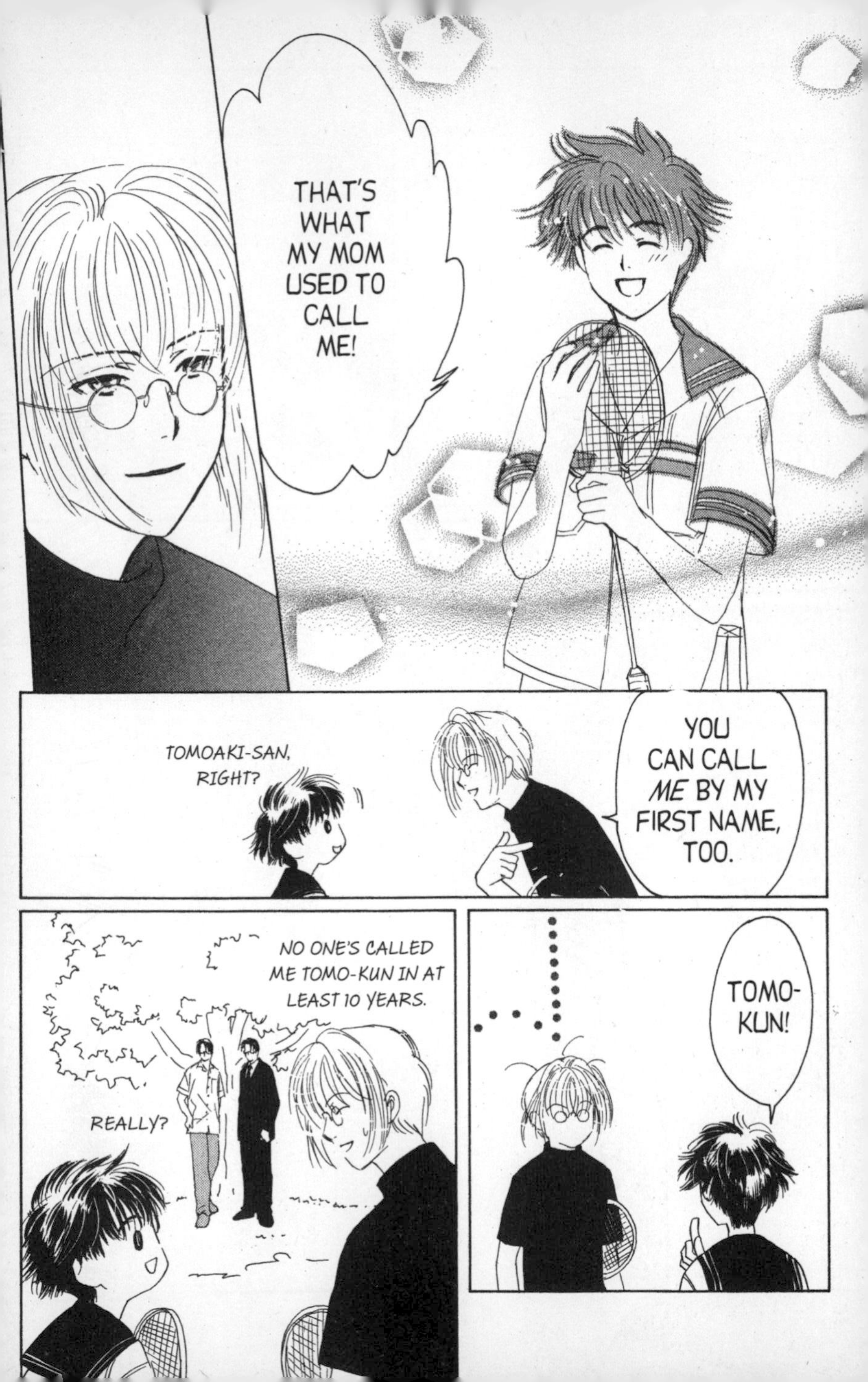
THAT'S WHAT MY MOM USED TO CALL ME!
YOU CAN CALL *ME* BY MY FIRST NAME, TOO.
TOMOAKI-SAN, RIGHT?
TOMO-KUN!
NO ONE'S CALLED ME TOMO-KUN IN AT LEAST 10 YEARS.
REALLY?

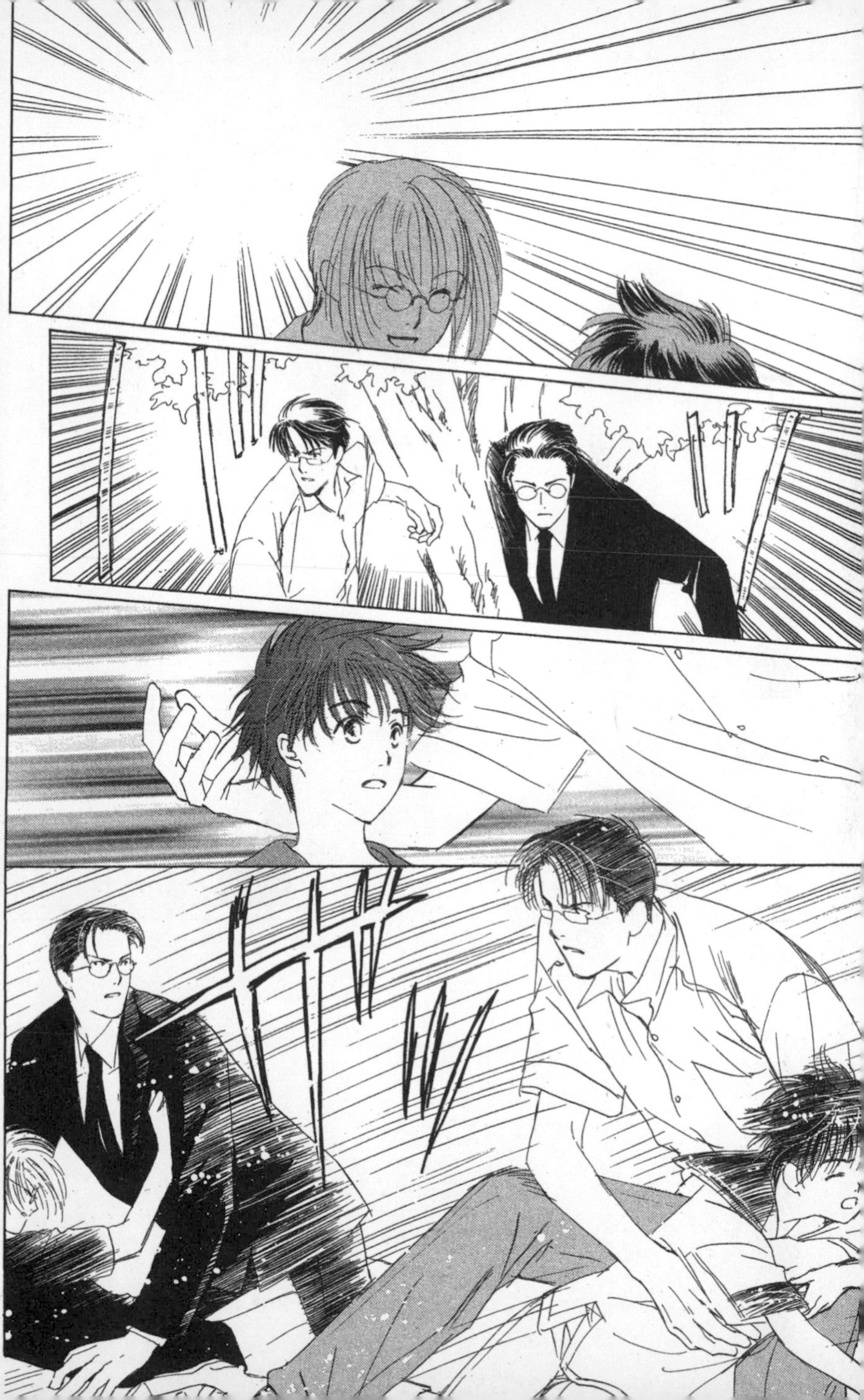

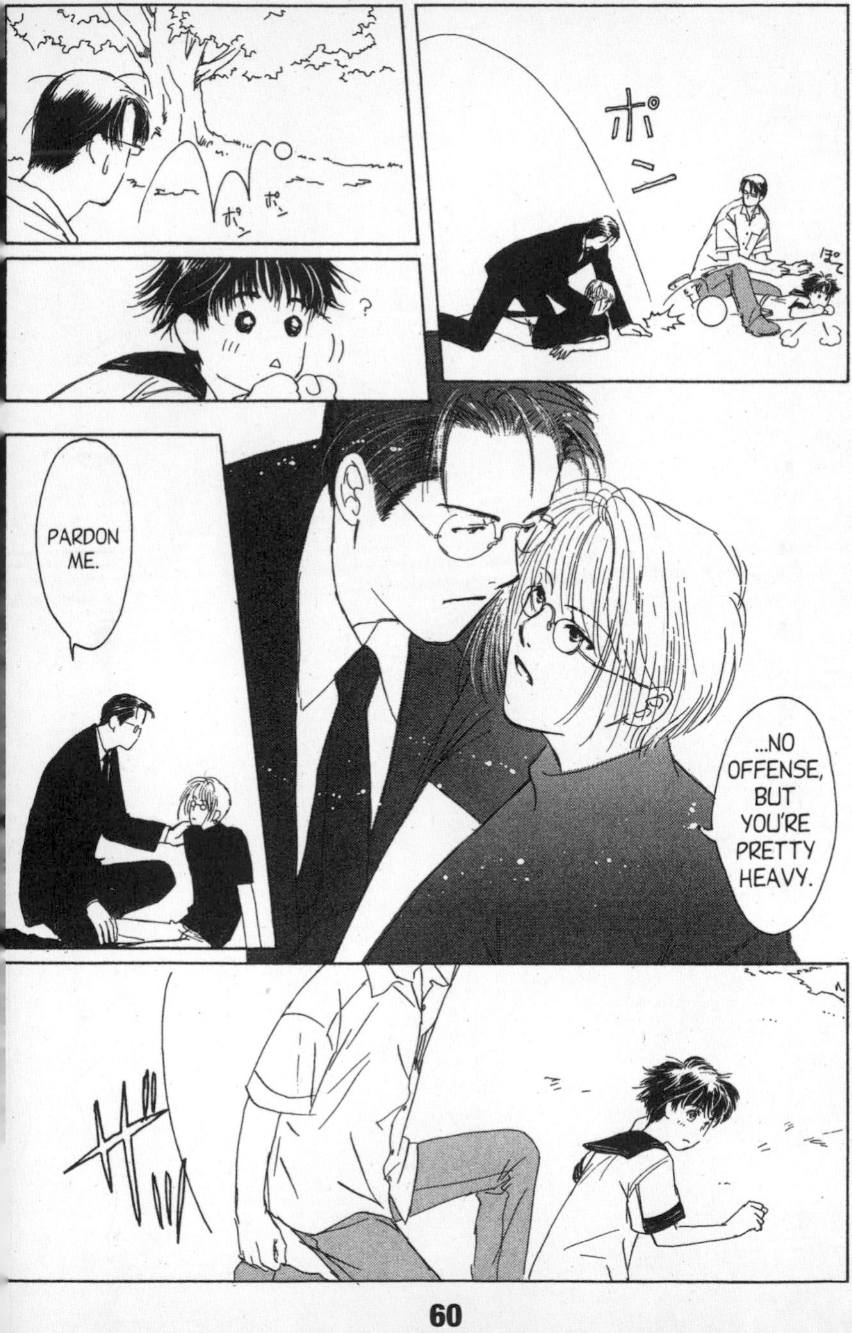
ポーン
ぽて
ポン
ポン
?
...NO OFFENSE, BUT YOU'RE PRETTY HEAVY.
PARDON ME.
...
...

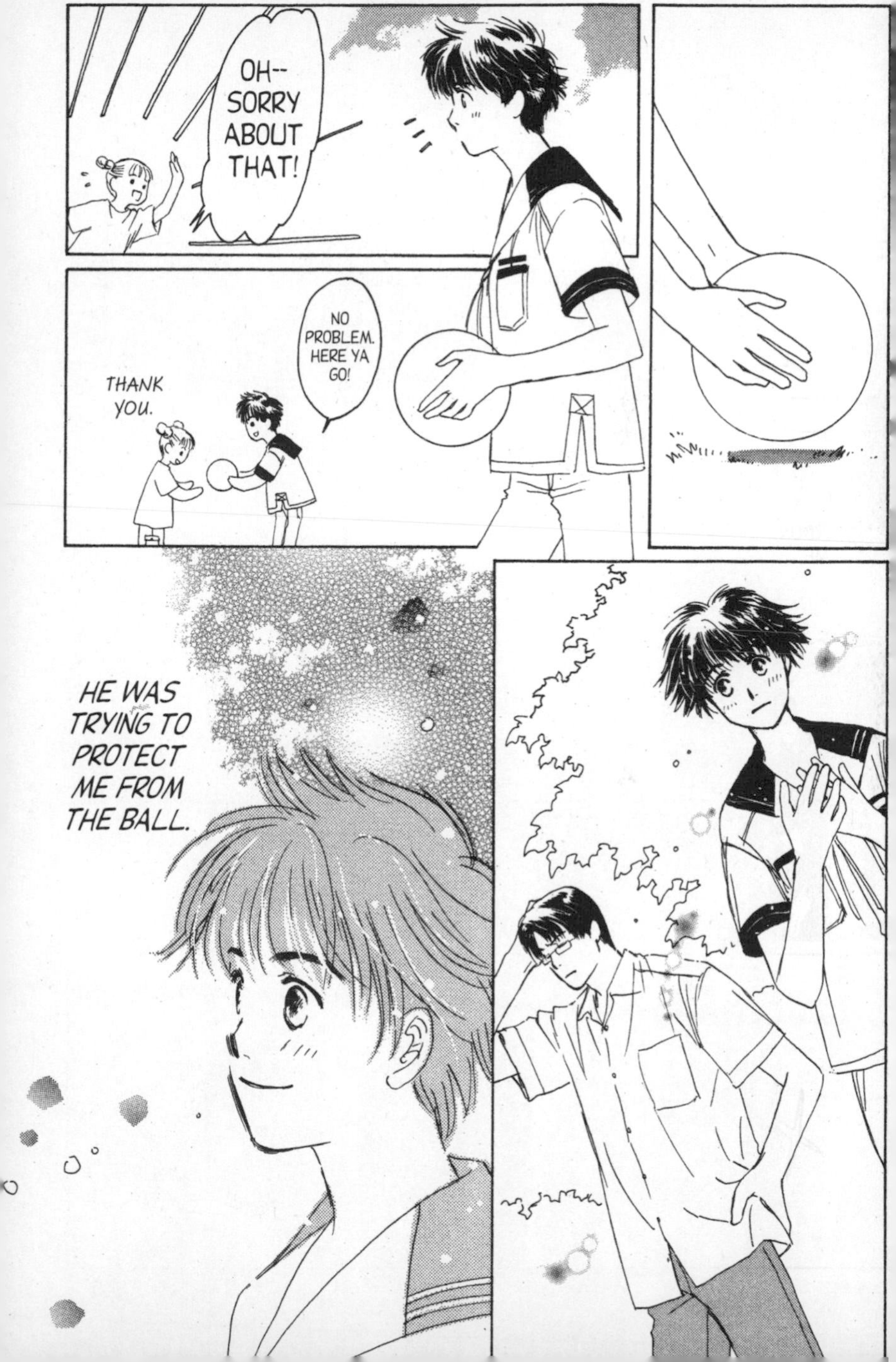
OH-- SORRY ABOUT THAT!
NO PROBLEM. HERE YA GO!
THANK YOU.
HE WAS TRYING TO PROTECT ME FROM THE BALL.

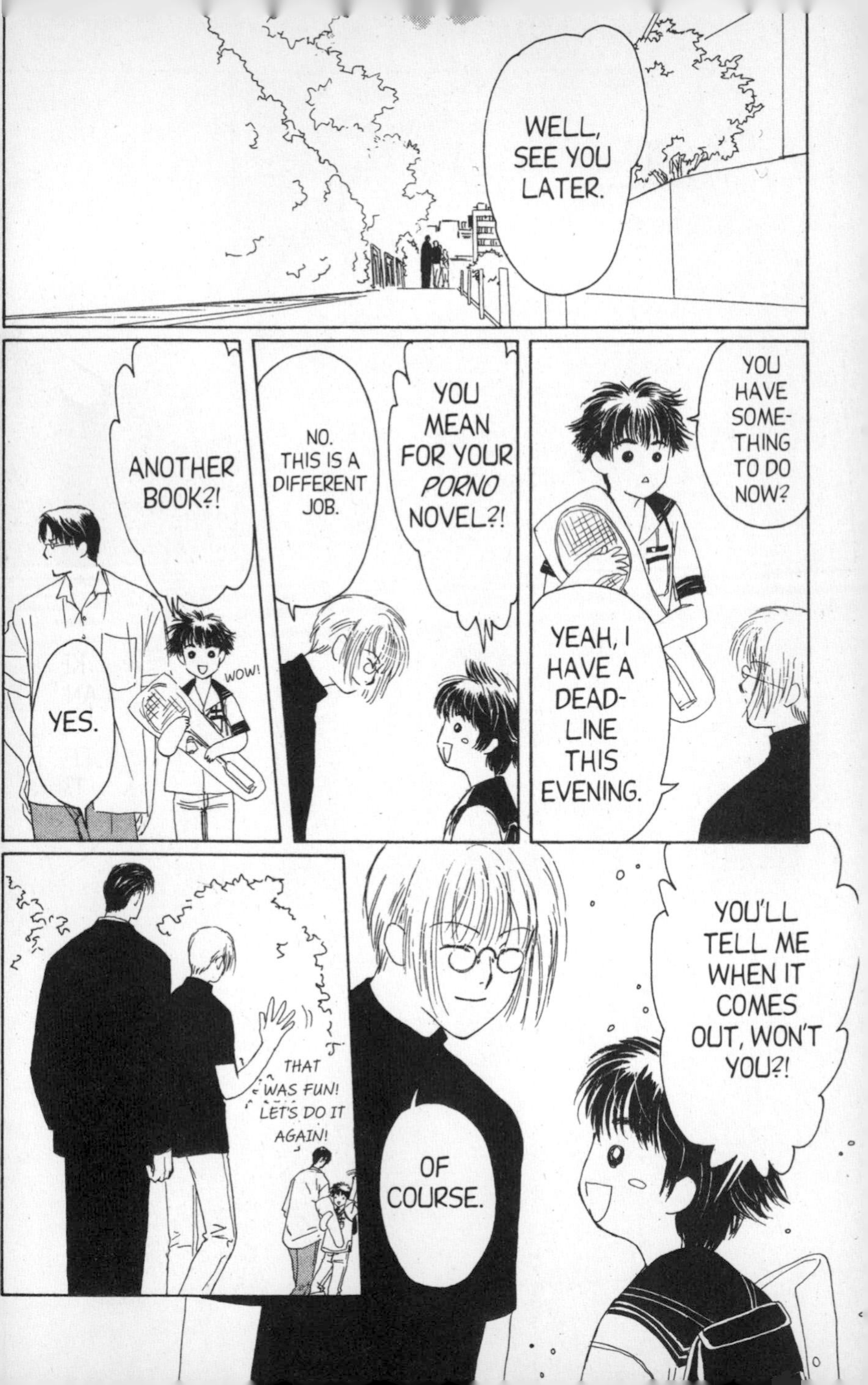
WELL, SEE YOU LATER.
YOU HAVE SOMETHING TO DO NOW?
YEAH, I HAVE A DEADLINE THIS EVENING.
YOU MEAN FOR YOUR *PORNO* NOVEL?!
NO. THIS IS A DIFFERENT JOB.
ANOTHER BOOK?!
WOW!
YES.
YOU'LL TELL ME WHEN IT COMES OUT, WON'T YOU?!
OF COURSE.
THAT WAS FUN! LET'S DO IT AGAIN!

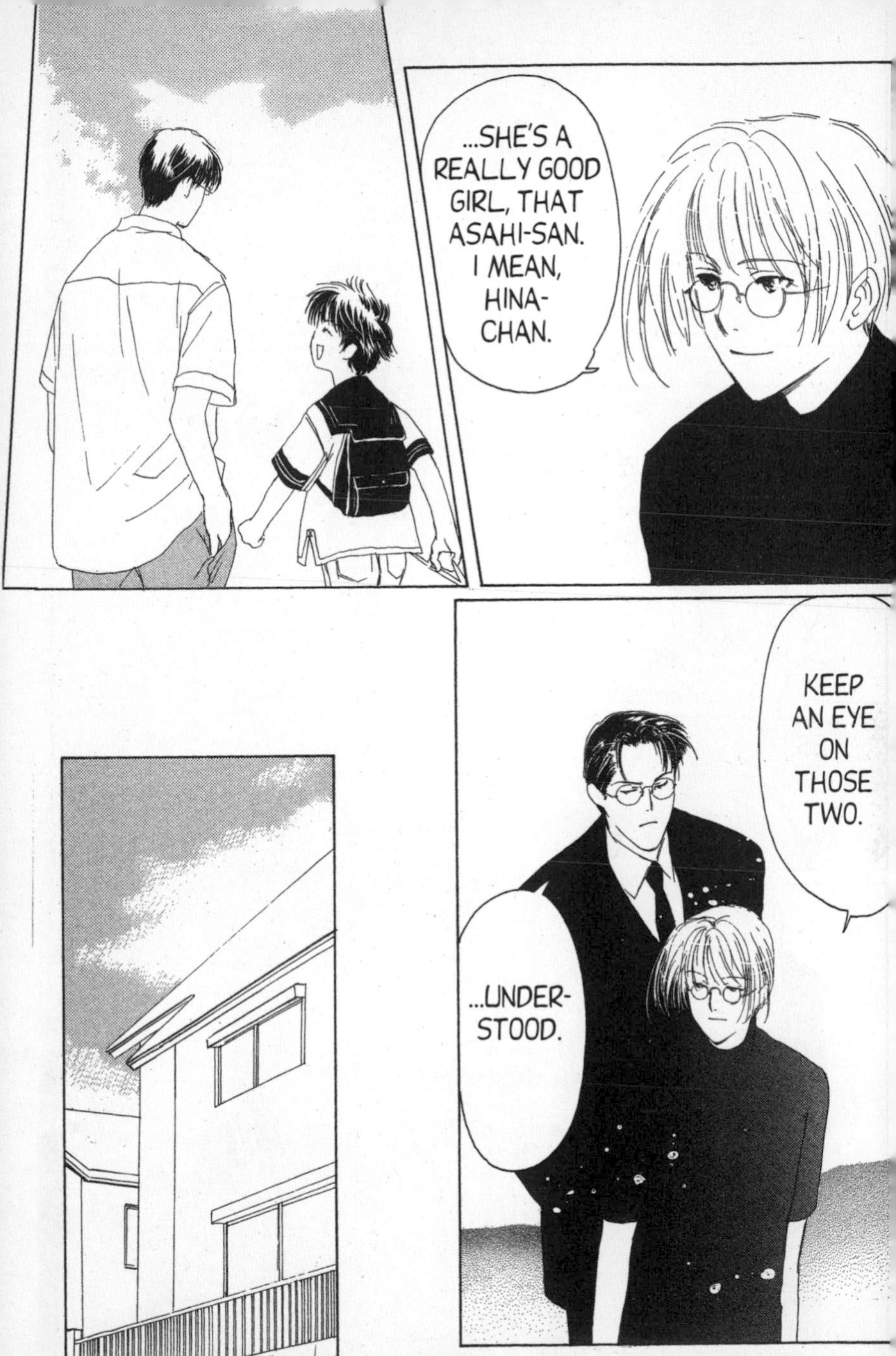
...SHE'S A REALLY GOOD GIRL, THAT ASAHI-SAN. I MEAN, HINA-CHAN.
KEEP AN EYE ON THOSE TWO.
...UNDER-STOOD.

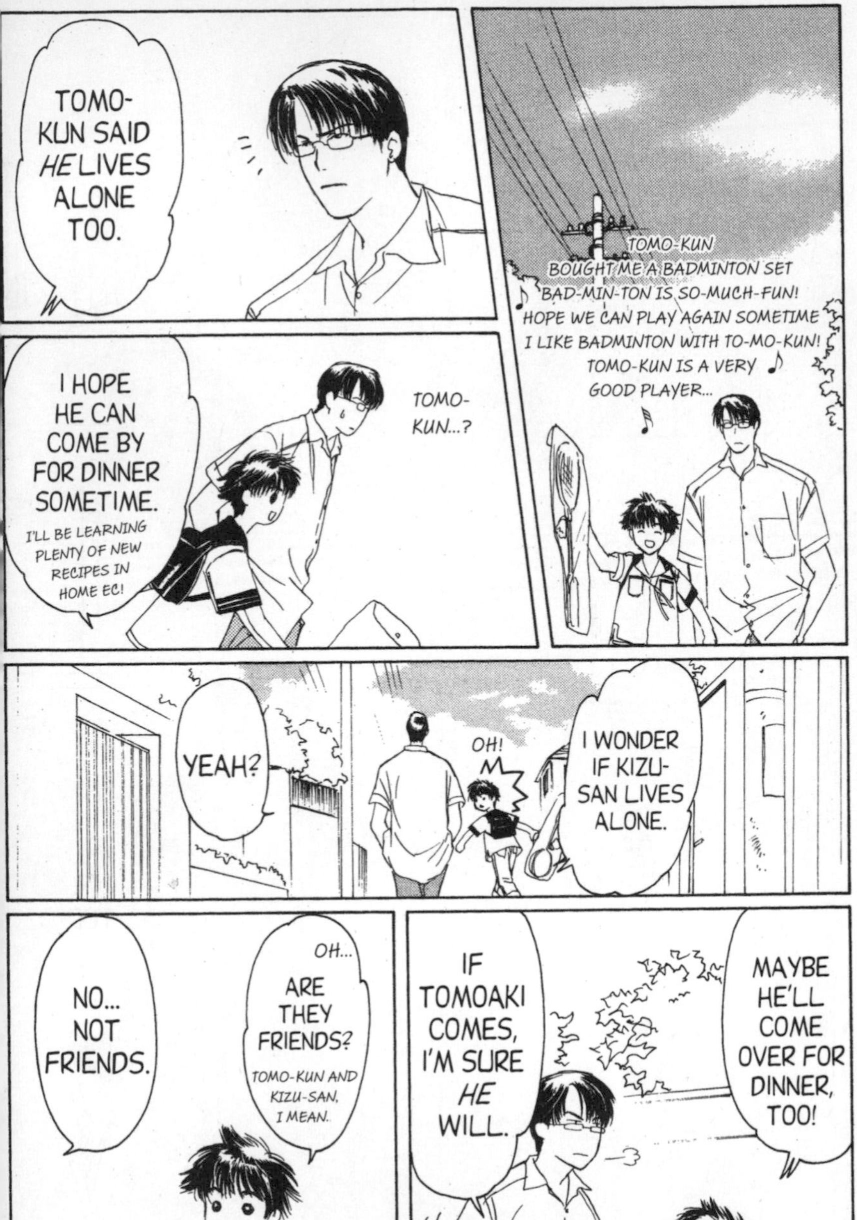
TOMO-KUN
BOUGHT ME A BADMINTON SET
BAD-MIN-TON IS SO-MUCH-FUN!
HOPE WE CAN PLAY AGAIN SOMETIME
I LIKE BADMINTON WITH TO-MO-KUN!
TOMO-KUN IS A VERY
GOOD PLAYER...
TOMO-KUN SAID *HE* LIVES ALONE TOO.
TOMO-KUN...?
I HOPE HE CAN COME BY FOR DINNER SOMETIME.
I'LL BE LEARNING PLENTY OF NEW RECIPES IN HOME EC!
I WONDER IF KIZU-SAN LIVES ALONE.
OH!
YEAH?
MAYBE HE'LL COME OVER FOR DINNER, TOO!
IF TOMOAKI COMES, I'M SURE *HE* WILL.
OH...
ARE THEY FRIENDS?
TOMO-KUN AND KIZU-SAN, I MEAN.
NO... NOT FRIENDS.

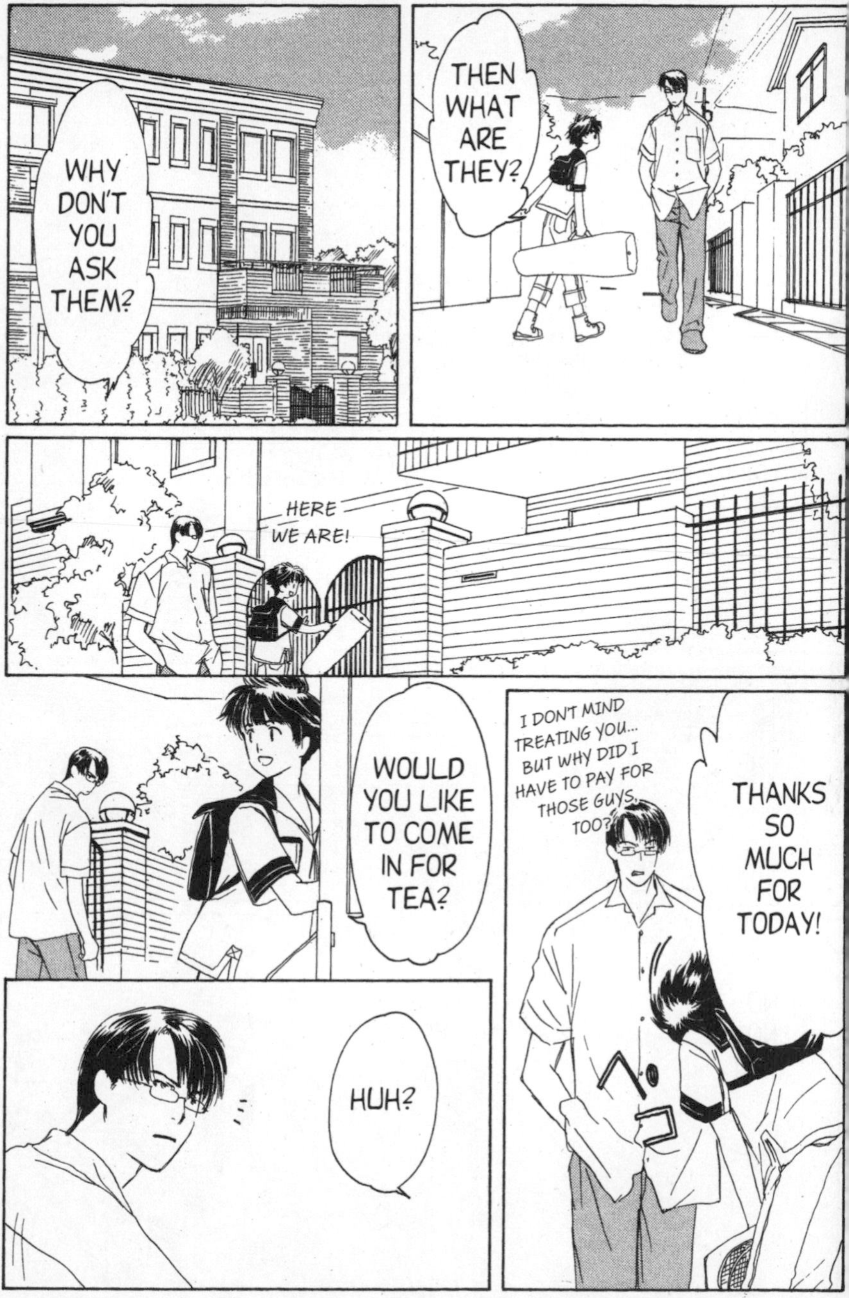
THEN WHAT ARE THEY?
WHY DON'T YOU ASK THEM?
HERE WE ARE!
THANKS SO MUCH FOR TODAY!
I DON'T MIND TREATING YOU... BUT WHY DID I HAVE TO PAY FOR THOSE GUYS, TOO?
WOULD YOU LIKE TO COME IN FOR TEA?
HUH?

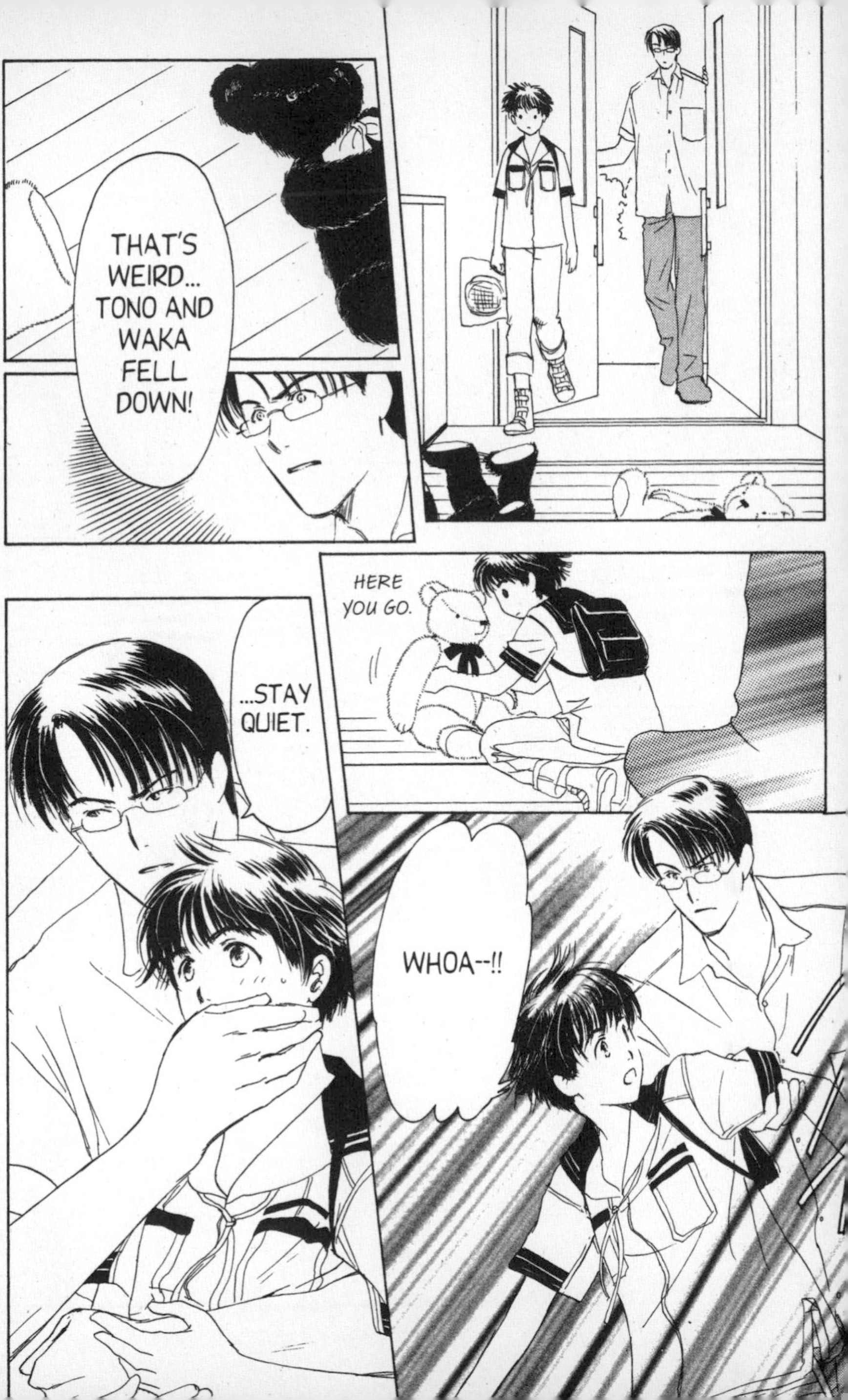
THAT'S WEIRD... TONO AND WAKA FELL DOWN!
HERE YOU GO.
WHOA--!!
...STAY QUIET.

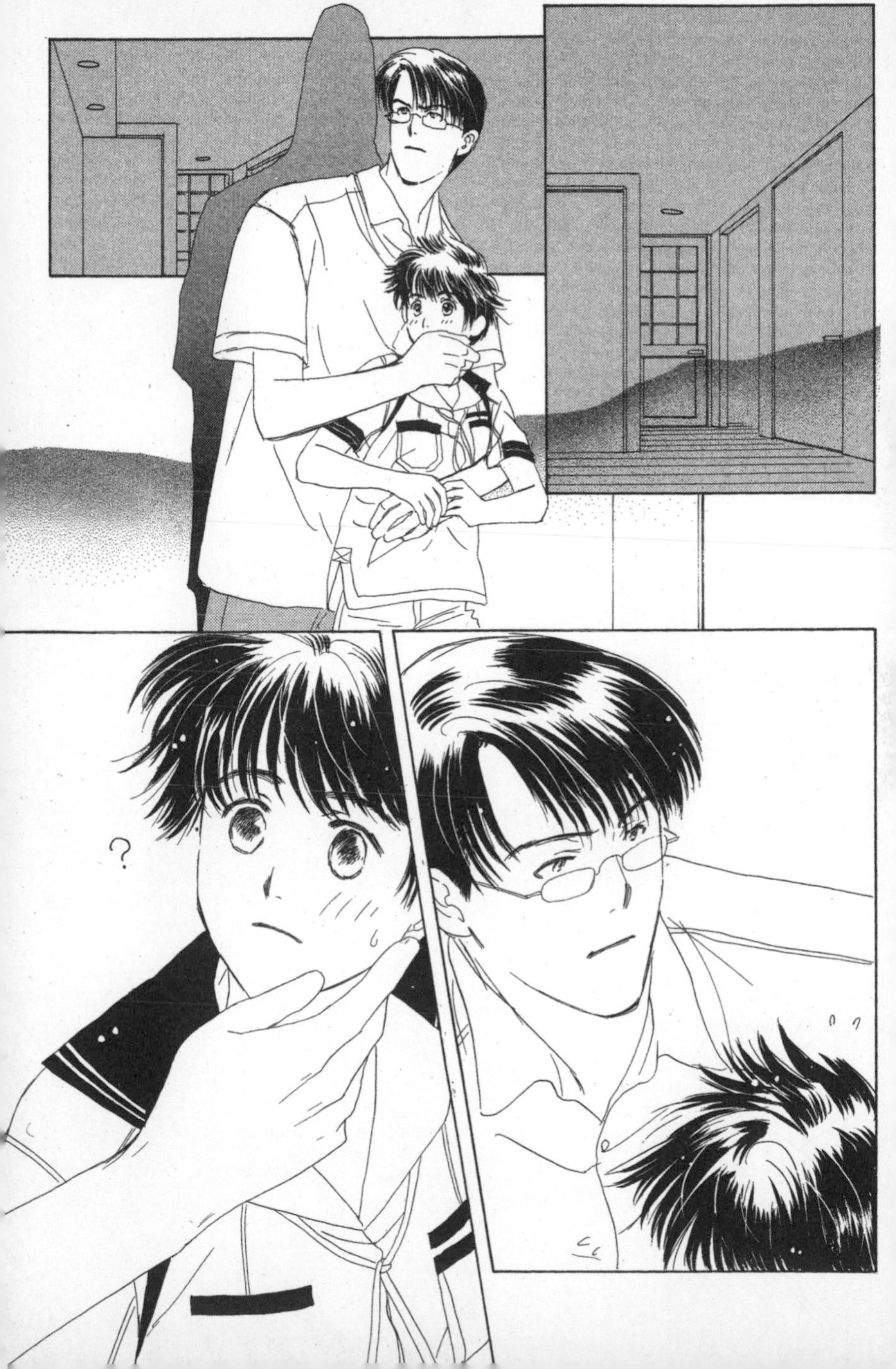
?

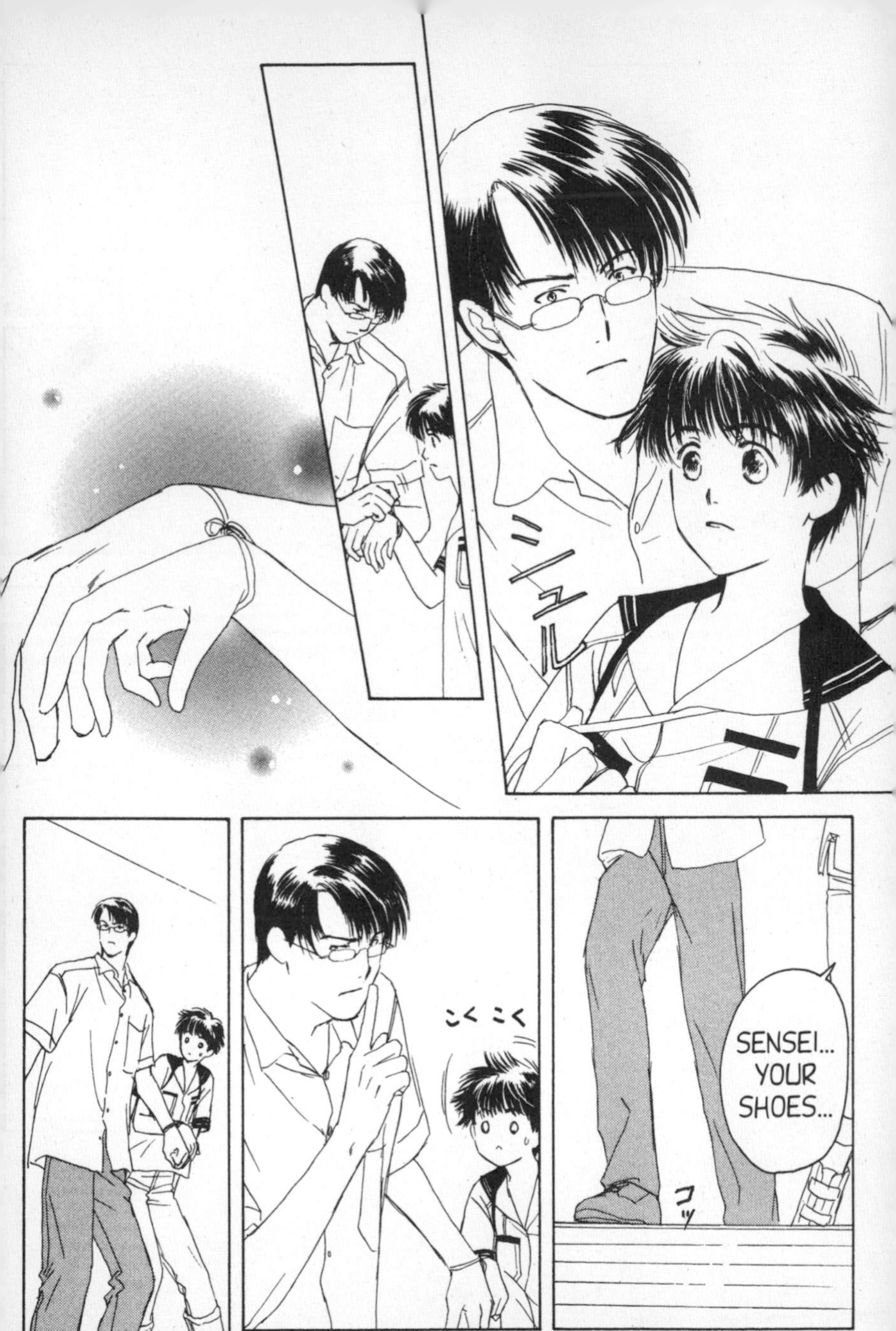
シュル
SENSEI... YOUR SHOES...
コッ
こくこく

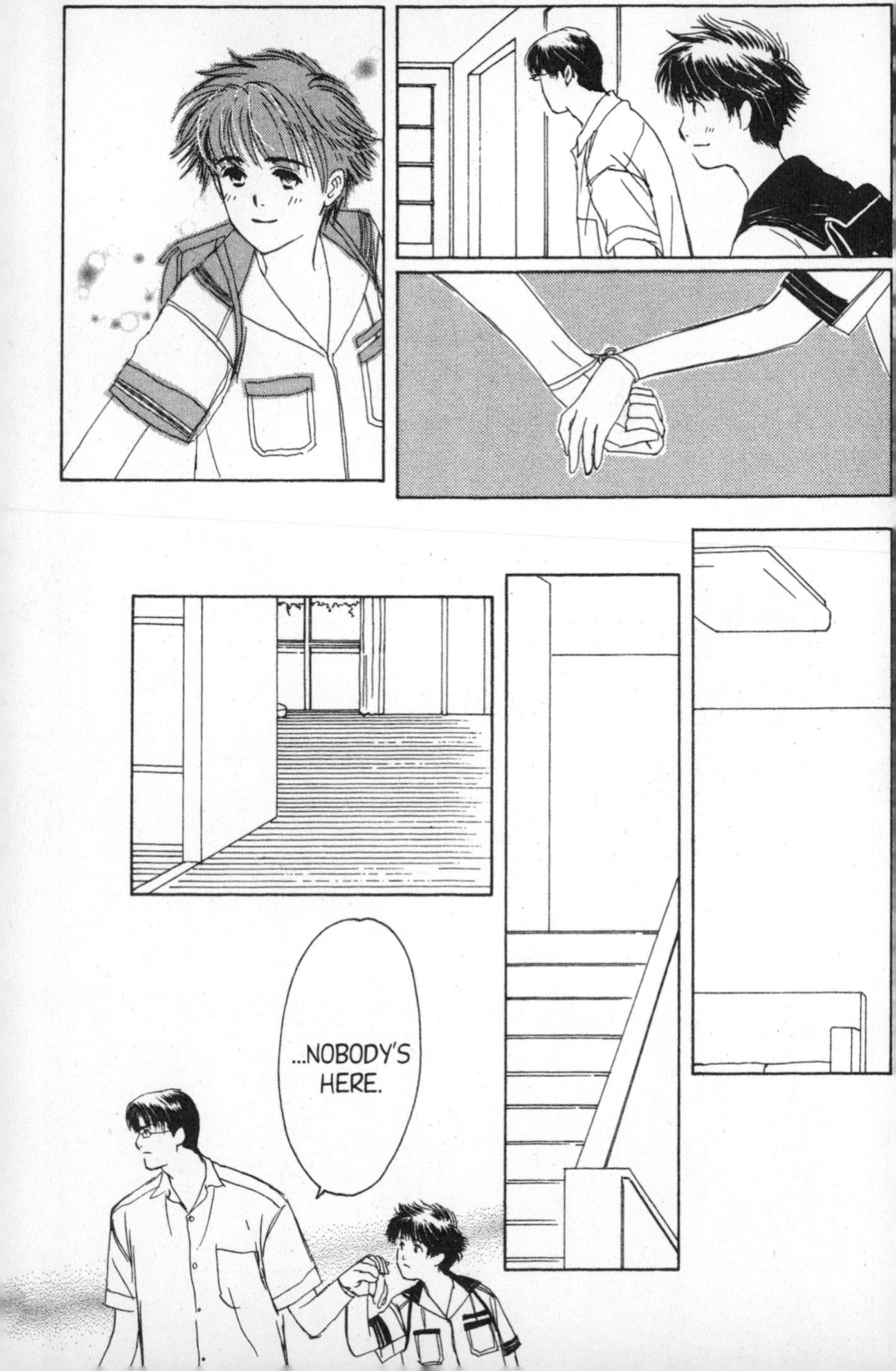
...NOBODY'S HERE.

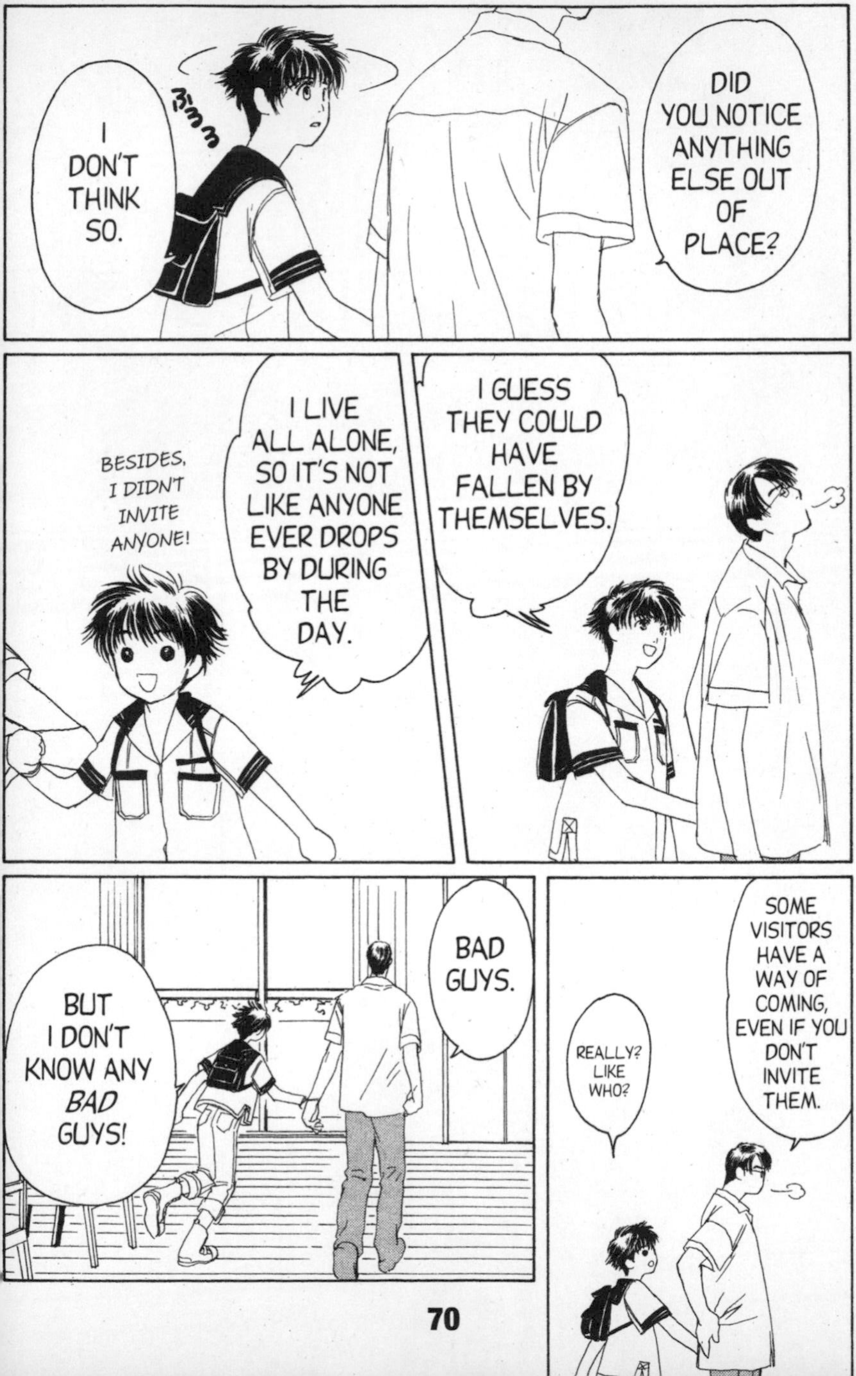
DID YOU NOTICE ANYTHING ELSE OUT OF PLACE?
I DON'T THINK SO.
I GUESS THEY COULD HAVE FALLEN BY THEMSELVES.
I LIVE ALL ALONE, SO IT'S NOT LIKE ANYONE EVER DROPS BY DURING THE DAY.
BESIDES, I DIDN'T INVITE ANYONE!
SOME VISITORS HAVE A WAY OF COMING, EVEN IF YOU DON'T INVITE THEM.
REALLY? LIKE WHO?
BAD GUYS.
BUT I DON'T KNOW ANY *BAD* GUYS!

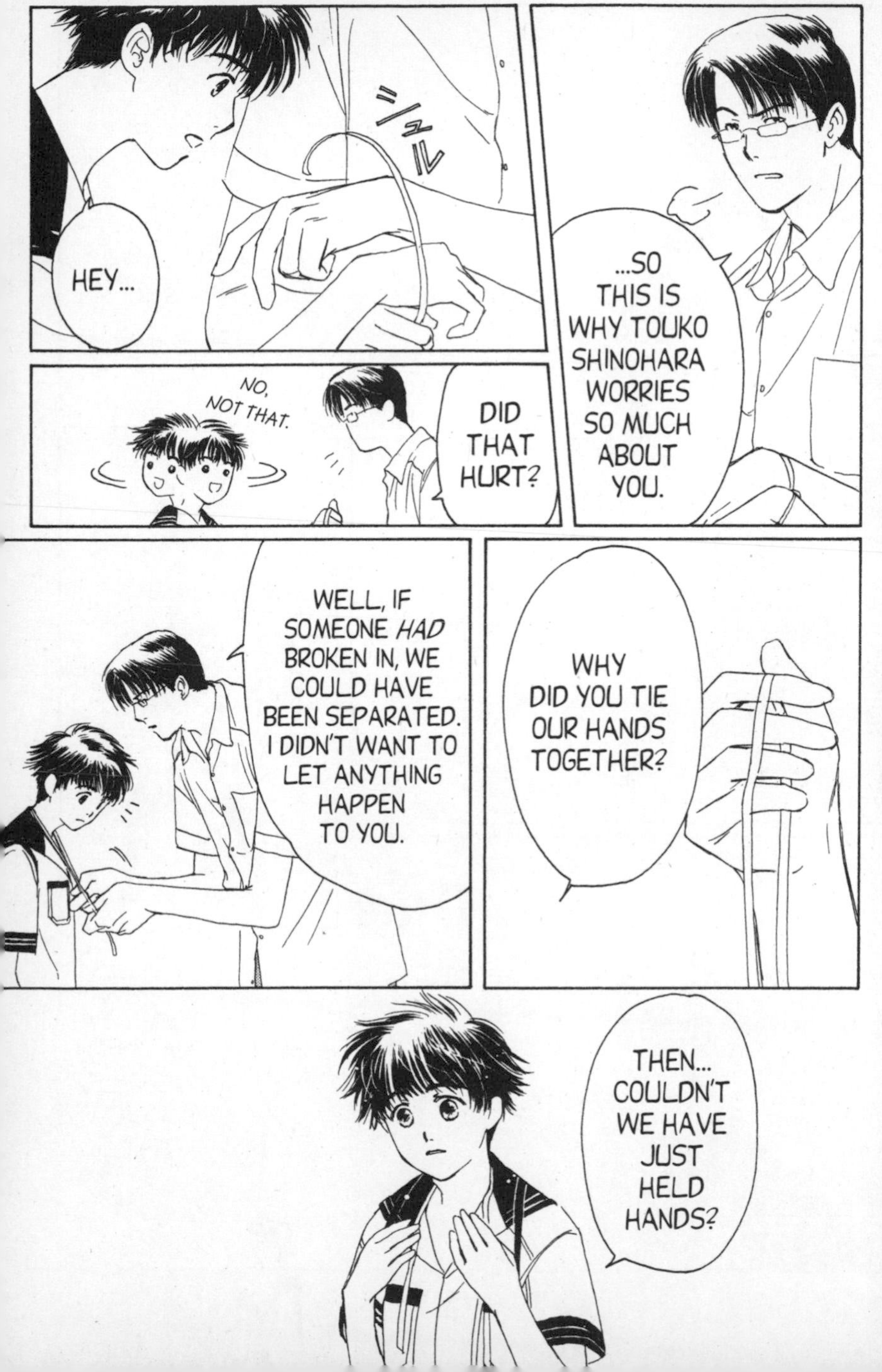
...SO THIS IS WHY TOUKO SHINOHARA WORRIES SO MUCH ABOUT YOU.
シュル
HEY...
DID THAT HURT?
NO, NOT THAT.
WHY DID YOU TIE OUR HANDS TOGETHER?
WELL, IF SOMEONE *HAD* BROKEN IN, WE COULD HAVE BEEN SEPARATED. I DIDN'T WANT TO LET ANYTHING HAPPEN TO YOU.
THEN... COULDN'T WE HAVE JUST HELD HANDS?

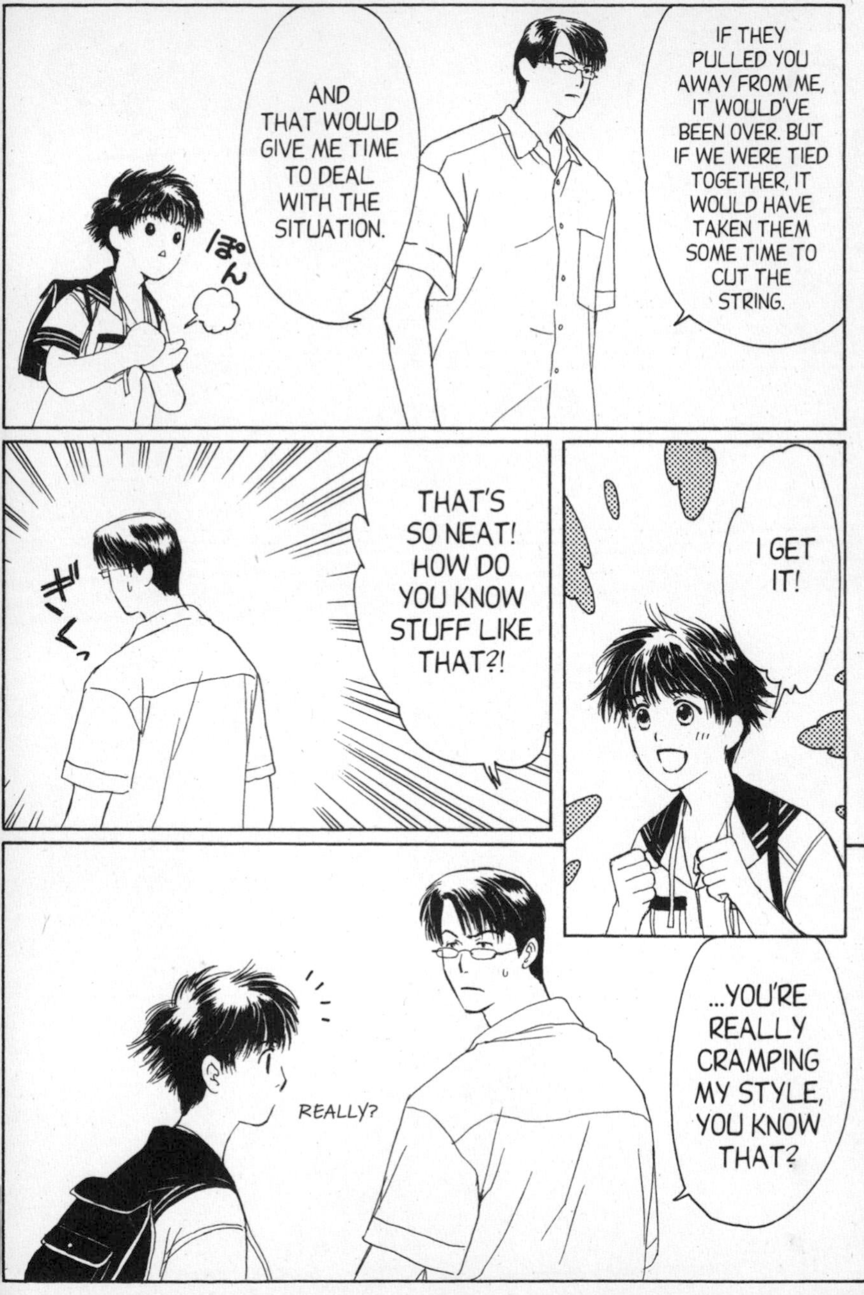
IF THEY PULLED YOU AWAY FROM ME, IT WOULD'VE BEEN OVER. BUT IF WE WERE TIED TOGETHER, IT WOULD HAVE TAKEN THEM SOME TIME TO CUT THE STRING.
AND THAT WOULD GIVE ME TIME TO DEAL WITH THE SITUATION.
ぽん
I GET IT!
THAT'S SO NEAT! HOW DO YOU KNOW STUFF LIKE THAT?!
ぎくっ
...YOU'RE REALLY CRAMPING MY STYLE, YOU KNOW THAT?
REALLY?

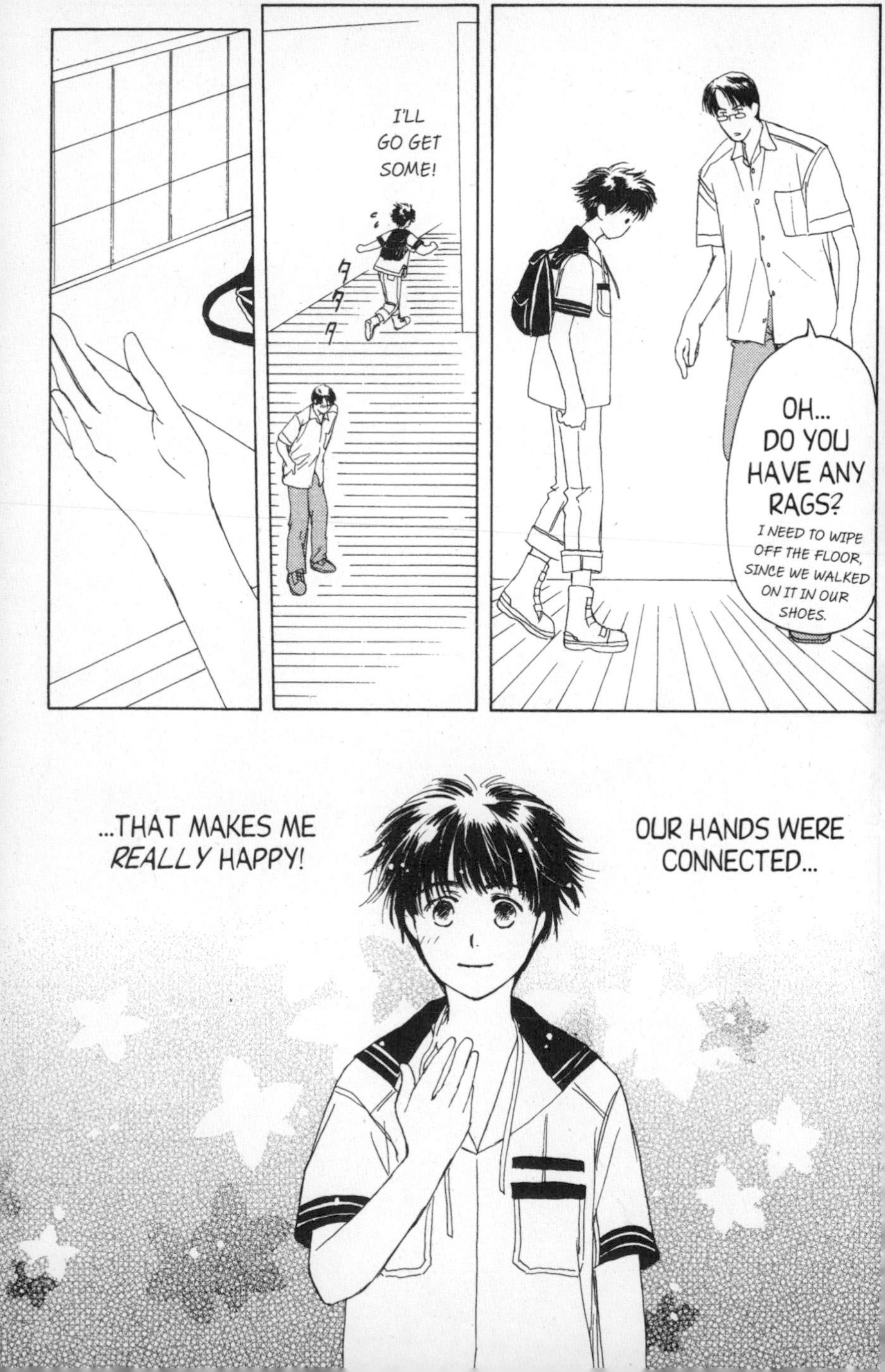
OH... DO YOU HAVE ANY RAGS?
I NEED TO WIPE OFF THE FLOOR, SINCE WE WALKED ON IT IN OUR SHOES.
I'LL GO GET SOME!
タタタ
OUR HANDS WERE CONNECTED...
...THAT MAKES ME *REALLY* HAPPY!

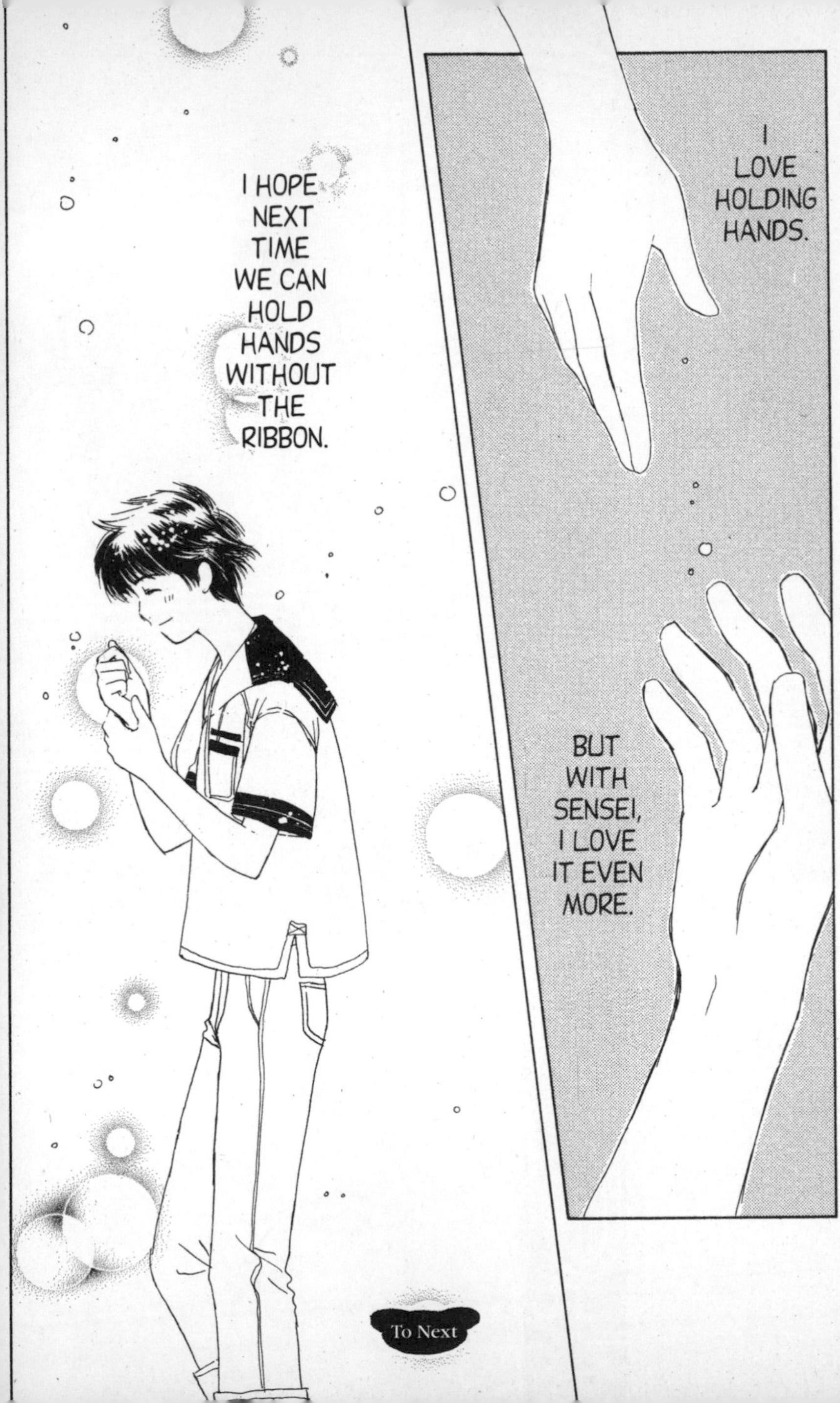
I LOVE HOLDING HANDS.
BUT WITH SENSEI, I LOVE IT EVEN MORE.
I HOPE NEXT TIME WE CAN HOLD HANDS WITHOUT THE RIBBON.
To Next

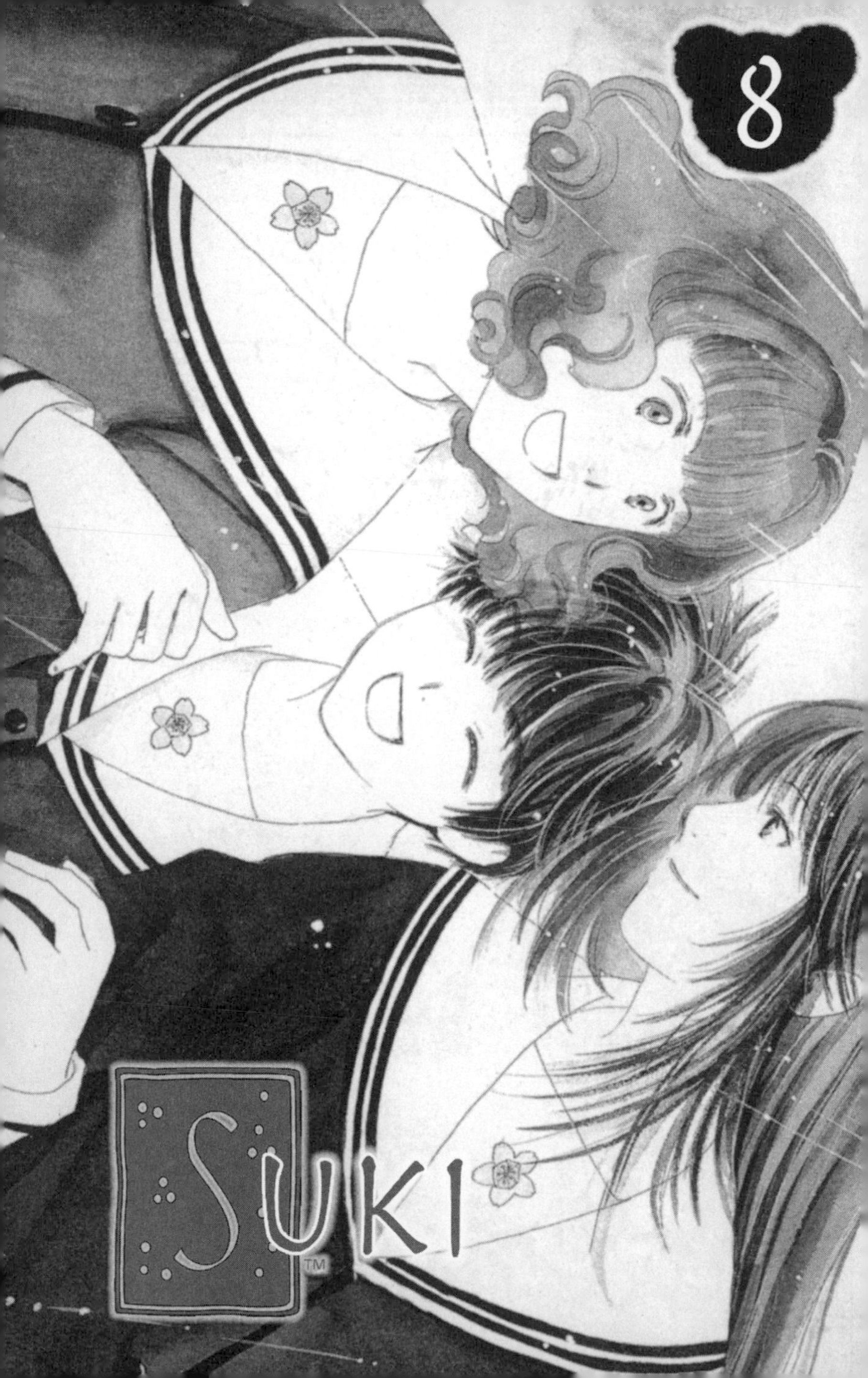
8
SUKI™

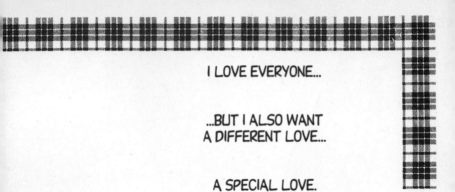

I LOVE EVERYONE...

...BUT I ALSO WANT
A DIFFERENT LOVE...

A SPECIAL LOVE.

I WANT TO LOVE YOU THE MOST.

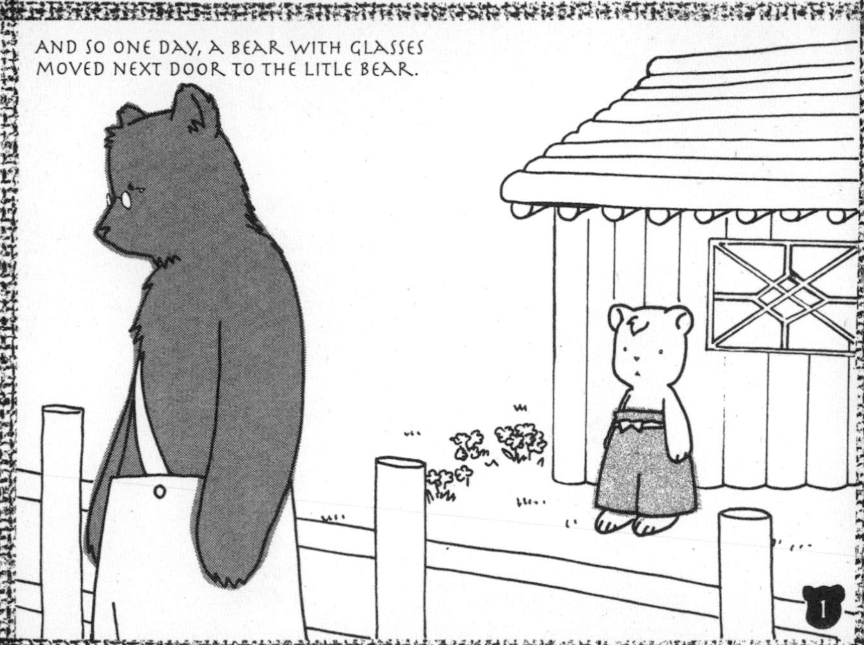
AND SO ONE DAY, A BEAR WITH GLASSES MOVED NEXT DOOR TO THE LITLE BEAR.
1

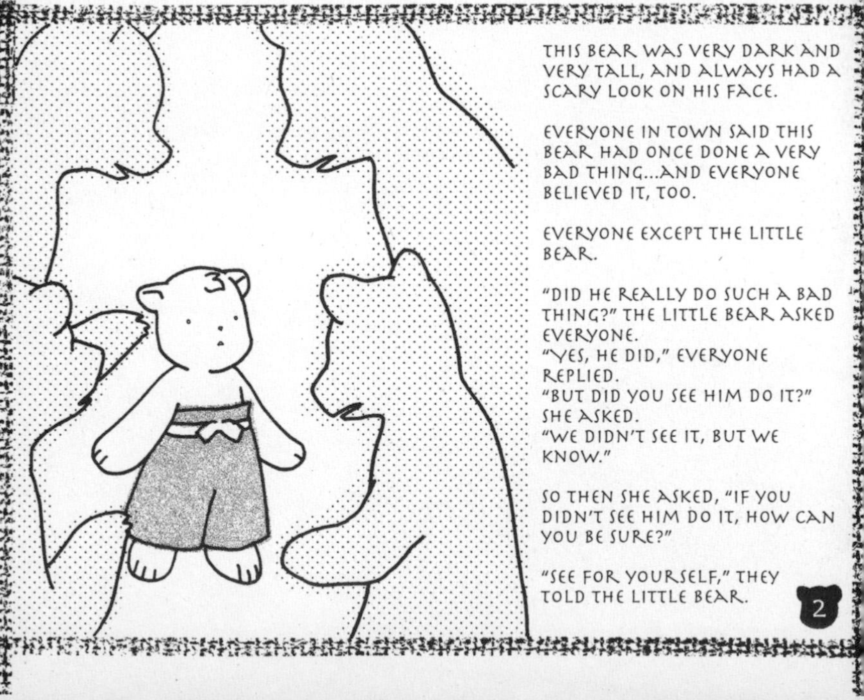
THIS BEAR WAS VERY DARK AND VERY TALL, AND ALWAYS HAD A SCARY LOOK ON HIS FACE.
EVERYONE IN TOWN SAID THIS BEAR HAD ONCE DONE A VERY BAD THING...AND EVERYONE BELIEVED IT, TOO.
EVERYONE EXCEPT THE LITTLE BEAR.
"DID HE REALLY DO SUCH A BAD THING?" THE LITTLE BEAR ASKED EVERYONE.
"YES, HE DID," EVERYONE REPLIED.
"BUT DID YOU SEE HIM DO IT?" SHE ASKED.
"WE DIDN'T SEE IT, BUT WE KNOW."
SO THEN SHE ASKED, "IF YOU DIDN'T SEE HIM DO IT, HOW CAN YOU BE SURE?"
"SEE FOR YOURSELF," THEY TOLD THE LITTLE BEAR.
2

"HE NEVER TALKS TO ANYONE," THEY SAID. "HE ALWAYS LOOKS MAD, STAYS AT HOME AND NEVER SMILES. HOW COULD HE BE ANYTHING BUT A BAD BEAR?"

BUT THE LITTLE BEAR WASN'T SURE.

"HOW CAN YOU TELL HE'S A BAD BEAR JUST BECAUSE HE DOESN'T TALK?" SHE PRESSED ON. "IF HE DOESN'T LOOK LIKE HE'S HAVING FUN, DOES THAT MAKE HIM A BAD BEAR?"

"WHO KNOWS WHAT THAT BEAR IS THINKING?" EVERYONE REPLIED. "THE ONLY POSSIBLE ANSWER IS THAT HE'S A BAD BEAR."

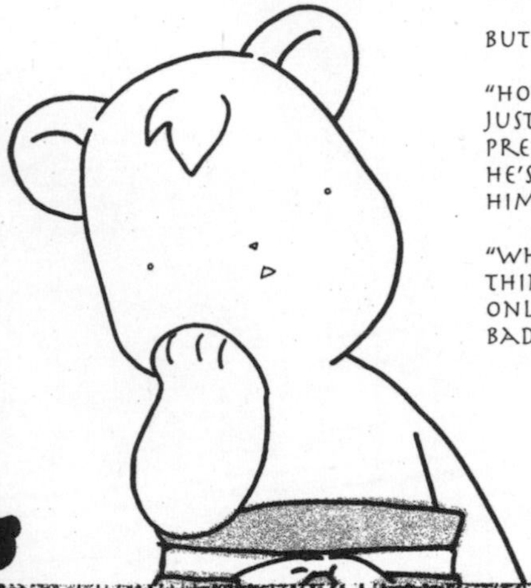

3

"JUST BECAUSE YOU DON'T UNDERSTAND HIM, DOESN'T MAKE HIM A BAD BEAR," THE LITTLE BEAR PROTESTED.

SHE JUST COULDN'T BELIEVE WHAT THE OTHER BEARS WERE SAYING WITHOUT PROOF.

"I WANT TO FIND OUT FOR MYSELF WHAT KIND OF BEAR THE BEAR WITH GLASSES IS," THE LITTLE BEAR DECIDED.

AND THEN, SHE BEGAN TO GET EXCITED.

"I KNOW...*I'LL* GO TALK TO HIM! THEN MAYBE I WILL UNDERSTAND HIM."

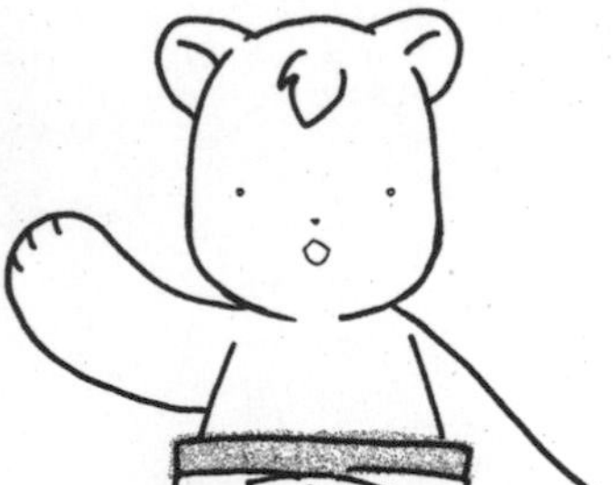

4

EVERYONE TRIED TO STOP THE LITTLE BEAR.
"YOU SHOULDN'T DO THAT," THEY SAID.
"WHO KNOWS WHAT HE MIGHT DO TO YOU?
YOU MIGHT NEVER RETURN."

BUT THE LITTLE BEAR SAID, "I'LL BE FINE."

"YOU SEE, I PASSED BY HIS WINDOW ONCE,
AND OUR EYES MET, BUT HE DIDN'T DO
ANYTHING BAD TO ME. SO I'M SURE I'LL
BE ALL RIGHT," SHE SAID.

"BEHIND HIS GLASSES, I COULD SEE HE HAD
VERY KIND EYES."

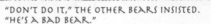

"DON'T DO IT," THE OTHER BEARS INSISTED.
"HE'S A BAD BEAR."

BUT THE LITTLE BEAR IGNORED THEM AND HEADED
FOR HER NEIGHBOR'S HOUSE.
AND AS SHE DID, SHE THOUGHT TO HERSELF, "I JUST
WANT TO MEET THAT BEAR WITH GLASSES. I JUST
WANT TO TALK WITH HIM."

THE LITTLE BEAR DIDN'T KNOW WHY SHE THOUGHT
THIS...BUT THAT IS WHAT SHE THOUGHT.

FOR THE LITTLE BEAR DID WANT TO KNOW
MORE ABOUT THE BEAR WITH THE GLASSES.
SHE WANTED VERY MUCH TO KNOW IF HE TRULY WAS A BAD BEAR
LIKE EVERYONE SAID.

BECAUSE SHE COULDN'T FORGET THE KIND LOOK IN HIS EYES THE ONE
TIME THEIR EYES HAD MET.

AND SO THE LITTLE BEAR ARRIVED AT THE HOUSE OF THE BEAR WITH GLASSES.

NERVOUSLY, SHE KNOCKED ON THE DOOR.

AFTER SOME TIME, THE TALL BEAR WITH GLASSES ANSWERED.
"HELLO," SAID THE LITTLE BEAR.

"WHAT DO YOU WANT?" DEMANDED THE BEAR WITH GLASSES. HE LOOKED MEAN AS HE ALWAYS DID.

THE LITTLE BEAR ANSWERED WITH A SMILE, "NOTHING. I JUST CAME BY TO HAVE A CHAT."

BUT THE BEAR WITH GLASSES ANSWERED GRUFFLY, "I HAVE NOTHING TO TALK ABOUT."

AND WITH THAT, HE SHUT THE DOOR.

THE LITTLE BEAR KNOCKED ON THE DOOR AGAIN SEVERAL TIMES.
"REALLY, I JUST CAME TO TALK. PLEASE... OPEN THE DOOR."

BUT THERE WAS NO ANSWER.

FINALLY, THE LITTLE BEAR GAVE UP.

"I'M SORRY. YOU MUST BE VERY BUSY TODAY. I'LL JUST TRY AGAIN TOMORROW."

BUT FROM INSIDE CAME THE BEAR WITH GLASSES' VOICE: "I'M GOING TO BE BUSY TOMORROW TOO."

SO THE LITTLE BEAR SAID, "THE DAY AFTER TOMORROW, THEN."

"I'M BUSY THE DAY AFTER TOMORROW TOO," THE BEAR WITH GLASSES SAID.

"THEN WHAT ABOUT THE DAY AFTER THE DAY AFTER TOMORROW?"

THE LITTLE BEAR WAS JUST HAPPY THAT THE BEAR WITH GLASSES WAS SPEAKING TO HER.

FINALLY, SHE SAID, "I'LL COME BY EVERY DAY UNTIL YOU DECIDE TO TALK TO ME."

9

THE BEAR WITH GLASSES GAVE NO ANSWER. BUT HE DIDN'T SAY TO NOT COME, SO THE LITTLE BEAR WAS SATISFIED.

SHE THOUGHT TO HERSELF, "ONE DAY, HE'LL LET ME IN...AND UNTIL THEN, I'LL JUST KEEP TRYING."

AND WITH THAT, THE LITTLE BEAR BEGAN TO FEEL VERY HAPPY INDEED.

10

TO BE CONTINUED

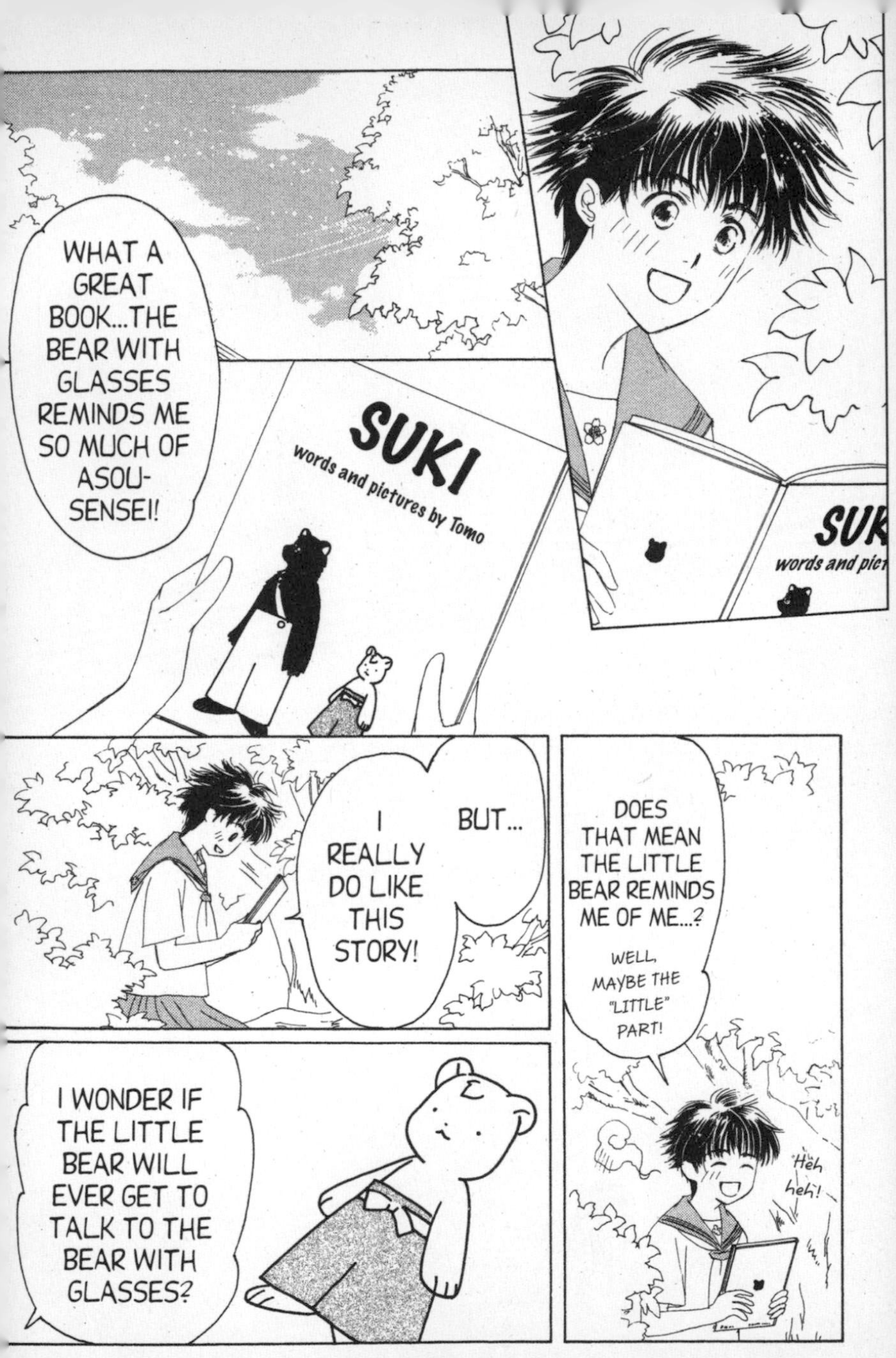
WHAT A GREAT BOOK...THE BEAR WITH GLASSES REMINDS ME SO MUCH OF ASOU-SENSEI!
SUKI
words and pictures by Tomo
DOES THAT MEAN THE LITTLE BEAR REMINDS ME OF ME...?
WELL, MAYBE THE "LITTLE" PART!
Heh heh!
BUT... I REALLY DO LIKE THIS STORY!
I WONDER IF THE LITTLE BEAR WILL EVER GET TO TALK TO THE BEAR WITH GLASSES?

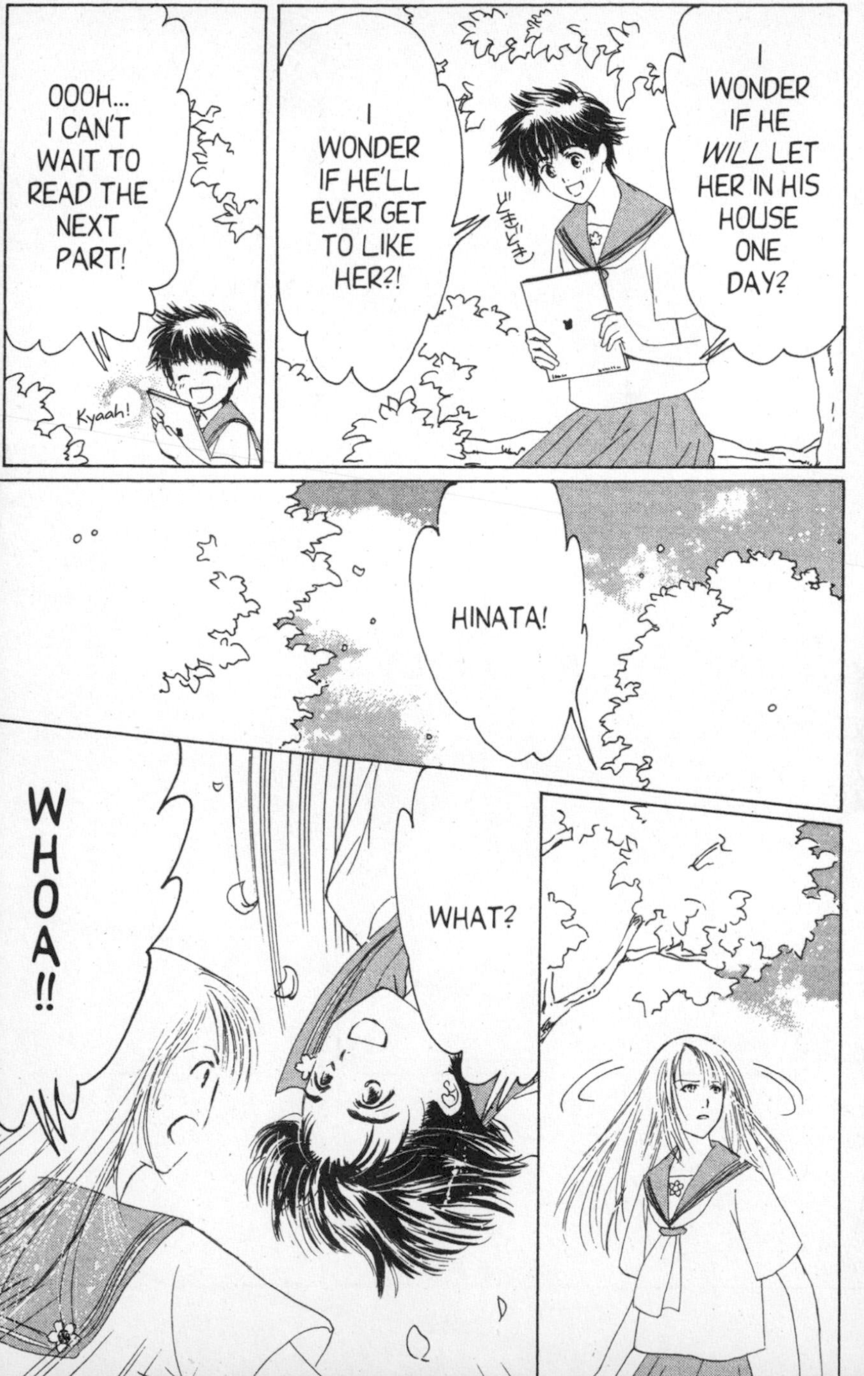
I WONDER IF HE *WILL* LET HER IN HIS HOUSE ONE DAY?
I WONDER IF HE'LL EVER GET TO LIKE HER?!
どきどき
OOOH... I CAN'T WAIT TO READ THE NEXT PART!
Kyaah!
HINATA!
WHAT?
WHOA!!

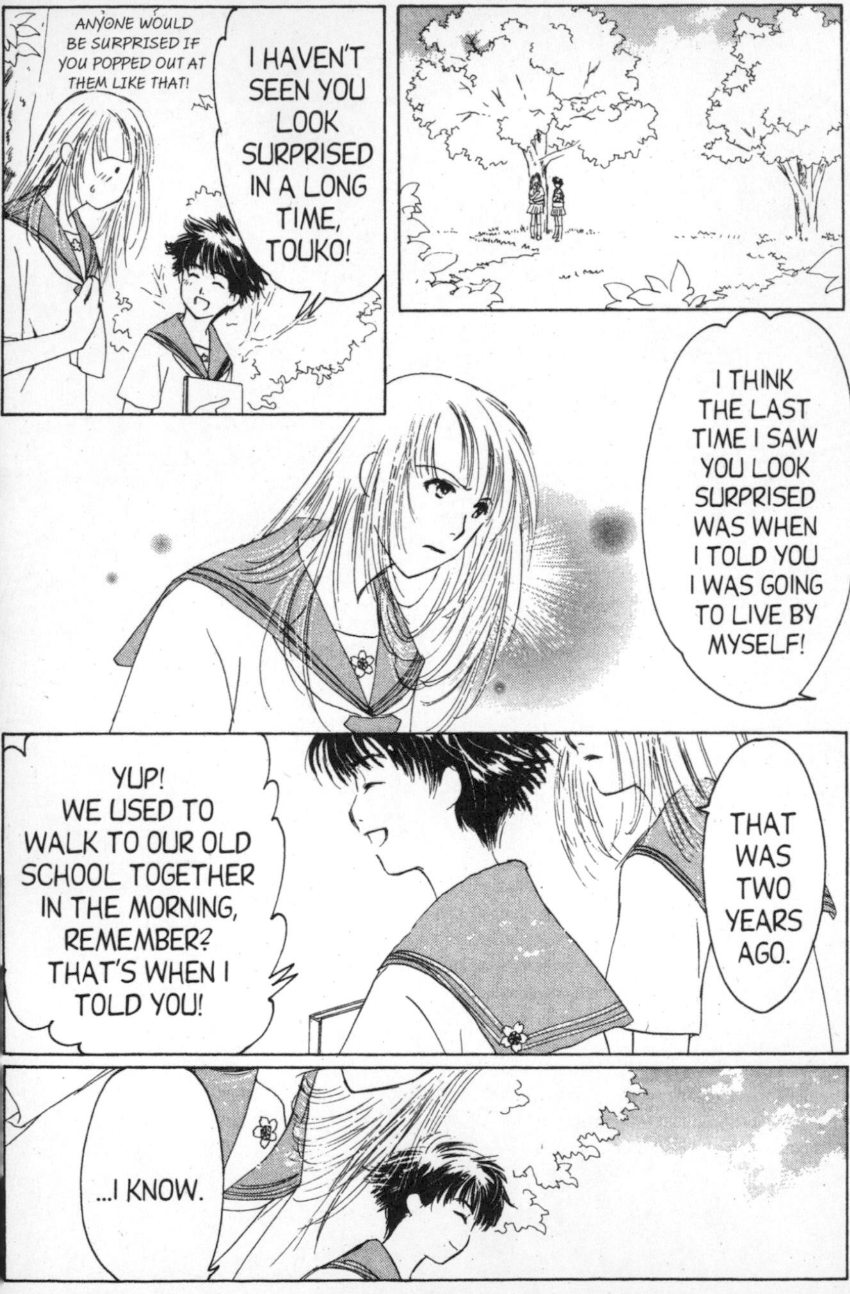
I HAVEN'T SEEN YOU LOOK SURPRISED IN A LONG TIME, TOUKO!
ANYONE WOULD BE SURPRISED IF YOU POPPED OUT AT THEM LIKE THAT!
I THINK THE LAST TIME I SAW YOU LOOK SURPRISED WAS WHEN I TOLD YOU I WAS GOING TO LIVE BY MYSELF!
THAT WAS TWO YEARS AGO.
YUP! WE USED TO WALK TO OUR OLD SCHOOL TOGETHER IN THE MORNING, REMEMBER? THAT'S WHEN I TOLD YOU!
...I KNOW.

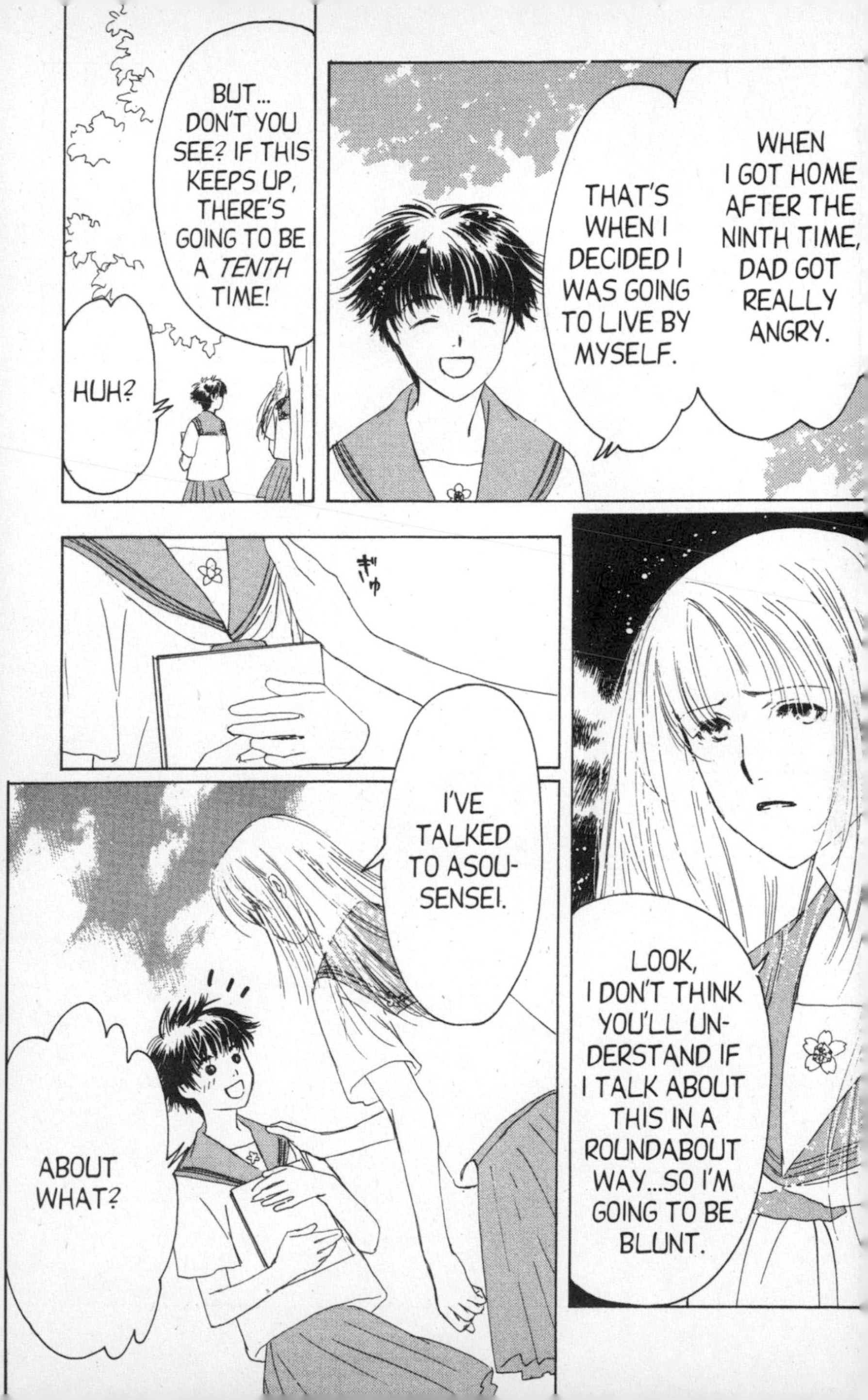
WHEN I GOT HOME AFTER THE NINTH TIME, DAD GOT REALLY ANGRY.
THAT'S WHEN I DECIDED I WAS GOING TO LIVE BY MYSELF.
BUT... DON'T YOU SEE? IF THIS KEEPS UP, THERE'S GOING TO BE A *TENTH* TIME!
HUH?
LOOK, I DON'T THINK YOU'LL UN-DERSTAND IF I TALK ABOUT THIS IN A ROUNDABOUT WAY...SO I'M GOING TO BE BLUNT.
ぎゅ
I'VE TALKED TO ASOU-SENSEI.
ABOUT WHAT?

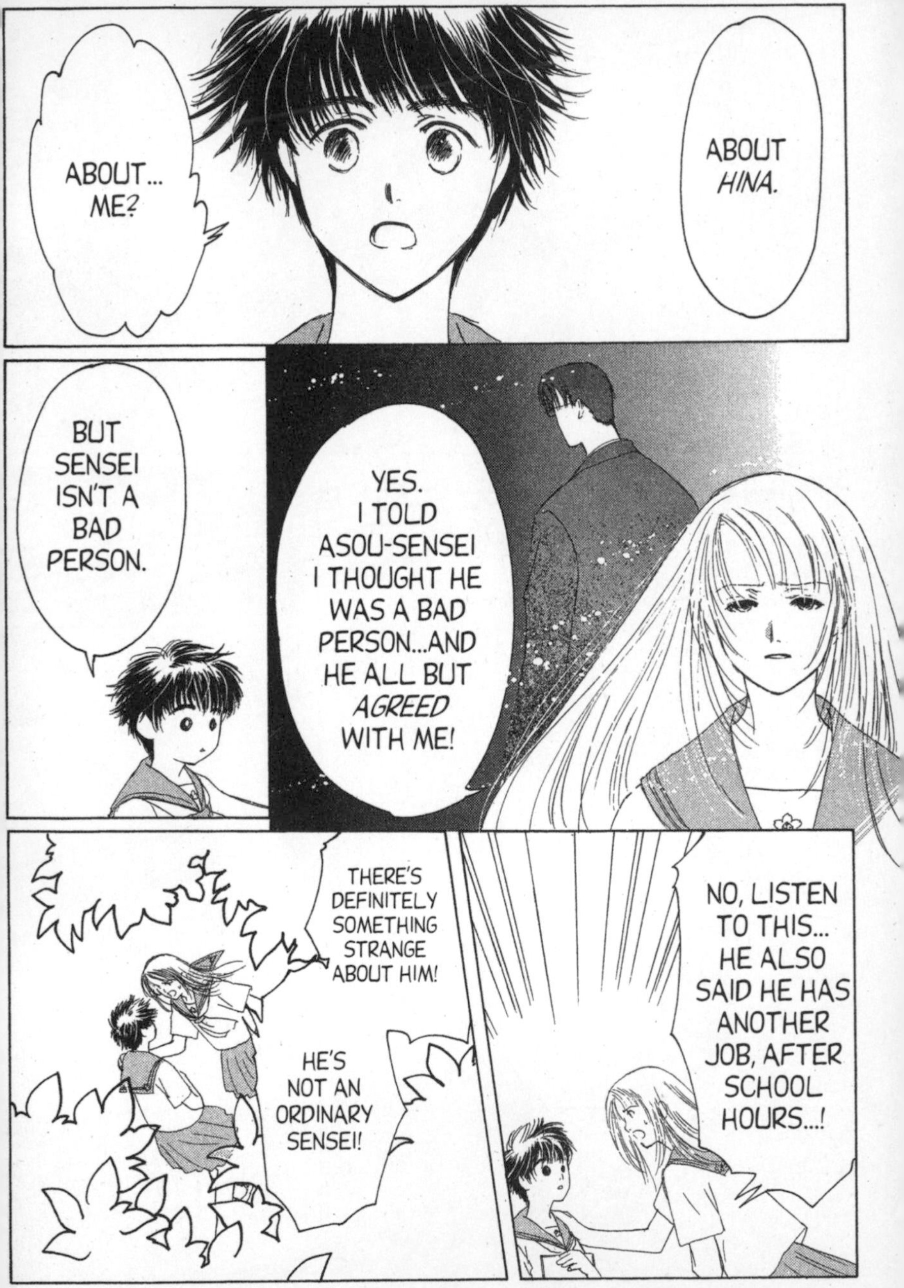
ABOUT *HINA.*
ABOUT... ME?
YES. I TOLD ASOU-SENSEI I THOUGHT HE WAS A BAD PERSON...AND HE ALL BUT *AGREED* WITH ME!
BUT SENSEI ISN'T A BAD PERSON.
NO, LISTEN TO THIS... HE ALSO SAID HE HAS ANOTHER JOB, AFTER SCHOOL HOURS...!
THERE'S DEFINITELY SOMETHING STRANGE ABOUT HIM!
HE'S NOT AN ORDINARY SENSEI!

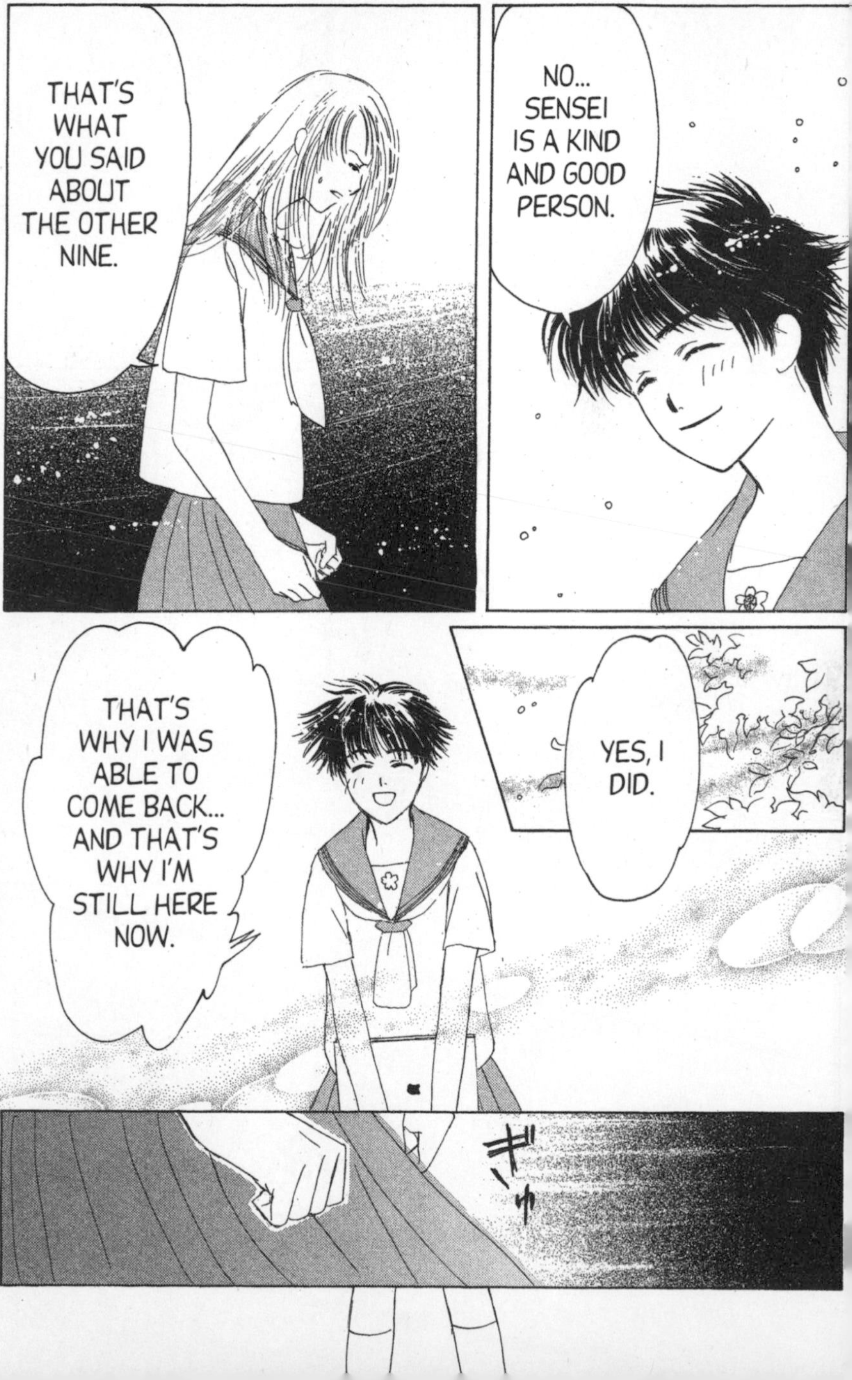
NO... SENSEI IS A KIND AND GOOD PERSON.
THAT'S WHAT YOU SAID ABOUT THE OTHER NINE.
YES, I DID.
THAT'S WHY I WAS ABLE TO COME BACK... AND THAT'S WHY I'M STILL HERE NOW.

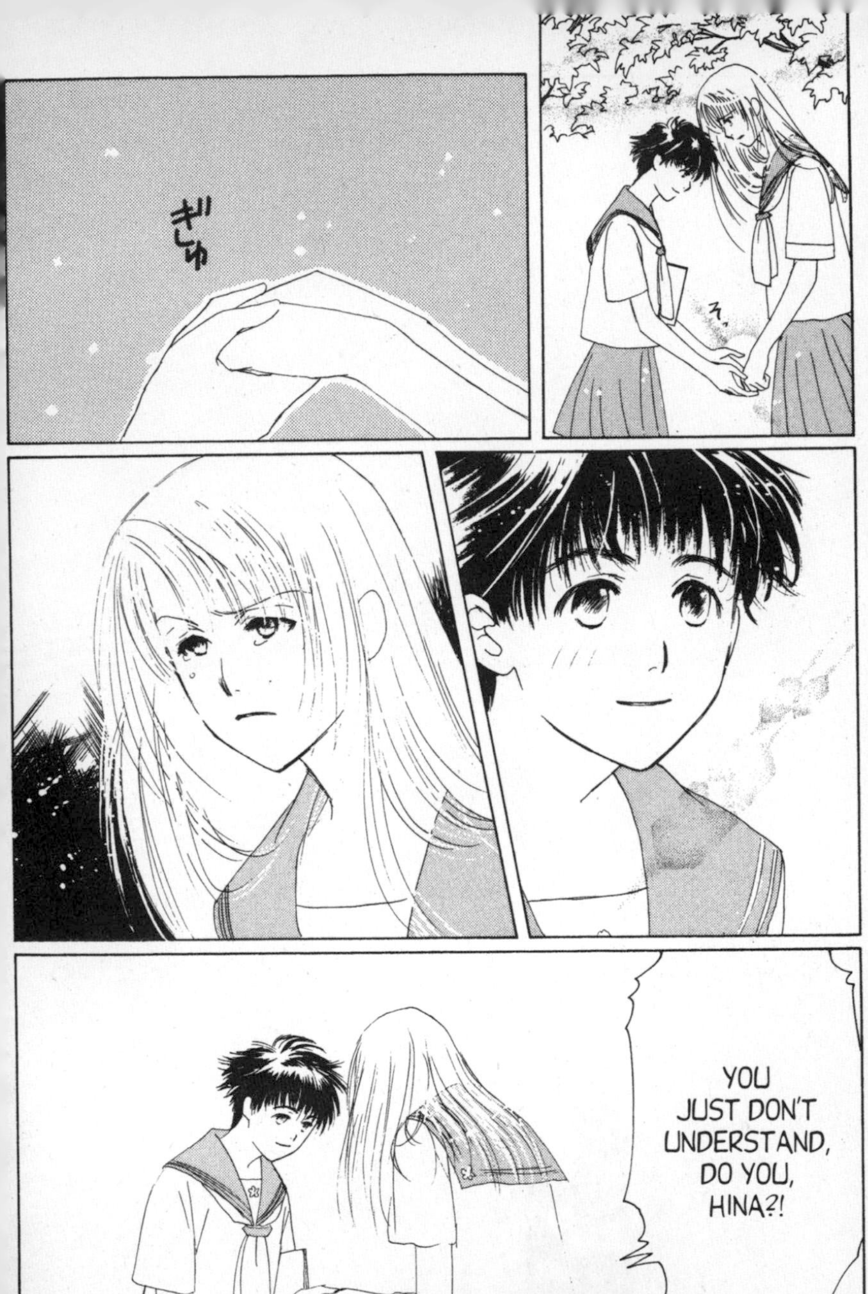
ぎしゅ
YOU JUST DON'T UNDERSTAND, DO YOU, HINA?!

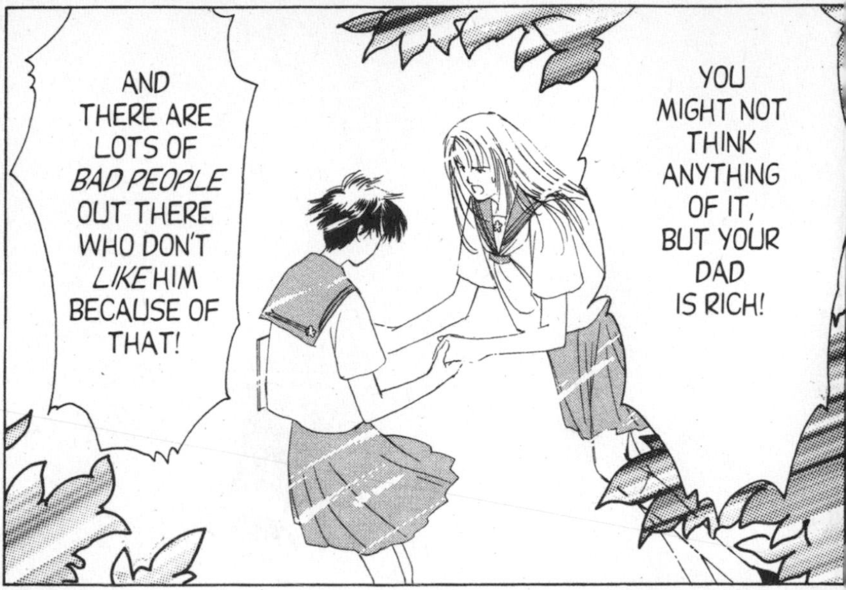
YOU MIGHT NOT THINK ANYTHING OF IT, BUT YOUR DAD IS RICH!
AND THERE ARE LOTS OF *BAD PEOPLE* OUT THERE WHO DON'T *LIKE* HIM BECAUSE OF THAT!

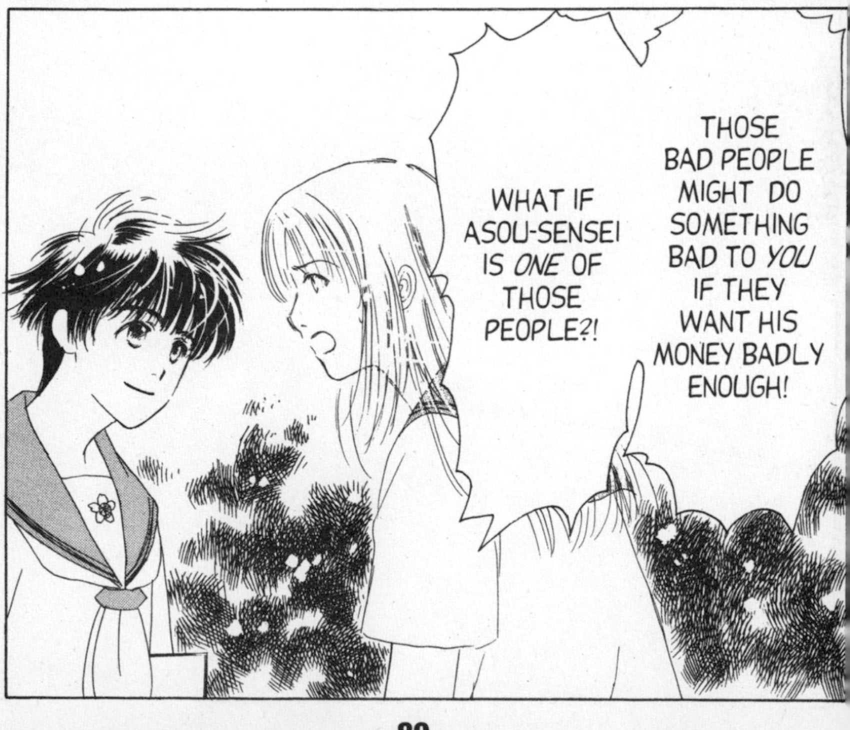
THOSE BAD PEOPLE MIGHT DO SOMETHING BAD TO *YOU* IF THEY WANT HIS MONEY BADLY ENOUGH!
WHAT IF ASOU-SENSEI IS *ONE* OF THOSE PEOPLE?!

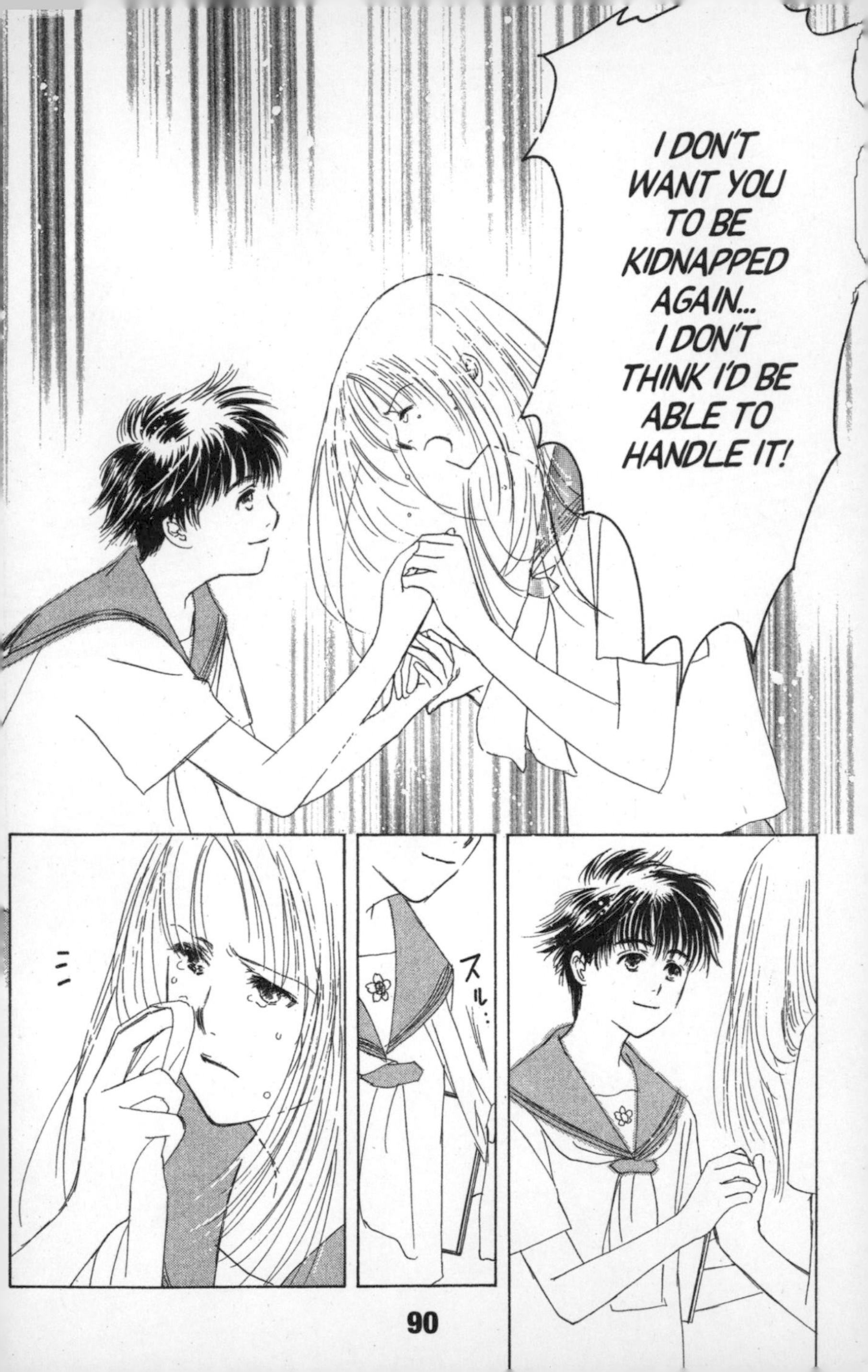
I DON'T WANT YOU TO BE KIDNAPPED AGAIN... I DON'T THINK I'D BE ABLE TO HANDLE IT!
スル‥

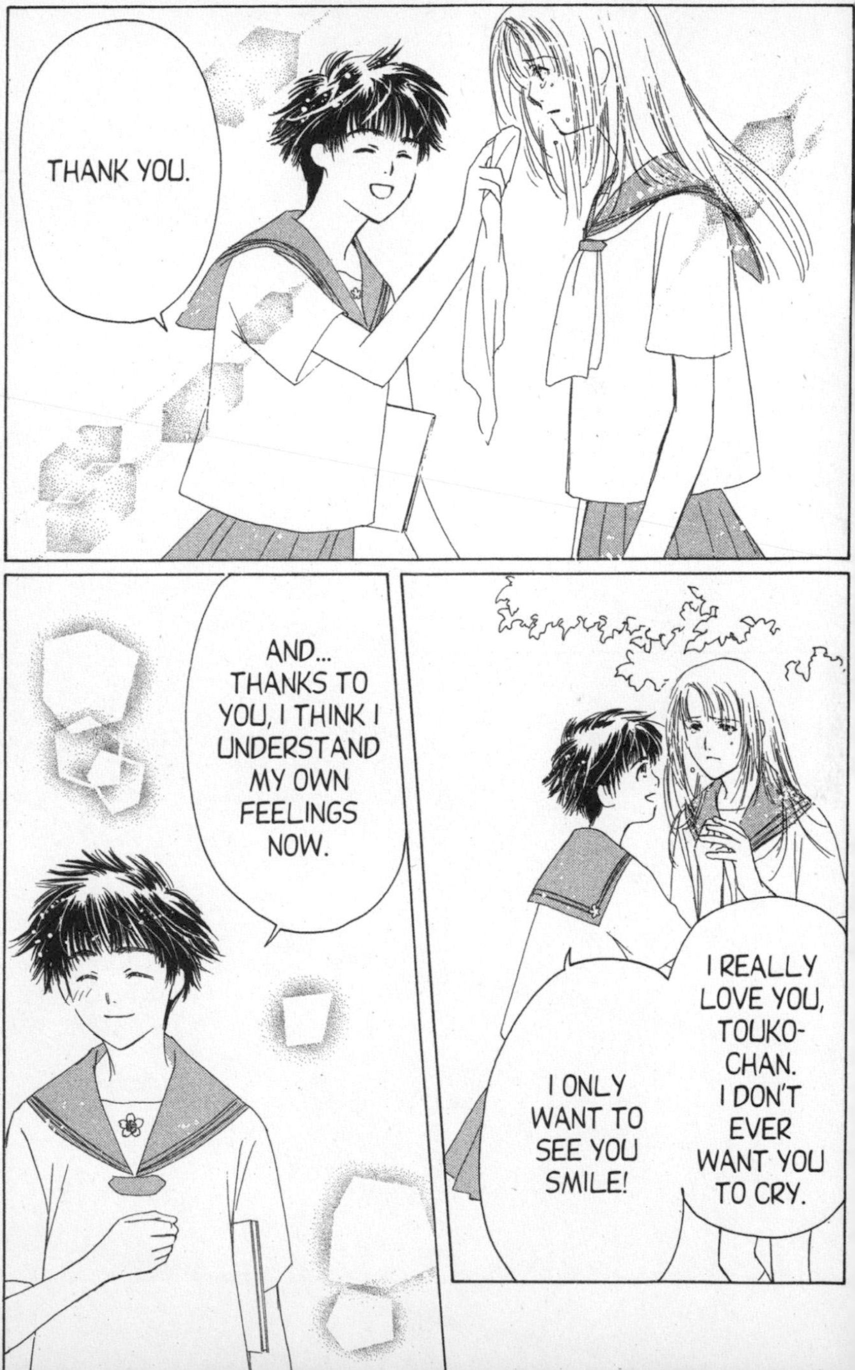
THANK YOU.
I REALLY LOVE YOU, TOUKO-CHAN. I DON'T EVER WANT YOU TO CRY.
I ONLY WANT TO SEE YOU SMILE!
AND... THANKS TO YOU, I THINK I UNDERSTAND MY OWN FEELINGS NOW.

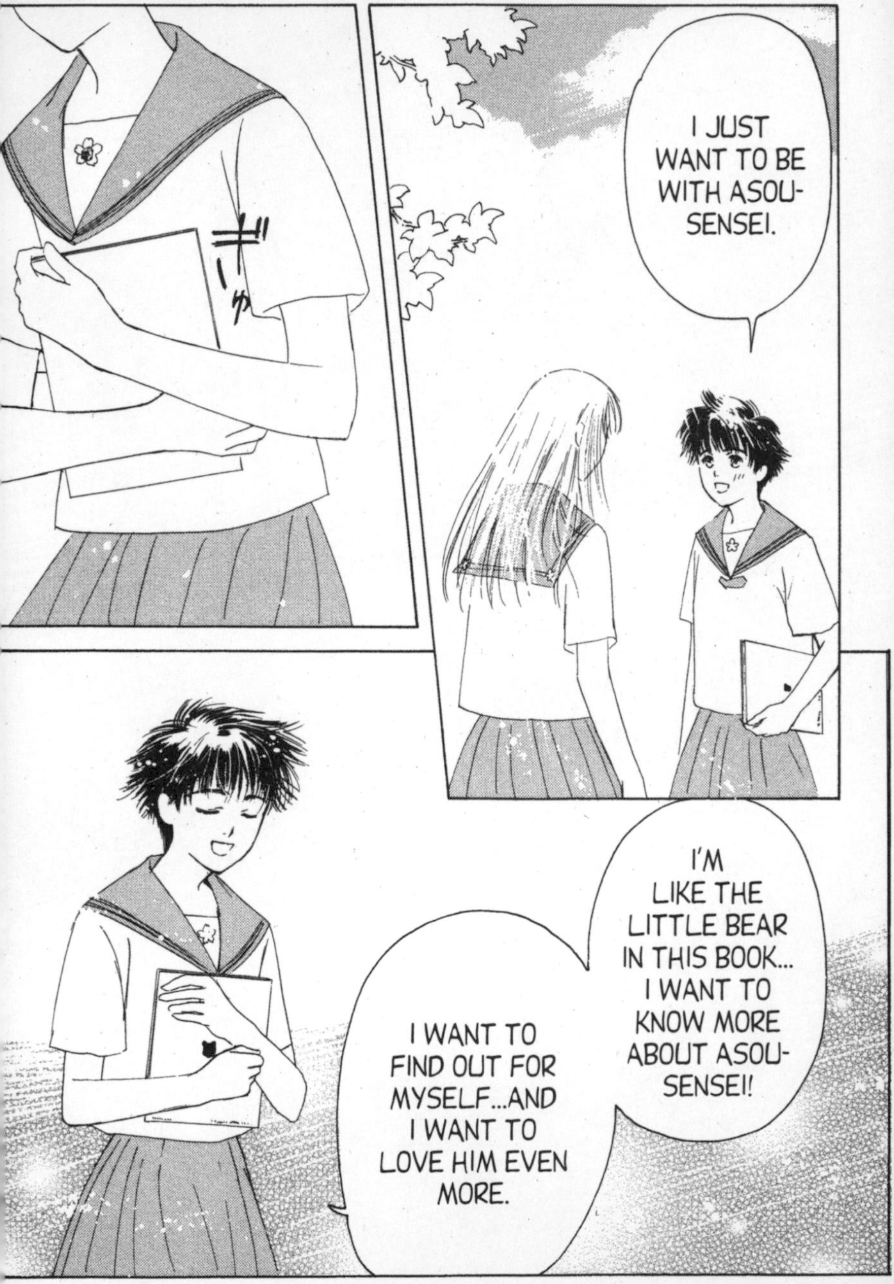
I JUST WANT TO BE WITH ASOU-SENSEI.
I'M LIKE THE LITTLE BEAR IN THIS BOOK... I WANT TO KNOW MORE ABOUT ASOU-SENSEI!
I WANT TO FIND OUT FOR MYSELF...AND I WANT TO LOVE HIM EVEN MORE.

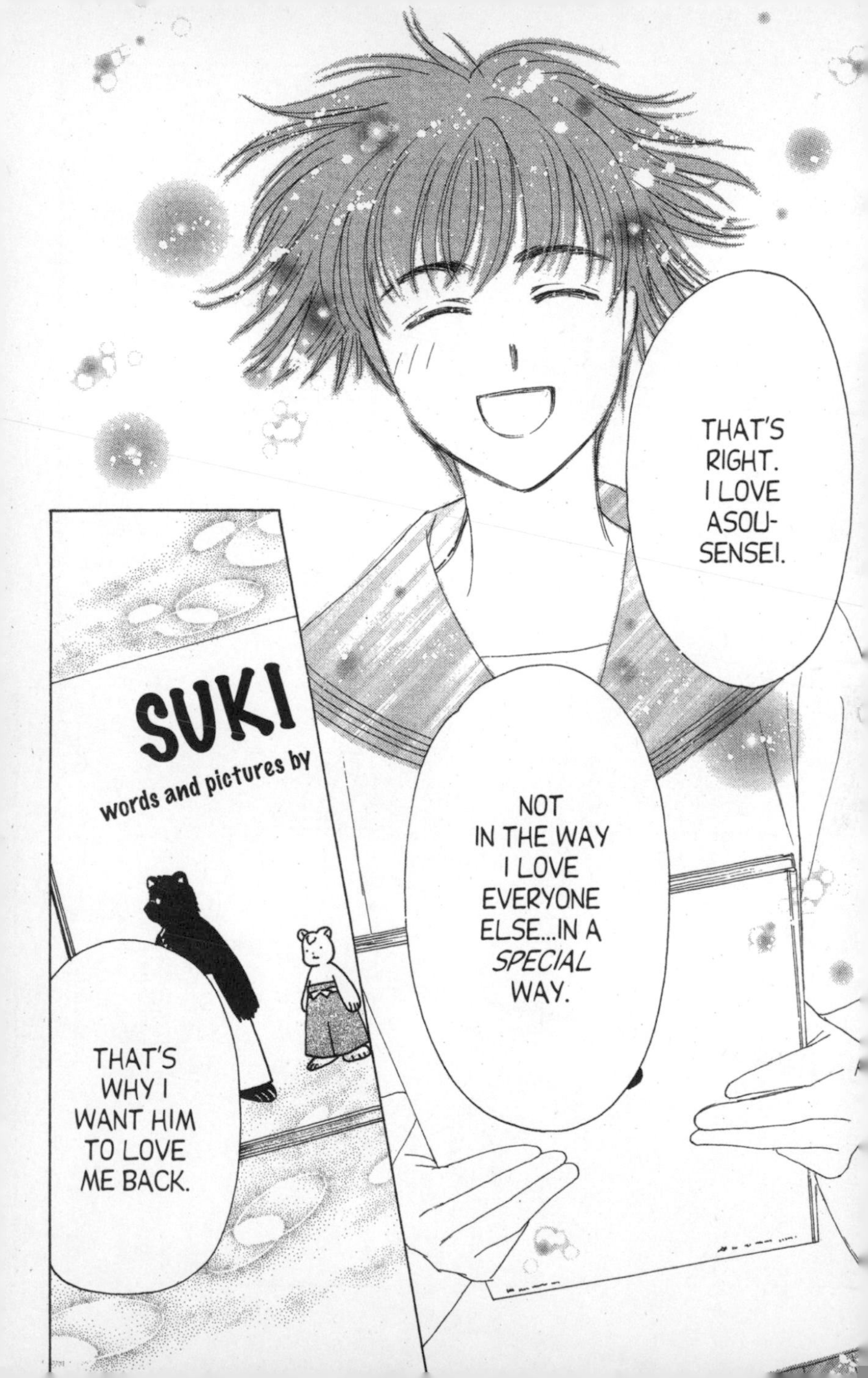
THAT'S RIGHT. I LOVE ASOU-SENSEI.
NOT IN THE WAY I LOVE EVERYONE ELSE...IN A *SPECIAL* WAY.
SUKI
words and pictures by
THAT'S WHY I WANT HIM TO LOVE ME BACK.

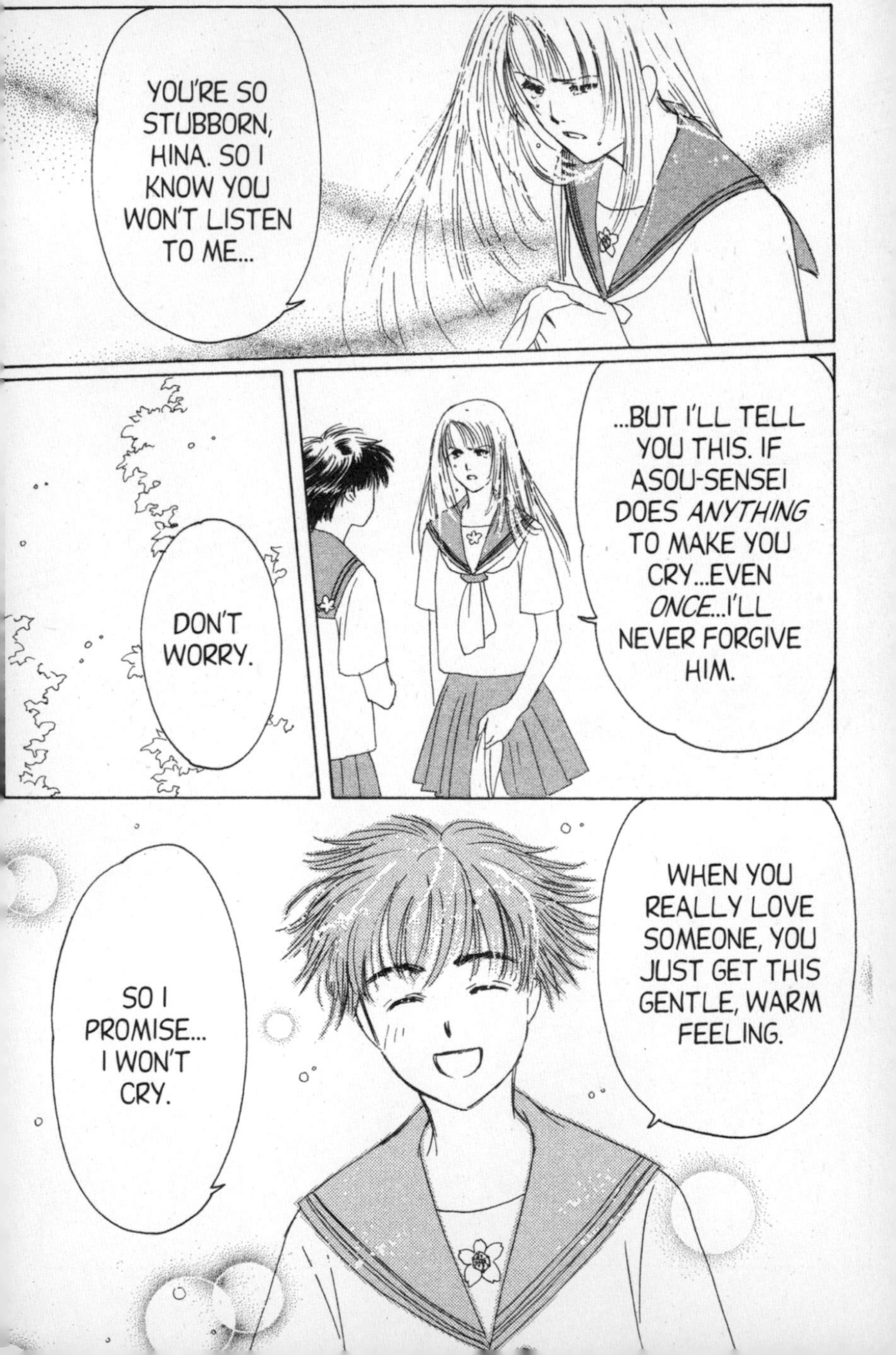
YOU'RE SO STUBBORN, HINA. SO I KNOW YOU WON'T LISTEN TO ME...
...BUT I'LL TELL YOU THIS. IF ASOU-SENSEI DOES *ANYTHING* TO MAKE YOU CRY...EVEN *ONCE*...I'LL NEVER FORGIVE HIM.
DON'T WORRY.
WHEN YOU REALLY LOVE SOMEONE, YOU JUST GET THIS GENTLE, WARM FEELING.
SO I PROMISE... I WON'T CRY.

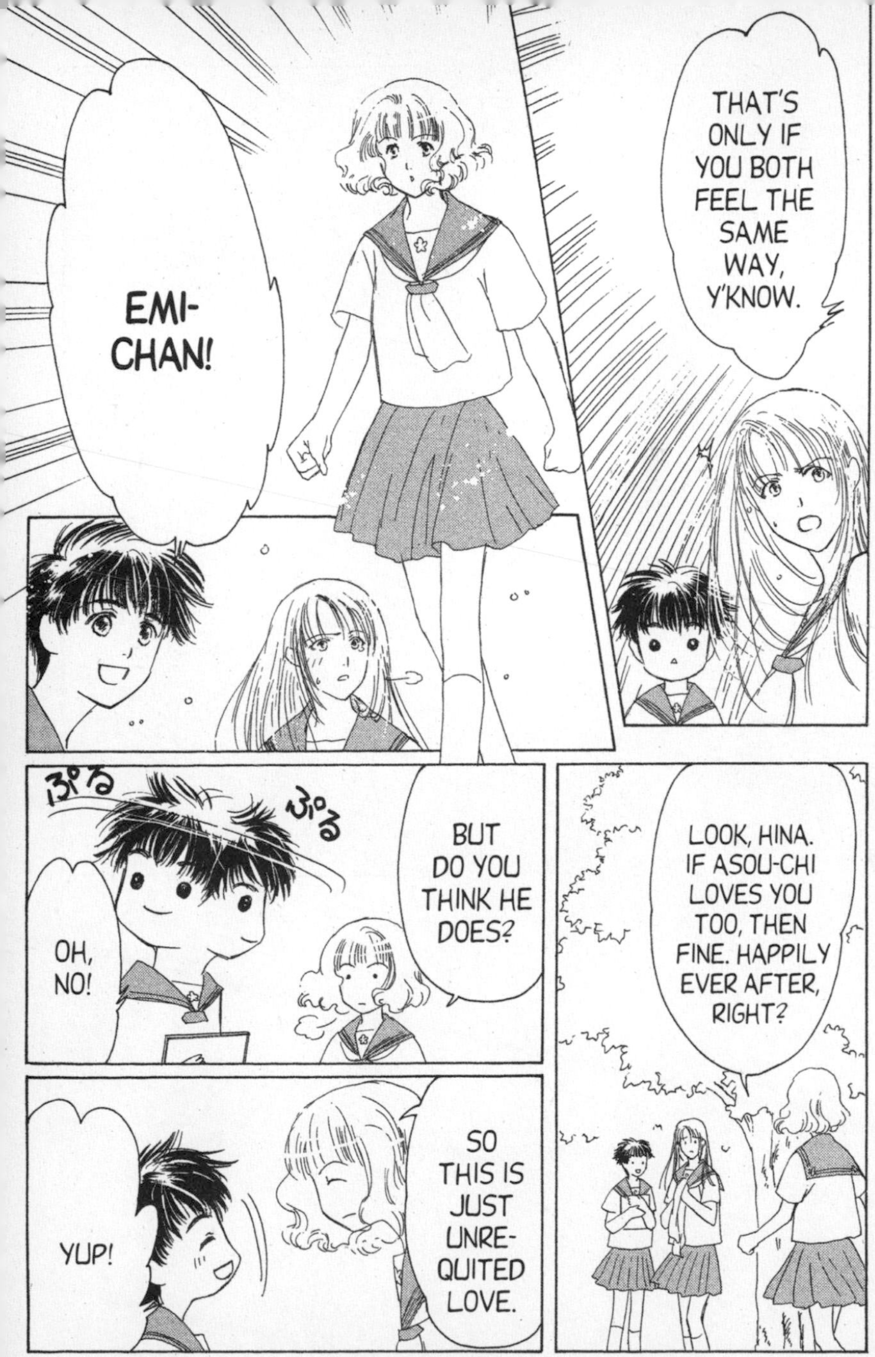
THAT'S ONLY IF YOU BOTH FEEL THE SAME WAY, Y'KNOW.
EMI-CHAN!
LOOK, HINA. IF ASOU-CHI LOVES YOU TOO, THEN FINE. HAPPILY EVER AFTER, RIGHT?
BUT DO YOU THINK HE DOES?
ぷる
ぷる
OH, NO!
SO THIS IS JUST UNRE-QUITED LOVE.
YUP!

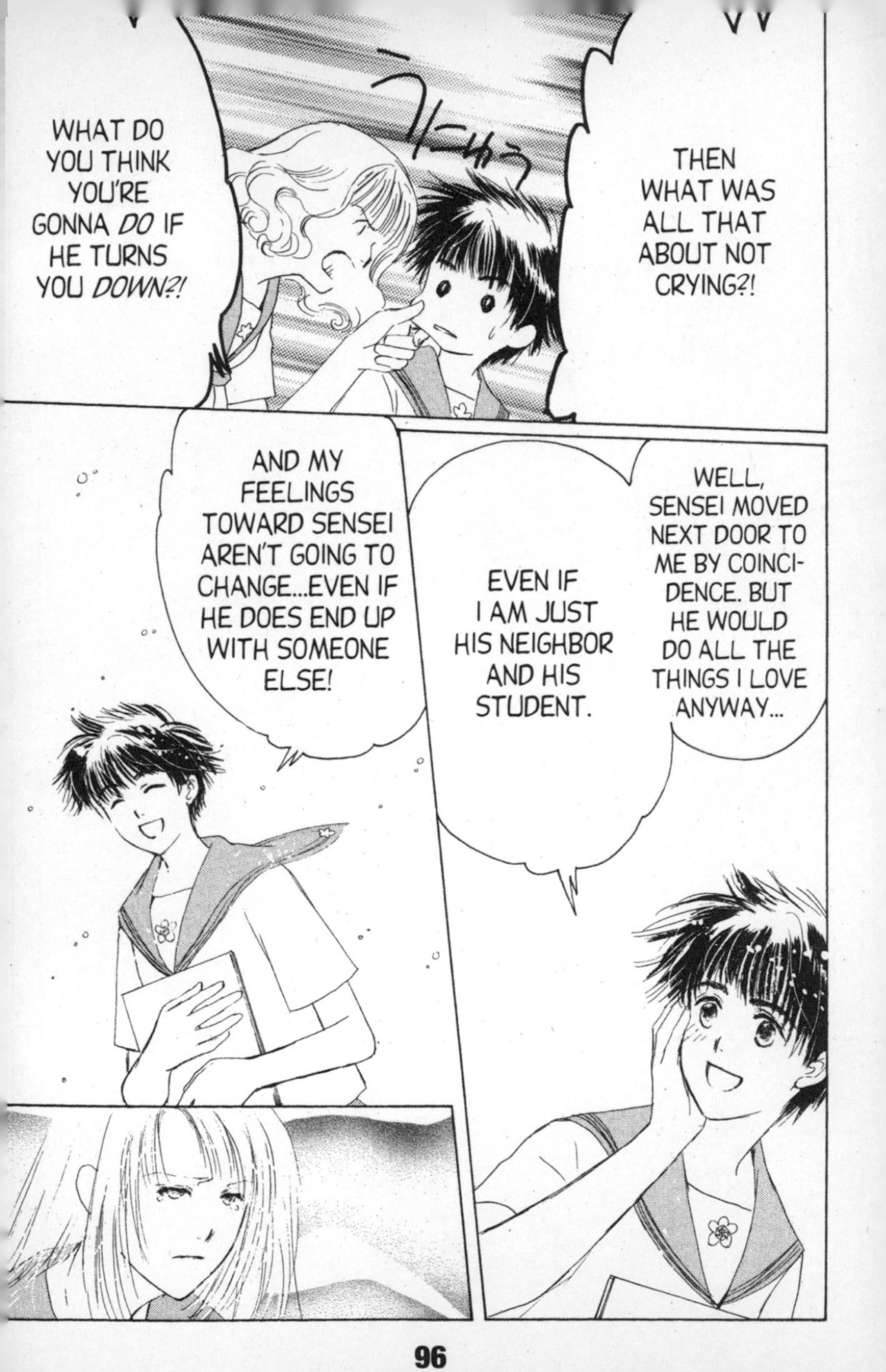
THEN WHAT WAS ALL THAT ABOUT NOT CRYING?!
WHAT DO YOU THINK YOU'RE GONNA *DO* IF HE TURNS YOU *DOWN*?!
WELL, SENSEI MOVED NEXT DOOR TO ME BY COINCI-DENCE. BUT HE WOULD DO ALL THE THINGS I LOVE ANYWAY...
EVEN IF I AM JUST HIS NEIGHBOR AND HIS STUDENT.
AND MY FEELINGS TOWARD SENSEI AREN'T GOING TO CHANGE...EVEN IF HE DOES END UP WITH SOMEONE ELSE!

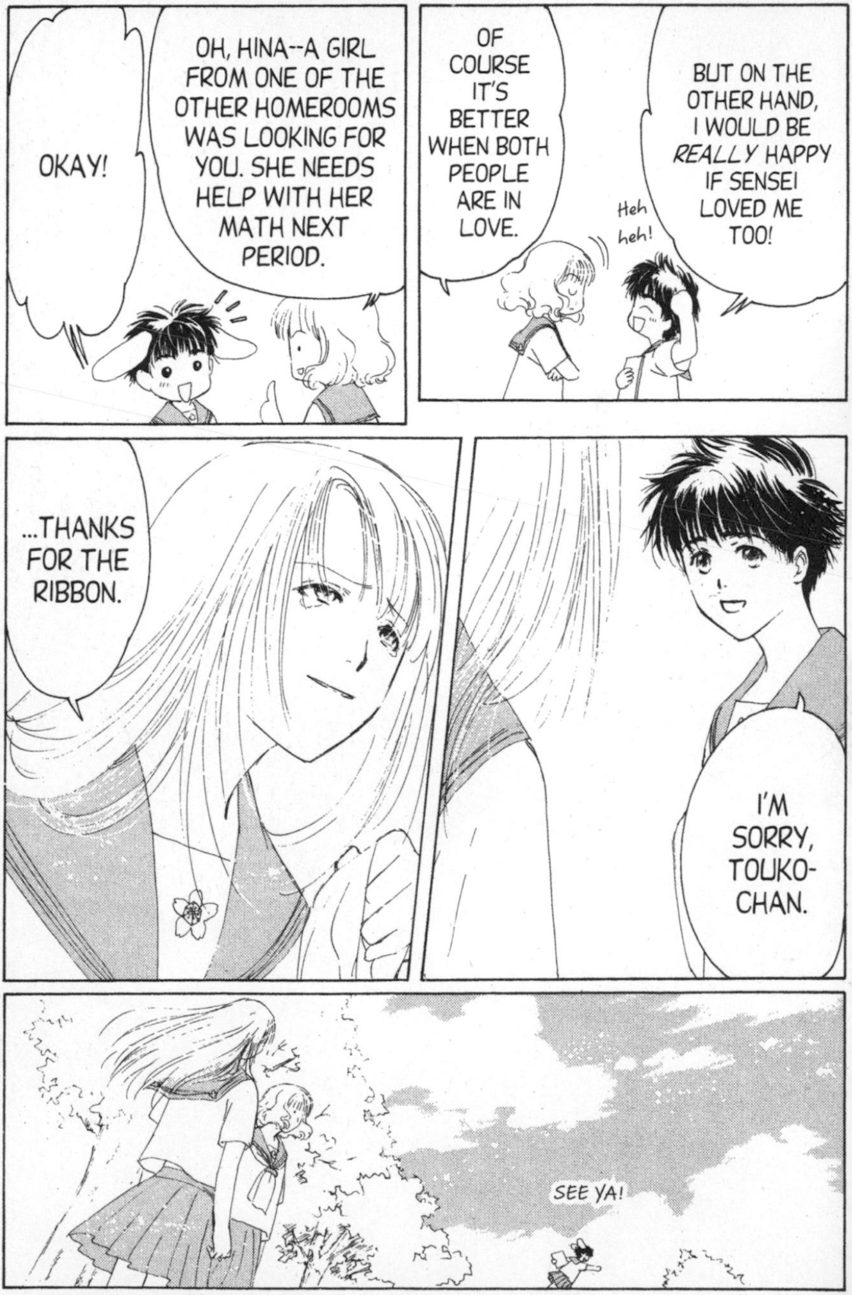
OF COURSE IT'S BETTER WHEN BOTH PEOPLE ARE IN LOVE.
Heh heh!
BUT ON THE OTHER HAND, I WOULD BE *REALLY* HAPPY IF SENSEI LOVED ME TOO!
OH, HINA--A GIRL FROM ONE OF THE OTHER HOMEROOMS WAS LOOKING FOR YOU. SHE NEEDS HELP WITH HER MATH NEXT PERIOD.
OKAY!
I'M SORRY, TOUKO-CHAN.
...THANKS FOR THE RIBBON.
SEE YA!

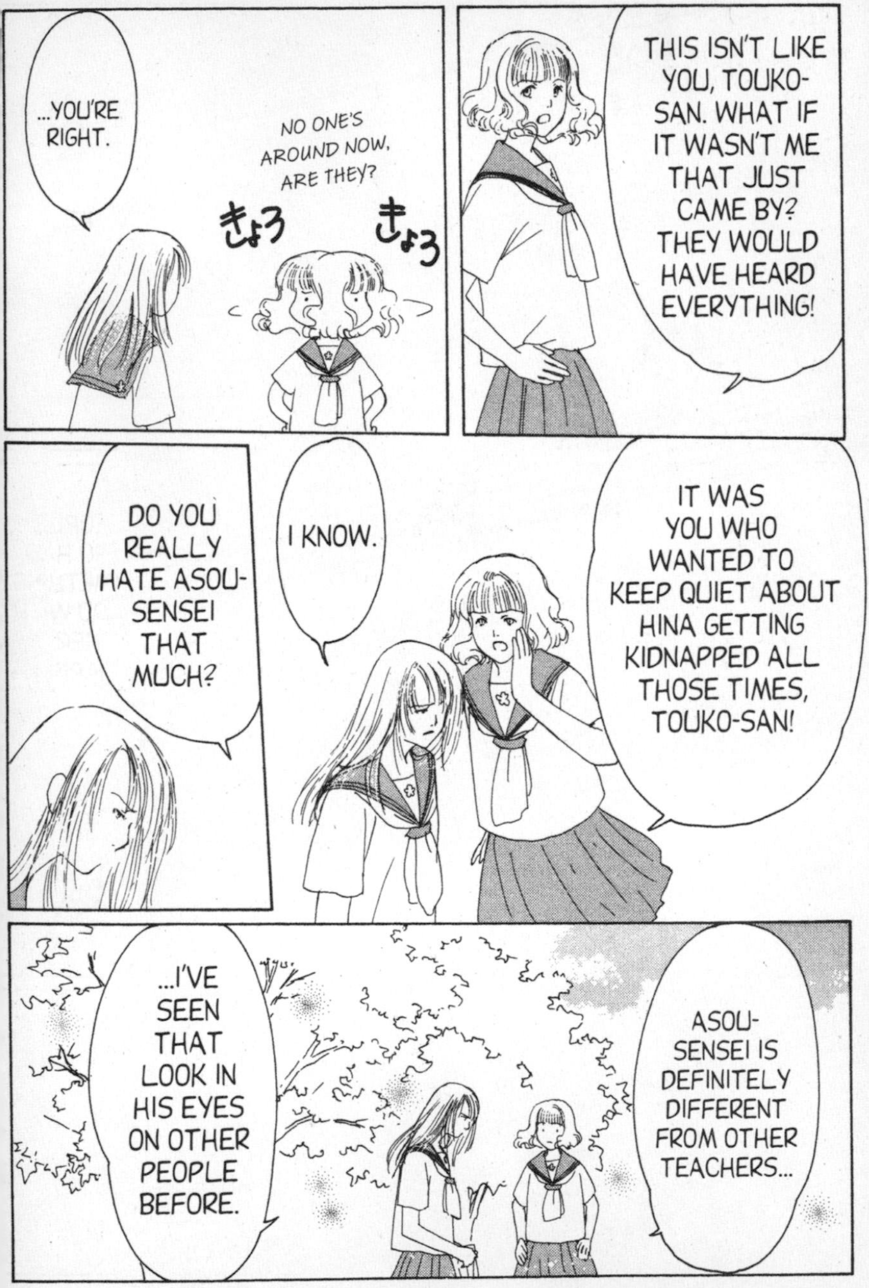
THIS ISN'T LIKE YOU, TOUKO-SAN. WHAT IF IT WASN'T ME THAT JUST CAME BY? THEY WOULD HAVE HEARD EVERYTHING!
...YOU'RE RIGHT.
NO ONE'S AROUND NOW, ARE THEY?
きょろ
きょろ
IT WAS YOU WHO WANTED TO KEEP QUIET ABOUT HINA GETTING KIDNAPPED ALL THOSE TIMES, TOUKO-SAN!
I KNOW.
DO YOU REALLY HATE ASOU-SENSEI THAT MUCH?
ASOU-SENSEI IS DEFINITELY DIFFERENT FROM OTHER TEACHERS...
...I'VE SEEN THAT LOOK IN HIS EYES ON OTHER PEOPLE BEFORE.

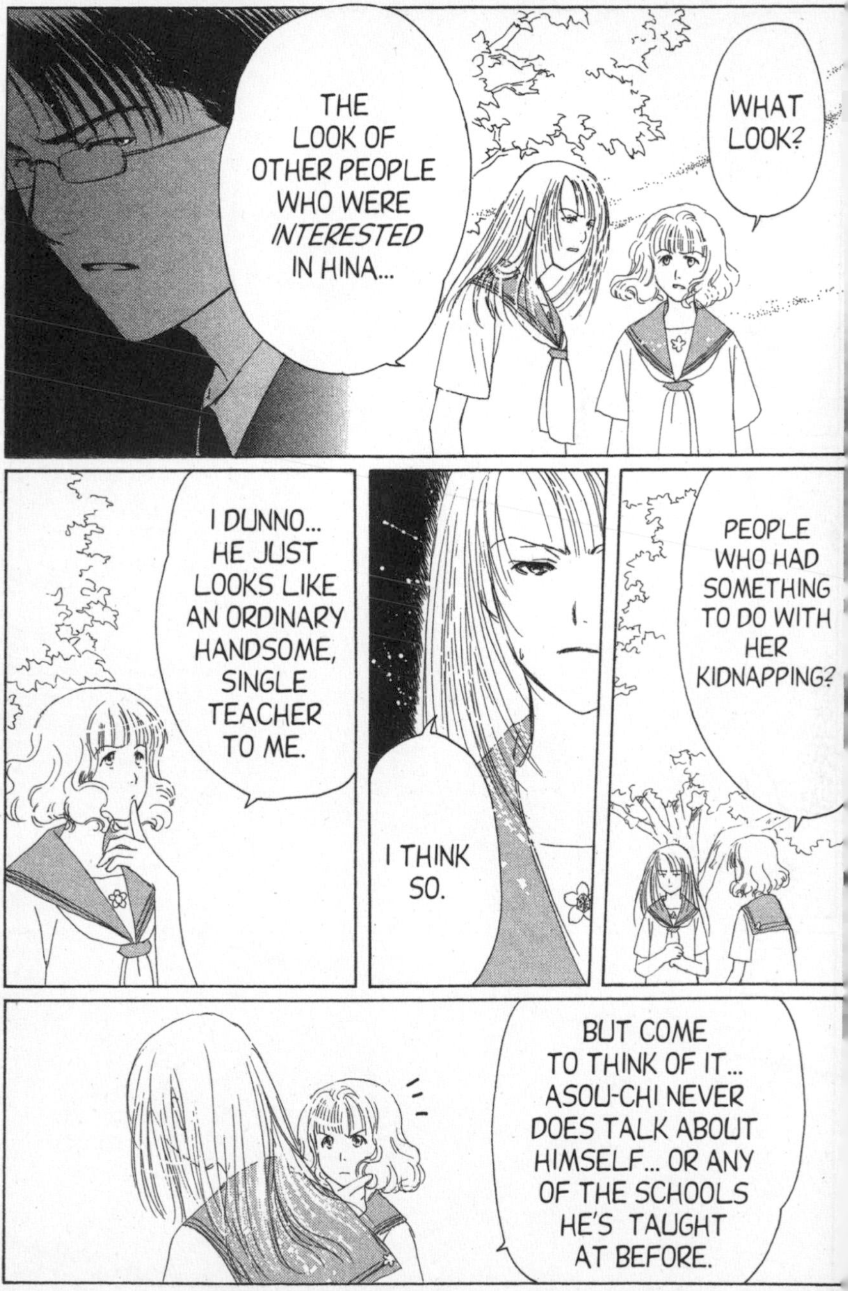
WHAT LOOK?
THE LOOK OF OTHER PEOPLE WHO WERE *INTERESTED* IN HINA...
PEOPLE WHO HAD SOMETHING TO DO WITH HER KIDNAPPING?
I THINK SO.
I DUNNO... HE JUST LOOKS LIKE AN ORDINARY HANDSOME, SINGLE TEACHER TO ME.
BUT COME TO THINK OF IT... ASOU-CHI NEVER DOES TALK ABOUT HIMSELF... OR ANY OF THE SCHOOLS HE'S TAUGHT AT BEFORE.

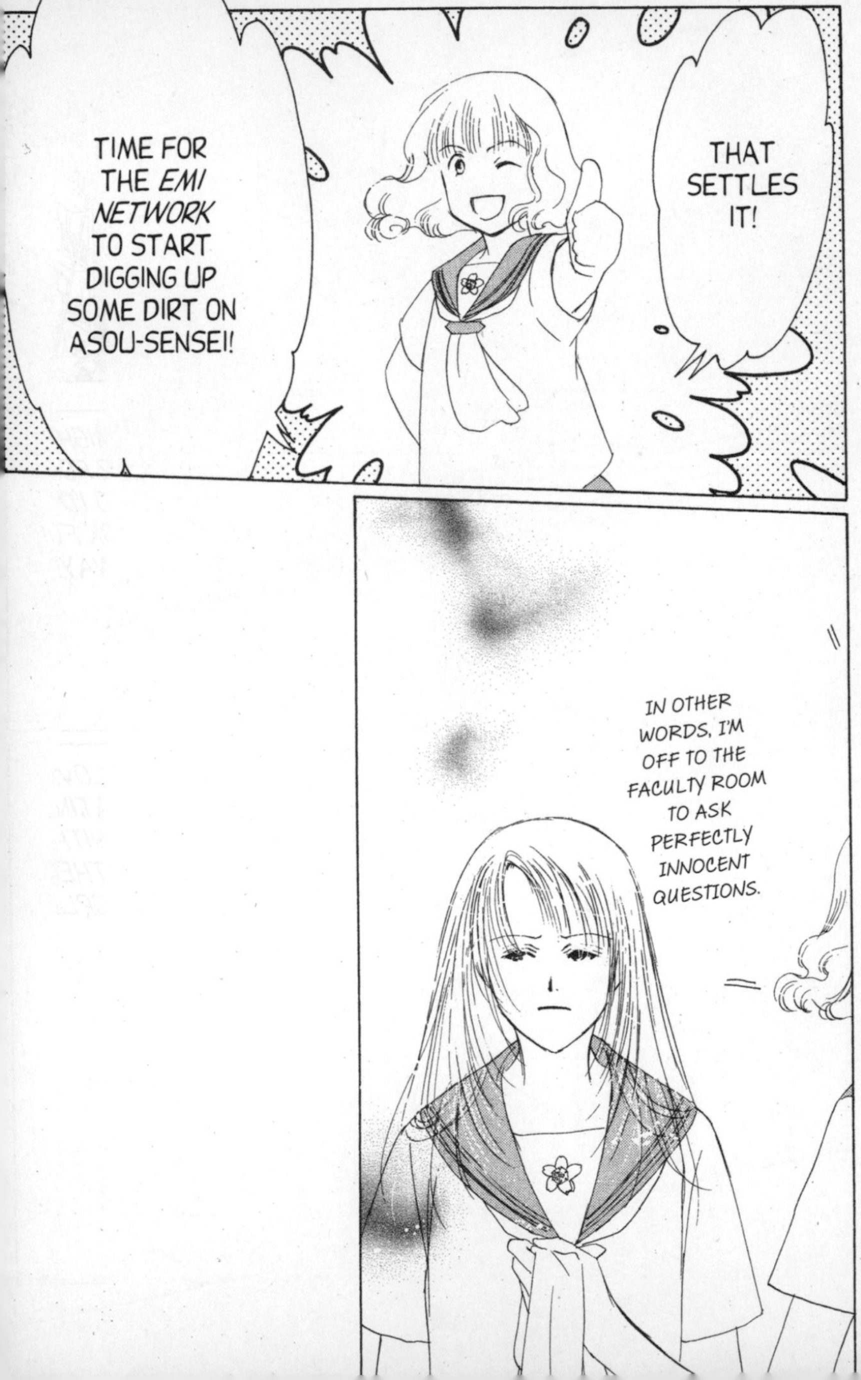
THAT SETTLES IT!
TIME FOR THE *EMI NETWORK* TO START DIGGING UP SOME DIRT ON ASOU-SENSEI!
IN OTHER WORDS, I'M OFF TO THE FACULTY ROOM TO ASK PERFECTLY INNOCENT QUESTIONS.

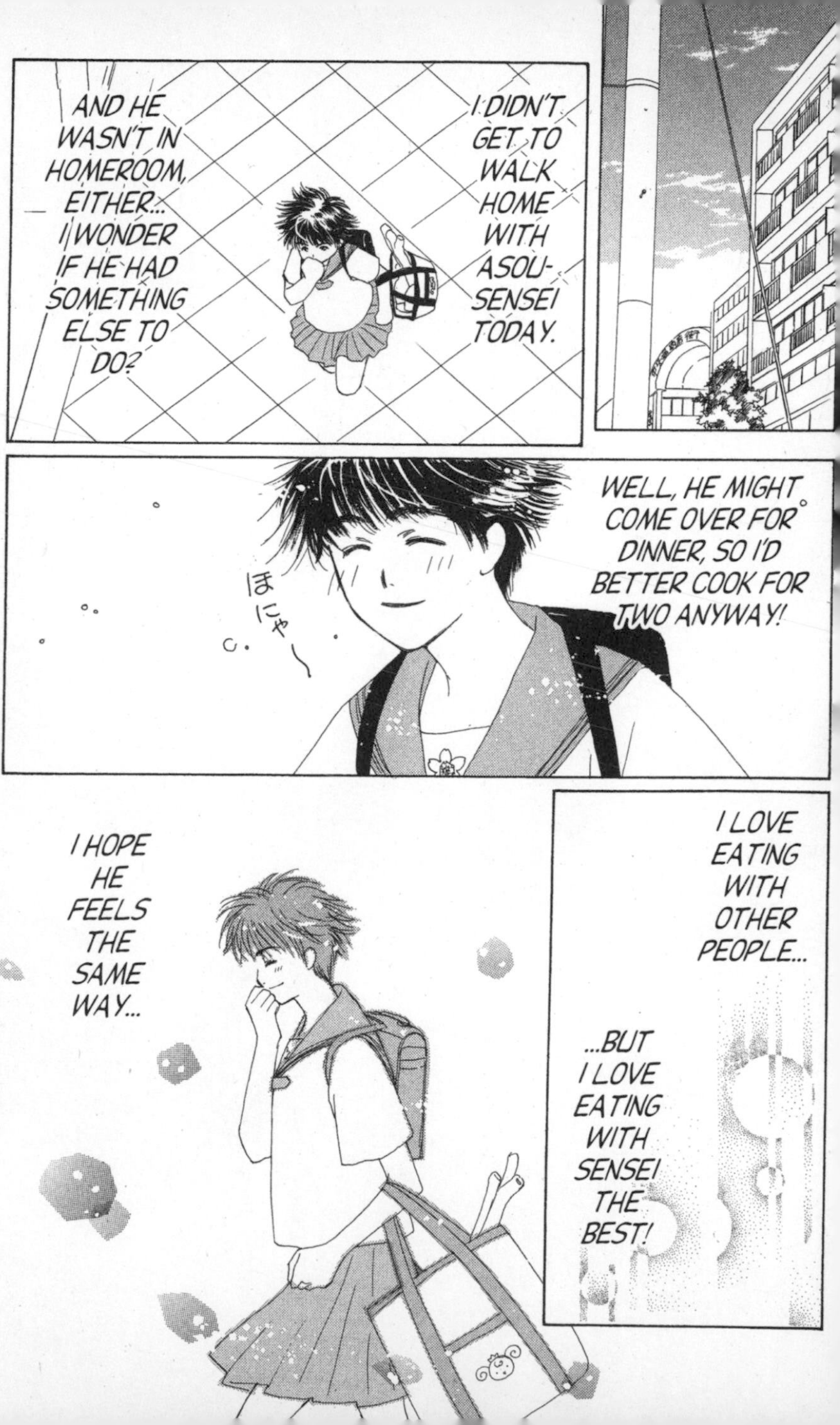
I DIDN'T GET TO WALK HOME WITH ASOU-SENSEI TODAY.
AND HE WASN'T IN HOMEROOM, EITHER... I WONDER IF HE HAD SOMETHING ELSE TO DO?
WELL, HE MIGHT COME OVER FOR DINNER, SO I'D BETTER COOK FOR TWO ANYWAY!
ほにゃ〜
I LOVE EATING WITH OTHER PEOPLE...
...BUT I LOVE EATING WITH SENSEI THE BEST!
I HOPE HE FEELS THE SAME WAY...

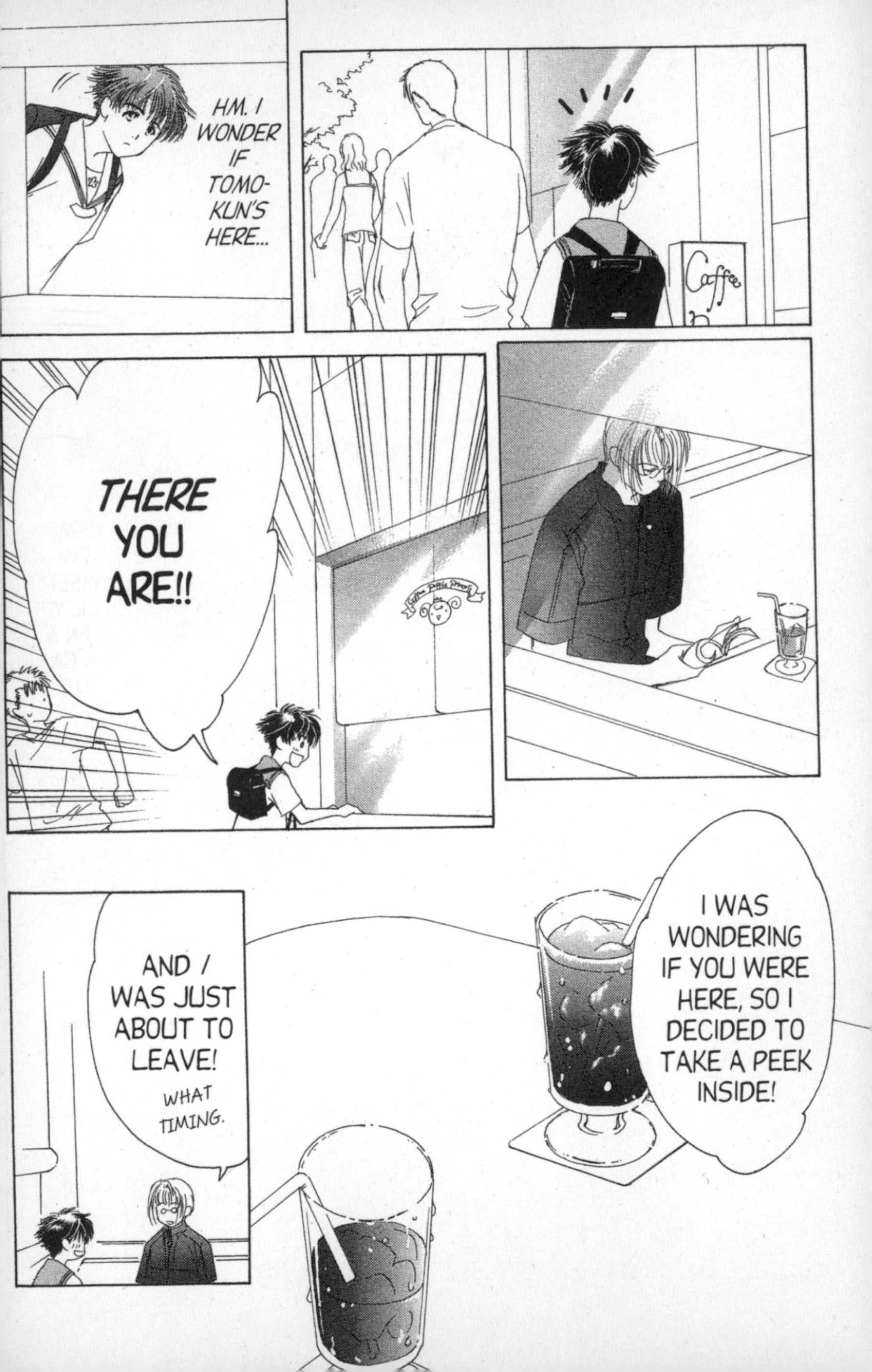
Coffee
HM. I WONDER IF TOMO-KUN'S HERE...
THERE YOU ARE!!
I WAS WONDERING IF YOU WERE HERE, SO I DECIDED TO TAKE A PEEK INSIDE!
AND I WAS JUST ABOUT TO LEAVE!
WHAT TIMING.

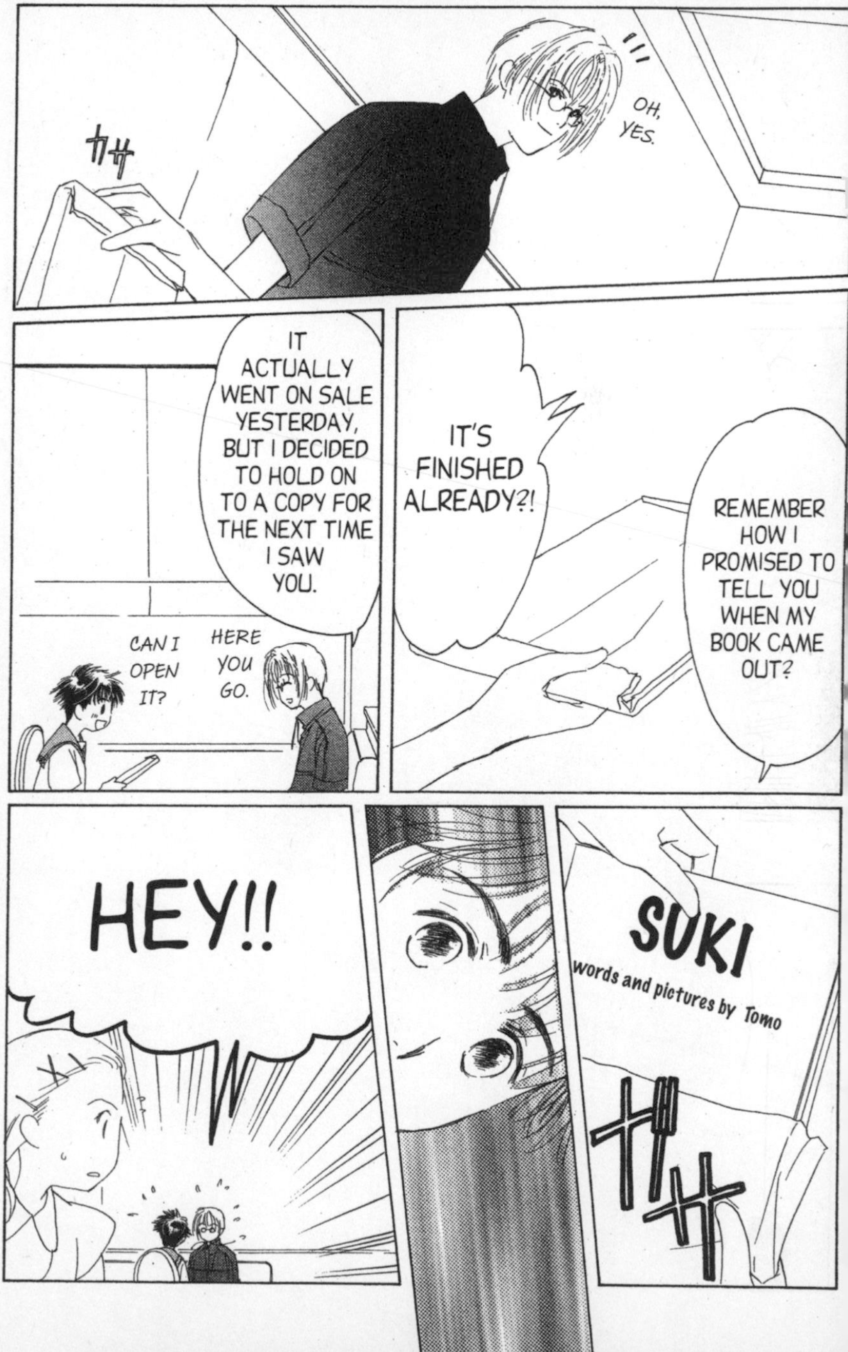
カサ
OH, YES.
REMEMBER HOW I PROMISED TO TELL YOU WHEN MY BOOK CAME OUT?
IT'S FINISHED ALREADY?!
IT ACTUALLY WENT ON SALE YESTERDAY, BUT I DECIDED TO HOLD ON TO A COPY FOR THE NEXT TIME I SAW YOU.
HERE YOU GO.
CAN I OPEN IT?
SUKI
words and pictures by Tomo
HEY!!

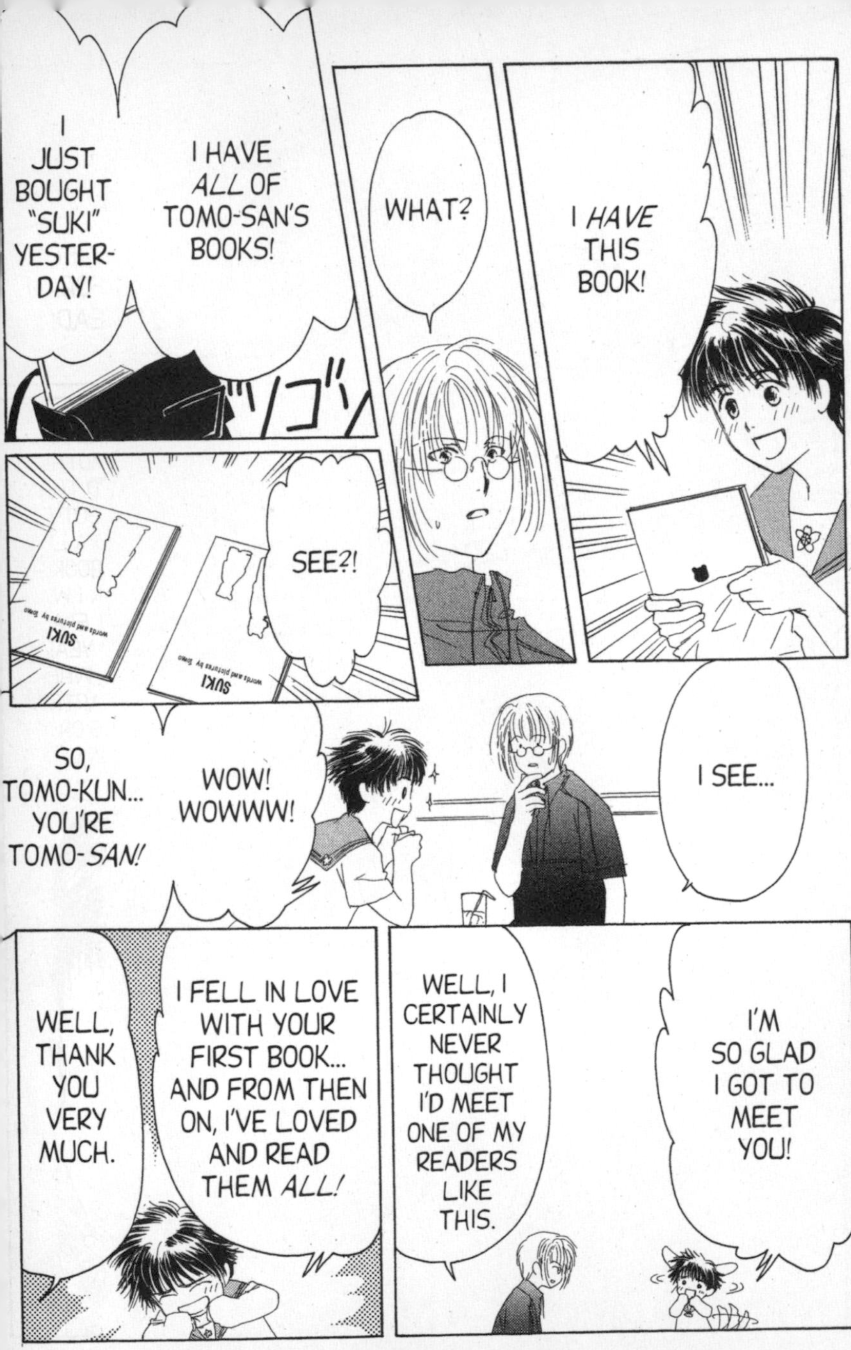

I *HAVE* THIS BOOK!
WHAT?
I HAVE *ALL* OF TOMO-SAN'S BOOKS!
I JUST BOUGHT "SUKI" YESTER-DAY!
SEE?!
SUKI
SUKI
I SEE...
WOW! WOWWW!
SO, TOMO-KUN... YOU'RE TOMO-*SAN*!
I'M SO GLAD I GOT TO MEET YOU!
WELL, I CERTAINLY NEVER THOUGHT I'D MEET ONE OF MY READERS LIKE THIS.
I FELL IN LOVE WITH YOUR FIRST BOOK... AND FROM THEN ON, I'VE LOVED AND READ THEM *ALL*!
WELL, THANK YOU VERY MUCH.

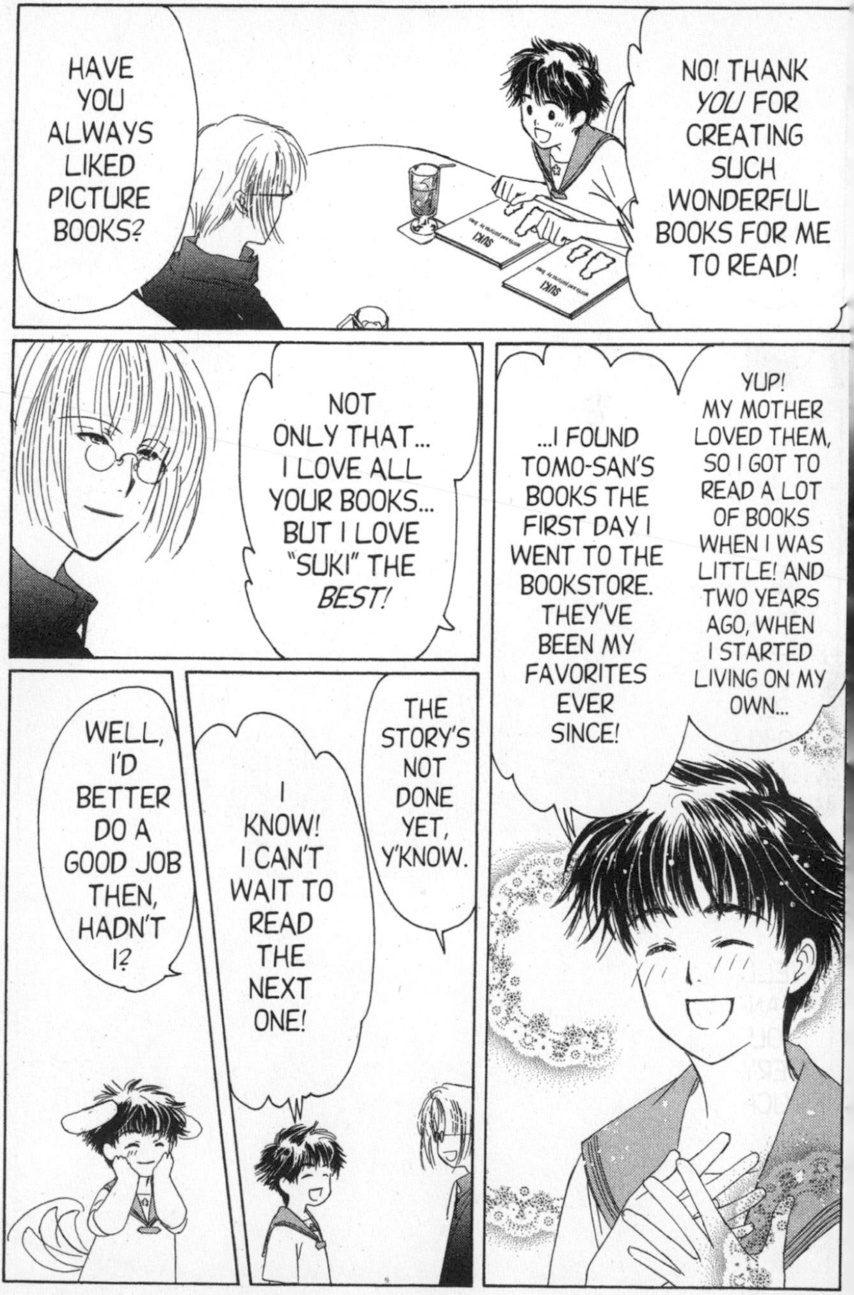
NO! THANK YOU FOR CREATING SUCH WONDERFUL BOOKS FOR ME TO READ!
HAVE YOU ALWAYS LIKED PICTURE BOOKS?
YUP! MY MOTHER LOVED THEM, SO I GOT TO READ A LOT OF BOOKS WHEN I WAS LITTLE! AND TWO YEARS AGO, WHEN I STARTED LIVING ON MY OWN...
...I FOUND TOMO-SAN'S BOOKS THE FIRST DAY I WENT TO THE BOOKSTORE. THEY'VE BEEN MY FAVORITES EVER SINCE!
NOT ONLY THAT... I LOVE ALL YOUR BOOKS... BUT I LOVE "SUKI" THE BEST!
THE STORY'S NOT DONE YET, Y'KNOW.
I KNOW! I CAN'T WAIT TO READ THE NEXT ONE!
WELL, I'D BETTER DO A GOOD JOB THEN, HADN'T I?

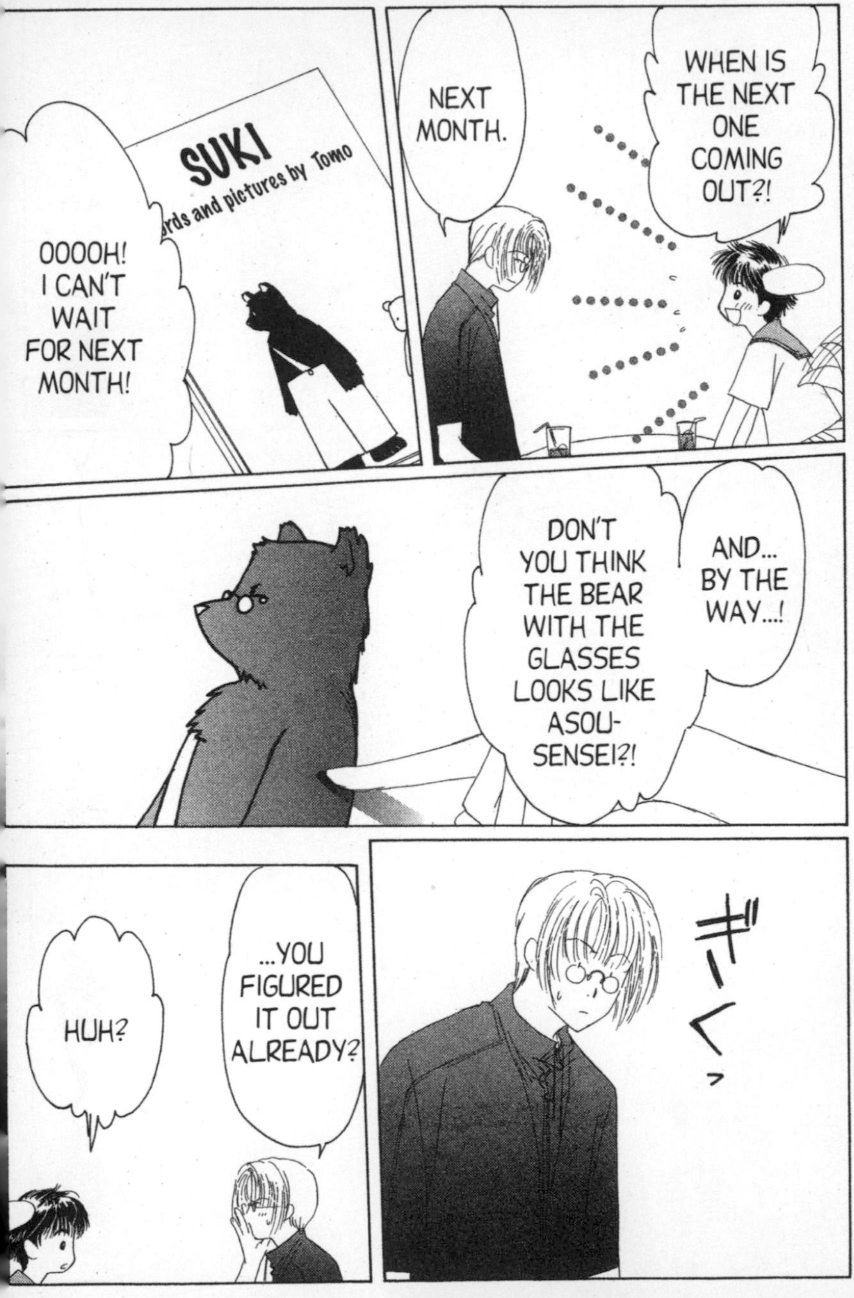
WHEN IS THE NEXT ONE COMING OUT?!
NEXT MONTH.
SUKI
rds and pictures by Tomo
OOOOH! I CAN'T WAIT FOR NEXT MONTH!
AND... BY THE WAY...!
DON'T YOU THINK THE BEAR WITH THE GLASSES LOOKS LIKE ASOU-SENSEI?!
ぎくっ
...YOU FIGURED IT OUT ALREADY?
HUH?

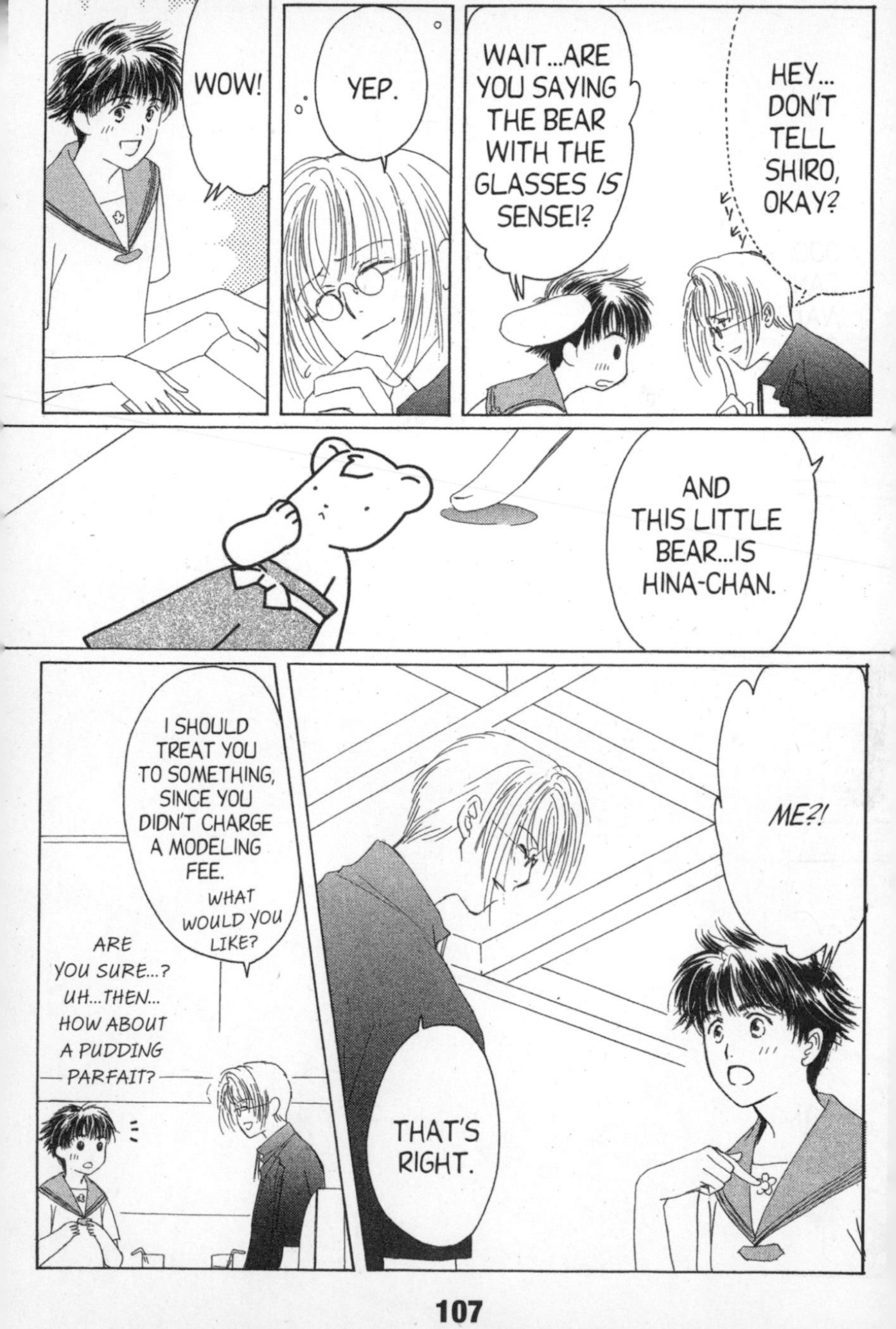
HEY... DON'T TELL SHIRO, OKAY?
WAIT...ARE YOU SAYING THE BEAR WITH THE GLASSES *IS* SENSEI?
YEP.
WOW!
AND THIS LITTLE BEAR...IS HINA-CHAN.
ME?!
THAT'S RIGHT.
I SHOULD TREAT YOU TO SOMETHING, SINCE YOU DIDN'T CHARGE A MODELING FEE.
WHAT WOULD YOU LIKE?
ARE YOU SURE...? UH...THEN... HOW ABOUT A PUDDING PARFAIT?

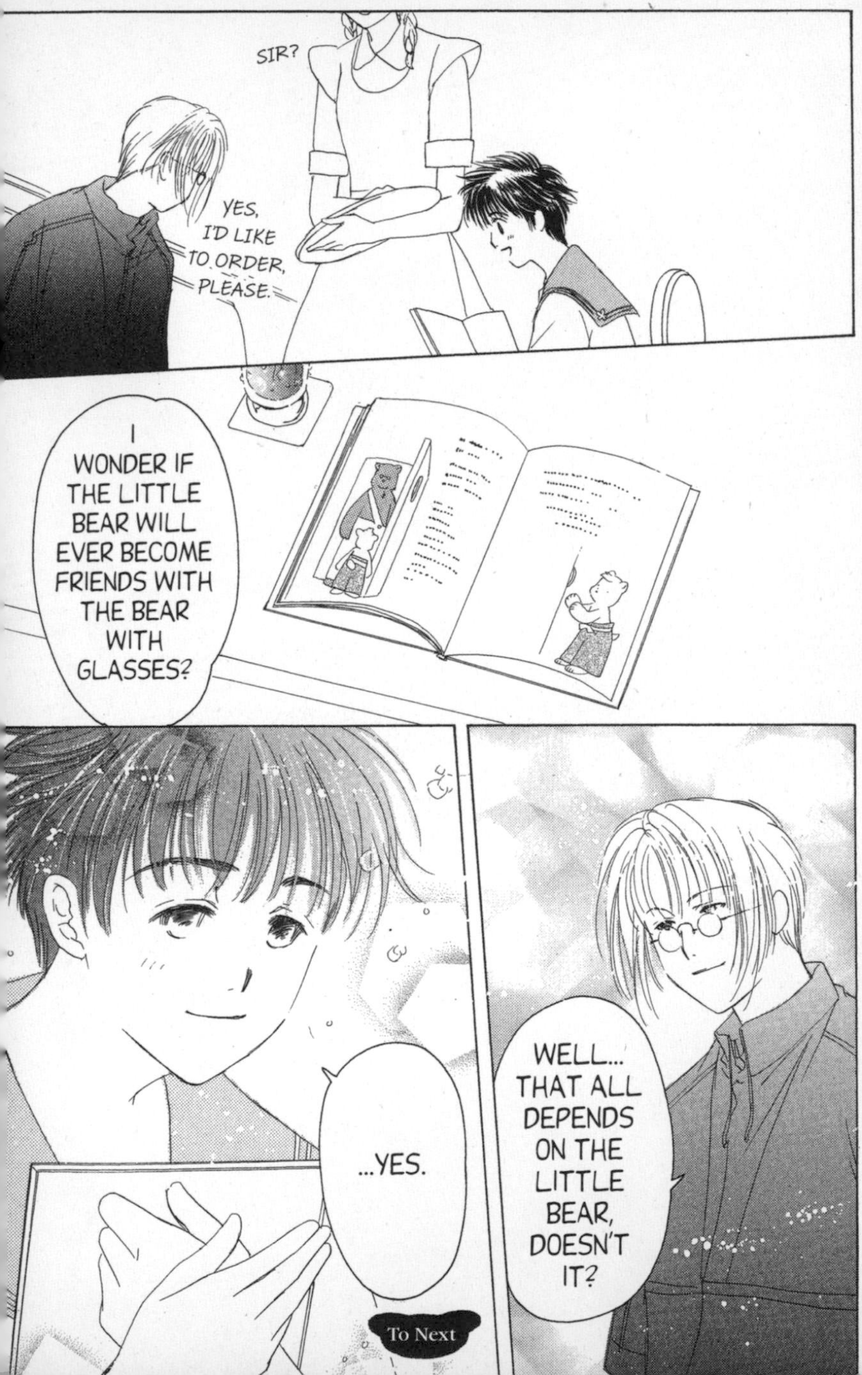
SIR?
YES, I'D LIKE TO ORDER, PLEASE.
I WONDER IF THE LITTLE BEAR WILL EVER BECOME FRIENDS WITH THE BEAR WITH GLASSES?
WELL... THAT ALL DEPENDS ON THE LITTLE BEAR, DOESN'T IT?
...YES.
To Next

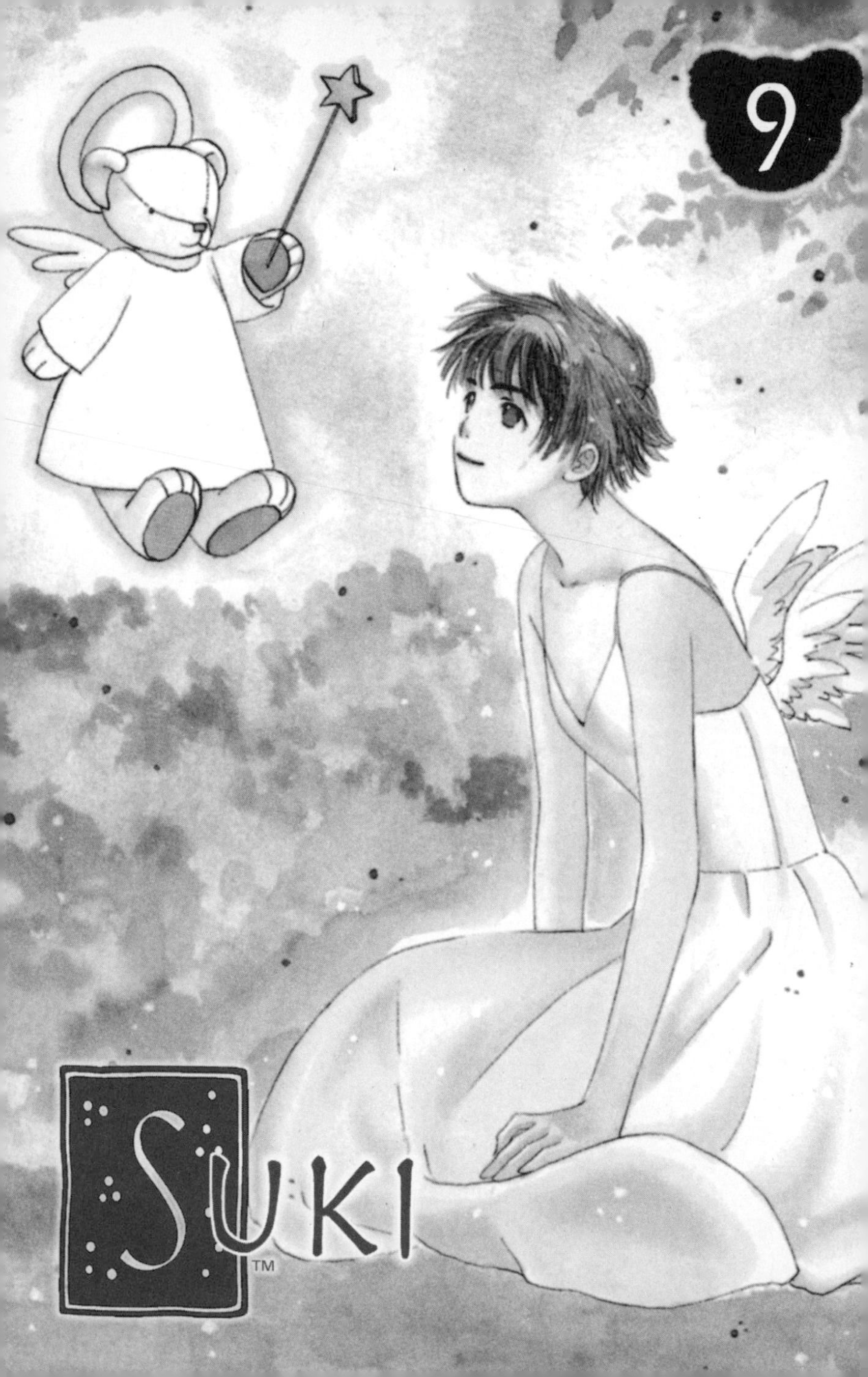
9
SUKI™

I LOVE IT WHEN YOU'RE KIND TO ME.

I EVEN LOVE IT WHEN YOU'RE BRUSQUE.

THAT'S WHY I WANT
SO MUCH TO SAY...

THAT I LOVE YOU.

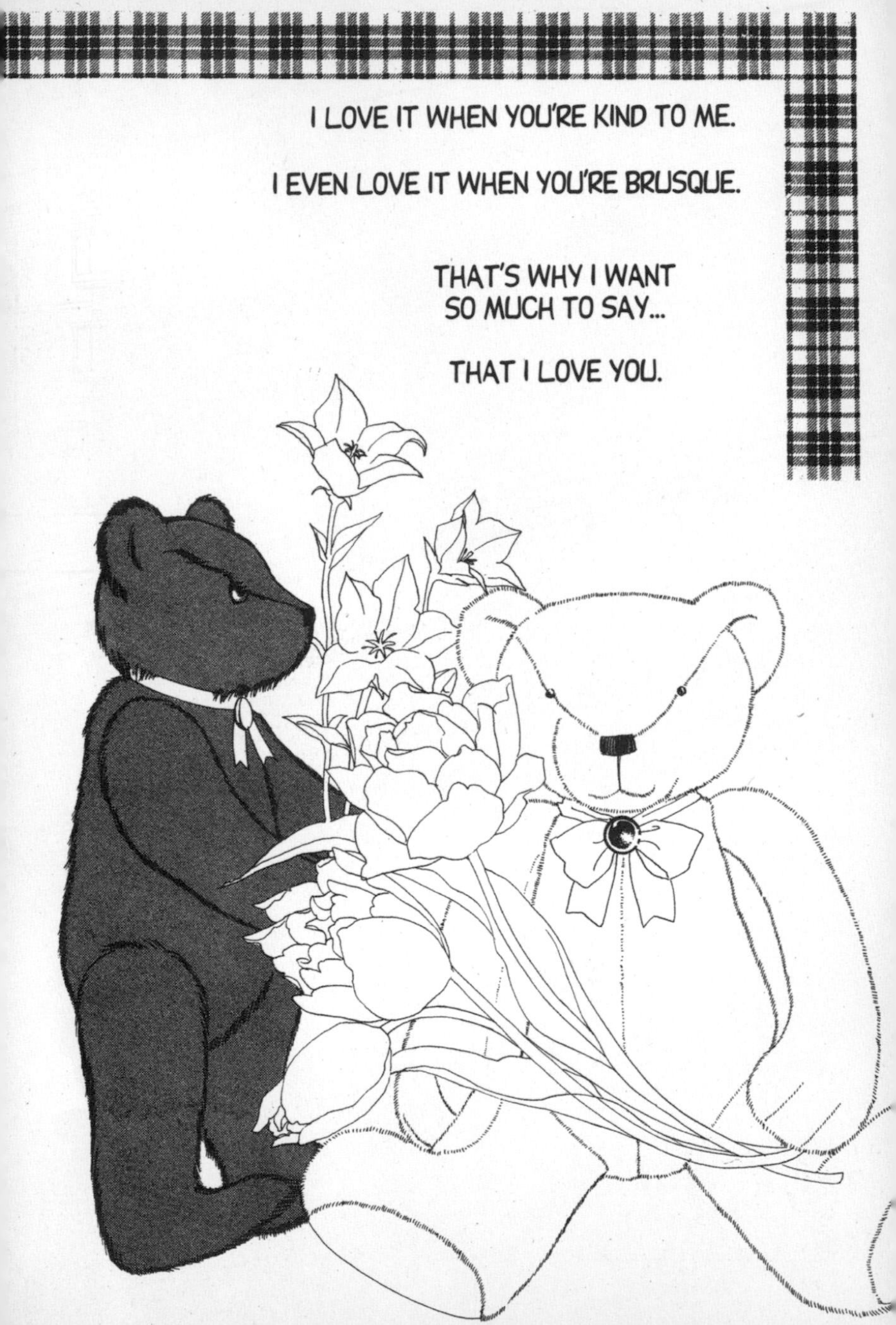

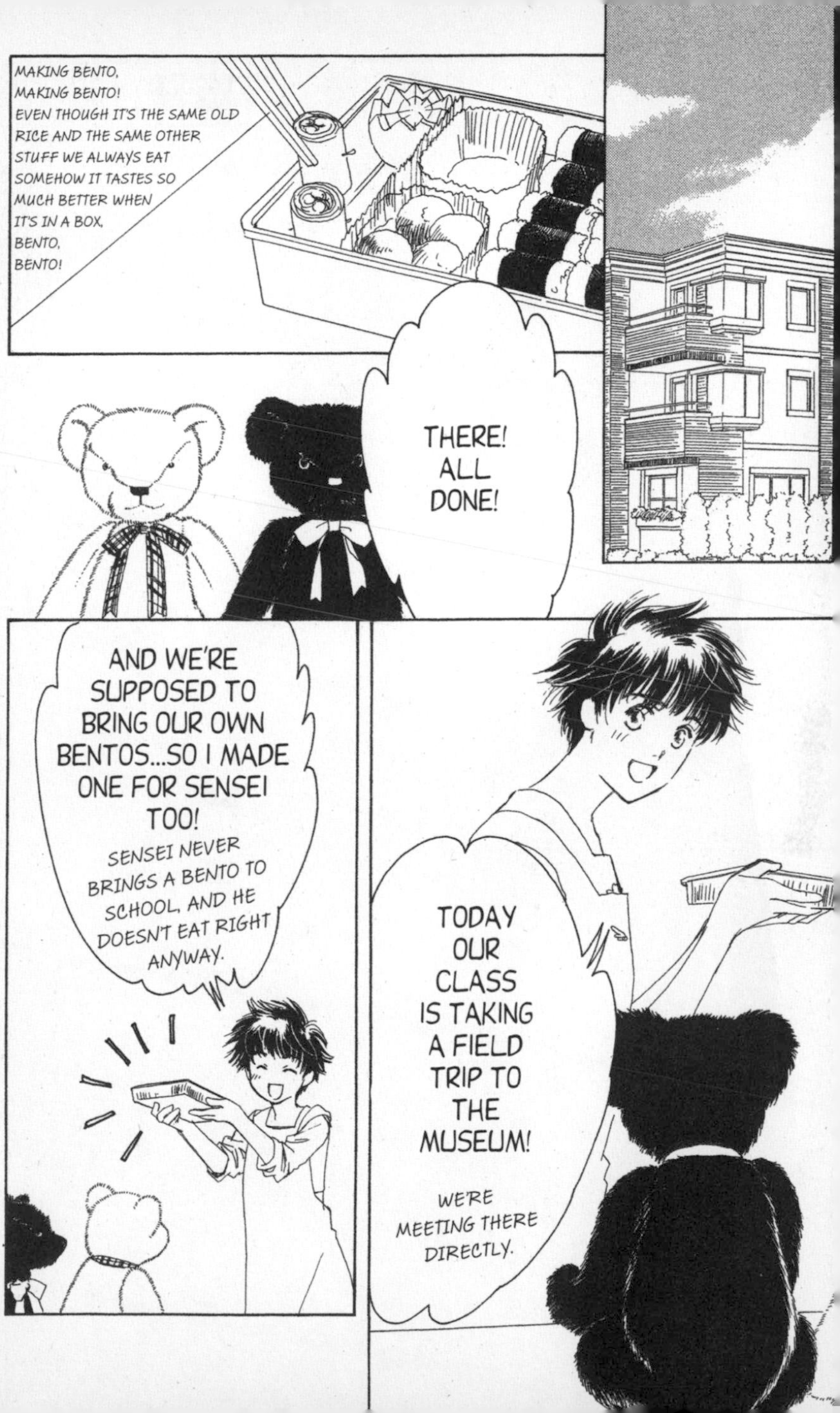
MAKING BENTO, MAKING BENTO! EVEN THOUGH IT'S THE SAME OLD RICE AND THE SAME OTHER STUFF WE ALWAYS EAT SOMEHOW IT TASTES SO MUCH BETTER WHEN IT'S IN A BOX. BENTO, BENTO!
THERE! ALL DONE!
TODAY OUR CLASS IS TAKING A FIELD TRIP TO THE MUSEUM!
WE'RE MEETING THERE DIRECTLY.
AND WE'RE SUPPOSED TO BRING OUR OWN BENTOS...SO I MADE ONE FOR SENSEI TOO!
SENSEI NEVER BRINGS A BENTO TO SCHOOL, AND HE DOESN'T EAT RIGHT ANYWAY.

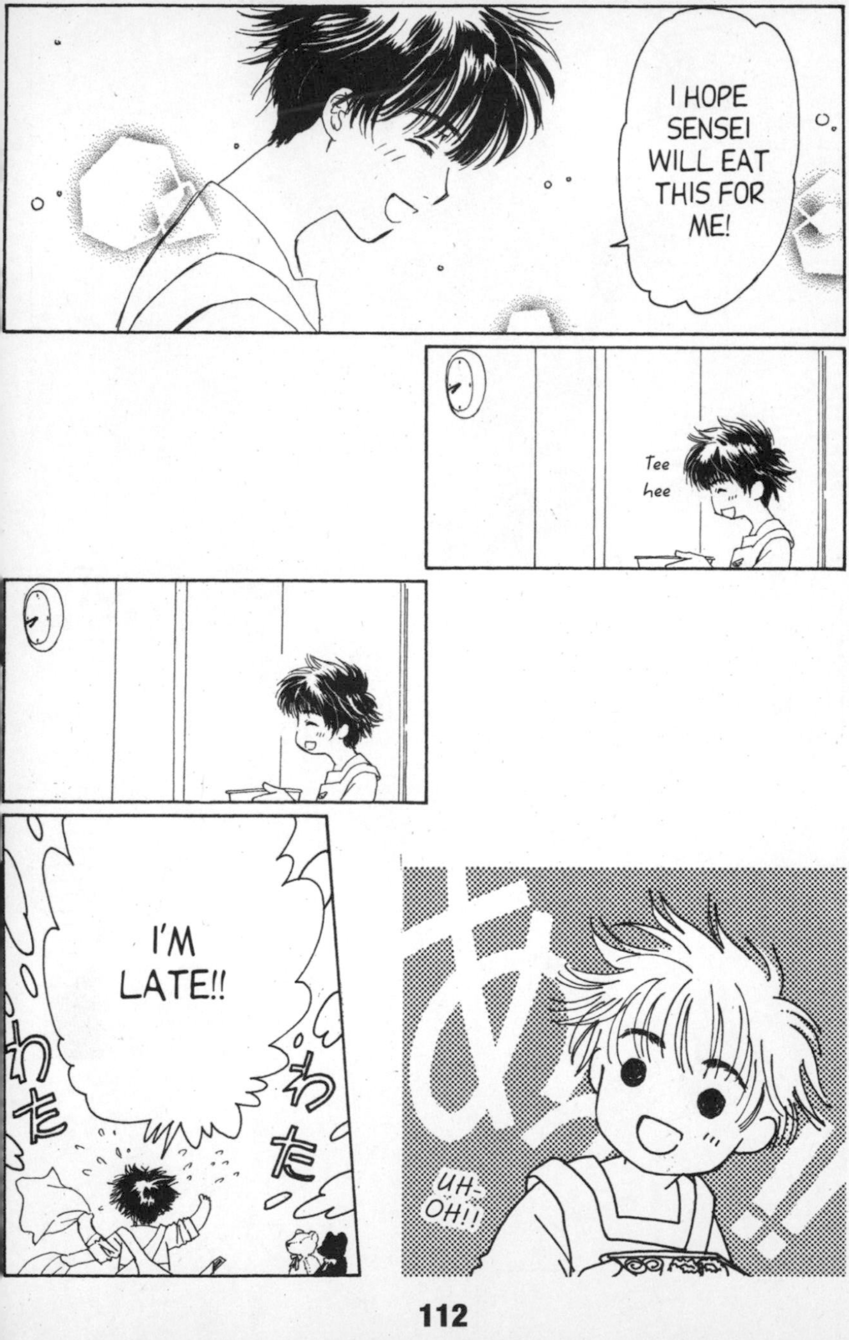
I HOPE SENSEI WILL EAT THIS FOR ME!
Tee hee
あ
UH-OH!!
I'M LATE!!
わた
わた

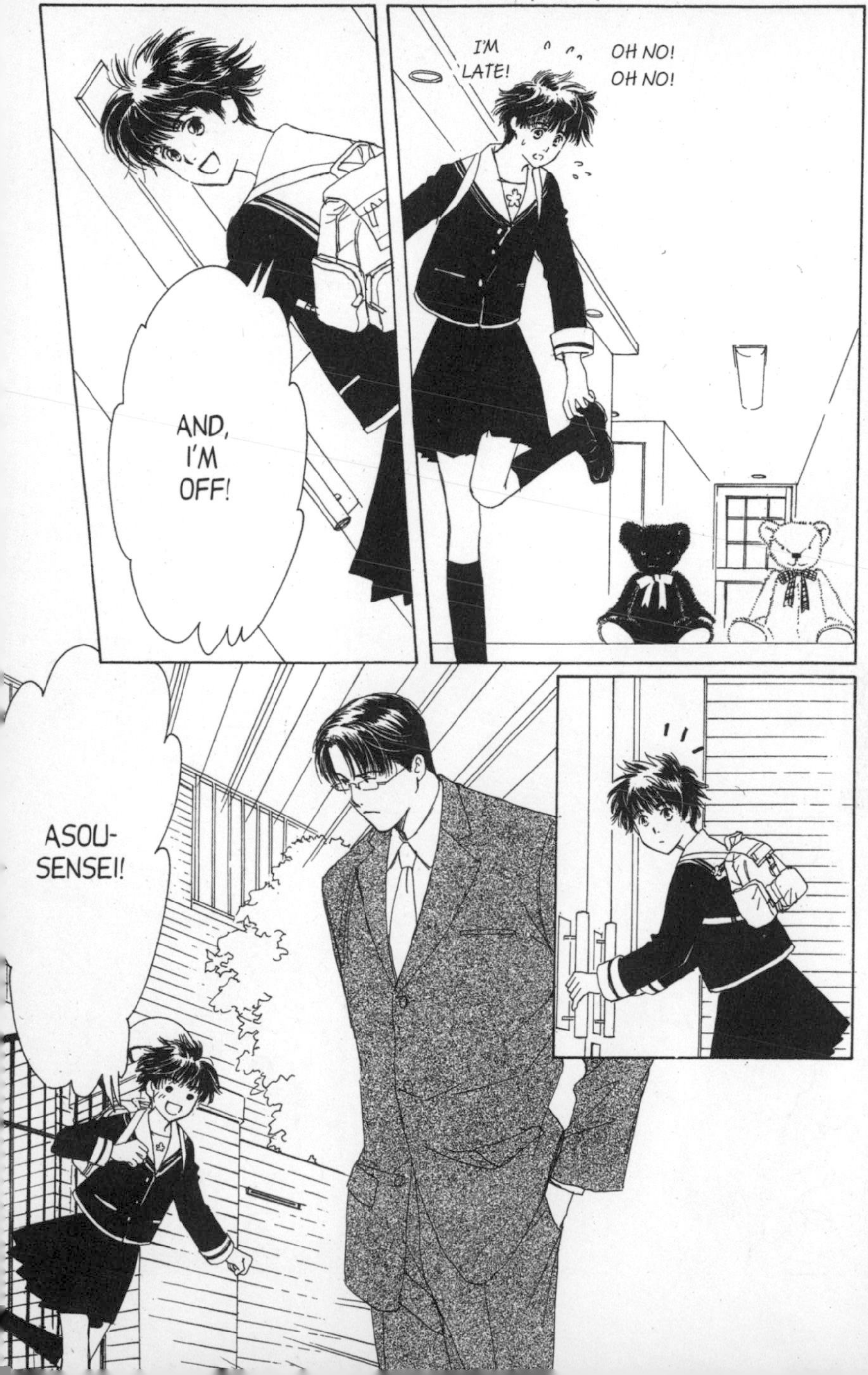
OH NO! OH NO!
I'M LATE!
AND, I'M OFF!
ASOU-SENSEI!

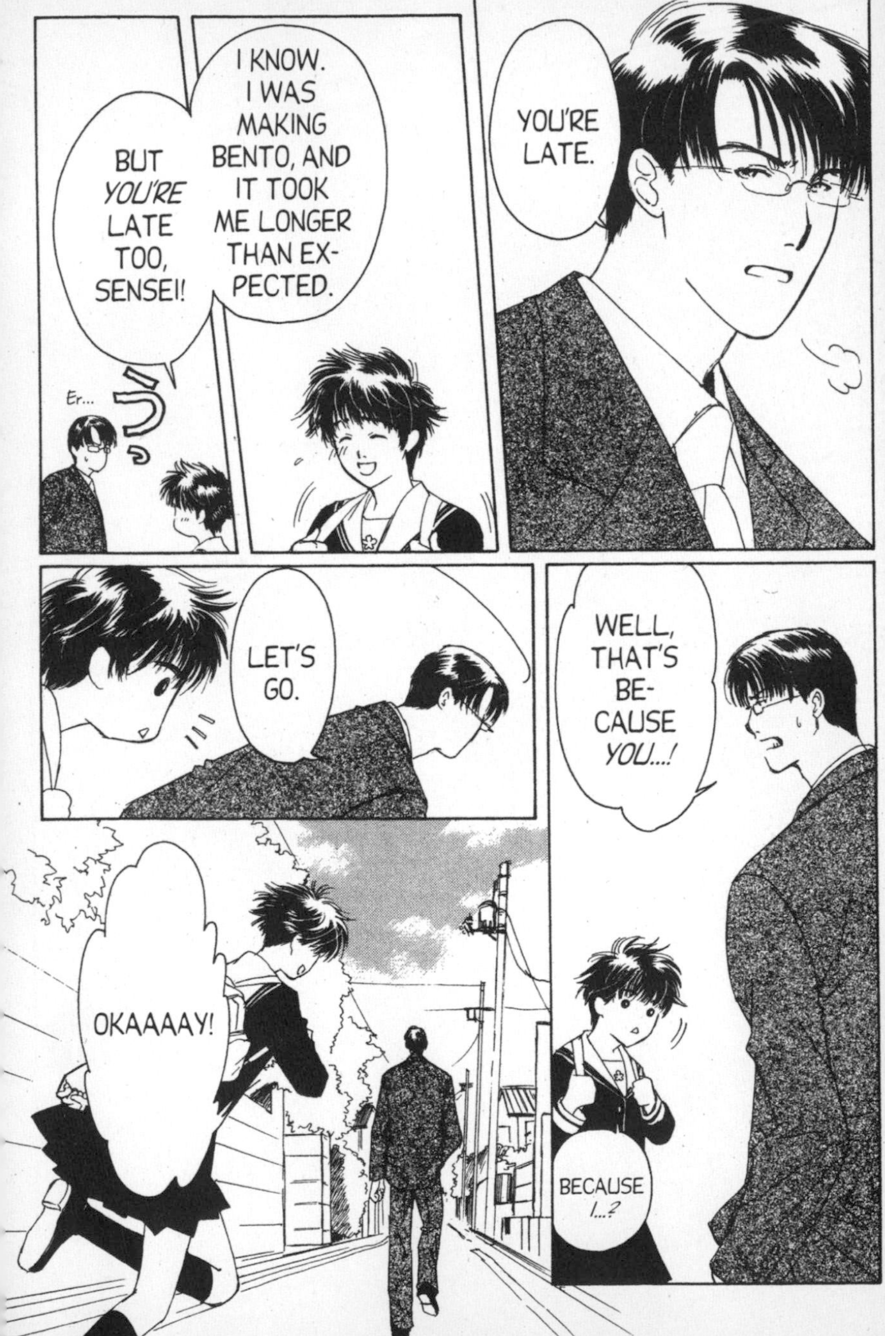
YOU'RE LATE.
I KNOW. I WAS MAKING BENTO, AND IT TOOK ME LONGER THAN EX-PECTED.
BUT *YOU'RE* LATE TOO, SENSEI!
Er...
う
WELL, THAT'S BE-CAUSE *YOU*...!
BECAUSE *I*...?
LET'S GO.
OKAAAAY!

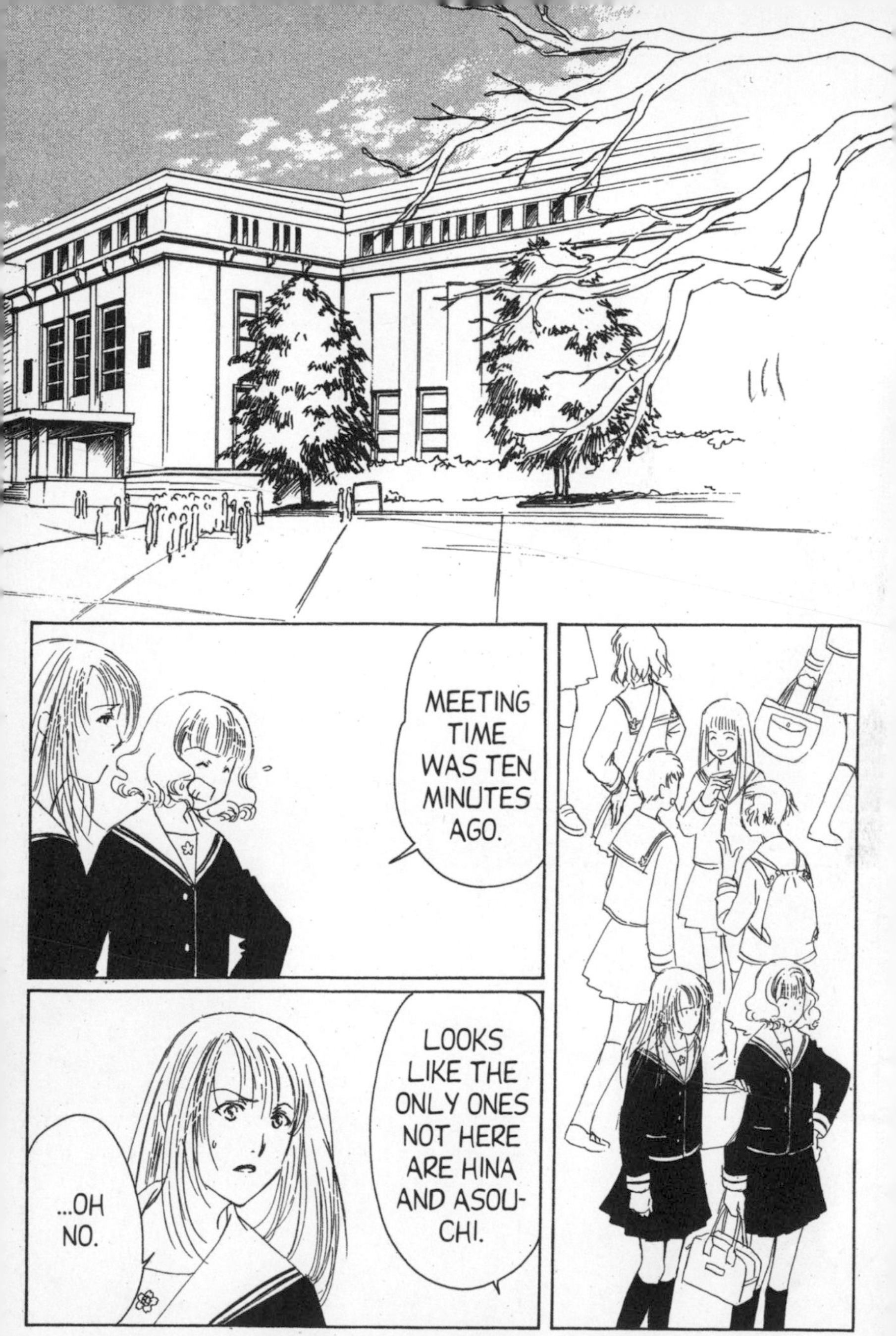
MEETING TIME WAS TEN MINUTES AGO.
LOOKS LIKE THE ONLY ONES NOT HERE ARE HINA AND ASOU-CHI.
...OH NO.

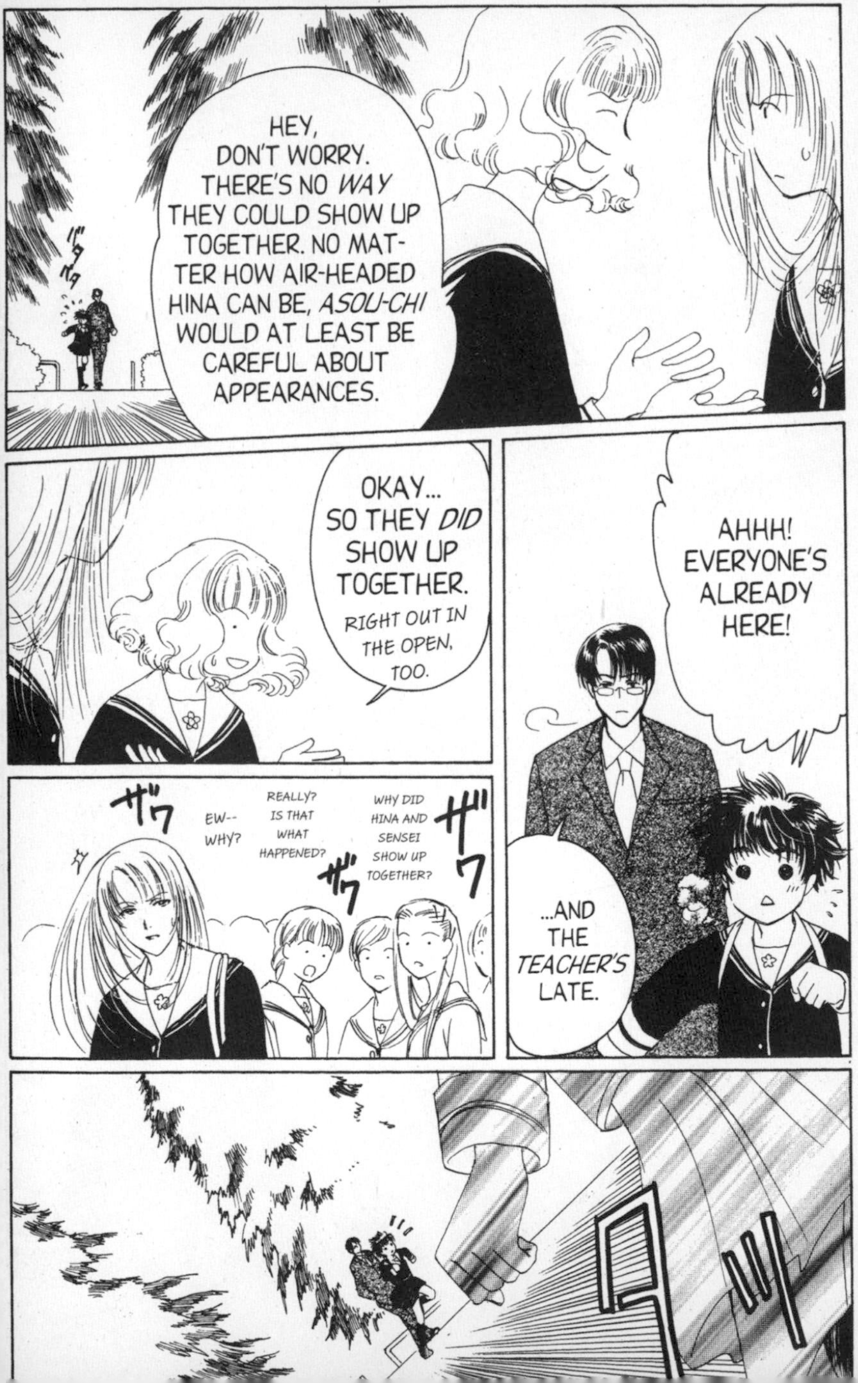
HEY, DON'T WORRY. THERE'S NO *WAY* THEY COULD SHOW UP TOGETHER. NO MATTER HOW AIR-HEADED HINA CAN BE, *ASOU-CHI* WOULD AT LEAST BE CAREFUL ABOUT APPEARANCES.
バタバタ
AHHH! EVERYONE'S ALREADY HERE!
...AND THE *TEACHER'S* LATE.
OKAY... SO THEY *DID* SHOW UP TOGETHER.
RIGHT OUT IN THE OPEN, TOO.
ザワ
WHY DID HINA AND SENSEI SHOW UP TOGETHER?
ザワ
REALLY? IS THAT WHAT HAPPENED?
EW-- WHY?
ザワ
ダッ

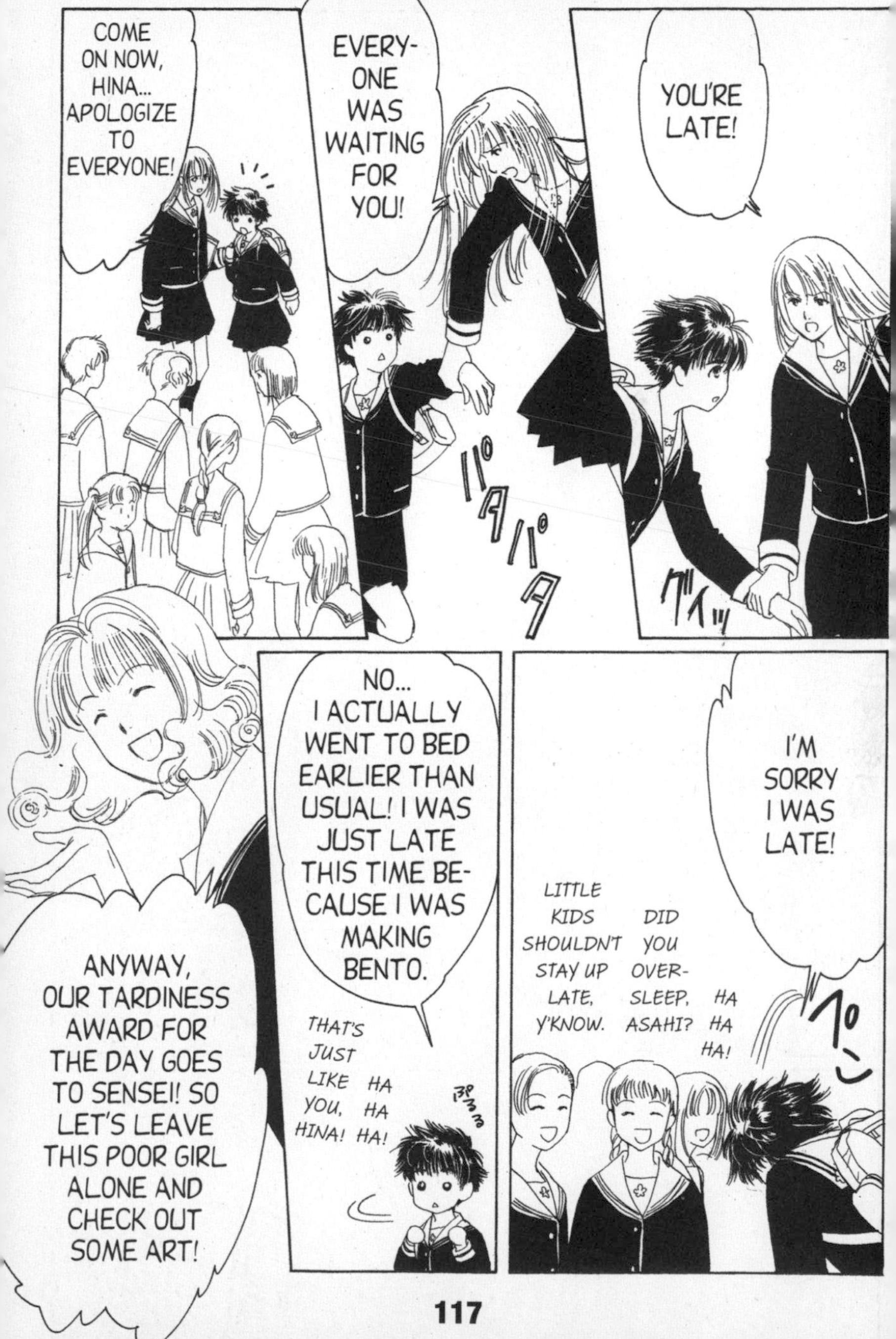
YOU'RE LATE!
グイッ
EVERY-ONE WAS WAITING FOR YOU!
パタパタ
COME ON NOW, HINA... APOLOGIZE TO EVERYONE!
I'M SORRY I WAS LATE!
ぺこ
DID YOU OVER-SLEEP, ASAHI? HA HA HA!
LITTLE KIDS SHOULDN'T STAY UP LATE, Y'KNOW.
NO... I ACTUALLY WENT TO BED EARLIER THAN USUAL! I WAS JUST LATE THIS TIME BE-CAUSE I WAS MAKING BENTO.
THAT'S JUST LIKE YOU, HINA! HA HA HA!
ANYWAY, OUR TARDINESS AWARD FOR THE DAY GOES TO SENSEI! SO LET'S LEAVE THIS POOR GIRL ALONE AND CHECK OUT SOME ART!

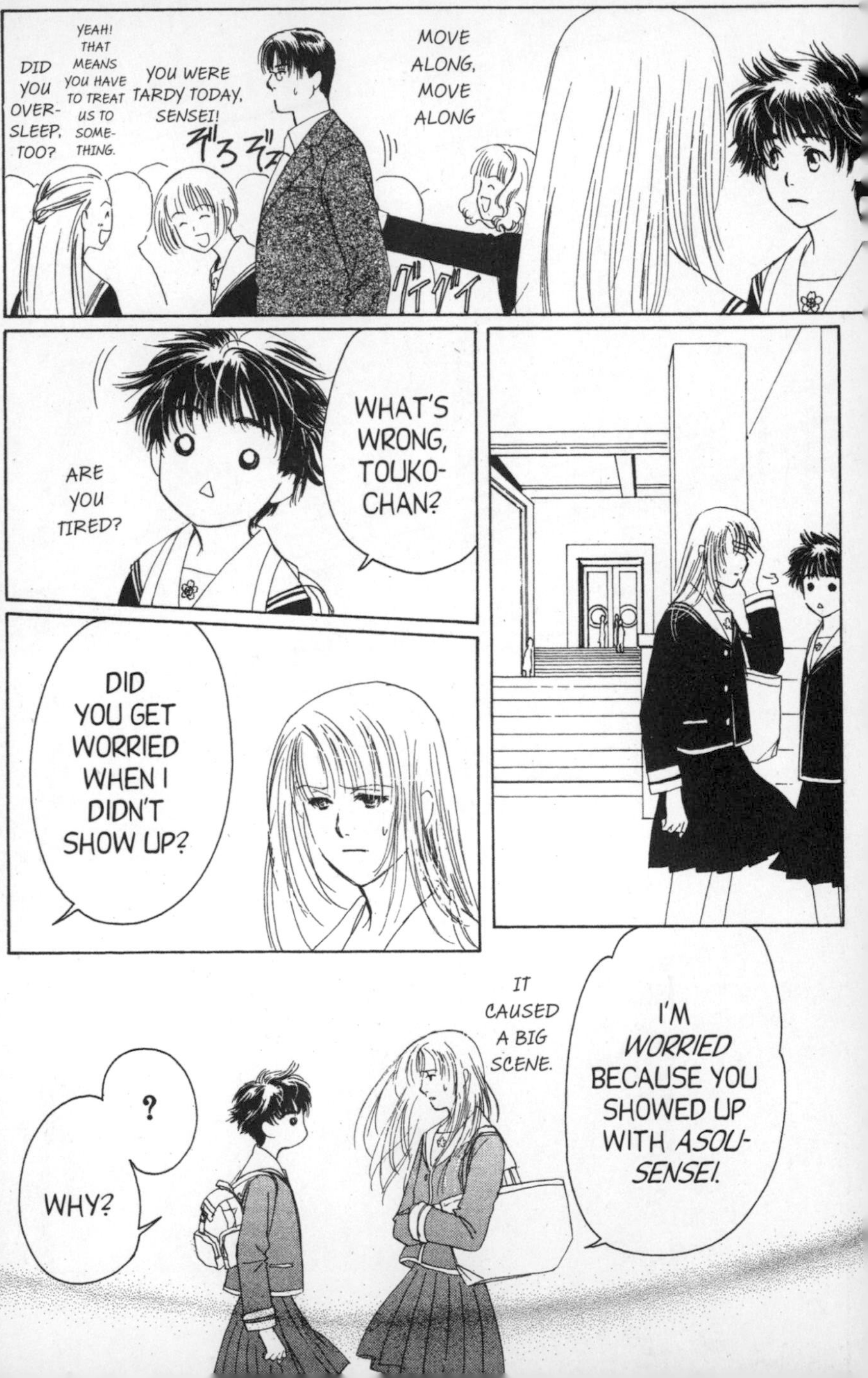
MOVE ALONG, MOVE ALONG
YOU WERE TARDY TODAY, SENSEI!
ぞろぞろ
YEAH! THAT MEANS YOU HAVE TO TREAT US TO SOMETHING.
DID YOU OVER-SLEEP, TOO?
グイグイ
WHAT'S WRONG, TOUKO-CHAN?
ARE YOU TIRED?
DID YOU GET WORRIED WHEN I DIDN'T SHOW UP?
I'M *WORRIED* BECAUSE YOU SHOWED UP WITH *ASOU-SENSEI.*
IT CAUSED A BIG SCENE.
?
WHY?

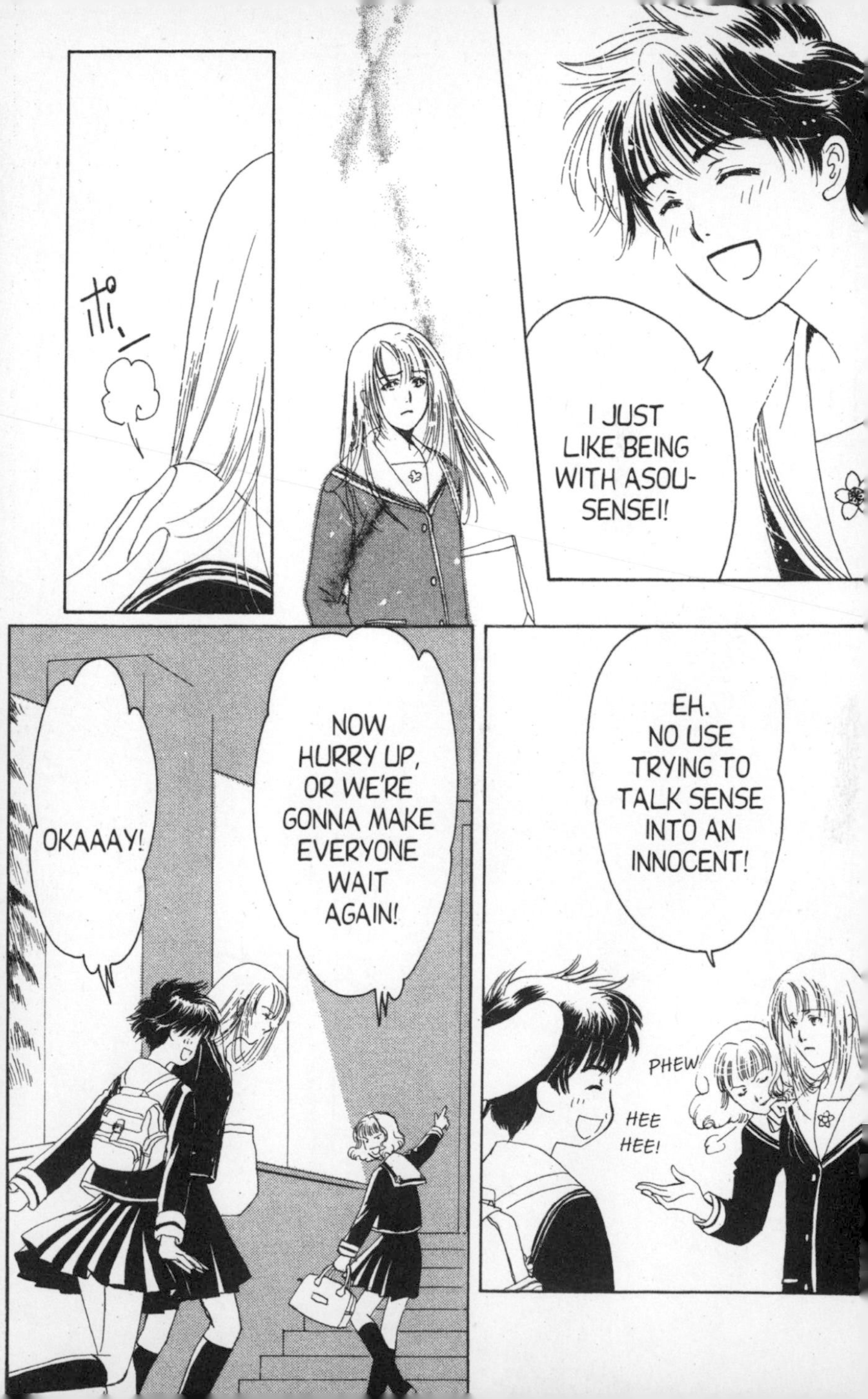
I JUST LIKE BEING WITH ASOU-SENSEI!
EH. NO USE TRYING TO TALK SENSE INTO AN INNOCENT!
PHEW
HEE HEE!
NOW HURRY UP, OR WE'RE GONNA MAKE EVERYONE WAIT AGAIN!
OKAAAY!

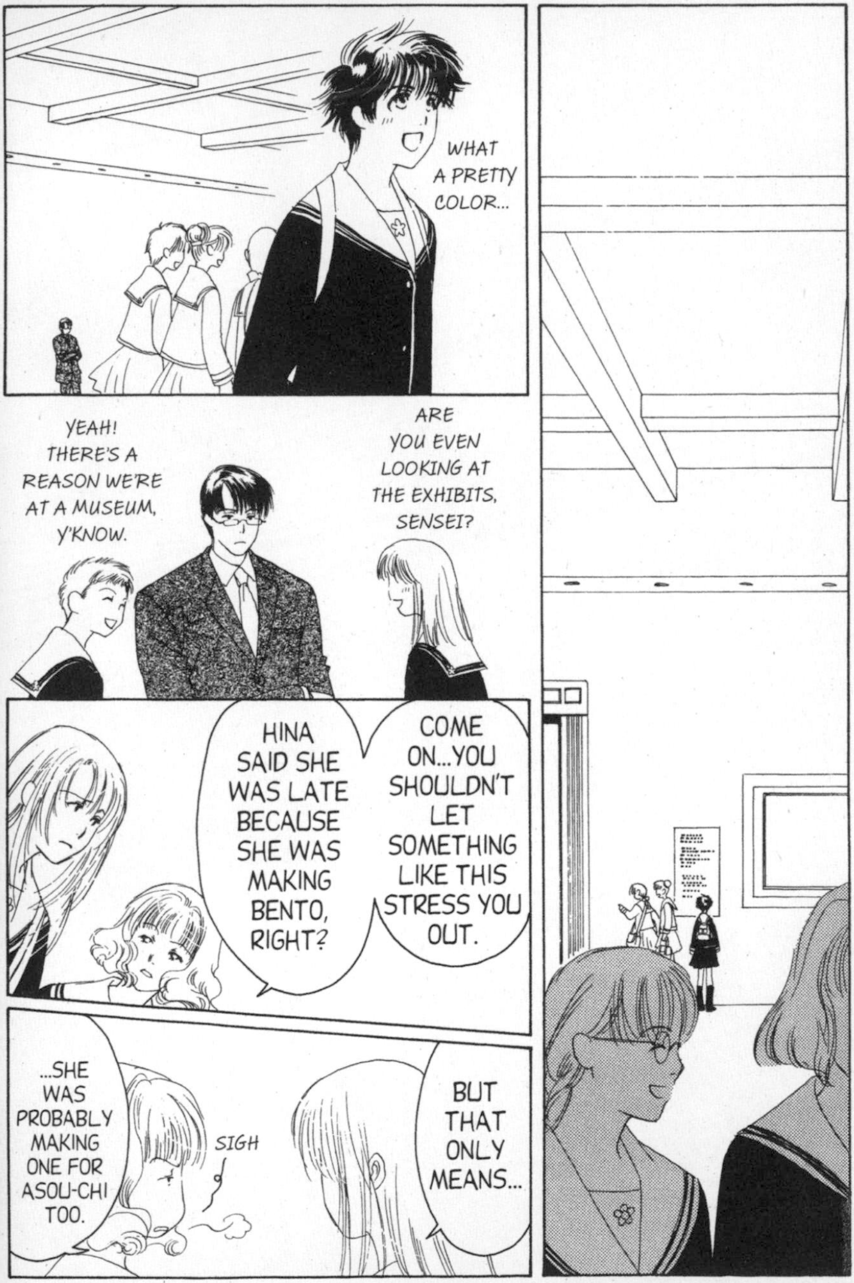
WHAT A PRETTY COLOR...
ARE YOU EVEN LOOKING AT THE EXHIBITS, SENSEI?
YEAH! THERE'S A REASON WE'RE AT A MUSEUM, Y'KNOW.
COME ON...YOU SHOULDN'T LET SOMETHING LIKE THIS STRESS YOU OUT.
HINA SAID SHE WAS LATE BECAUSE SHE WAS MAKING BENTO, RIGHT?
BUT THAT ONLY MEANS...
SIGH
...SHE WAS PROBABLY MAKING ONE FOR ASOU-CHI TOO.

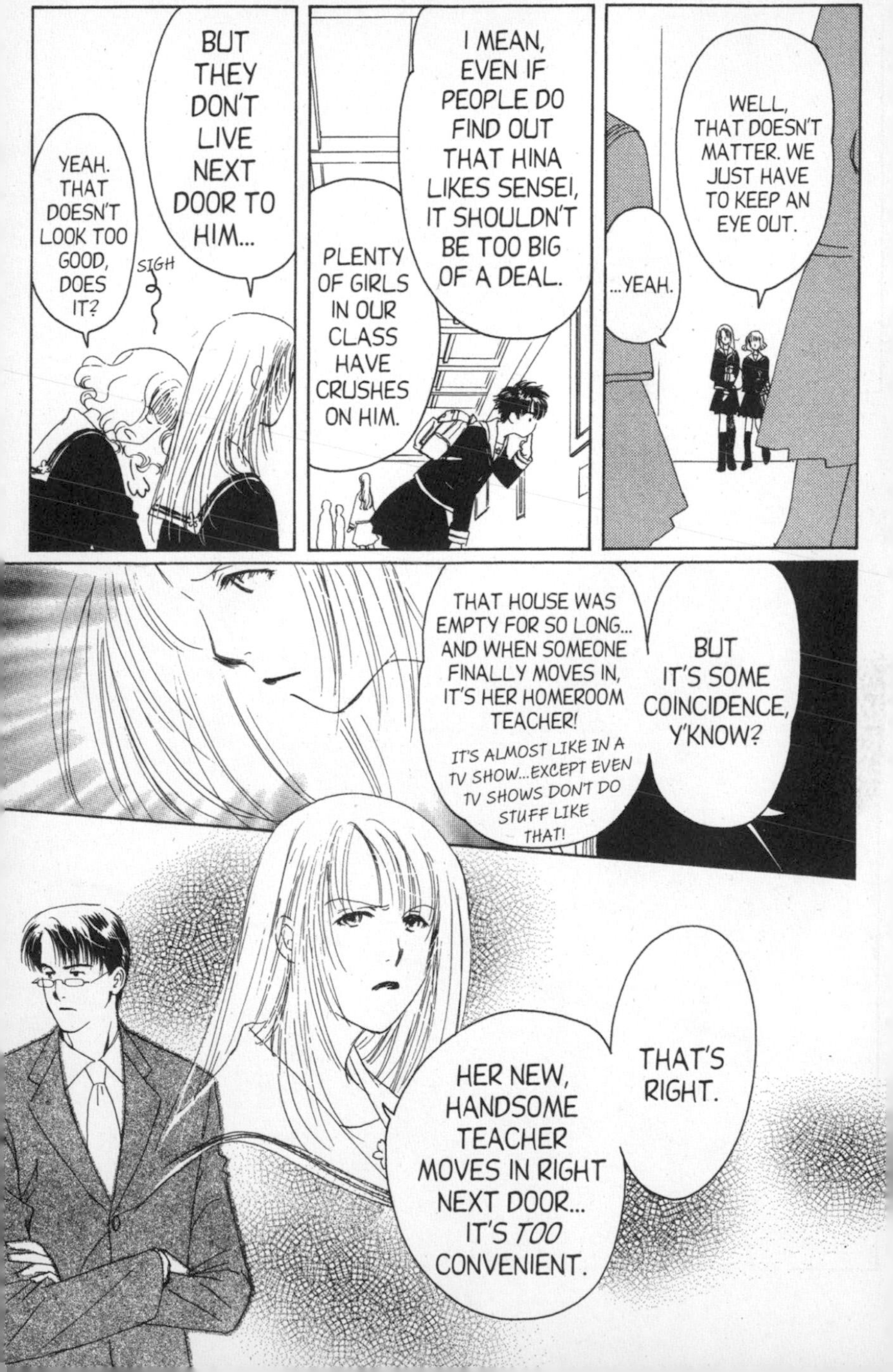
WELL, THAT DOESN'T MATTER. WE JUST HAVE TO KEEP AN EYE OUT.
...YEAH.
I MEAN, EVEN IF PEOPLE DO FIND OUT THAT HINA LIKES SENSEI, IT SHOULDN'T BE TOO BIG OF A DEAL.
PLENTY OF GIRLS IN OUR CLASS HAVE CRUSHES ON HIM.
BUT THEY DON'T LIVE NEXT DOOR TO HIM...
SIGH
YEAH. THAT DOESN'T LOOK TOO GOOD, DOES IT?
BUT IT'S SOME COINCIDENCE, Y'KNOW?
THAT HOUSE WAS EMPTY FOR SO LONG... AND WHEN SOMEONE FINALLY MOVES IN, IT'S HER HOMEROOM TEACHER!
IT'S ALMOST LIKE IN A TV SHOW...EXCEPT EVEN TV SHOWS DON'T DO STUFF LIKE THAT!
THAT'S RIGHT.
HER NEW, HANDSOME TEACHER MOVES IN RIGHT NEXT DOOR... IT'S *TOO* CONVENIENT.

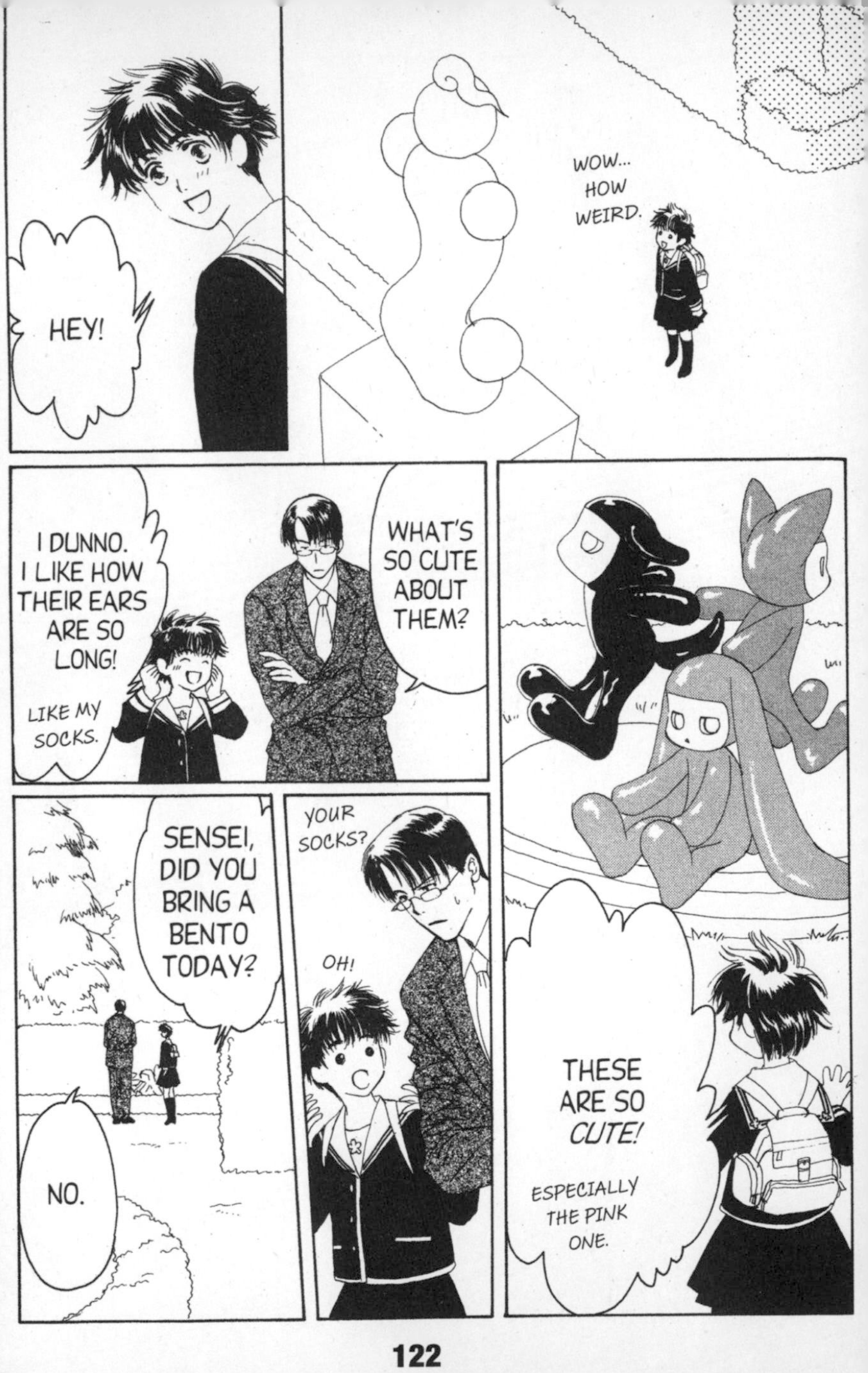
WOW... HOW WEIRD.
HEY!
THESE ARE SO *CUTE!*
ESPECIALLY THE PINK ONE.
WHAT'S SO CUTE ABOUT THEM?
I DUNNO. I LIKE HOW THEIR EARS ARE SO LONG!
LIKE MY SOCKS.
YOUR SOCKS?
OH!
SENSEI, DID YOU BRING A BENTO TODAY?
NO.

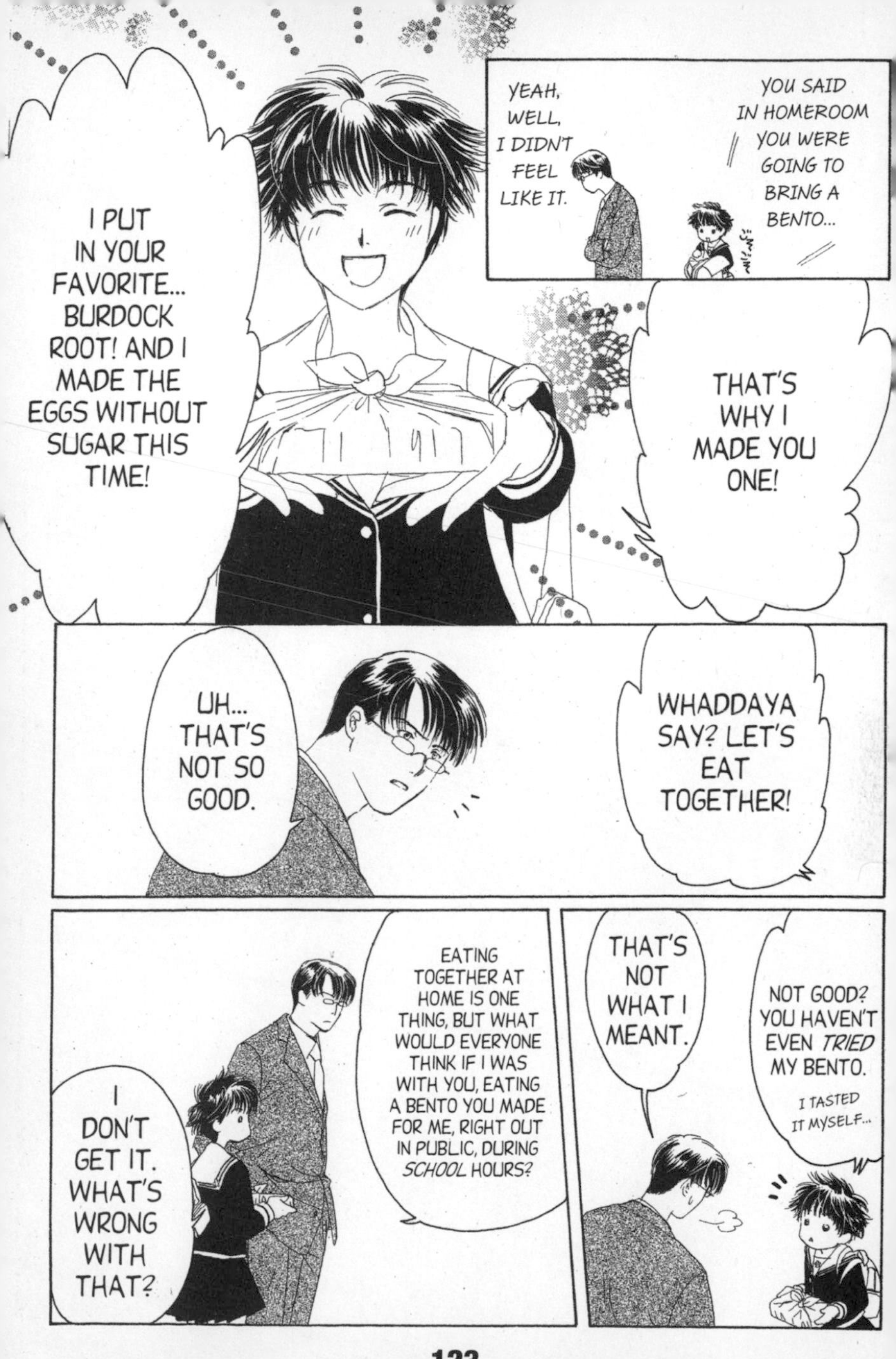
YOU SAID IN HOMEROOM YOU WERE GOING TO BRING A BENTO...
YEAH, WELL, I DIDN'T FEEL LIKE IT.
THAT'S WHY I MADE YOU ONE!
I PUT IN YOUR FAVORITE... BURDOCK ROOT! AND I MADE THE EGGS WITHOUT SUGAR THIS TIME!
WHADDAYA SAY? LET'S EAT TOGETHER!
UH... THAT'S NOT SO GOOD.
NOT GOOD? YOU HAVEN'T EVEN *TRIED* MY BENTO.
I TASTED IT MYSELF...
THAT'S NOT WHAT I MEANT.
EATING TOGETHER AT HOME IS ONE THING, BUT WHAT WOULD EVERYONE THINK IF I WAS WITH YOU, EATING A BENTO YOU MADE FOR ME, RIGHT OUT IN PUBLIC, DURING *SCHOOL* HOURS?
I DON'T GET IT. WHAT'S WRONG WITH THAT?

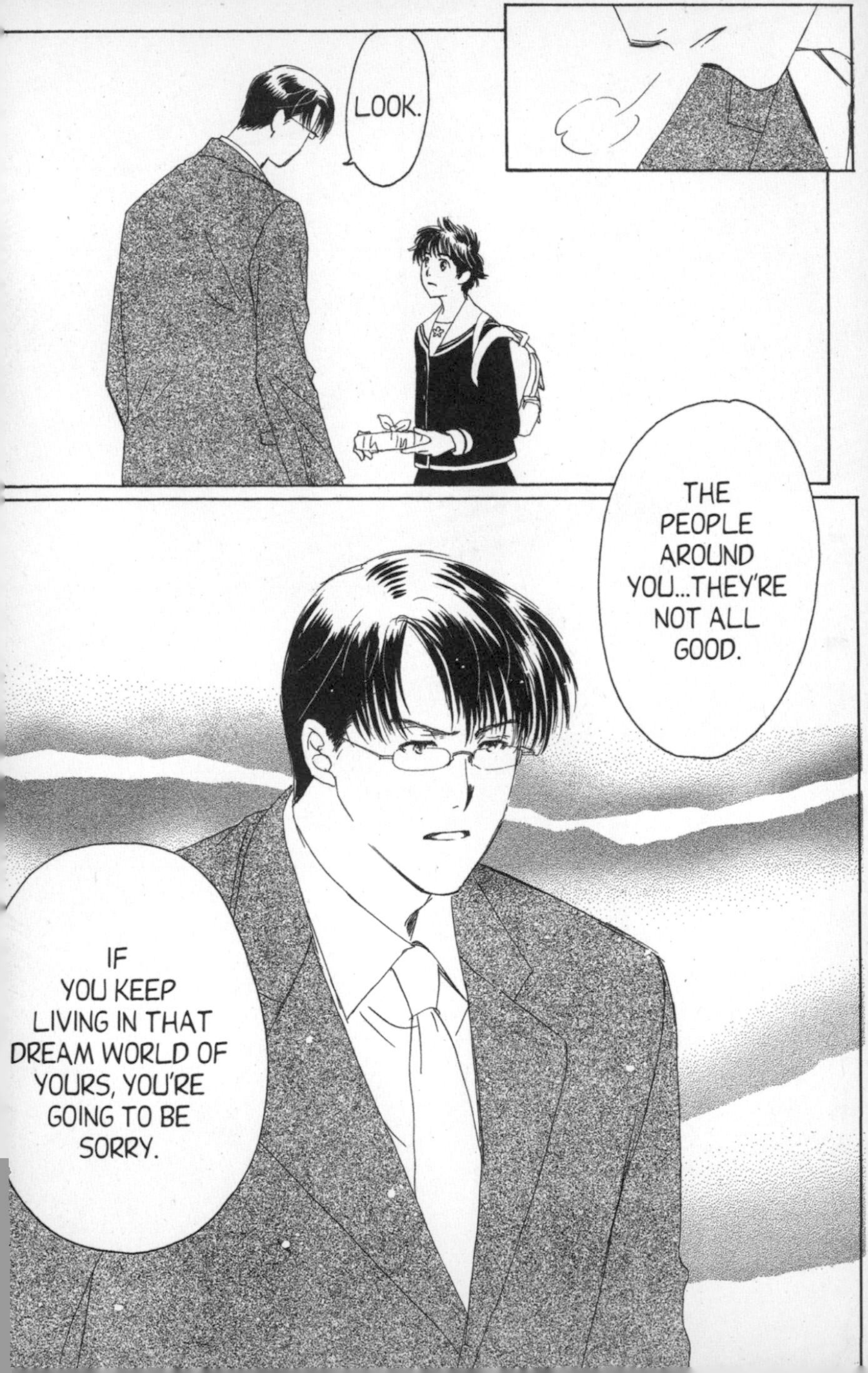
LOOK.
THE PEOPLE AROUND YOU...THEY'RE NOT ALL GOOD.
IF YOU KEEP LIVING IN THAT DREAM WORLD OF YOURS, YOU'RE GOING TO BE SORRY.

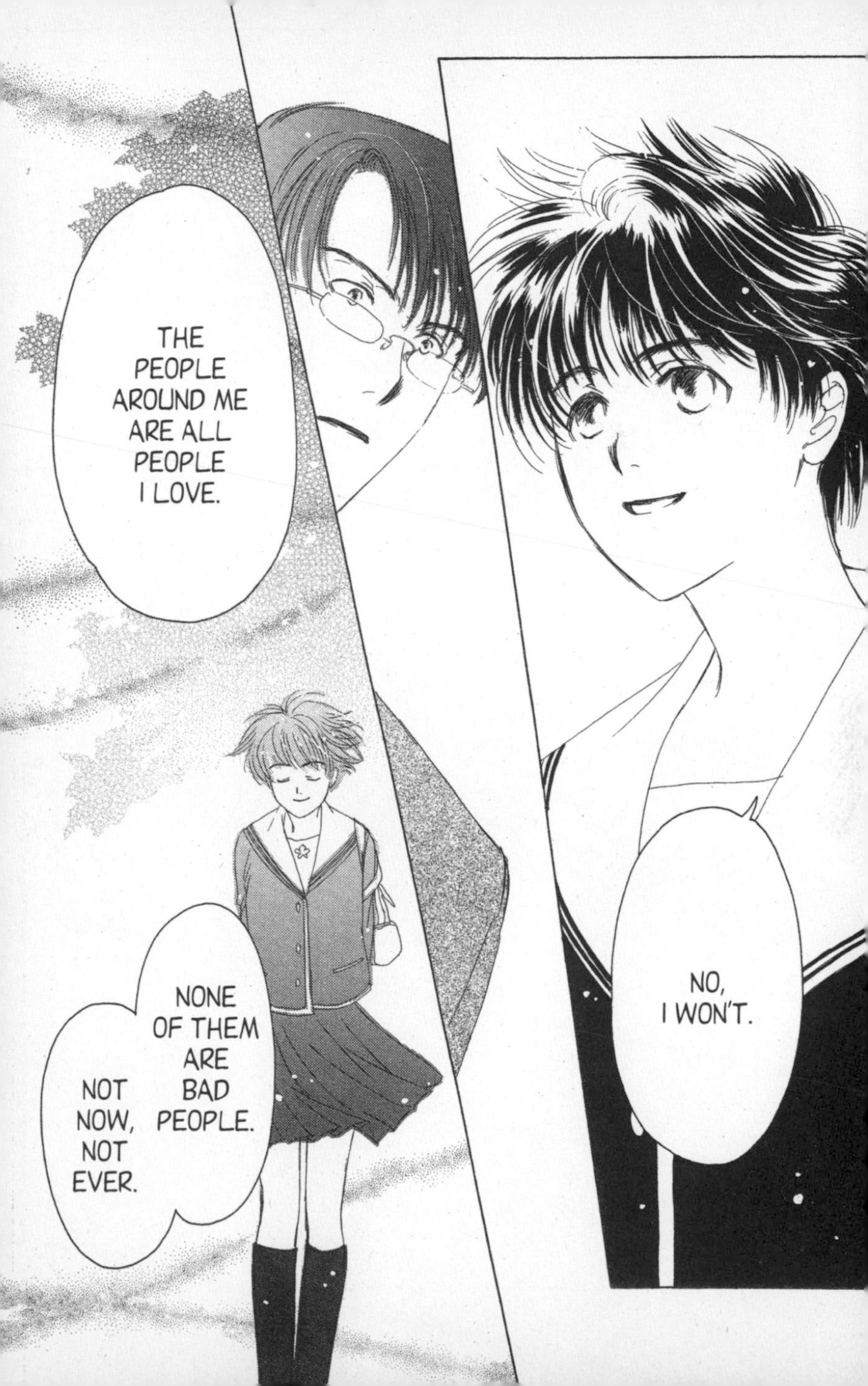
NO, I WON'T.
THE PEOPLE AROUND ME ARE ALL PEOPLE I LOVE.
NONE OF THEM ARE BAD PEOPLE.
NOT NOW, NOT EVER.

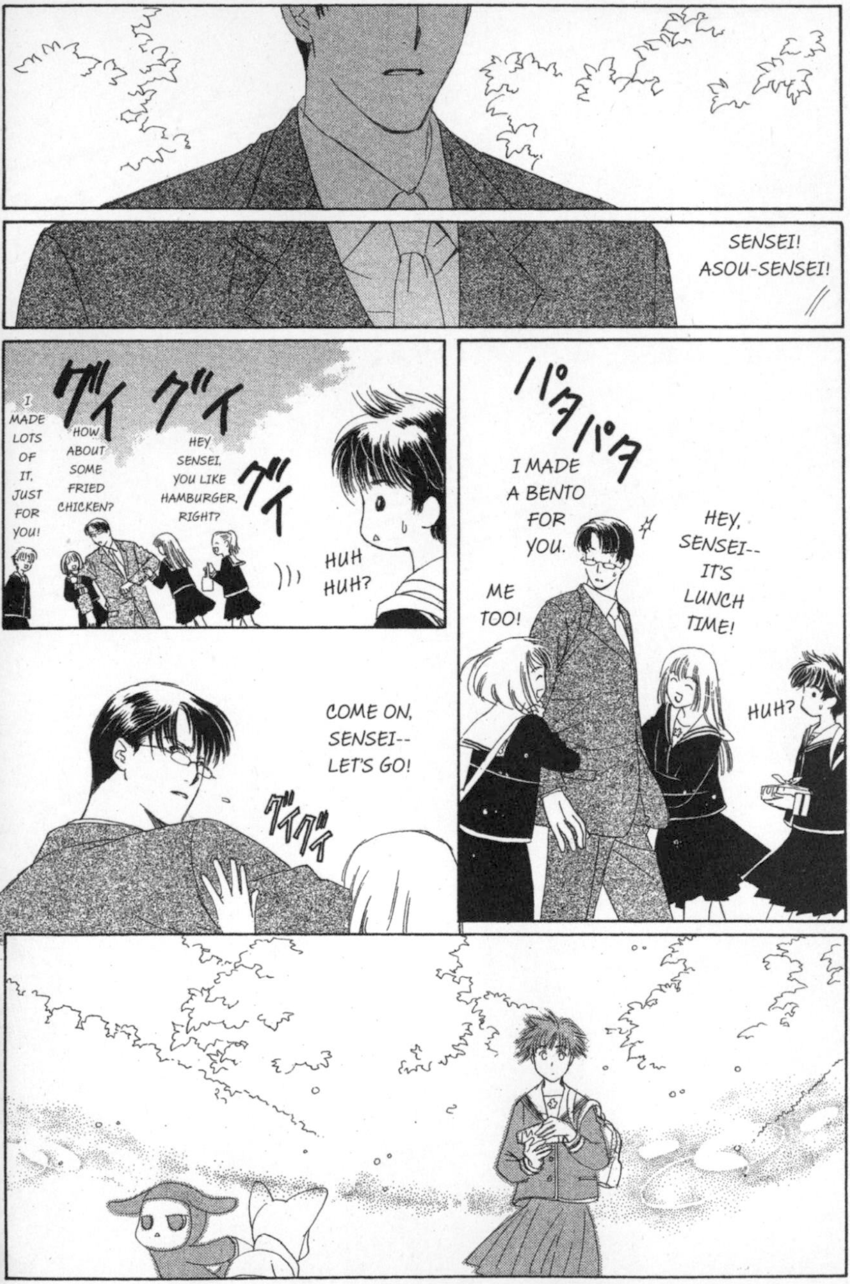
SENSEI! ASOU-SENSEI!
パタパタ
HEY, SENSEI-- IT'S LUNCH TIME!
I MADE A BENTO FOR YOU.
ME TOO!
HUH?
HUH HUH?
グイグイグイ
HEY SENSEI, YOU LIKE HAMBURGER, RIGHT?
HOW ABOUT SOME FRIED CHICKEN?
I MADE LOTS OF IT, JUST FOR YOU!
COME ON, SENSEI-- LET'S GO!
グイグイ

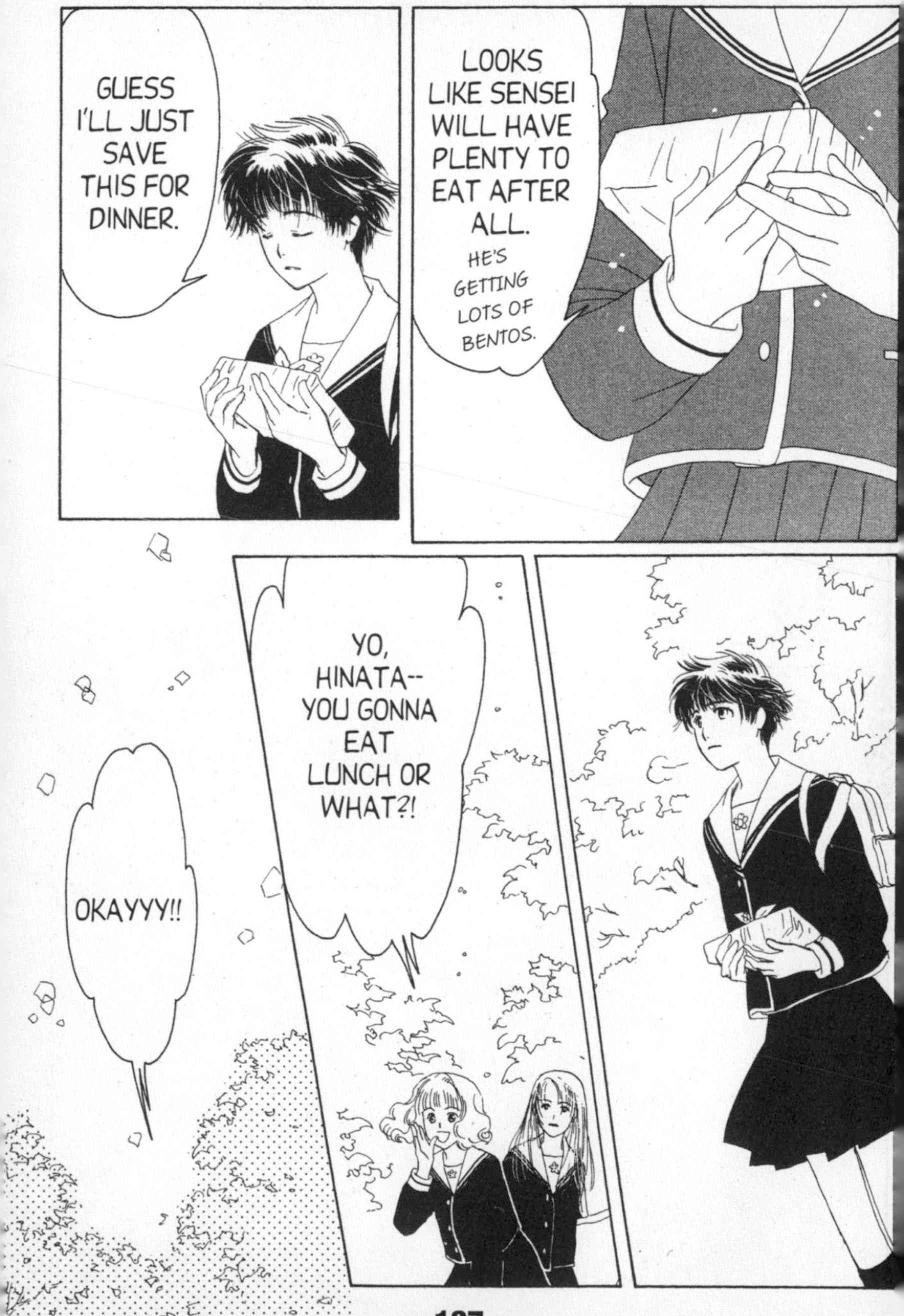
LOOKS LIKE SENSEI WILL HAVE PLENTY TO EAT AFTER ALL.
HE'S GETTING LOTS OF BENTOS.
GUESS I'LL JUST SAVE THIS FOR DINNER.
YO, HINATA-- YOU GONNA EAT LUNCH OR WHAT?!
OKAYYY!!

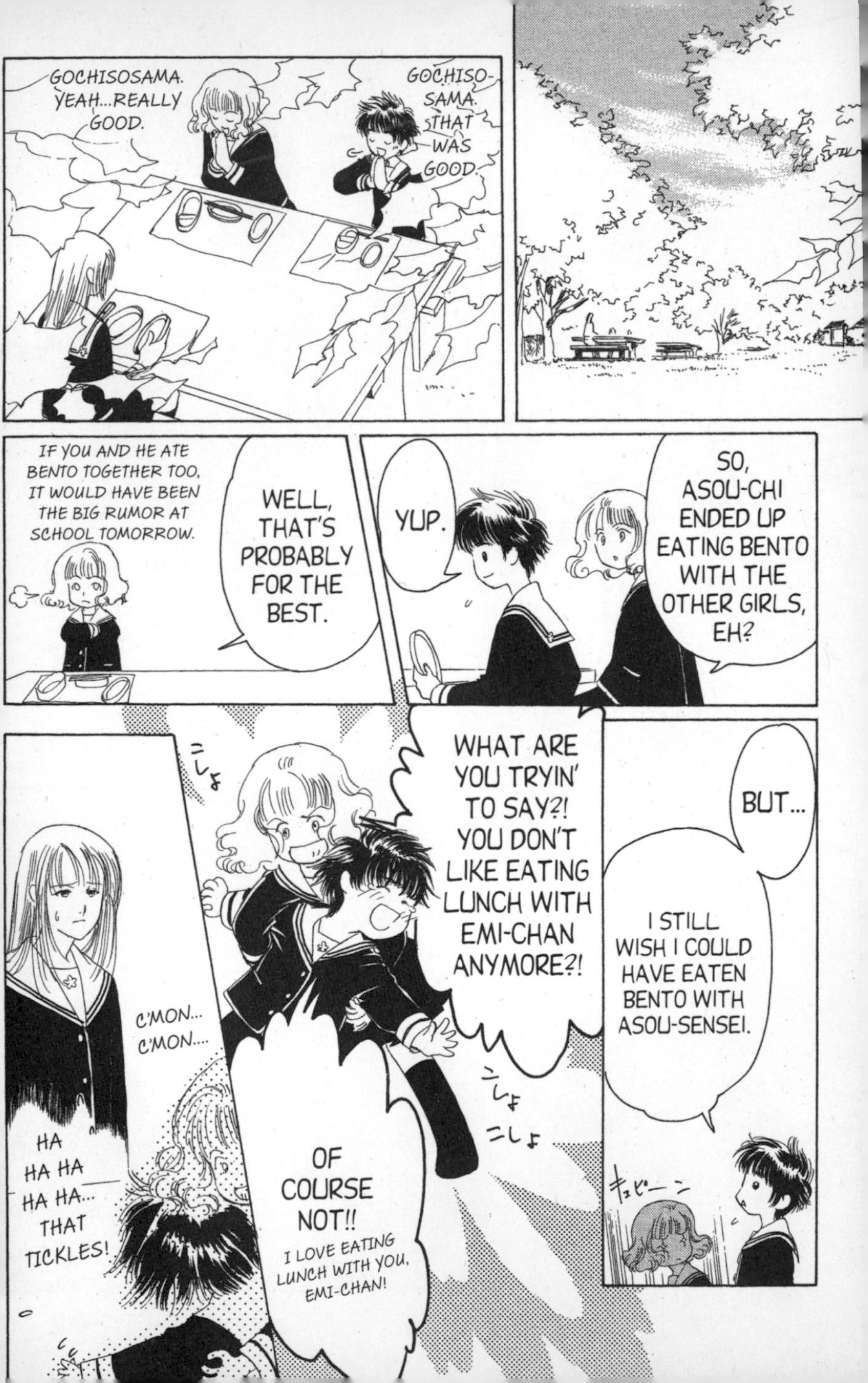
GOCHISO-SAMA. THAT WAS GOOD.
GOCHISOSAMA. YEAH...REALLY GOOD.
SO, ASOU-CHI ENDED UP EATING BENTO WITH THE OTHER GIRLS, EH?
YUP.
WELL, THAT'S PROBABLY FOR THE BEST.
IF YOU AND HE ATE BENTO TOGETHER TOO, IT WOULD HAVE BEEN THE BIG RUMOR AT SCHOOL TOMORROW.
BUT...
I STILL WISH I COULD HAVE EATEN BENTO WITH ASOU-SENSEI.
キュピーン
WHAT ARE YOU TRYIN' TO SAY?! YOU DON'T LIKE EATING LUNCH WITH EMI-CHAN ANYMORE?!
こしょ
こしょ
こしょ
OF COURSE NOT!!
I LOVE EATING LUNCH WITH YOU, EMI-CHAN!
C'MON... C'MON...
HA HA HA HA HA... THAT TICKLES!

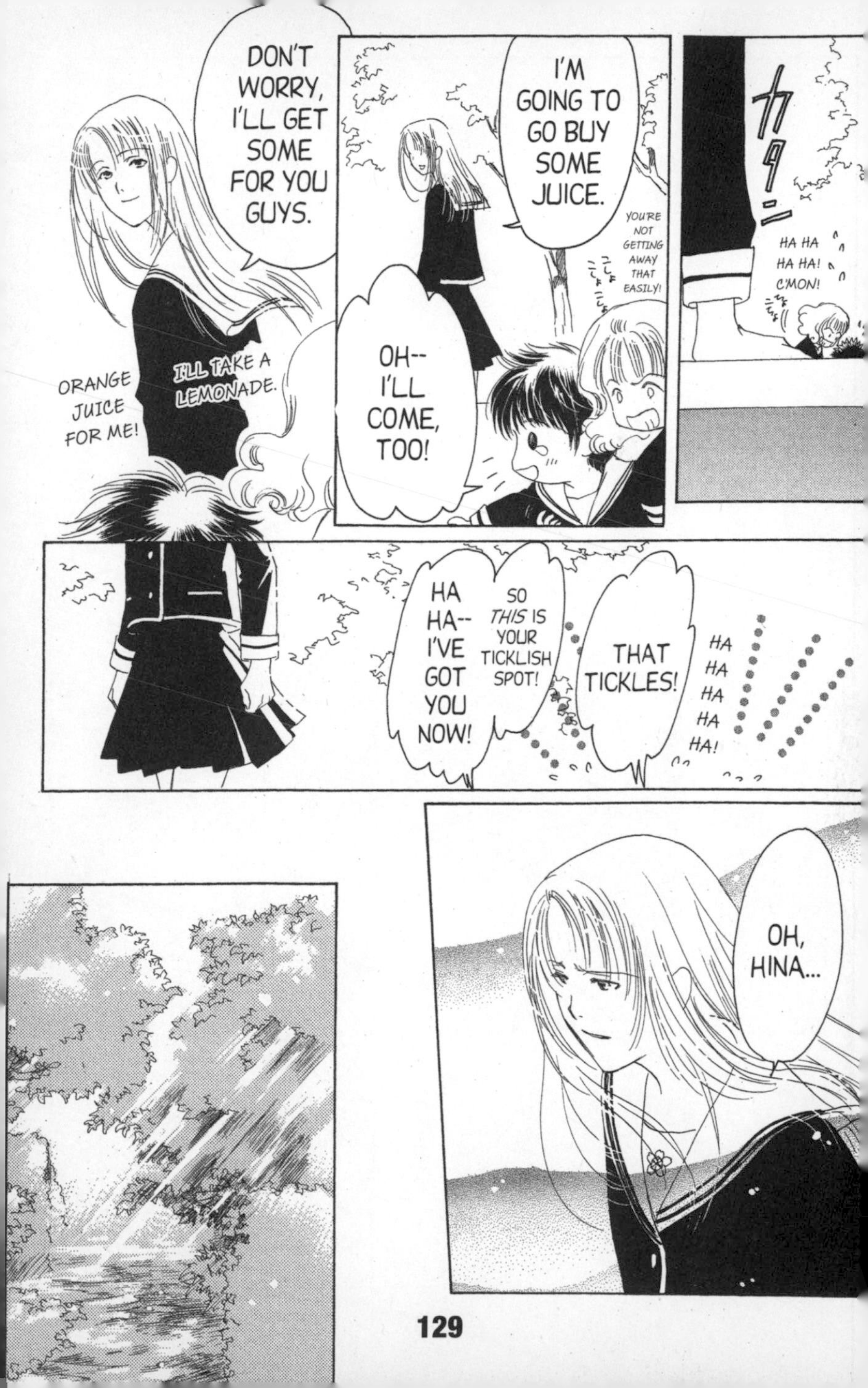
カタ
HA HA HA HA! C'MON!
I'M GOING TO GO BUY SOME JUICE.
YOU'RE NOT GETTING AWAY THAT EASILY!
OH-- I'LL COME, TOO!
DON'T WORRY, I'LL GET SOME FOR YOU GUYS.
I'LL TAKE A LEMONADE.
ORANGE JUICE FOR ME!
HA HA HA HA HA!
THAT TICKLES!
SO *THIS* IS YOUR TICKLISH SPOT!
HA HA-- I'VE GOT YOU NOW!
OH, HINA...

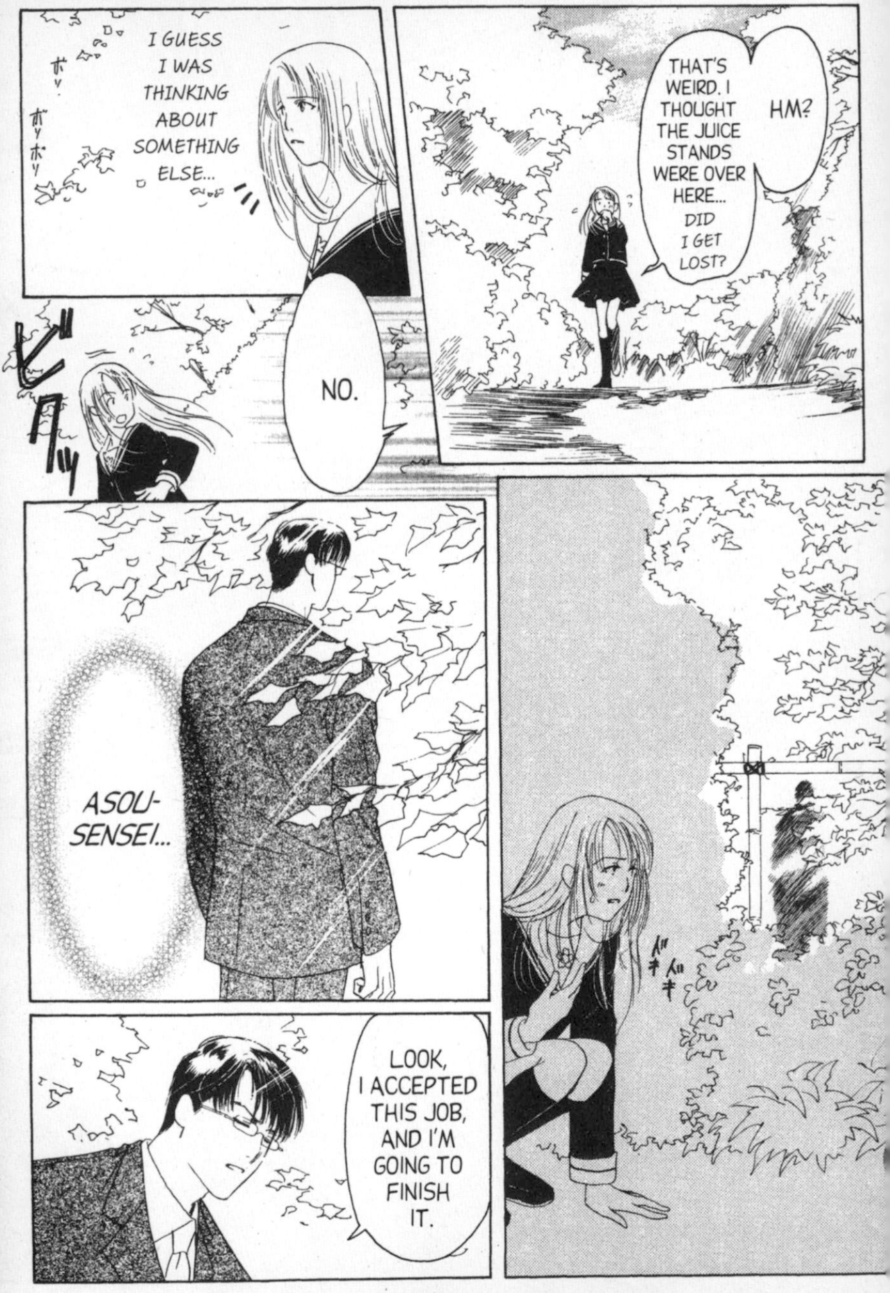
HM?
THAT'S WEIRD. I THOUGHT THE JUICE STANDS WERE OVER HERE...
DID I GET LOST?
I GUESS I WAS THINKING ABOUT SOMETHING ELSE...
NO.
ビクッ
ASOU-SENSEI...
LOOK, I ACCEPTED THIS JOB, AND I'M GOING TO FINISH IT.

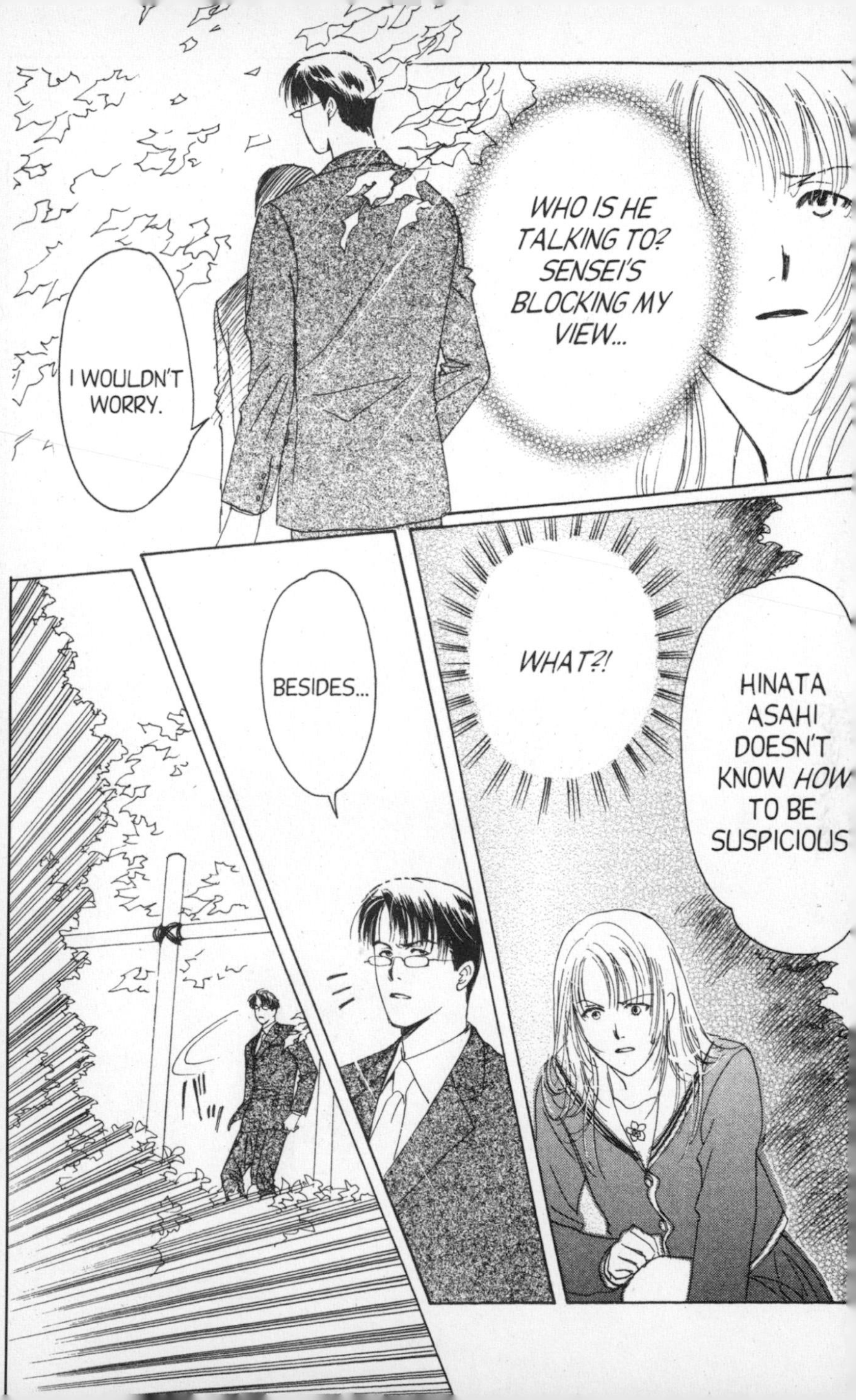
WHO IS HE TALKING TO? SENSEI'S BLOCKING MY VIEW...
I WOULDN'T WORRY.
HINATA ASAHI DOESN'T KNOW *HOW* TO BE SUSPICIOUS
WHAT?!
BESIDES...

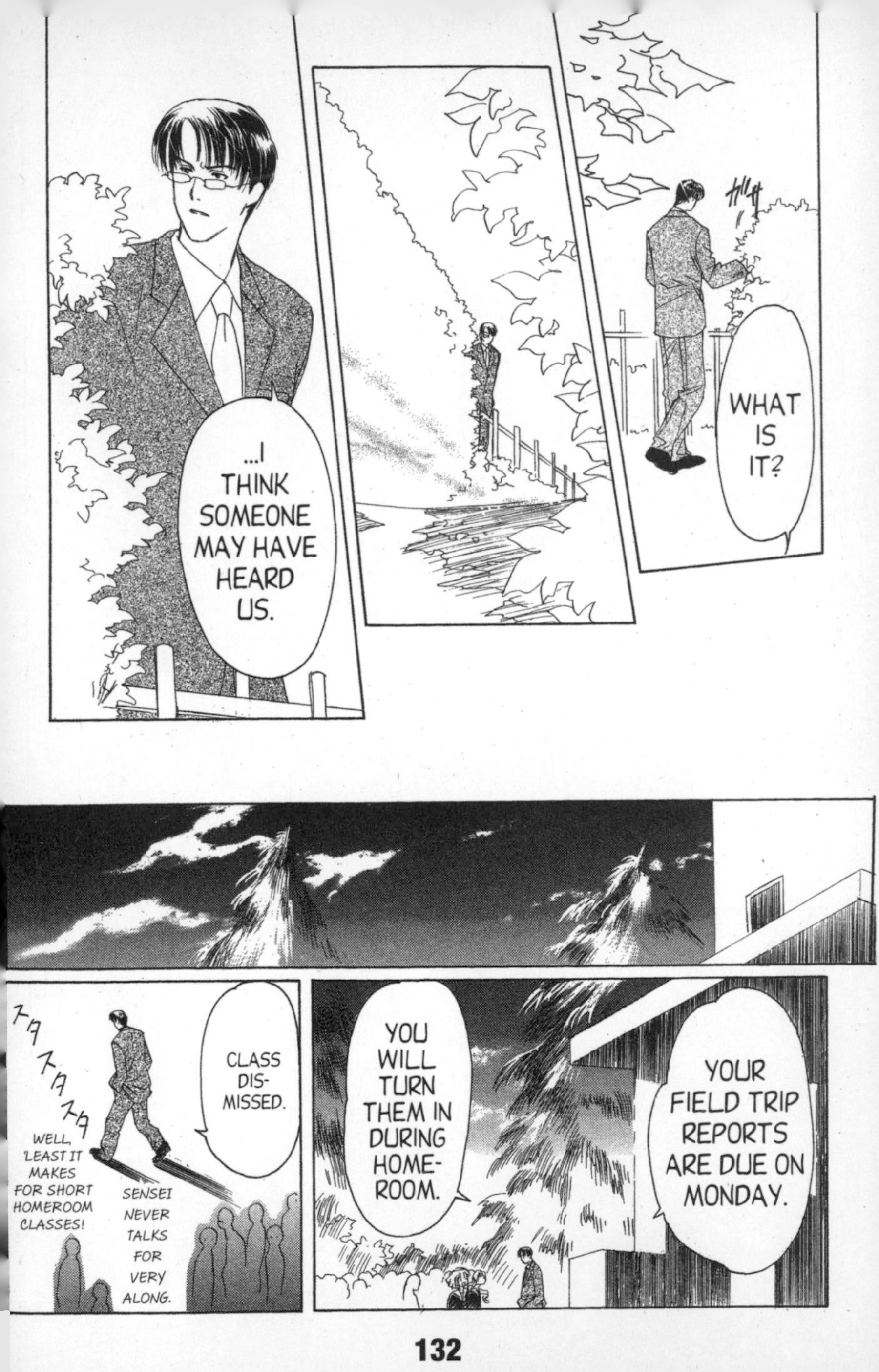
ガサ
WHAT IS IT?
...I THINK SOMEONE MAY HAVE HEARD US.
YOUR FIELD TRIP REPORTS ARE DUE ON MONDAY.
YOU WILL TURN THEM IN DURING HOME-ROOM.
CLASS DIS-MISSED.
スタスタスタ
SENSEI NEVER TALKS FOR VERY ALONG.
WELL, 'LEAST IT MAKES FOR SHORT HOMEROOM CLASSES!

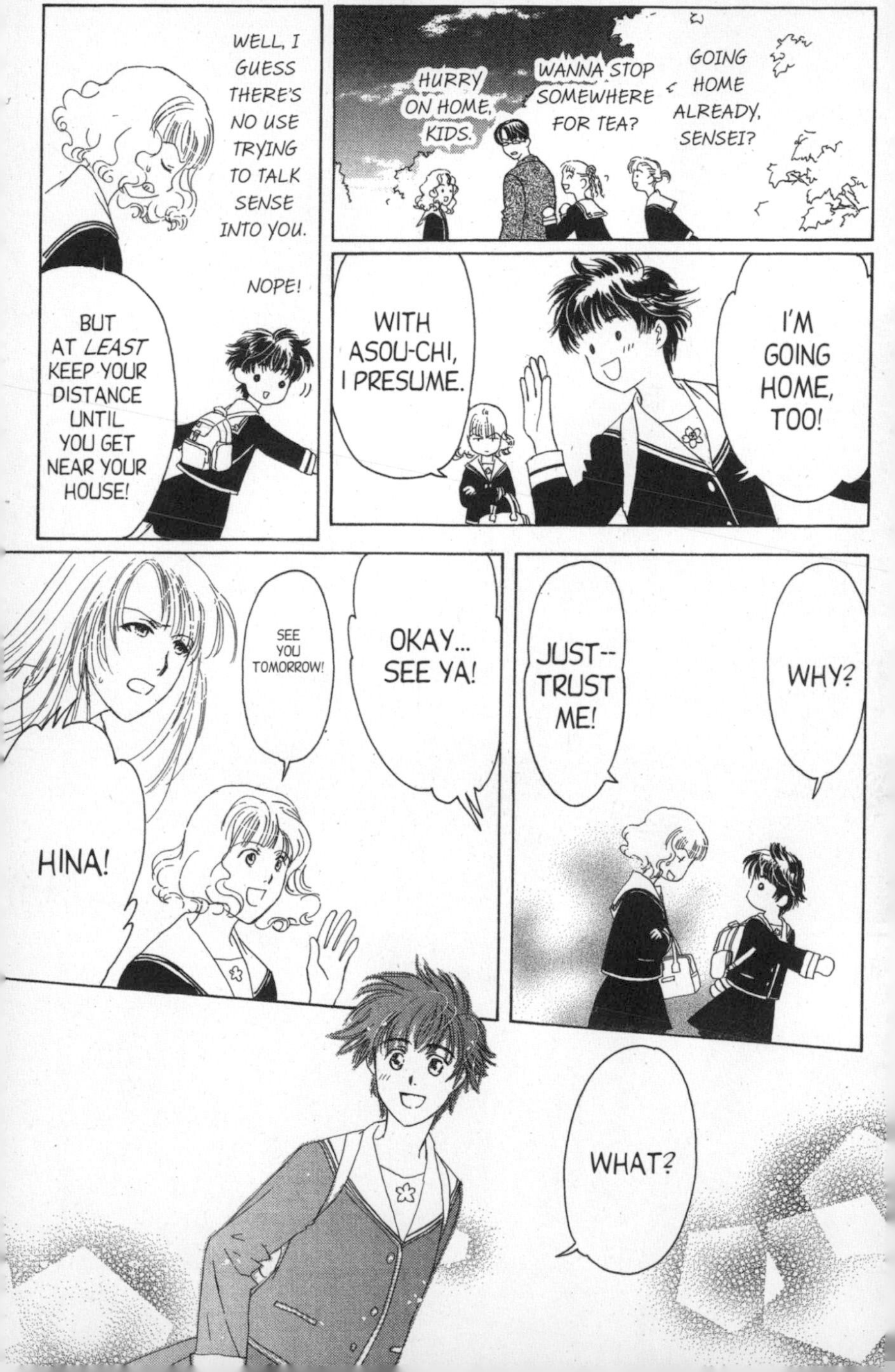
GOING HOME ALREADY, SENSEI?
WANNA STOP SOMEWHERE FOR TEA?
HURRY ON HOME, KIDS.
I'M GOING HOME, TOO!
WITH ASOU-CHI, I PRESUME.
WELL, I GUESS THERE'S NO USE TRYING TO TALK SENSE INTO YOU.
NOPE!
BUT AT *LEAST* KEEP YOUR DISTANCE UNTIL YOU GET NEAR YOUR HOUSE!
WHY?
JUST-- TRUST ME!
OKAY... SEE YA!
SEE YOU TOMORROW!
HINA!
WHAT?

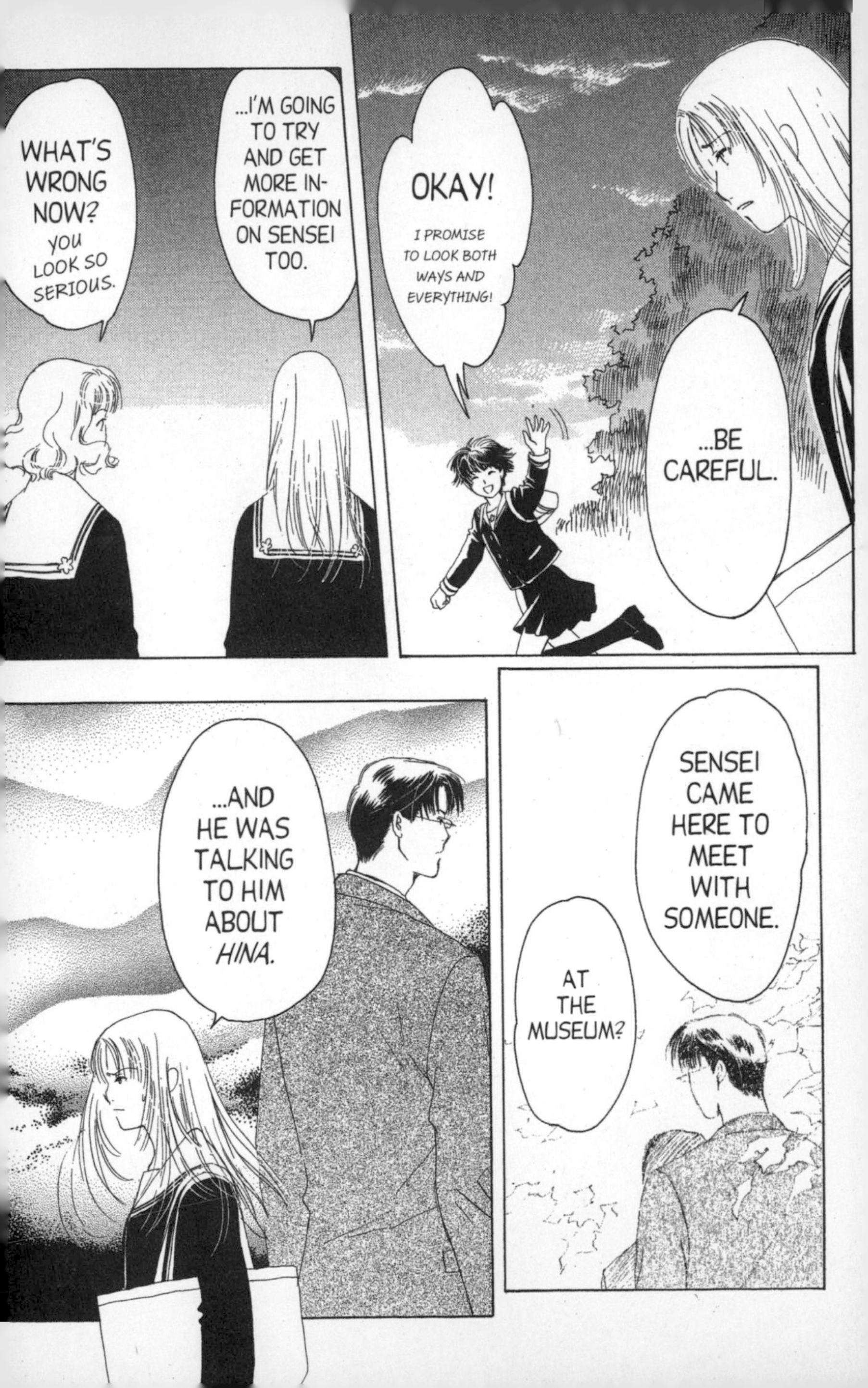
...BE CAREFUL.
OKAY!
I PROMISE TO LOOK BOTH WAYS AND EVERYTHING!
...I'M GOING TO TRY AND GET MORE IN-FORMATION ON SENSEI TOO.
WHAT'S WRONG NOW?
YOU LOOK SO SERIOUS.
SENSEI CAME HERE TO MEET WITH SOMEONE.
AT THE MUSEUM?
...AND HE WAS TALKING TO HIM ABOUT *HINA*.

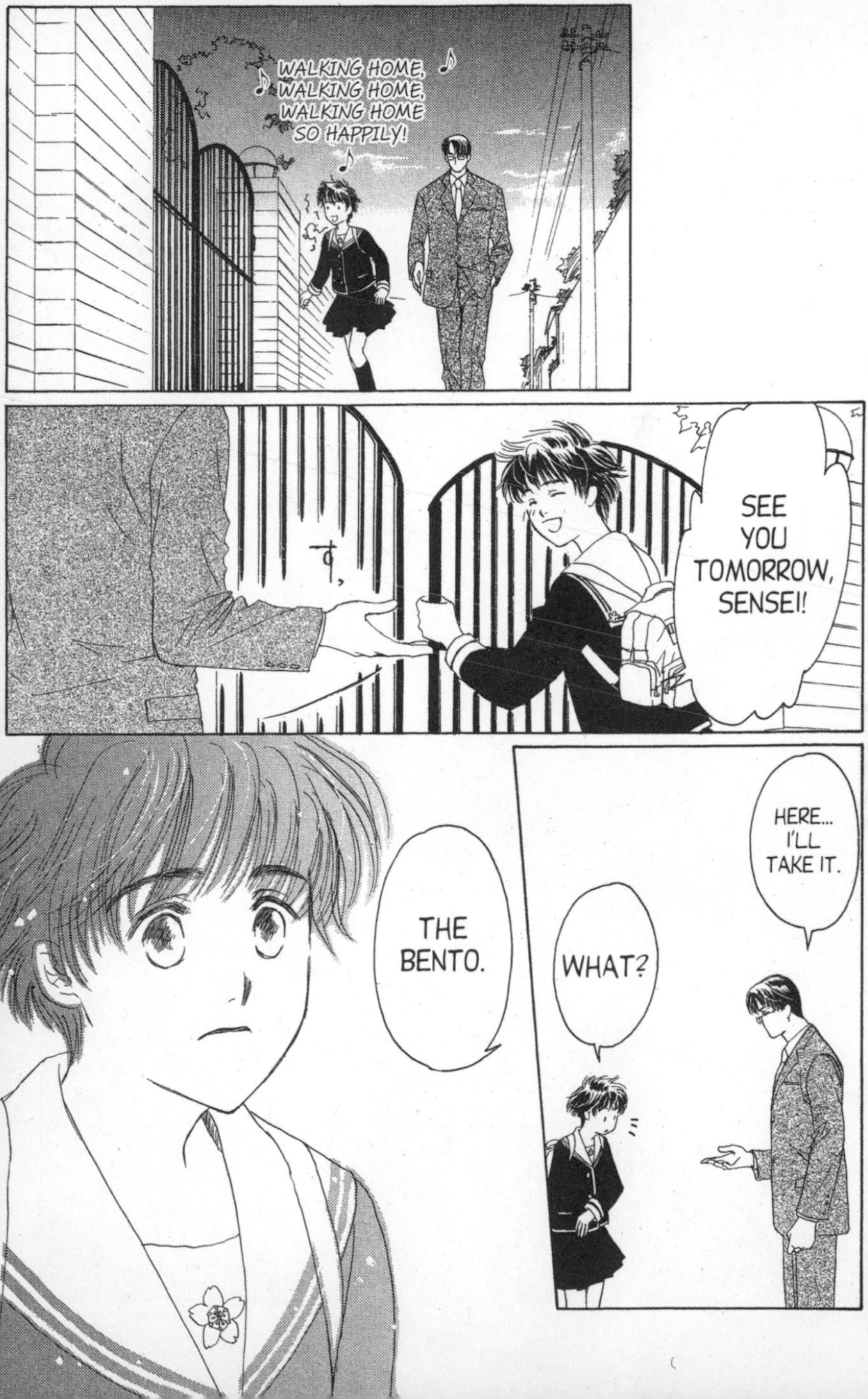
♪ WALKING HOME, WALKING HOME, WALKING HOME SO HAPPILY! ♪
SEE YOU TOMORROW, SENSEI!
す
HERE... I'LL TAKE IT.
WHAT?
THE BENTO.

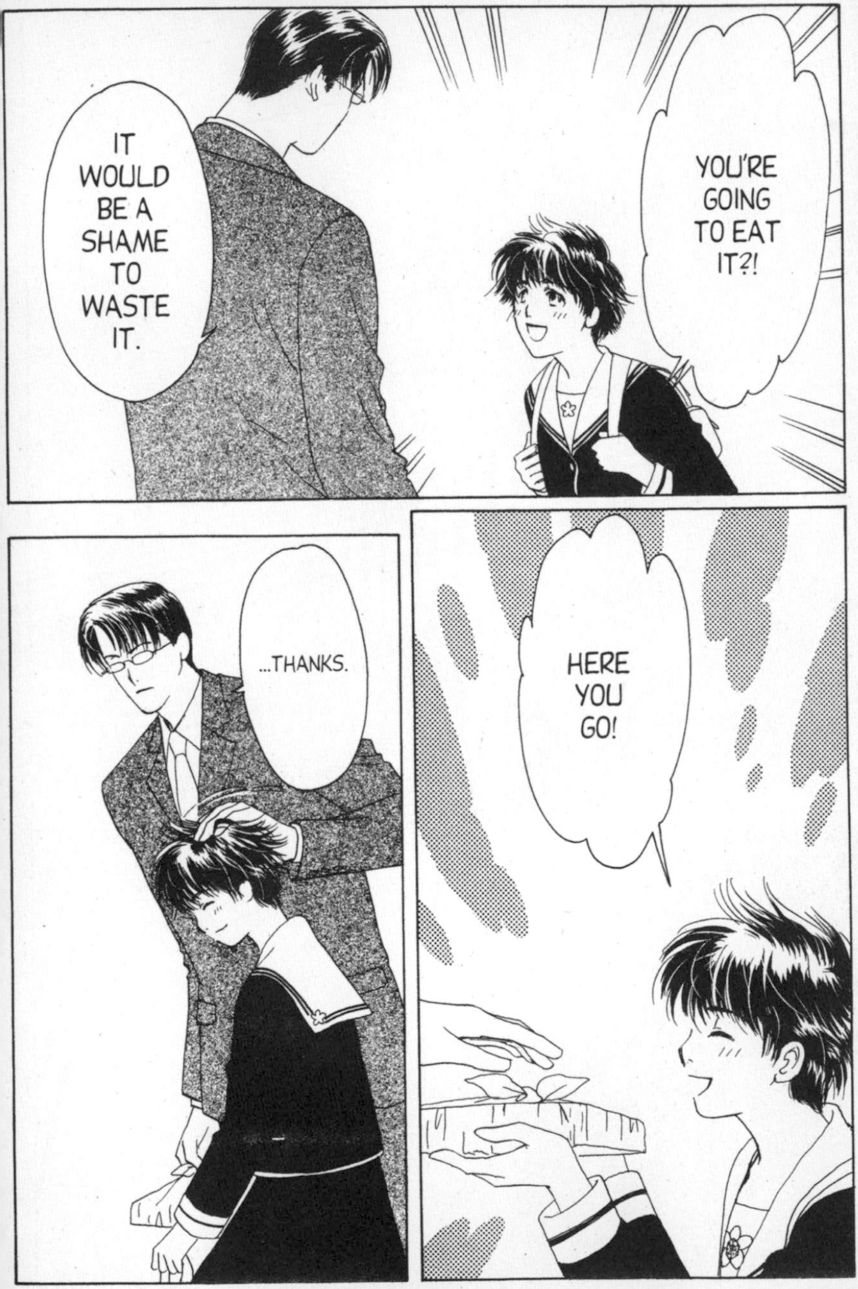
YOU'RE GOING TO EAT IT?!
IT WOULD BE A SHAME TO WASTE IT.
HERE YOU GO!
...THANKS.

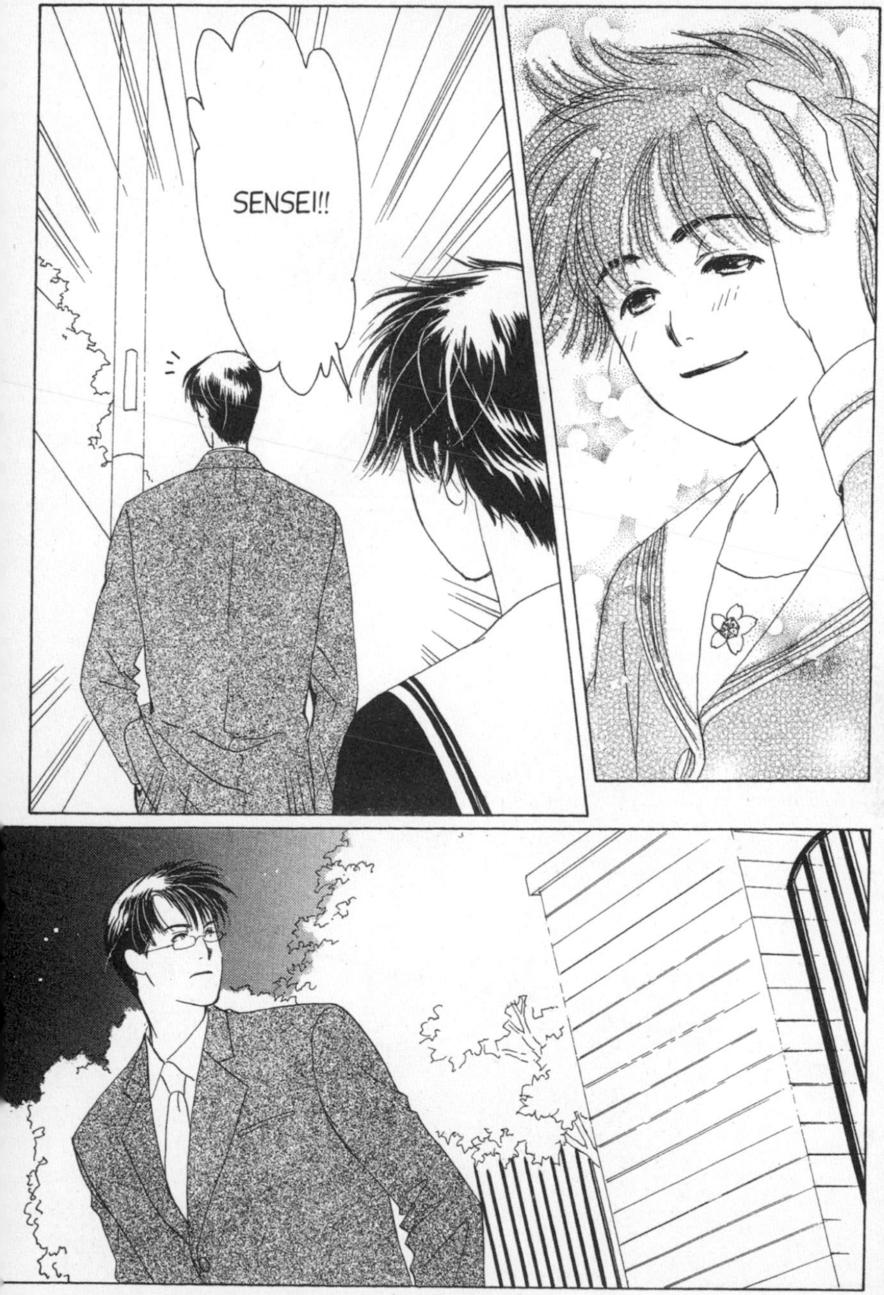

SENSEI!!

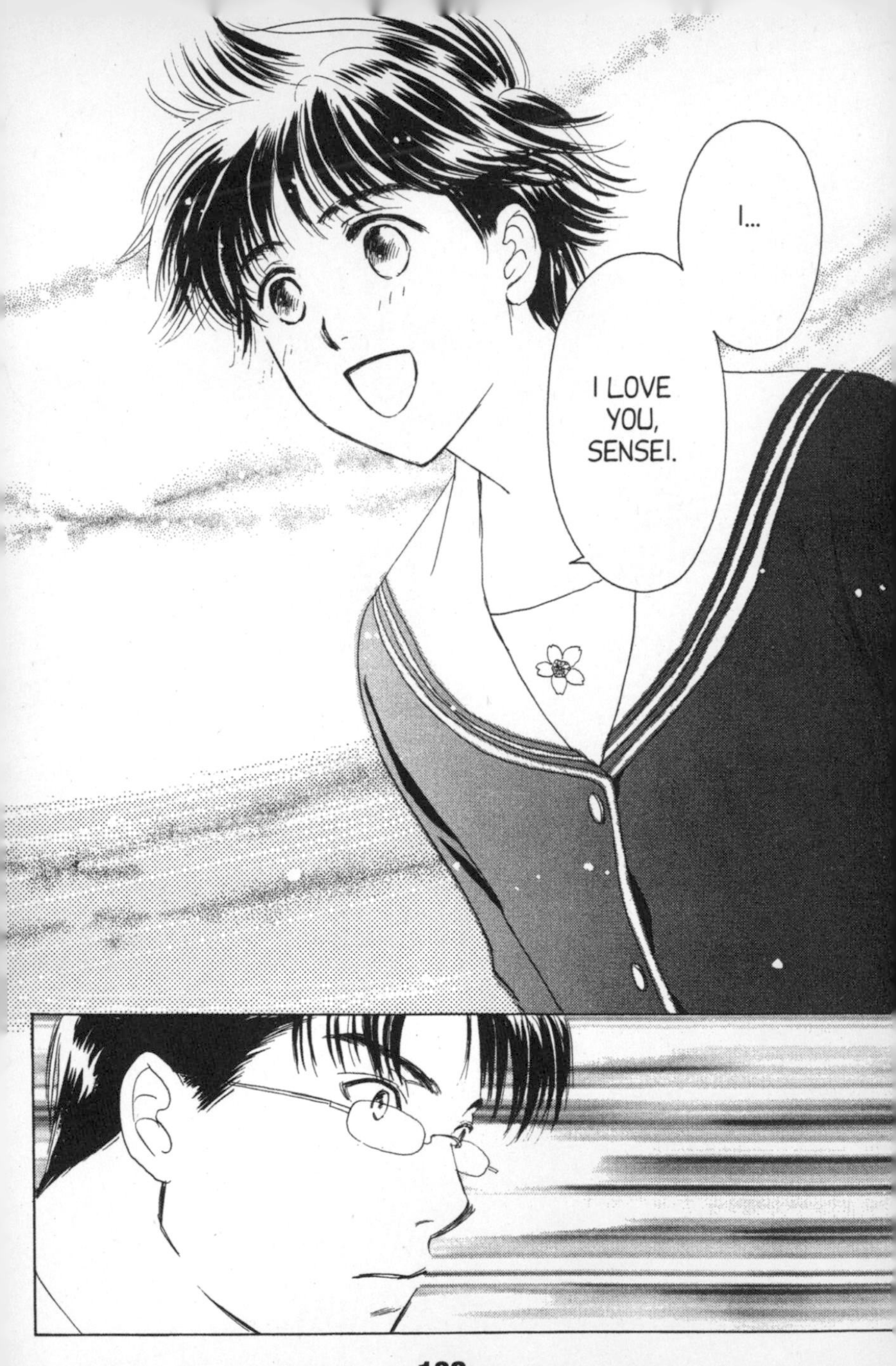
I...
I LOVE YOU, SENSEI.

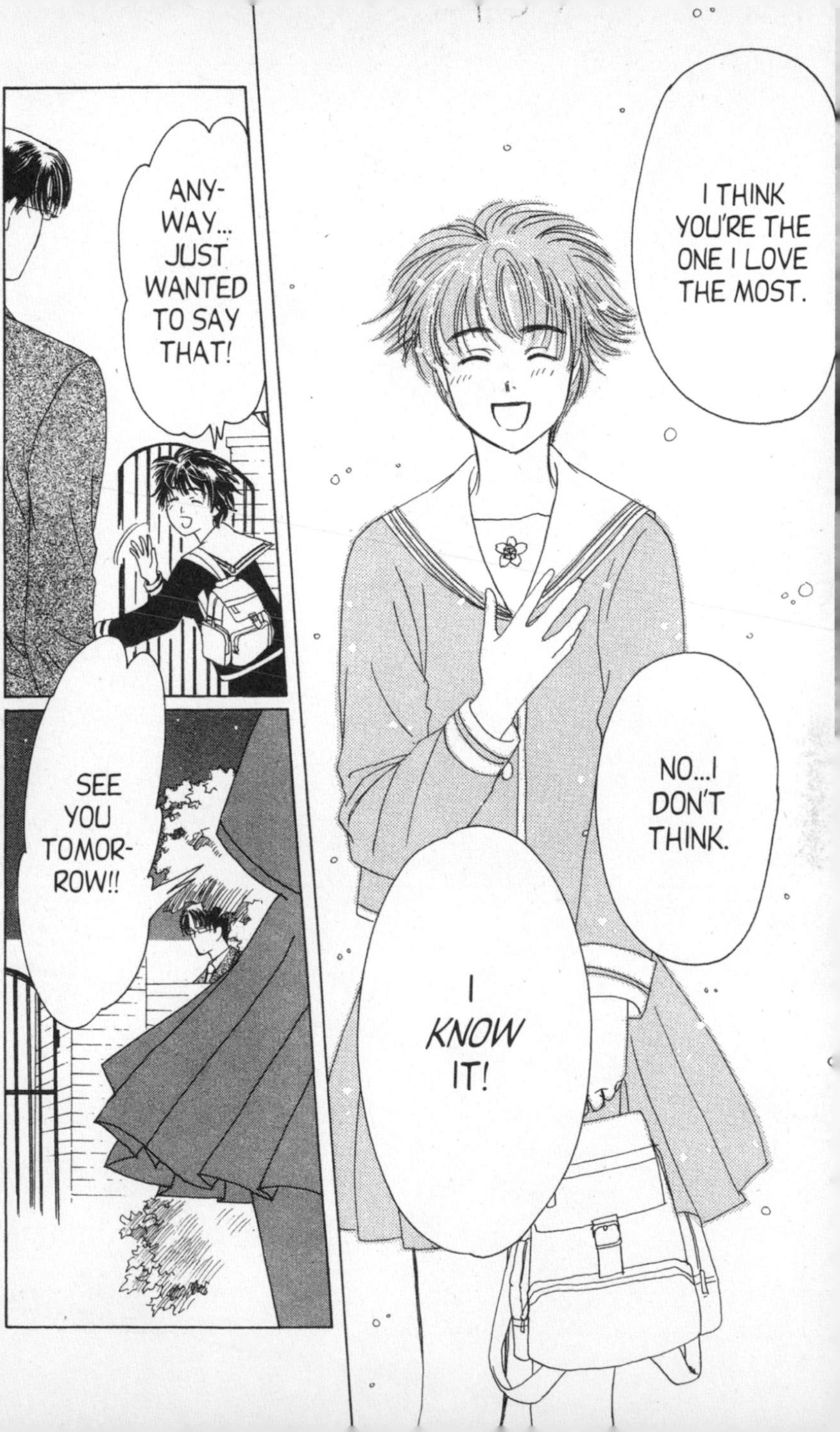
I THINK YOU'RE THE ONE I LOVE THE MOST.
NO...I DON'T THINK.
I *KNOW* IT!
ANY-WAY... JUST WANTED TO SAY THAT!
SEE YOU TOMOR-ROW!!

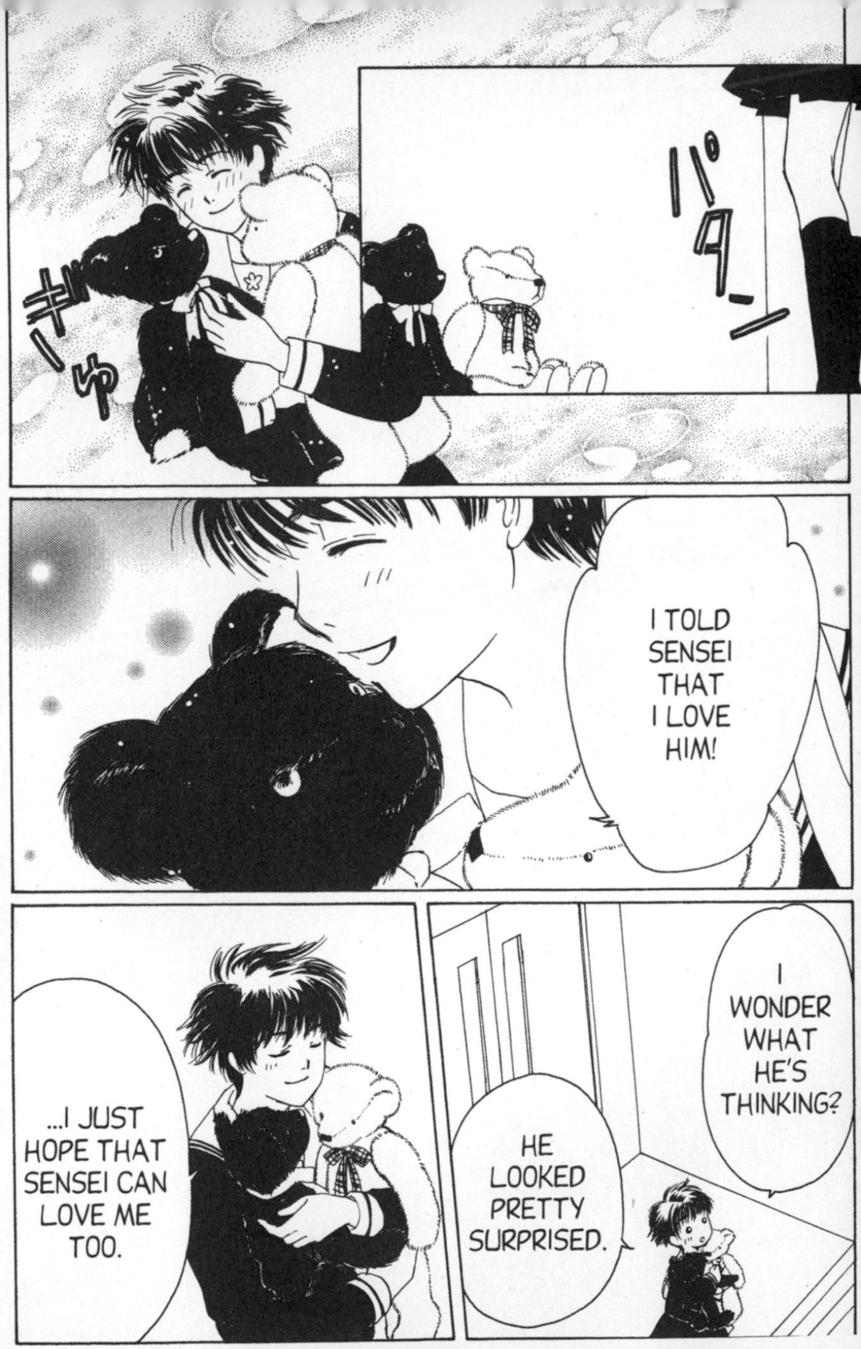
パターン
I TOLD SENSEI THAT I LOVE HIM!
I WONDER WHAT HE'S THINKING?
HE LOOKED PRETTY SURPRISED.
...I JUST HOPE THAT SENSEI CAN LOVE ME TOO.

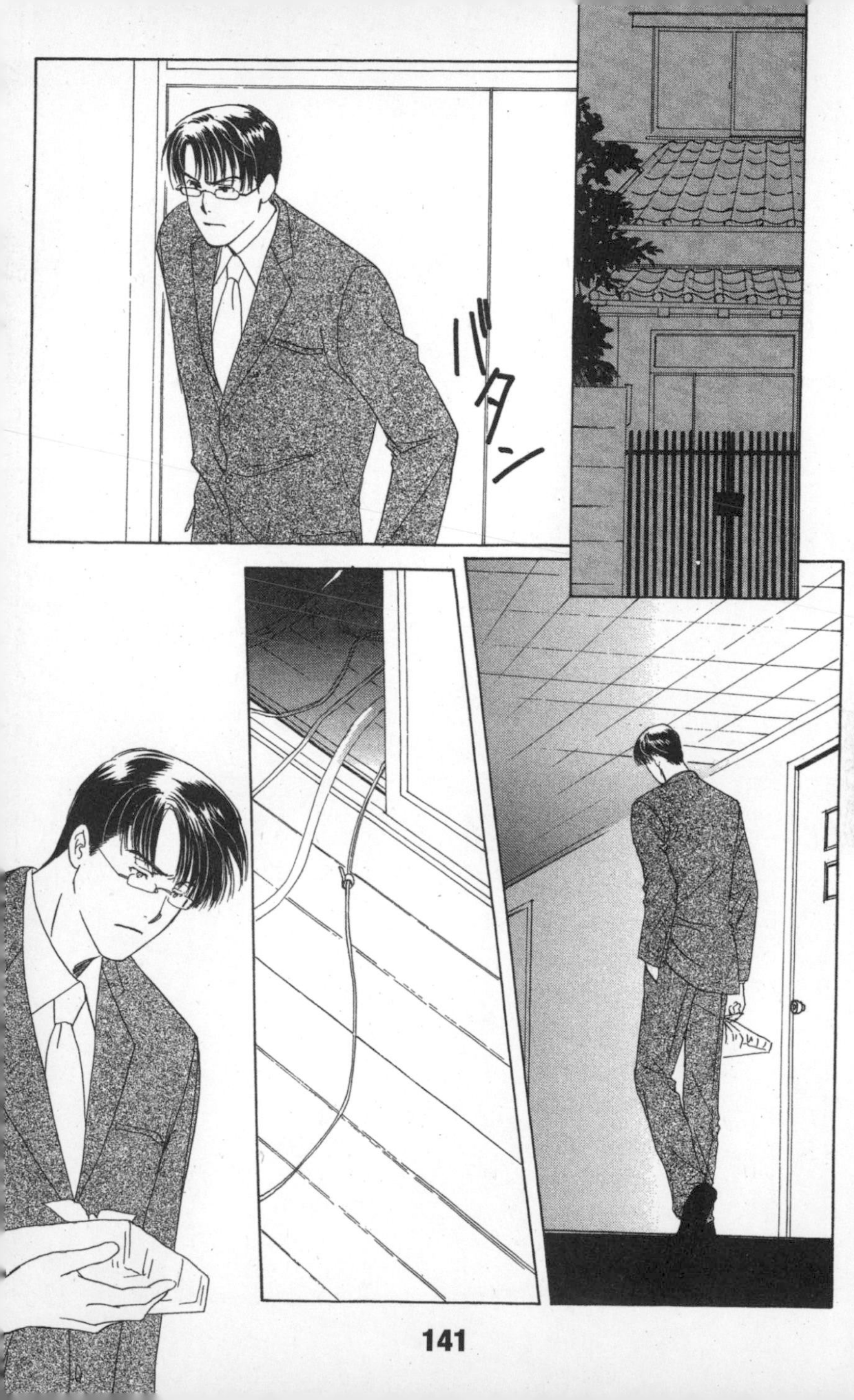
バタン

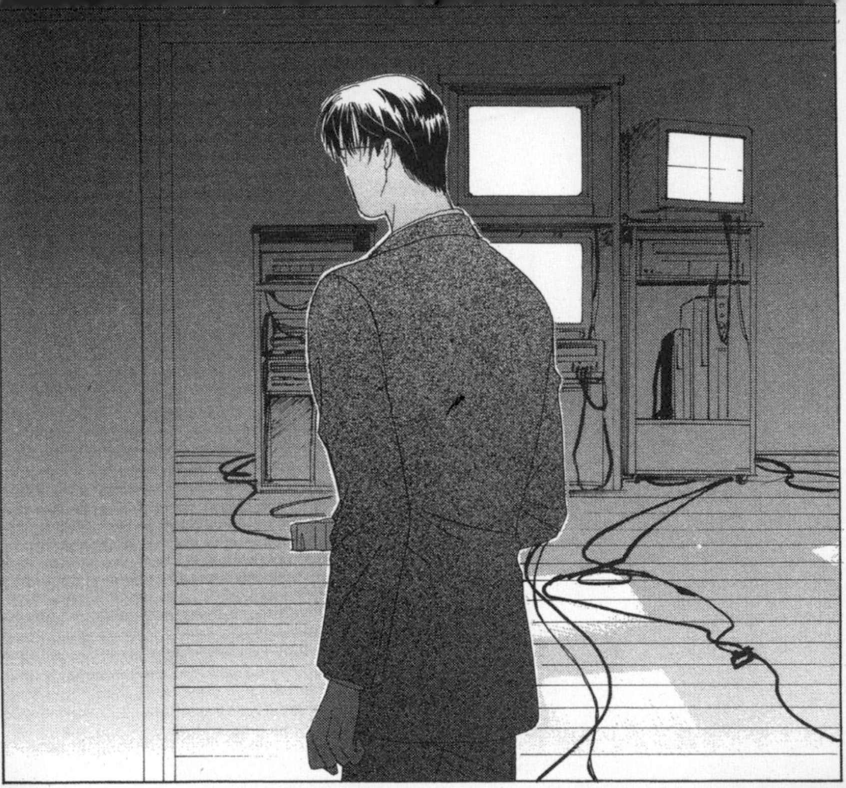

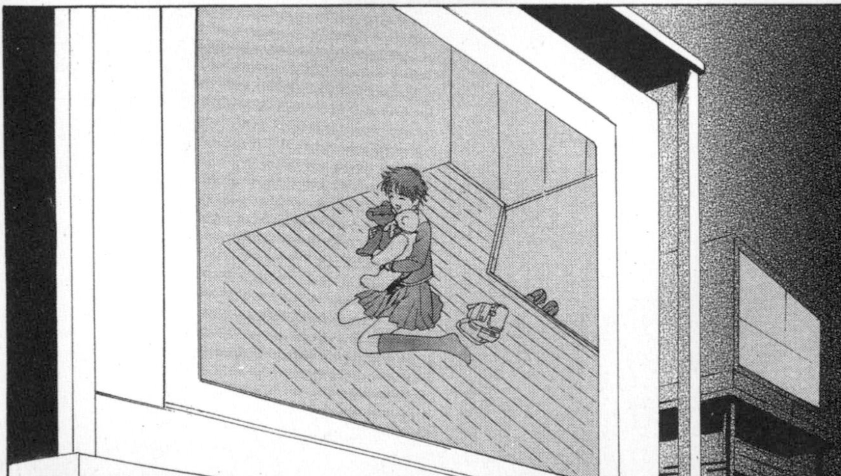

To Next

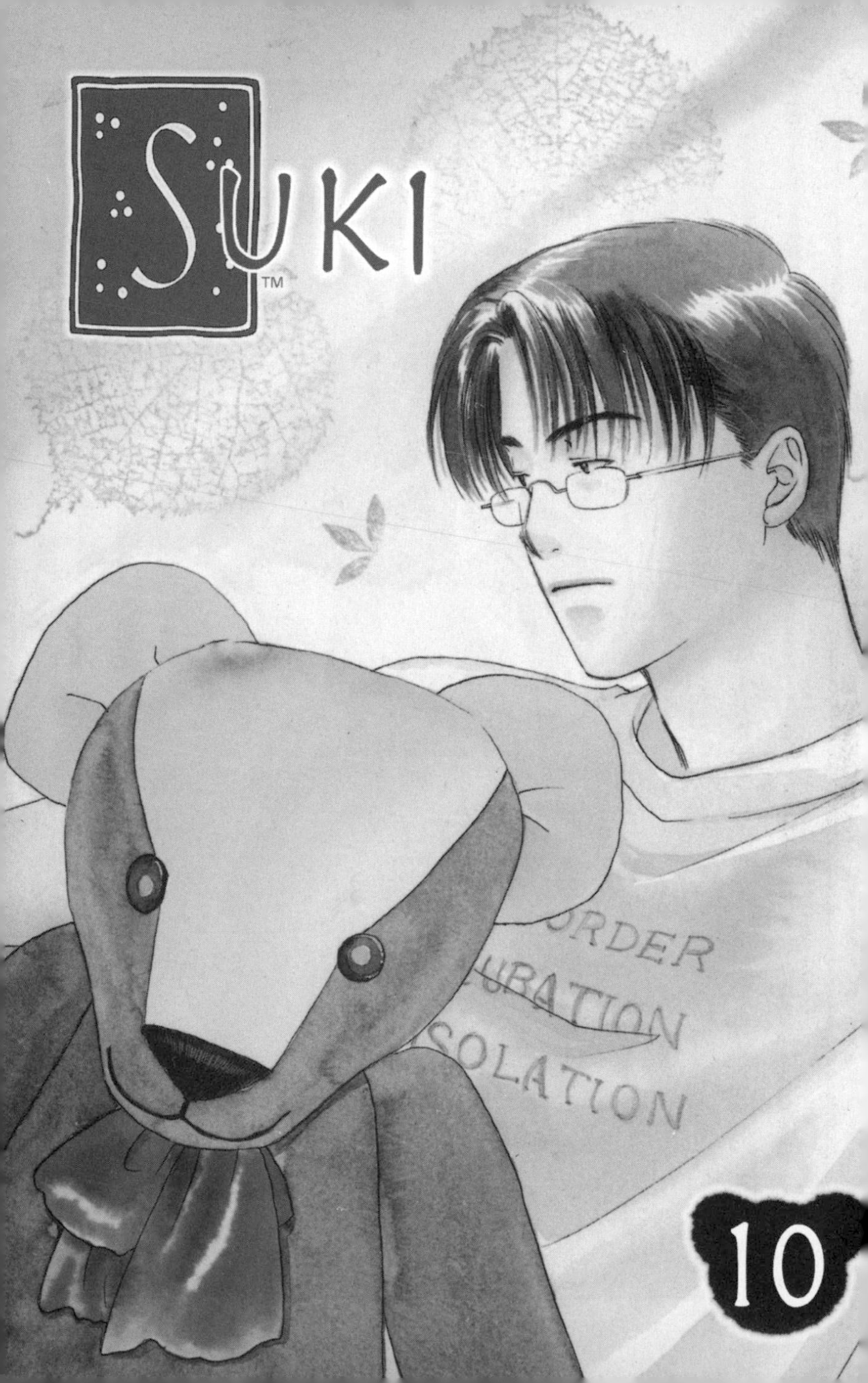
SUKI™
10

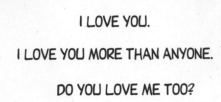

I LOVE YOU.

I LOVE YOU MORE THAN ANYONE.

DO YOU LOVE ME TOO?

AND SO THE LITTLE BEAR VISITED THE HOUSE OF THE BEAR WITH GLASSES EVERY DAY.

EACH TIME, SHE WOULD KNOCK ON HIS DOOR AND TRY TO TALK TO HIM.

BUT THE BEAR WITH GLASSES WOULD NOT OPEN HIS DOOR.

EVERYONE TOLD THE LITTLE BEAR,
"YOU SEE? IT'S IMPOSSIBLE."

"HE DOESN'T WANT TO TALK TO ANYONE."
"HE IS A BAD BEAR."

1

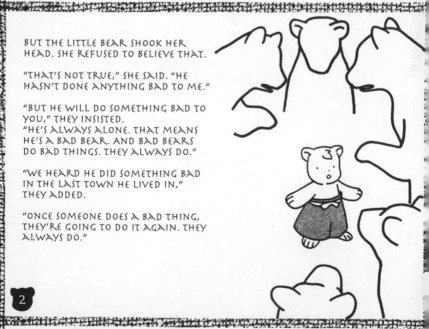

BUT THE LITTLE BEAR SHOOK HER HEAD. SHE REFUSED TO BELIEVE THAT.

"THAT'S NOT TRUE," SHE SAID. "HE HASN'T DONE ANYTHING BAD TO ME."

"BUT HE WILL DO SOMETHING BAD TO YOU," THEY INSISTED.
"HE'S ALWAYS ALONE. THAT MEANS HE'S A BAD BEAR. AND BAD BEARS DO BAD THINGS. THEY ALWAYS DO."

"WE HEARD HE DID SOMETHING BAD IN THE LAST TOWN HE LIVED IN," THEY ADDED.

"ONCE SOMEONE DOES A BAD THING, THEY'RE GOING TO DO IT AGAIN. THEY ALWAYS DO."

2

"THAT'S NOT TRUE," THE LITTLE BEAR SAID.
"KUMA-SAN HAS SUCH NICE, KIND EYES.
THERE'S NO WAY HE COULD BE A BAD BEAR."

SO THE LITTLE BEAR IGNORED EVERYONE'S WARNINGS
AND VISITED KUMA-SAN'S HOUSE EACH DAY.

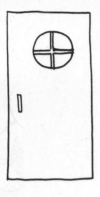

THEN, ONE MORNING...

...THE LITTLE BEAR VISITED KUMA-SAN'S
HOUSE ONCE MORE. BUT THIS TIME, SHE HELD
A BASKET IN HER HANDS.

"GOOD MORNING!" SHE CALLED OUT.

THERE WAS NO ANSWER.
THE LITTLE BEAR KNOCKED AGAIN.

"GOOD MORNING, KUMA-SAN. ARE YOU
HOME?" SHE ASKED.

THE LITTLE BEAR LISTENED CAREFULLY,
BUT NO ONE SEEMED TO BE INSIDE.

SO THE LITTLE BEAR TRIED PEEKING INTO
THE HOUSE THROUGH THE WINDOW.
BUT THE BEAR WITH GLASSES WASN'T IN
HIS USUAL CHAIR. AND HE WASN'T IN THE
BACKYARD, EITHER, WHERE HE USUALLY
CHOPPED HIS WOOD.

"MAYBE HE WENT OUT," THOUGHT THE
LITTLE BEAR.
SO SHE DECIDED TO DRAW A MESSAGE IN
THE DIRT WITH A NEARBY STICK.

"I'M GOING INTO THE WEST WOODS TO PICK
BERRIES," SHE WROTE. "I'LL PICK LOTS OF
BERRIES AND BRING YOU SOME TOO. PLEASE
WAIT FOR ME."

AND WITH THAT, THE LITTLE BEAR SET OFF
FOR THE WEST WOODS, HOPING TO GIVE
KUMA-SAN A GIFT OF BERRIES TO EAT.

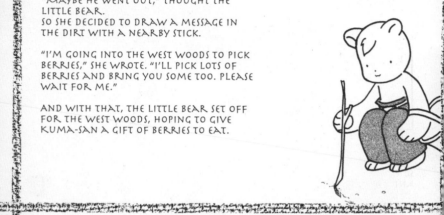

THE WEST WOODS WERE DARK, EVEN DURING
THE DAY. EVEN THE ADULT BEARS AVOIDED
GOING THERE.

BUT THE LITTLE BEAR WANTED TO GIVE
KUMA-SAN A GIFT OF BERRIES, SO SHE
WENT DEEPER AND DEEPER INTO THE TREES.

THE LITTLE BEAR WALKED AND WALKED
UNTIL SHE ARRIVED AT A TREE WITH BIG,
DELICIOUS BERRIES.

"I'LL PICK FROM THIS TREE," SAID THE
LITTLE BEAR.

THE LITTLE BEAR REACHED WAY UP HIGH
AND DID HER BEST TO PICK THE BERRIES.

SHE THOUGHT TO HERSELF, "I HOPE
KUMA-SAN LIKES MOUNTAIN BERRIES.
I HOPE HE'LL BE HAPPY WHEN HE SEES
THEM."

SUDDENLY, THE LITTLE BEAR HEARD LOUD FLAPPING
FROM ABOVE.
"I WONDER WHAT THAT IS?" SHE THOUGHT.

SHE LOOKED UP AND SAW SEVERAL LARGE BLACK CROWS
SITTING AT THE TOP OF THE TREE.

SHE HAD NEVER SEEN SUCH LARGE CROWS...
AND THEY STARED BACK DOWN AT HER JUST AS HARD.

IT WAS THE FIRST TIME THE LITTLE BEAR
HAD SEEN CROWS LIKE THAT. SO SHE
DECIDED TO INTRODUCE HERSELF.

"H-HELLO." SHE BOWED HER HEAD.
BUT THE CROWS SAID NOTHING...
ONLY STARED.

THE LITTLE BEAR THOUGHT, "I WONDER
IF CROWS SAY HELLO DIFFERENTLY
THAN BEARS DO?"

THEN WITHOUT WARNING, ALL OF THE
CROWS DIVED DOWN FROM THE TREE...
STRAIGHT FOR THE LITTLE BEAR.

"W-WHAT'S GOING ON?!" THE LITTLE
BEAR GASPED.

THE LITTLE BEAR FROZE WHERE SHE
STOOD, NOT UNDERSTANDING WHAT WAS
HAPPENING.

"MOVE, YOU FOOL!" SOMEONE BEHIND HER
YELLED. SHE FELT HER PAW BEING YANKED
BACK. SURPRISED, THE LITTLE BEAR LOOKED
BACK TO SEE THE BEAR WITH GLASSES.
"KUMA-SAN?" SHE SAID.

THE LITTLE BEAR DID NOT UNDERSTAND
WHY KUMA-SAN WAS THERE. SHE WAS
ABOUT TO ASK HIM, BUT HE BEGAN TO
SPEAK HIMSELF.

"WELL, DON'T STAND THERE! DO YOU WANT
TO BE EATEN BY CROWS?!"
AND AS HE SAID IT, KUMA-SAN GRABBED
THE LITTLE BEAR'S PAW AND BEGAN TO RUN.

THE LITTLE BEAR DIDN'T UNDERSTAND,
BUT LED BY KUMA-SAN, SHE TOO RAN
AS FAST AS SHE COULD.

SOMEHOW THEY MANAGED TO GET
OUT OF THE WOODS.
WHEN THEY FINALLY LOOKED BACK,
THE CROWS WERE NOWHERE TO BE SEEN.

KUMA-SAN SIGHED, THEN SAID TO THE
LITTLE BEAR:

"THERE ARE MANY CROWS LIVING IN
THE WEST WOODS. IF THEY CATCH A
CUB LIKE YOU WALKING THERE ALONE,
THEY'LL EAT YOU FOR DINNER."

KUMA-SAN WAS VERY ANGRY,
IT SEEMED.
THE LITTLE BEAR WAS VERY SORRY,
AND SHE APOLOGIZED.

"I'M SORRY. BUT, KUMA-SAN...
WHY DID YOU COME INTO THE
WEST WOODS?"

KUMA-SAN SAID NOTHING.

THE LITTLE BEAR THOUGHT FOR A
MOMENT, THEN HAPPILY SAID, "DID
YOU COME WHEN YOU SAW THE
NOTE I LEFT AT YOUR HOUSE?"

"...WE'RE GOING HOME," WAS THE
ONLY REPLY SHE GOT.

BUT AS KUMA-SAN STOMPED DOWN
TOWARD THE TOWN, THE LITTLE
BEAR FELT VERY HAPPY.

FOR ALTHOUGH HE WOULD SPEAK NOTHING OF IT, THE LITTLE BEAR KNEW THAT KUMA-SAN HAD COME TO RESCUE HER.

AND WITH THAT THOUGHT, SHE KNEW SHE HAD BEEN RIGHT. "HE ISN'T A BAD BEAR LIKE EVERYBODY SAID. HE IS A VERY KIND BEAR."

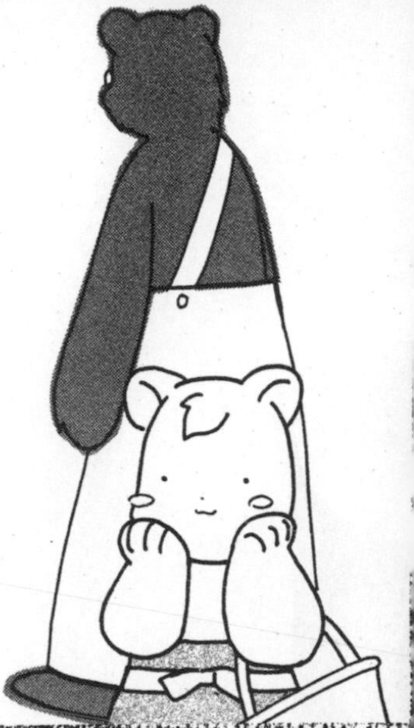

13

14

SO THE LITTLE BEAR WAS VERY HAPPY INDEED.

BUT EVEN AS SHE THOUGHT ALL THIS, SHE KNEW SHE WOULD BE EVEN HAPPIER IF KUMA-SAN WOULD EAT THE PLENTIFUL BERRIES SHE HAD PICKED THAT DAY.

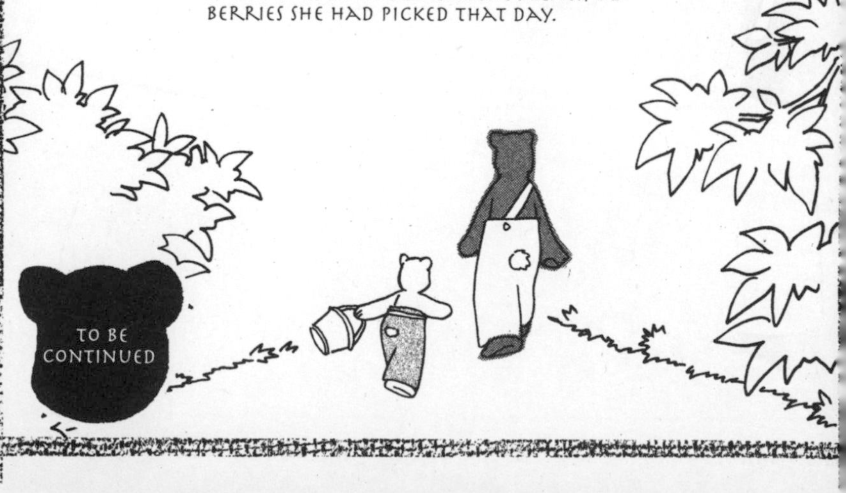

TO BE CONTINUED

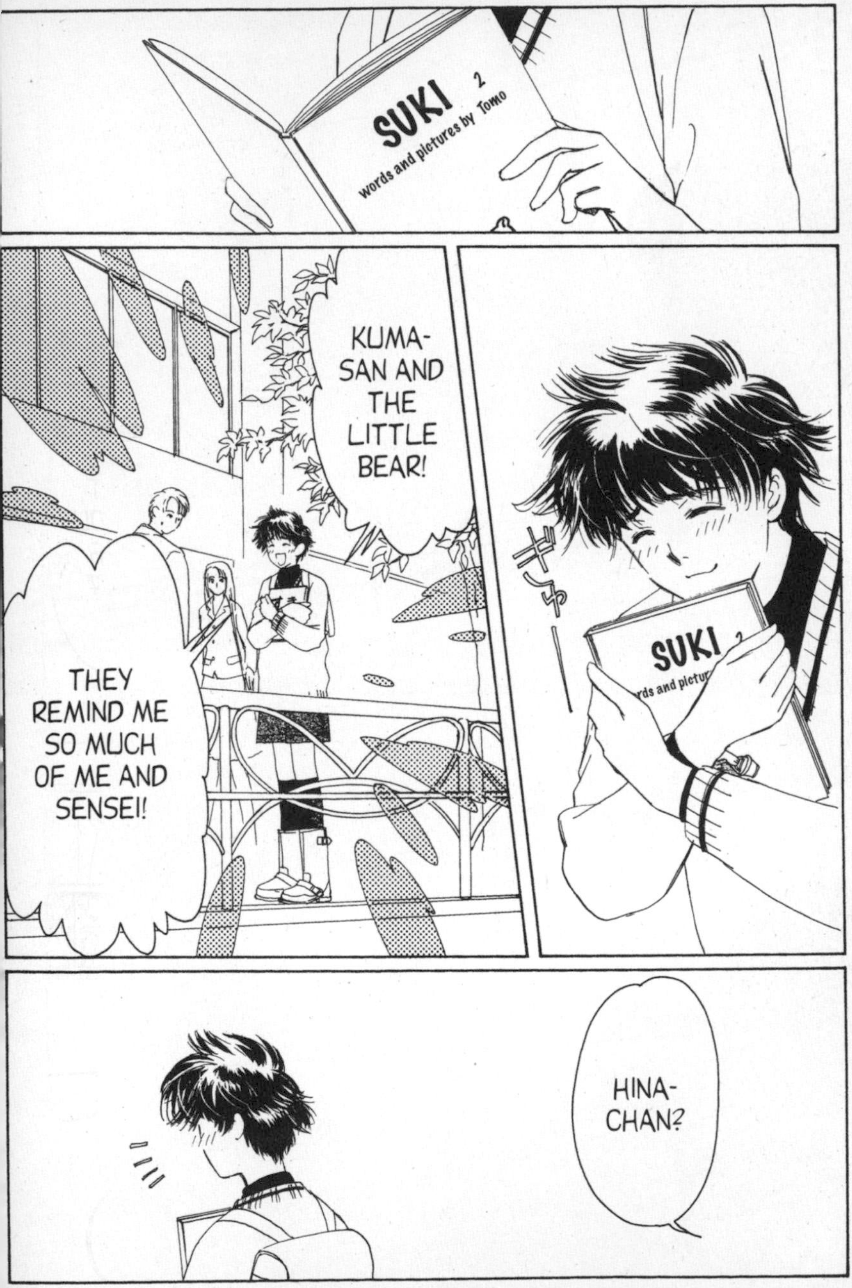
SUKI 2
words and pictures by Tomo
ギュー
SUKI 2
words and pictur
KUMA-SAN AND THE LITTLE BEAR!
THEY REMIND ME SO MUCH OF ME AND SENSEI!
HINA-CHAN?

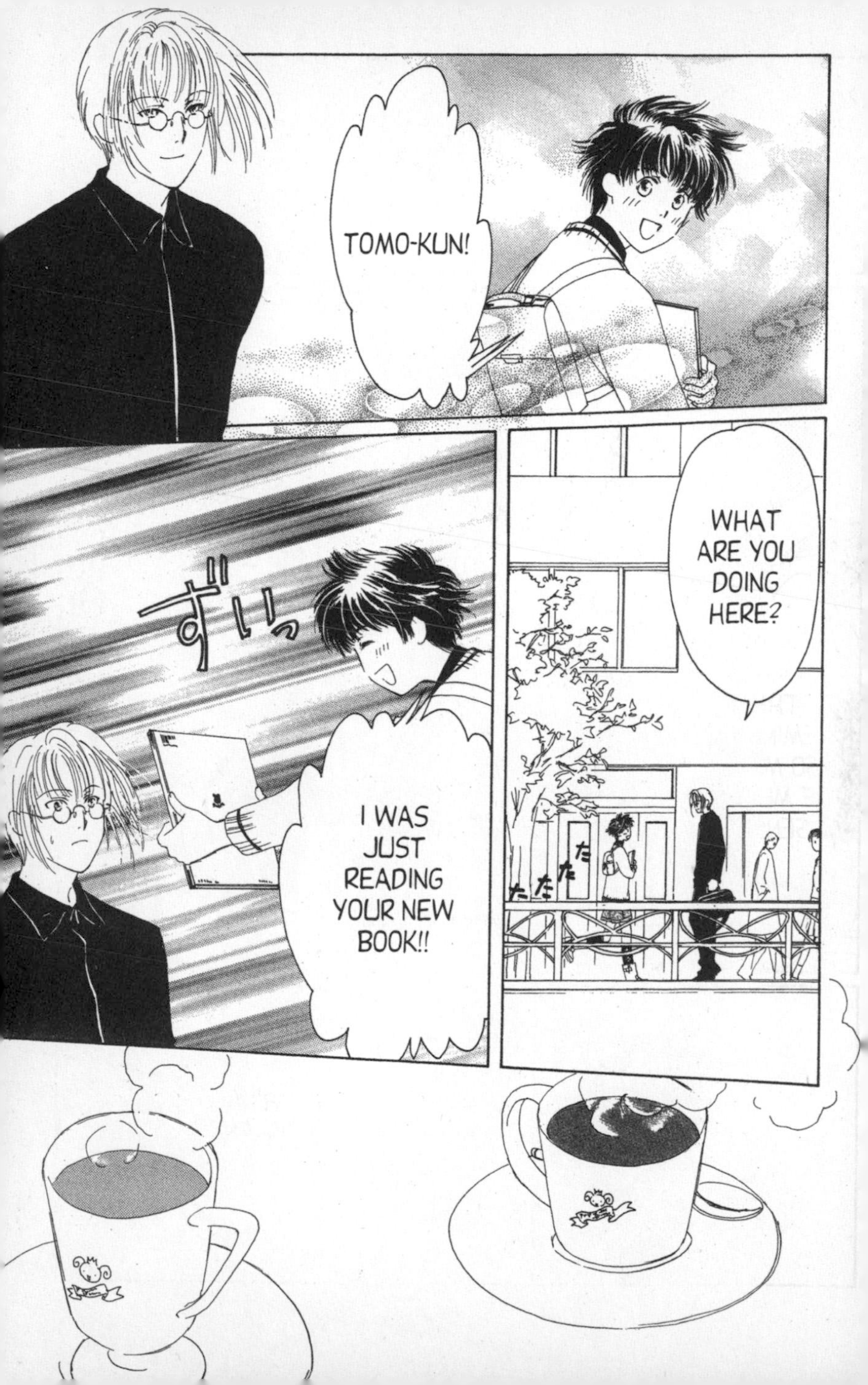
TOMO-KUN!
WHAT ARE YOU DOING HERE?
たたた
ずいっ
I WAS JUST READING YOUR NEW BOOK!!

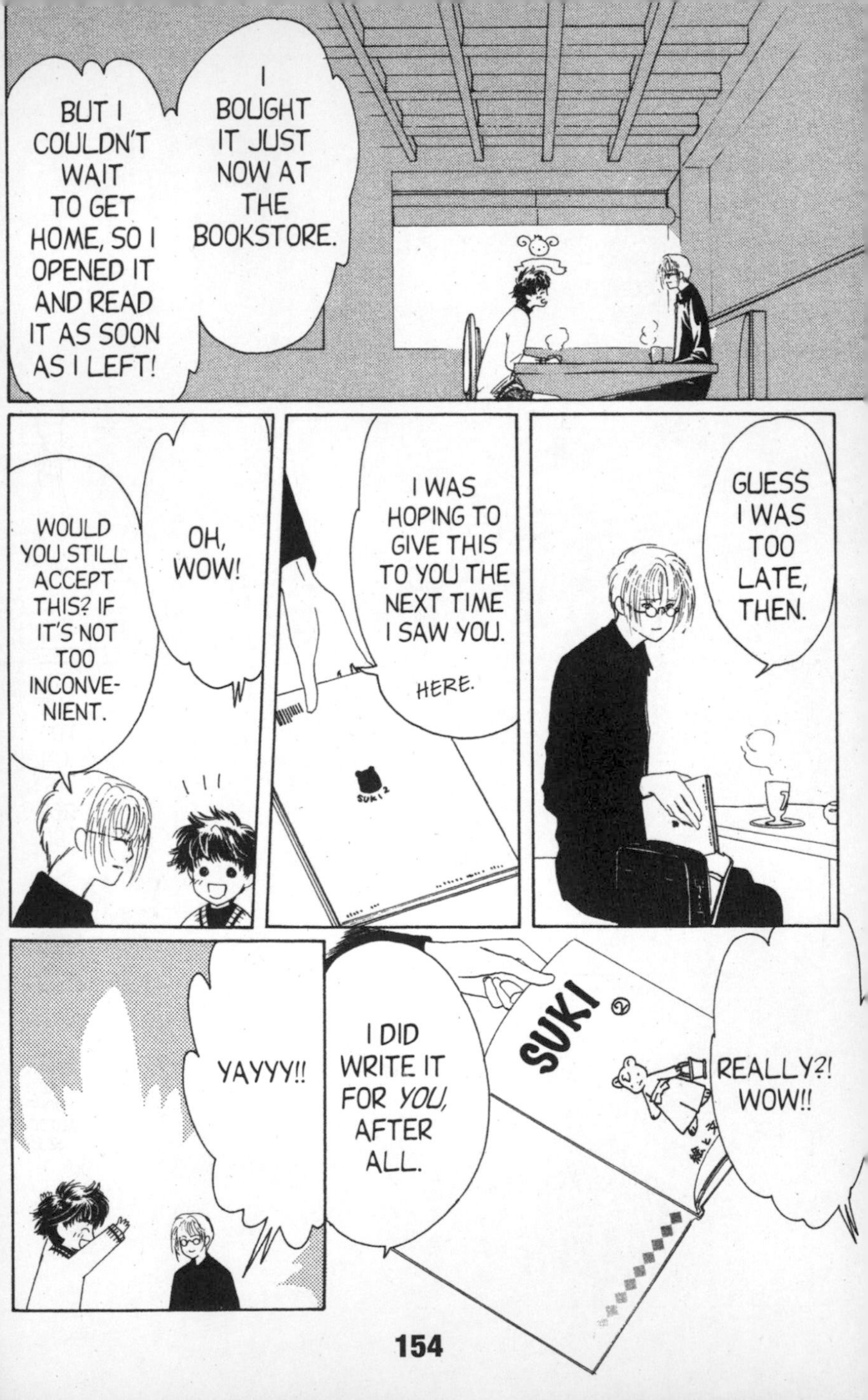
I BOUGHT IT JUST NOW AT THE BOOKSTORE.
BUT I COULDN'T WAIT TO GET HOME, SO I OPENED IT AND READ IT AS SOON AS I LEFT!
GUESS I WAS TOO LATE, THEN.
I WAS HOPING TO GIVE THIS TO YOU THE NEXT TIME I SAW YOU.
HERE.
OH, WOW!
WOULD YOU STILL ACCEPT THIS? IF IT'S NOT TOO INCONVENIENT.
REALLY?! WOW!!
SUKI
I DID WRITE IT FOR *YOU*, AFTER ALL.
YAYYY!!

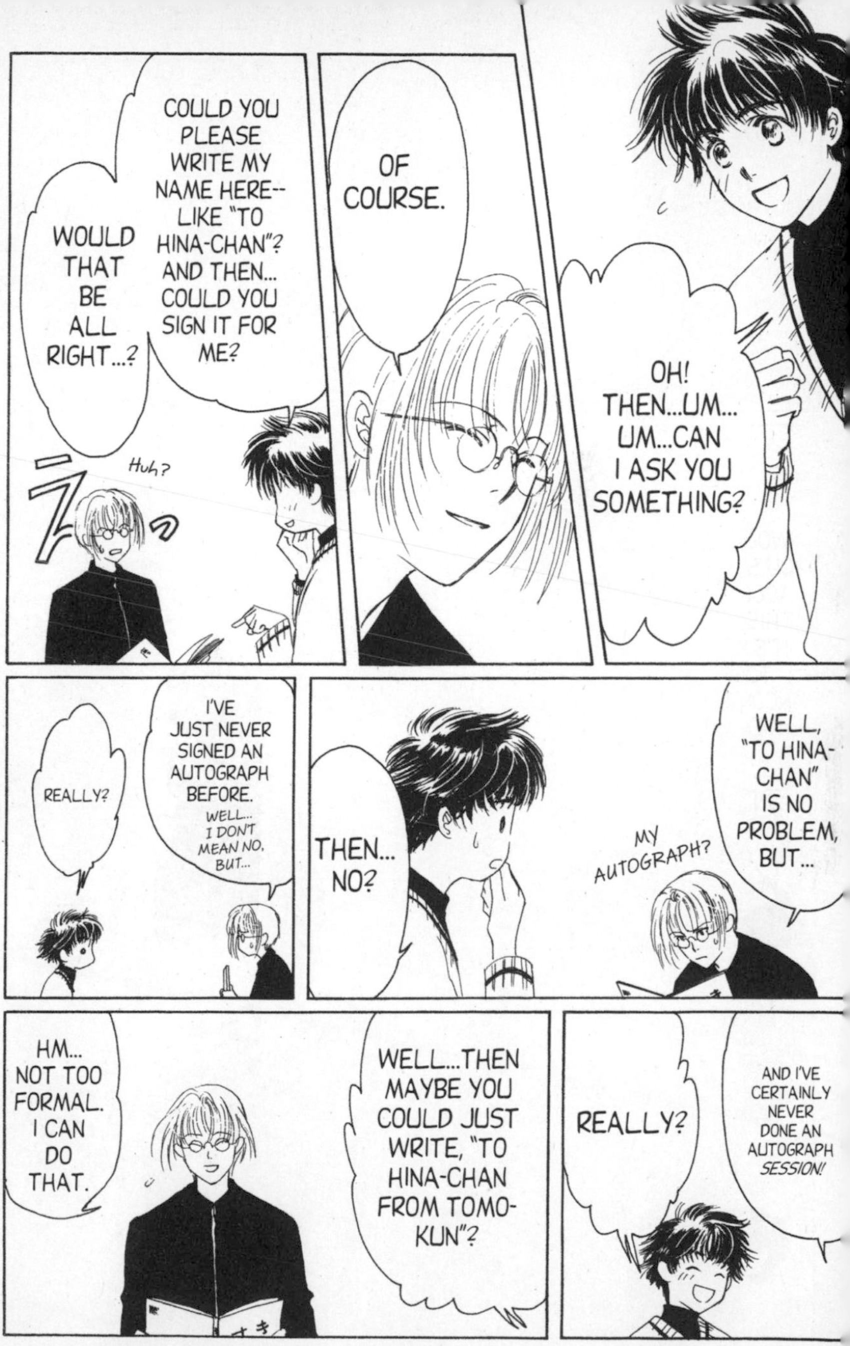
OH! THEN...UM... UM...CAN I ASK YOU SOMETHING?
OF COURSE.
COULD YOU PLEASE WRITE MY NAME HERE-- LIKE "TO HINA-CHAN"? AND THEN... COULD YOU SIGN IT FOR ME?
WOULD THAT BE ALL RIGHT...?
Huh?
WELL, "TO HINA-CHAN" IS NO PROBLEM, BUT...
MY AUTOGRAPH?
THEN... NO?
I'VE JUST NEVER SIGNED AN AUTOGRAPH BEFORE.
WELL... I DON'T MEAN NO, BUT...
REALLY?
AND I'VE CERTAINLY NEVER DONE AN AUTOGRAPH *SESSION!*
REALLY?
WELL...THEN MAYBE YOU COULD JUST WRITE, "TO HINA-CHAN FROM TOMO-KUN"?
HM... NOT TOO FORMAL. I CAN DO THAT.

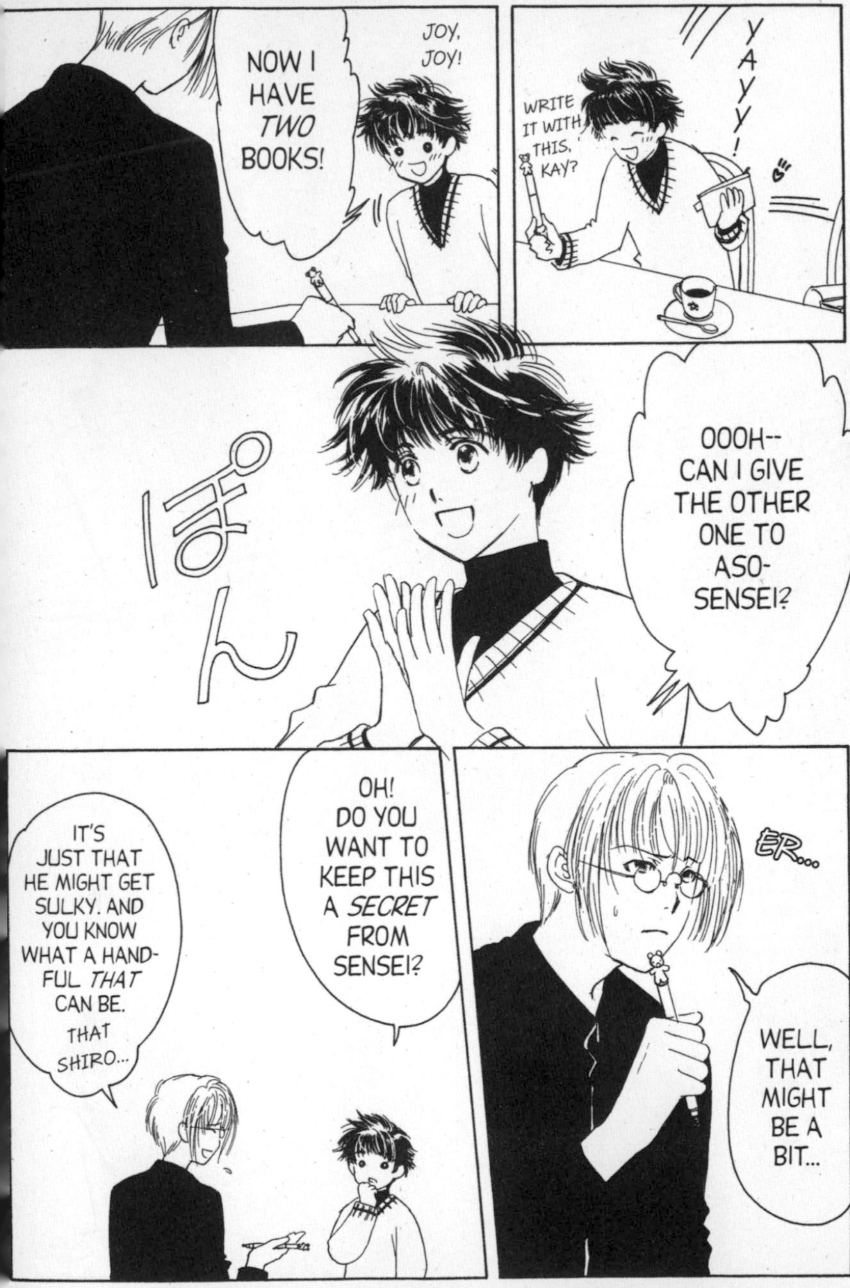
YAYY!
WRITE IT WITH THIS, KAY?
JOY, JOY!
NOW I HAVE *TWO* BOOKS!
OOOH-- CAN I GIVE THE OTHER ONE TO ASO-SENSEI?
ぽん
ER...
WELL, THAT MIGHT BE A BIT...
OH! DO YOU WANT TO KEEP THIS A *SECRET* FROM SENSEI?
IT'S JUST THAT HE MIGHT GET SULKY. AND YOU KNOW WHAT A HAND-FUL *THAT* CAN BE. THAT SHIRO...

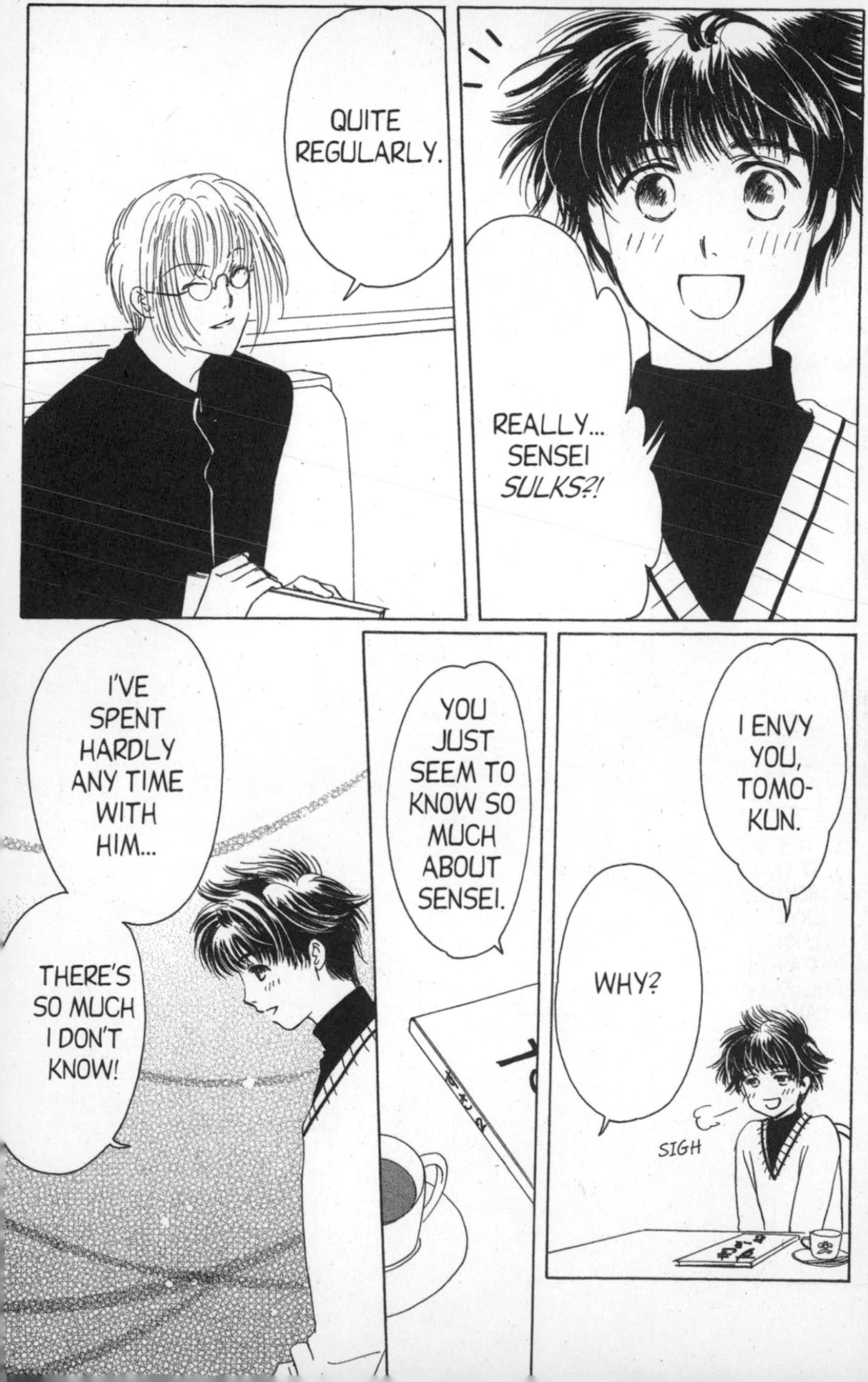
REALLY... SENSEI *SULKS?!*
QUITE REGULARLY.
I ENVY YOU, TOMO-KUN.
WHY?
SIGH
YOU JUST SEEM TO KNOW SO MUCH ABOUT SENSEI.
I'VE SPENT HARDLY ANY TIME WITH HIM...
THERE'S SO MUCH I DON'T KNOW!

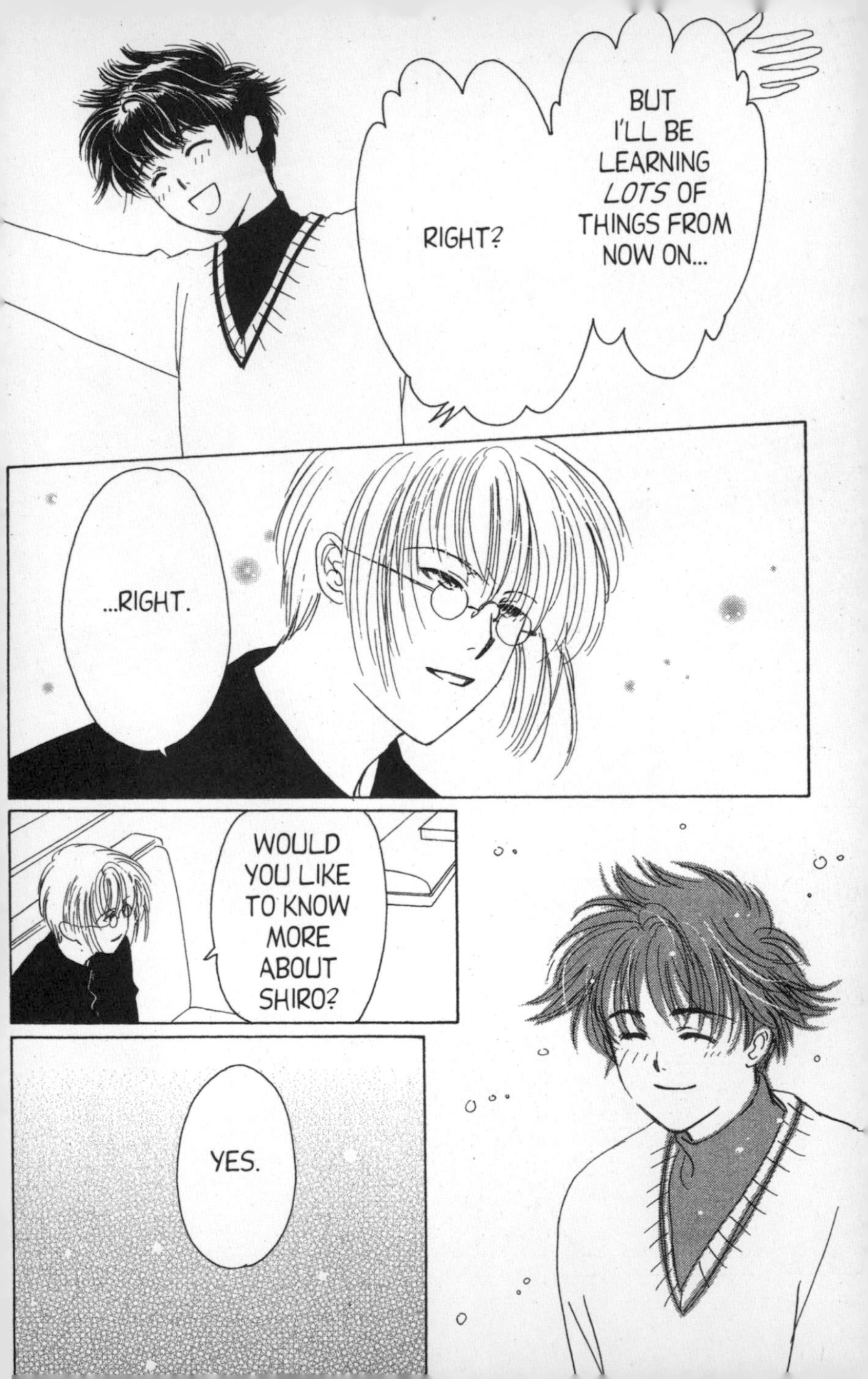
BUT I'LL BE LEARNING *LOTS* OF THINGS FROM NOW ON...
RIGHT?
...RIGHT.
WOULD YOU LIKE TO KNOW MORE ABOUT SHIRO?
YES.

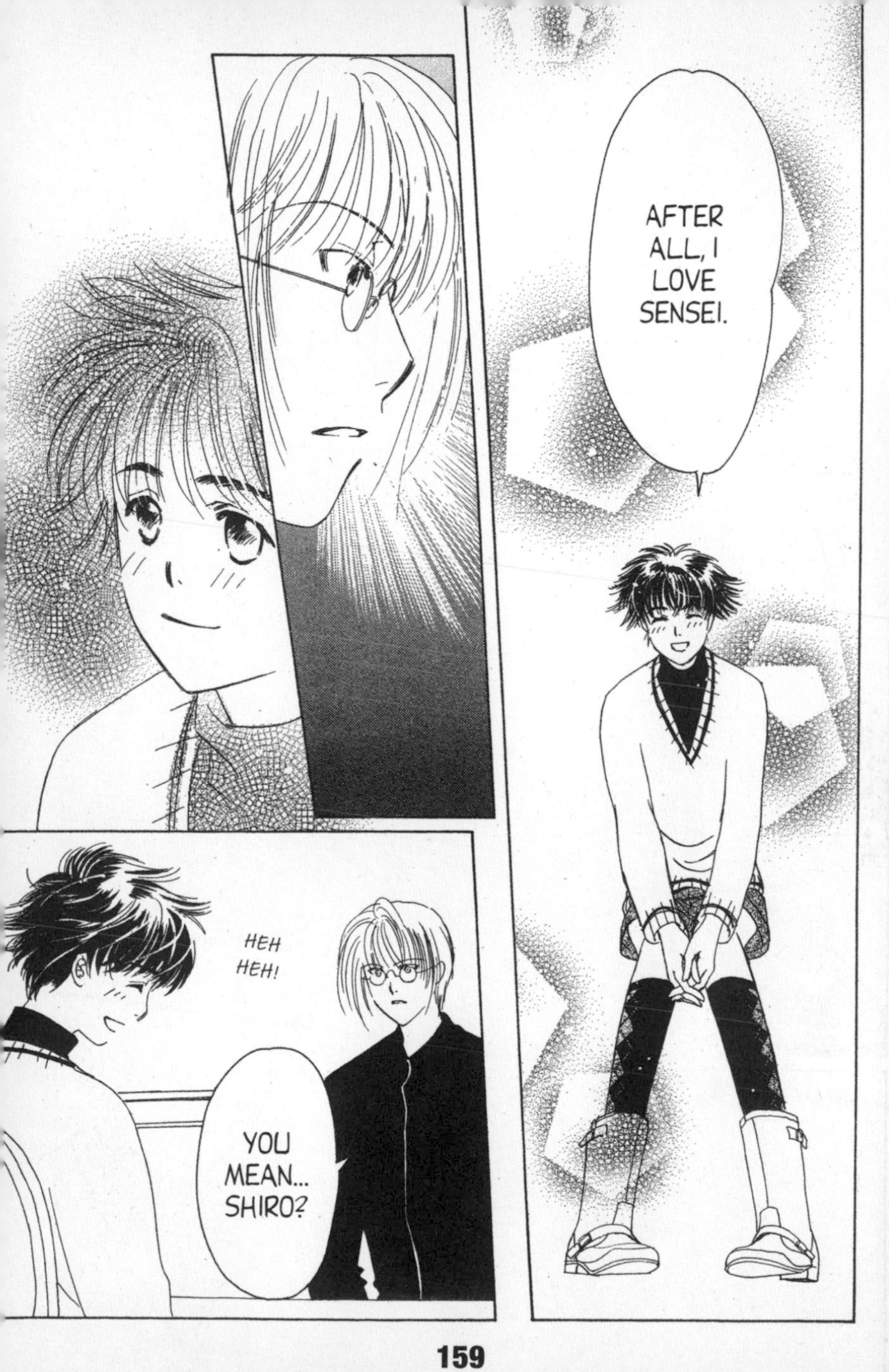
AFTER ALL, I LOVE SENSEI.
HEH HEH!
YOU MEAN... SHIRO?

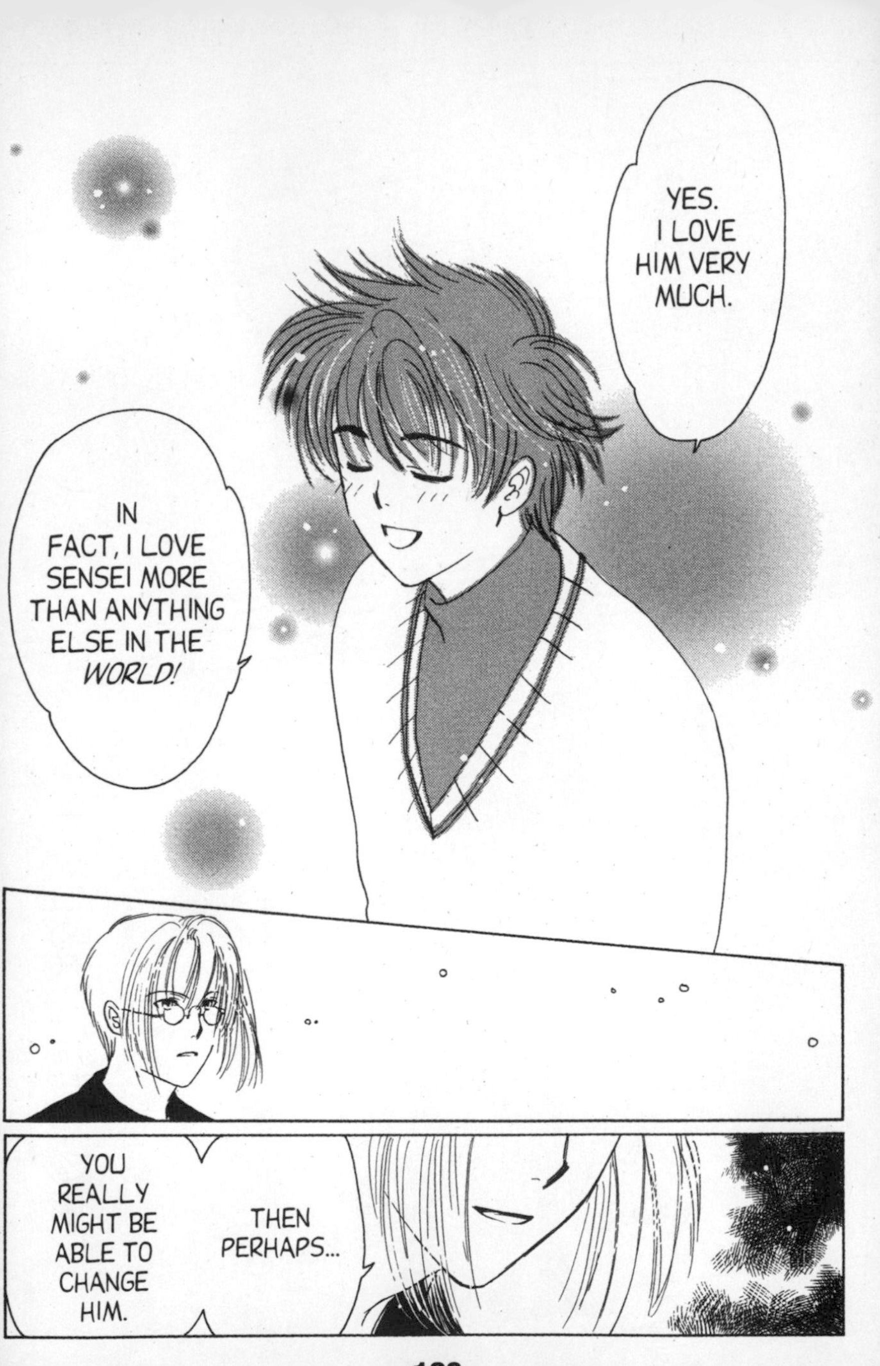
YES. I LOVE HIM VERY MUCH.
IN FACT, I LOVE SENSEI MORE THAN ANYTHING ELSE IN THE *WORLD!*
THEN PERHAPS...
YOU REALLY MIGHT BE ABLE TO CHANGE HIM.

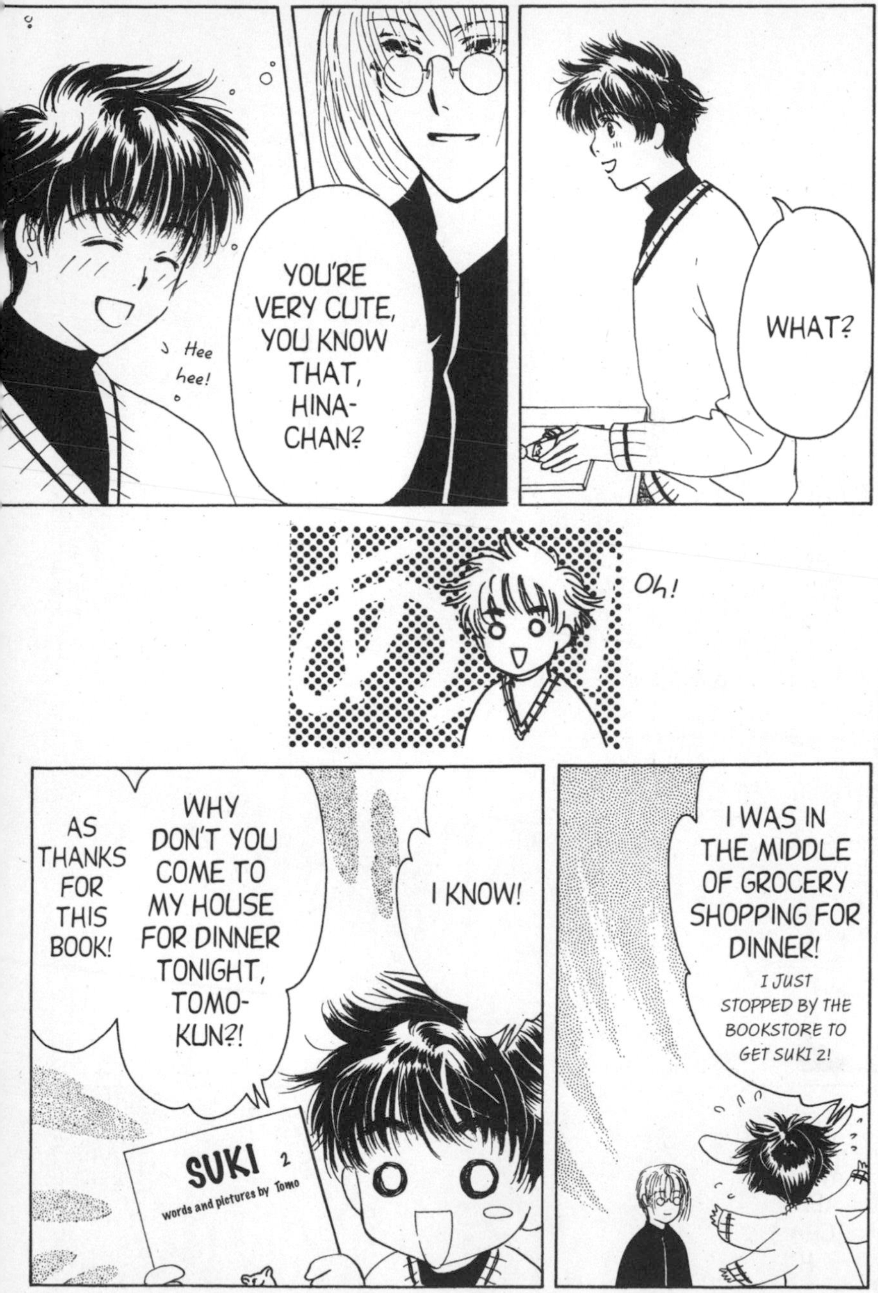
WHAT?
YOU'RE VERY CUTE, YOU KNOW THAT, HINA-CHAN?
Hee hee!
Oh!
I WAS IN THE MIDDLE OF GROCERY SHOPPING FOR DINNER!
I JUST STOPPED BY THE BOOKSTORE TO GET SUKI 2!
I KNOW!
WHY DON'T YOU COME TO MY HOUSE FOR DINNER TONIGHT, TOMO-KUN?!
AS THANKS FOR THIS BOOK!
SUKI 2
words and pictures by Tomo

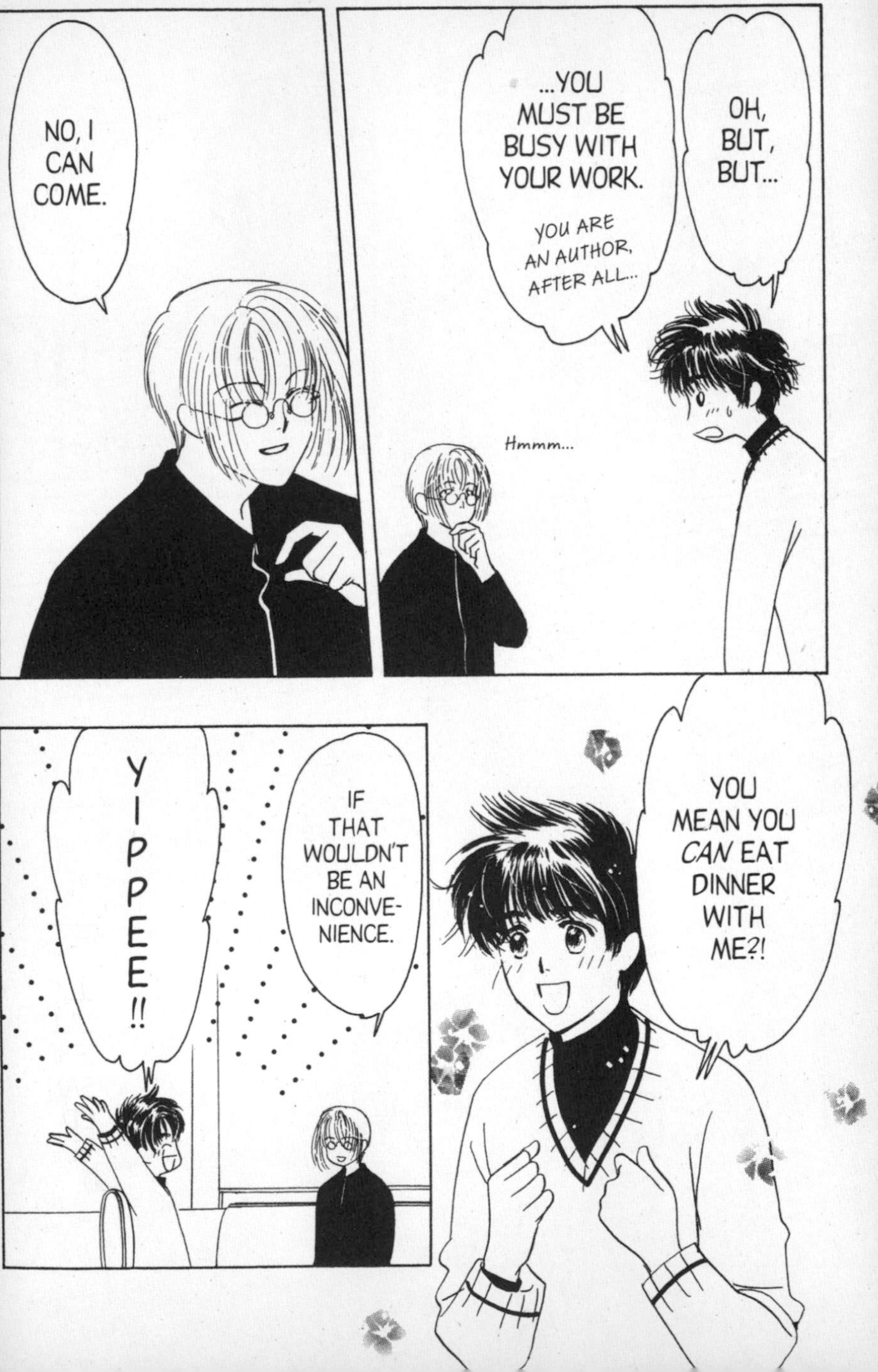
OH, BUT, BUT...
...YOU MUST BE BUSY WITH YOUR WORK.
YOU ARE AN AUTHOR, AFTER ALL...
Hmmm...
NO, I CAN COME.
YOU MEAN YOU CAN EAT DINNER WITH ME?!
IF THAT WOULDN'T BE AN INCONVENIENCE.
YIPPEE!!

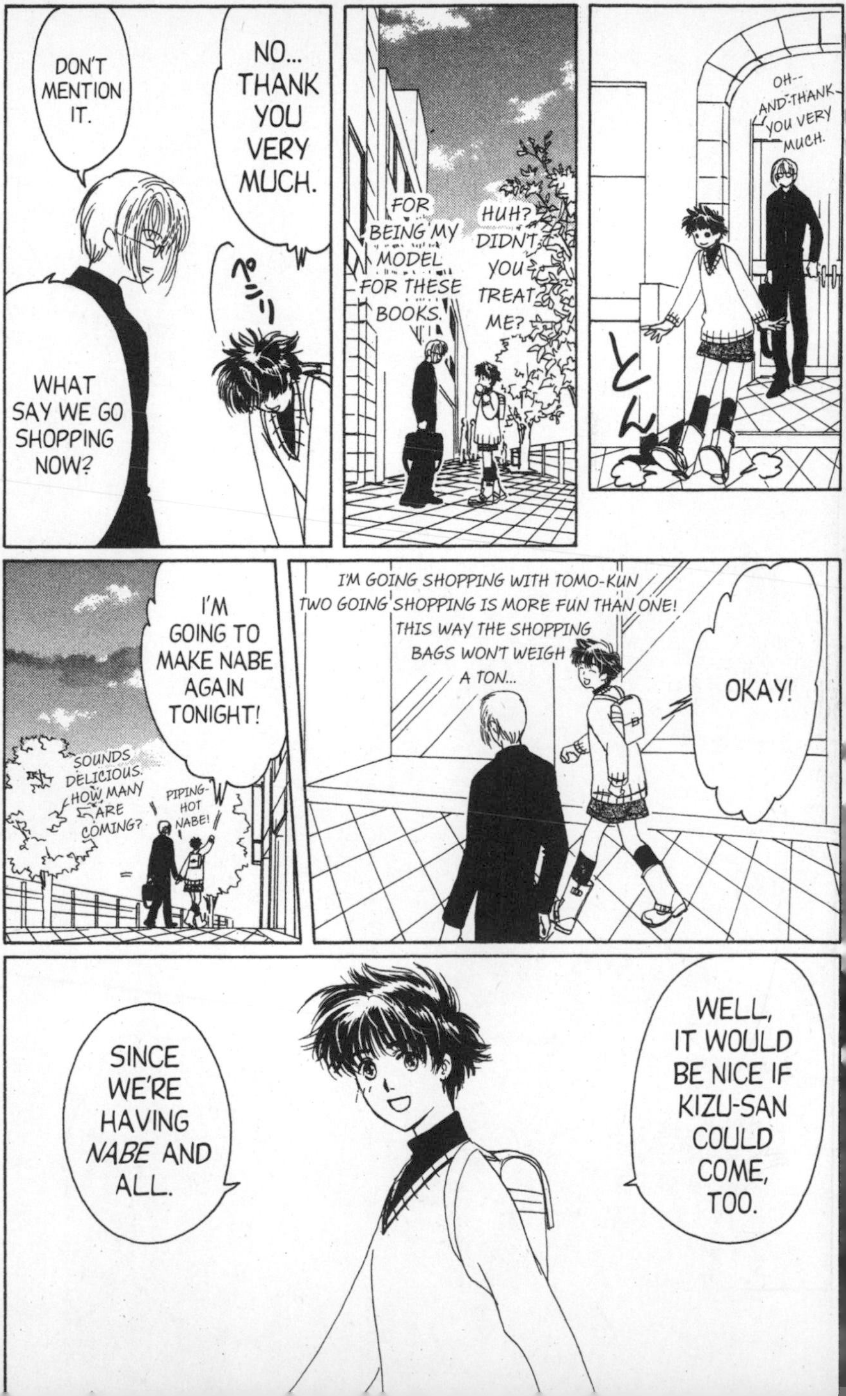
OH-- AND THANK YOU VERY MUCH.
とん
HUH? DIDN'T YOU TREAT ME?
FOR BEING MY MODEL FOR THESE BOOKS.
NO... THANK YOU VERY MUCH.
ぺこり
DON'T MENTION IT.
WHAT SAY WE GO SHOPPING NOW?
OKAY!
I'M GOING SHOPPING WITH TOMO-KUN
TWO GOING SHOPPING IS MORE FUN THAN ONE!
THIS WAY THE SHOPPING BAGS WON'T WEIGH A TON...
I'M GOING TO MAKE NABE AGAIN TONIGHT!
PIPING-HOT NABE!
SOUNDS DELICIOUS. HOW MANY ARE COMING?
WELL, IT WOULD BE NICE IF KIZU-SAN COULD COME, TOO.
SINCE WE'RE HAVING *NABE* AND ALL.

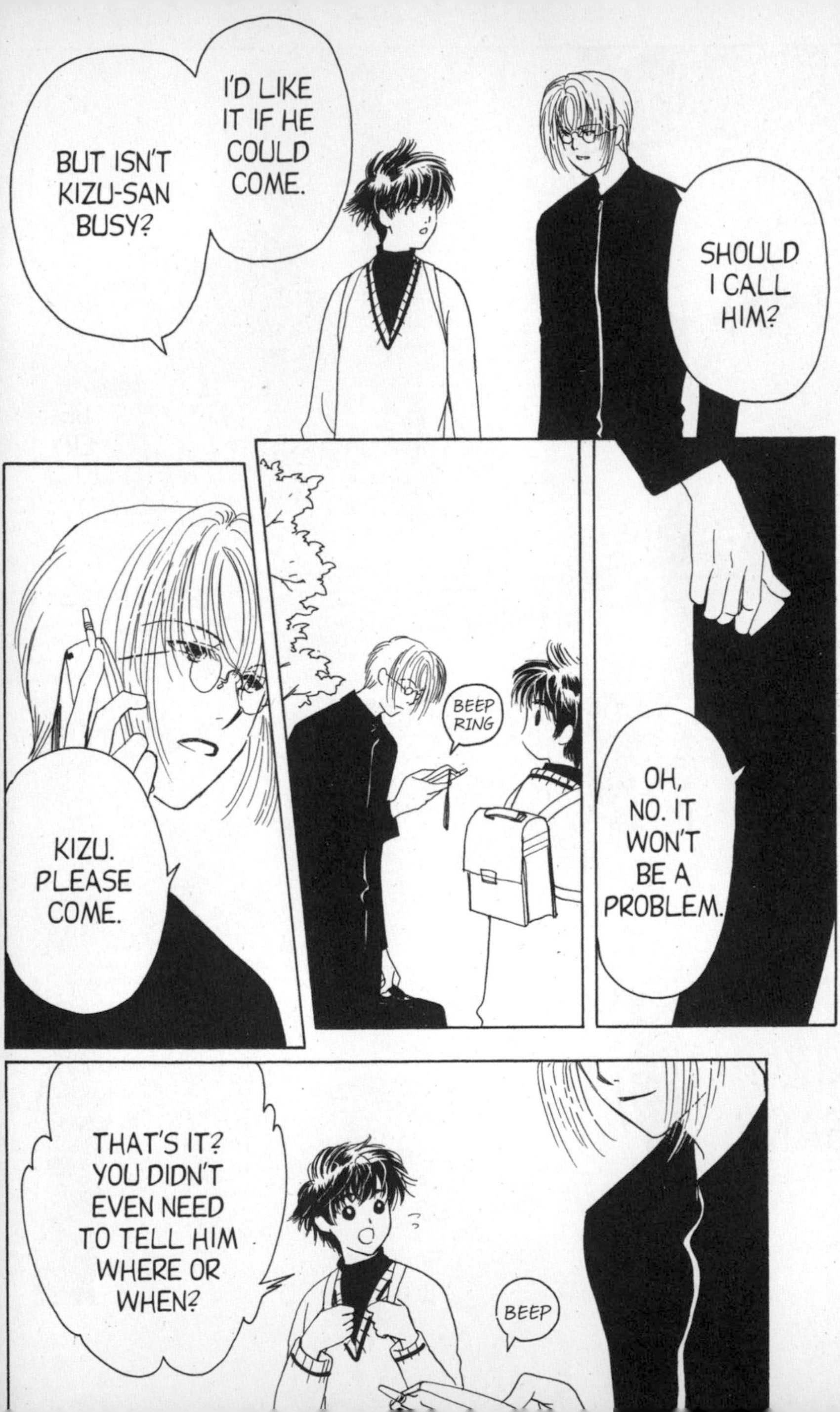
SHOULD I CALL HIM?
I'D LIKE IT IF HE COULD COME.
BUT ISN'T KIZU-SAN BUSY?
OH, NO. IT WON'T BE A PROBLEM.
BEEP RING
KIZU. PLEASE COME.
BEEP
THAT'S IT? YOU DIDN'T EVEN NEED TO TELL HIM WHERE OR WHEN?

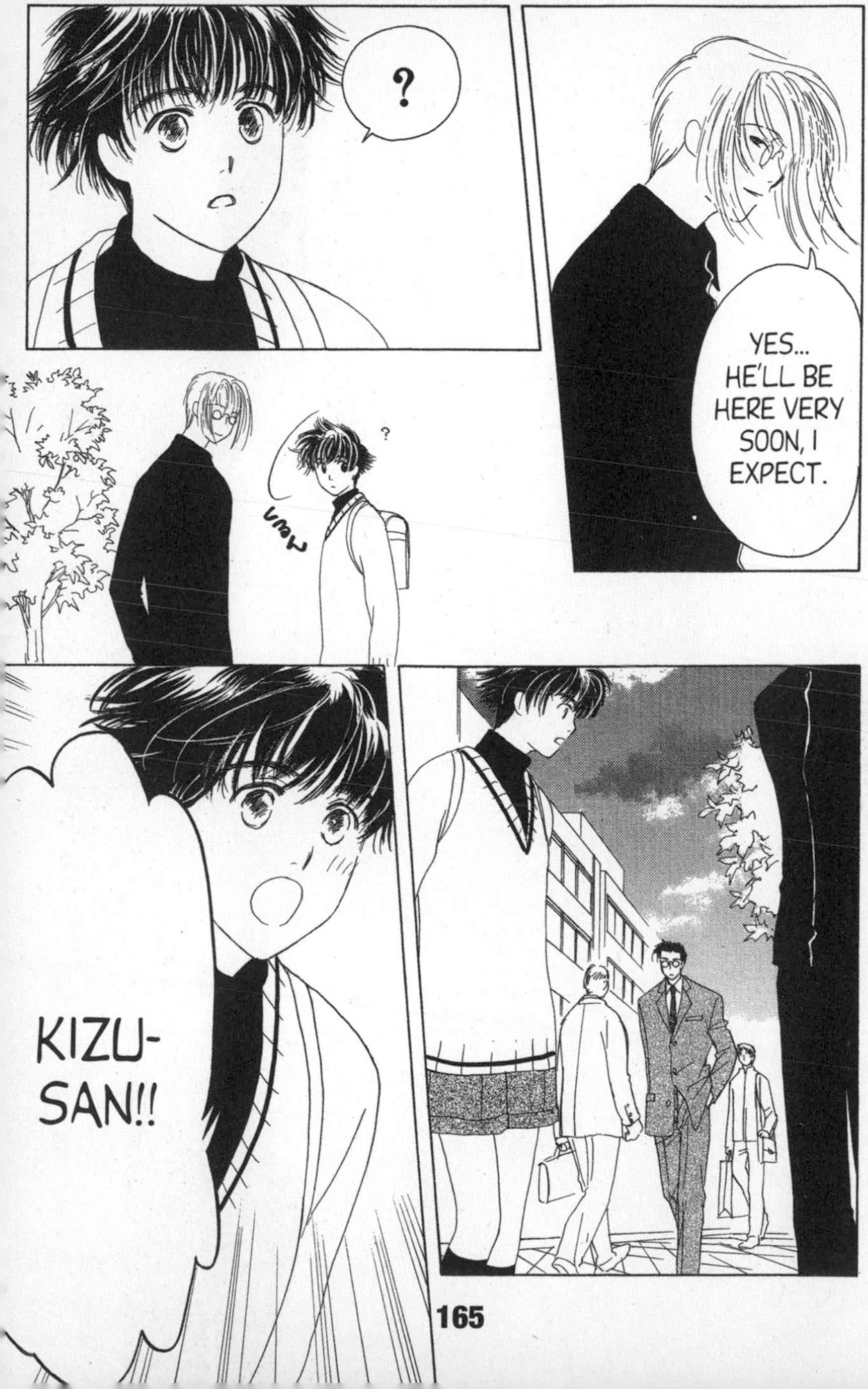
YES... HE'LL BE HERE VERY SOON, I EXPECT.
?
?
KIZU-SAN!!

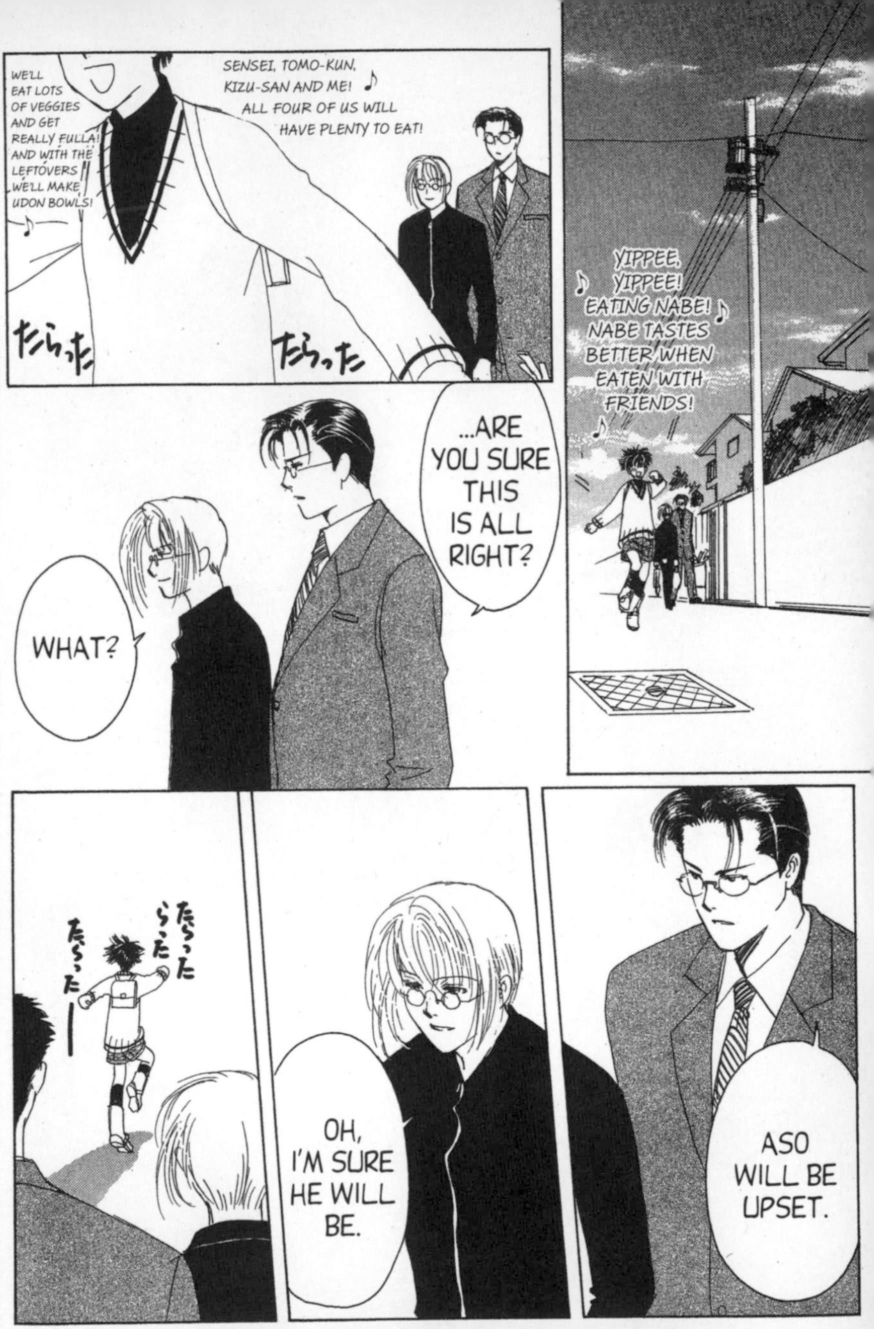

♪ YIPPEE, YIPPEE! EATING NABE! ♪ NABE TASTES BETTER WHEN EATEN WITH FRIENDS! ♪
SENSEI, TOMO-KUN, KIZU-SAN AND ME! ♪ ALL FOUR OF US WILL HAVE PLENTY TO EAT!
WE'LL EAT LOTS OF VEGGIES AND GET REALLY FULLA! AND WITH THE LEFTOVERS WE'LL MAKE UDON BOWLS! ♪
たらった
たらった
...ARE YOU SURE THIS IS ALL RIGHT?
WHAT?
ASO WILL BE UPSET.
OH, I'M SURE HE WILL BE.
たらった
らった
たらったー

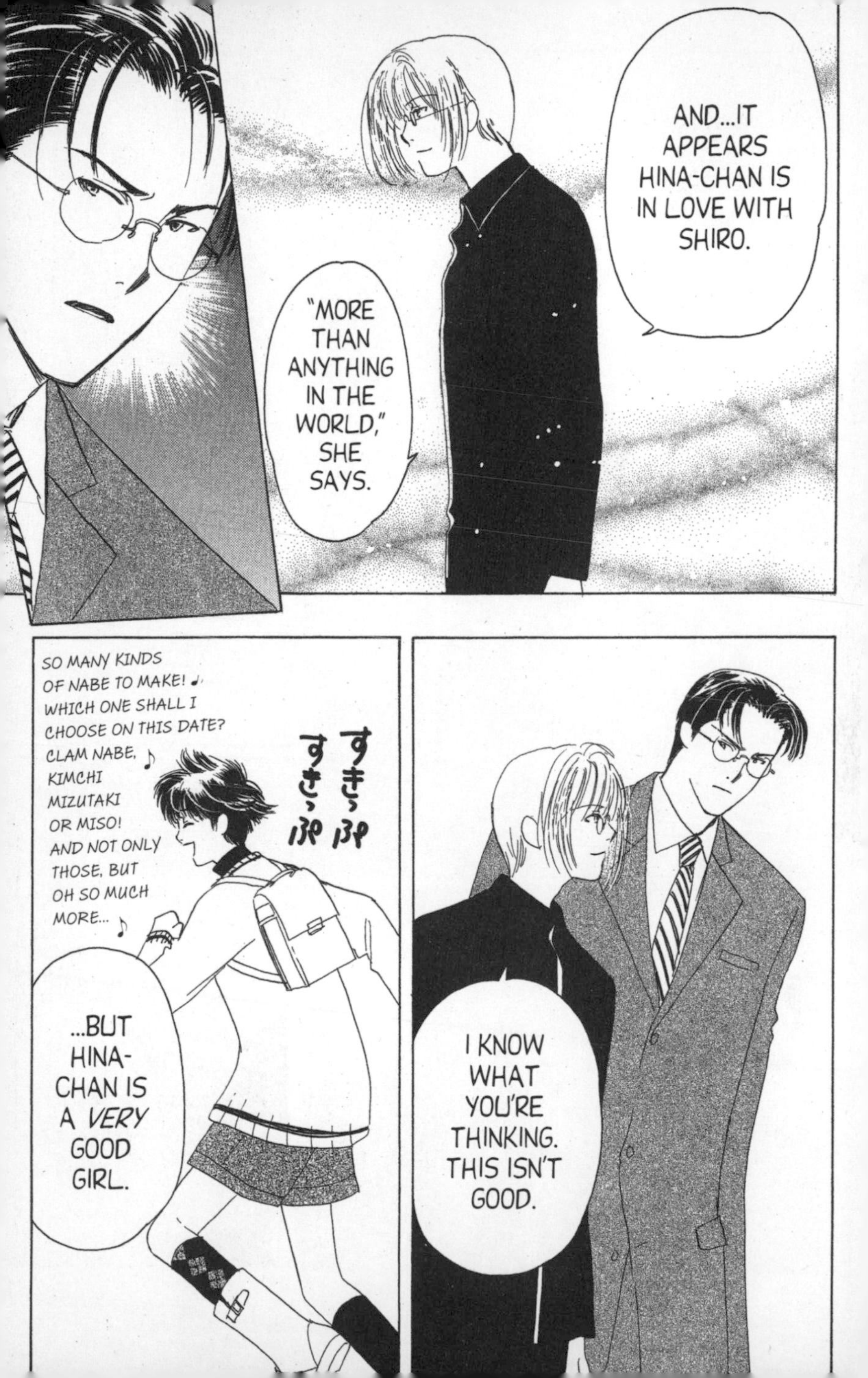
AND...IT APPEARS HINA-CHAN IS IN LOVE WITH SHIRO.
"MORE THAN ANYTHING IN THE WORLD," SHE SAYS.
I KNOW WHAT YOU'RE THINKING. THIS ISN'T GOOD.
すきっぷ すきっぷ
SO MANY KINDS OF NABE TO MAKE! ♪ WHICH ONE SHALL I CHOOSE ON THIS DATE? CLAM NABE, ♪ KIMCHI MIZUTAKI OR MISO! AND NOT ONLY THOSE, BUT OH SO MUCH MORE... ♪
...BUT HINA-CHAN IS A *VERY* GOOD GIRL.

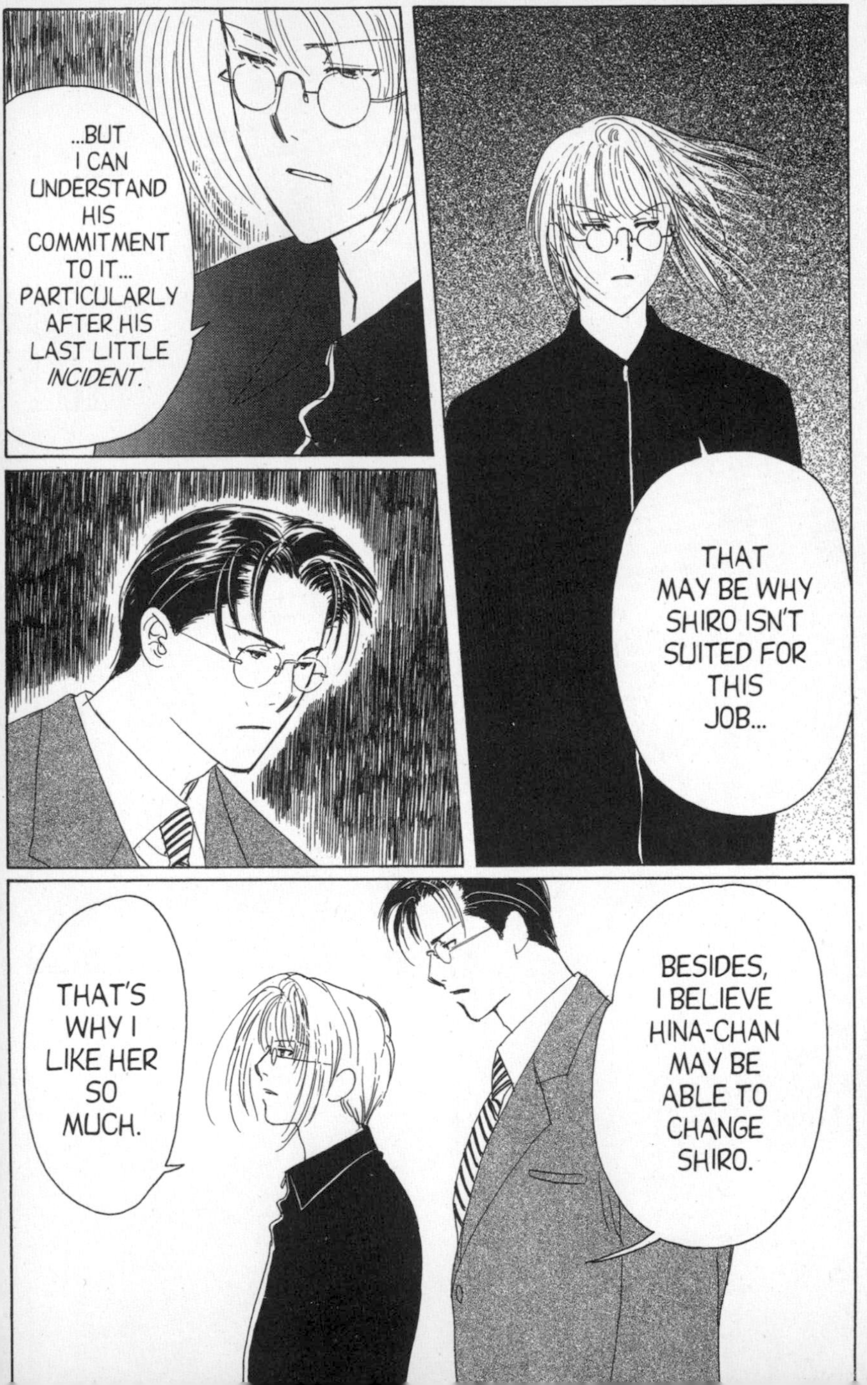
THAT MAY BE WHY SHIRO ISN'T SUITED FOR THIS JOB...
...BUT I CAN UNDERSTAND HIS COMMITMENT TO IT... PARTICULARLY AFTER HIS LAST LITTLE *INCIDENT*.
BESIDES, I BELIEVE HINA-CHAN MAY BE ABLE TO CHANGE SHIRO.
THAT'S WHY I LIKE HER SO MUCH.

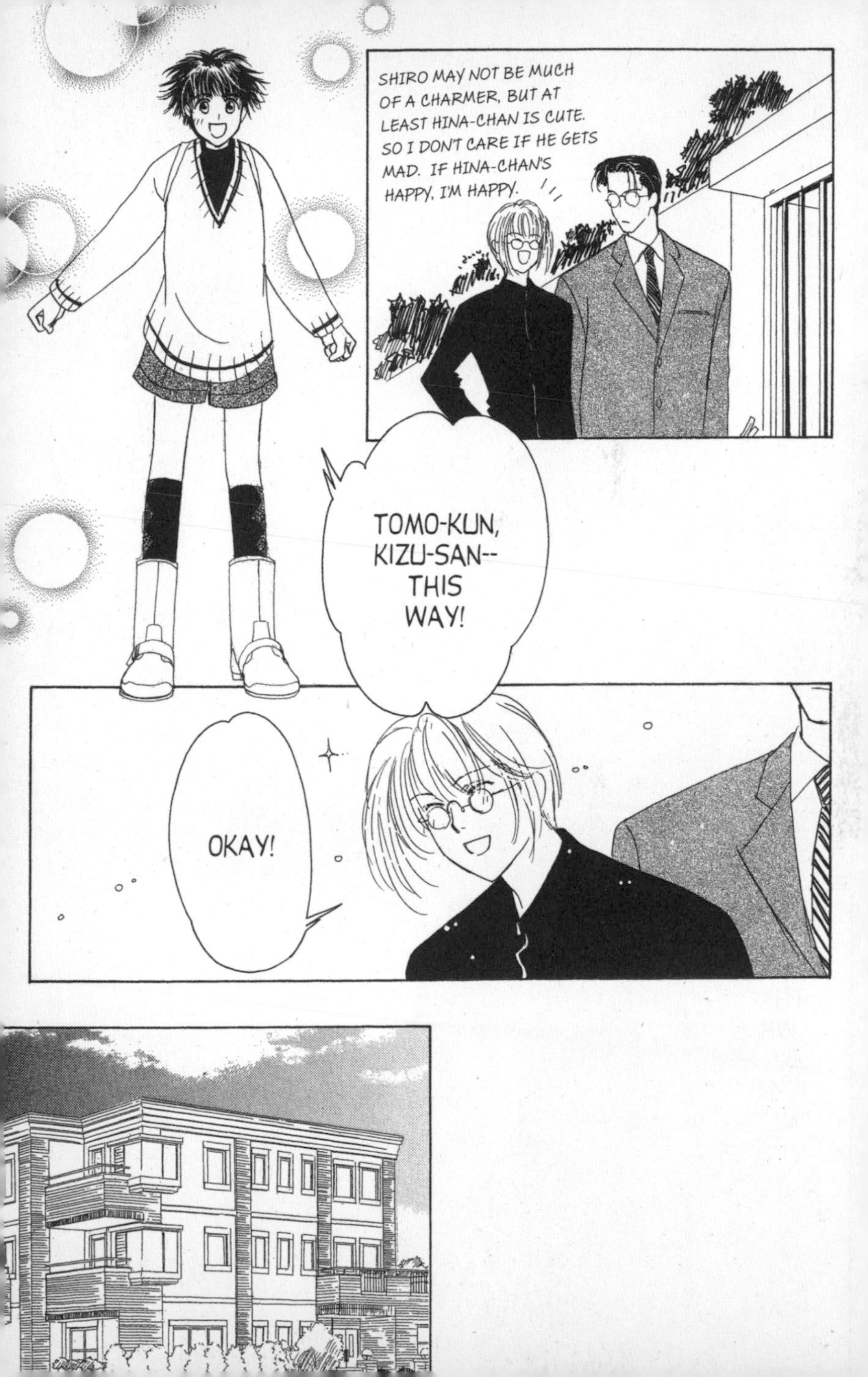
SHIRO MAY NOT BE MUCH OF A CHARMER, BUT AT LEAST HINA-CHAN IS CUTE. SO I DON'T CARE IF HE GETS MAD. IF HINA-CHAN'S HAPPY, I'M HAPPY.
TOMO-KUN, KIZU-SAN-- THIS WAY!
OKAY!

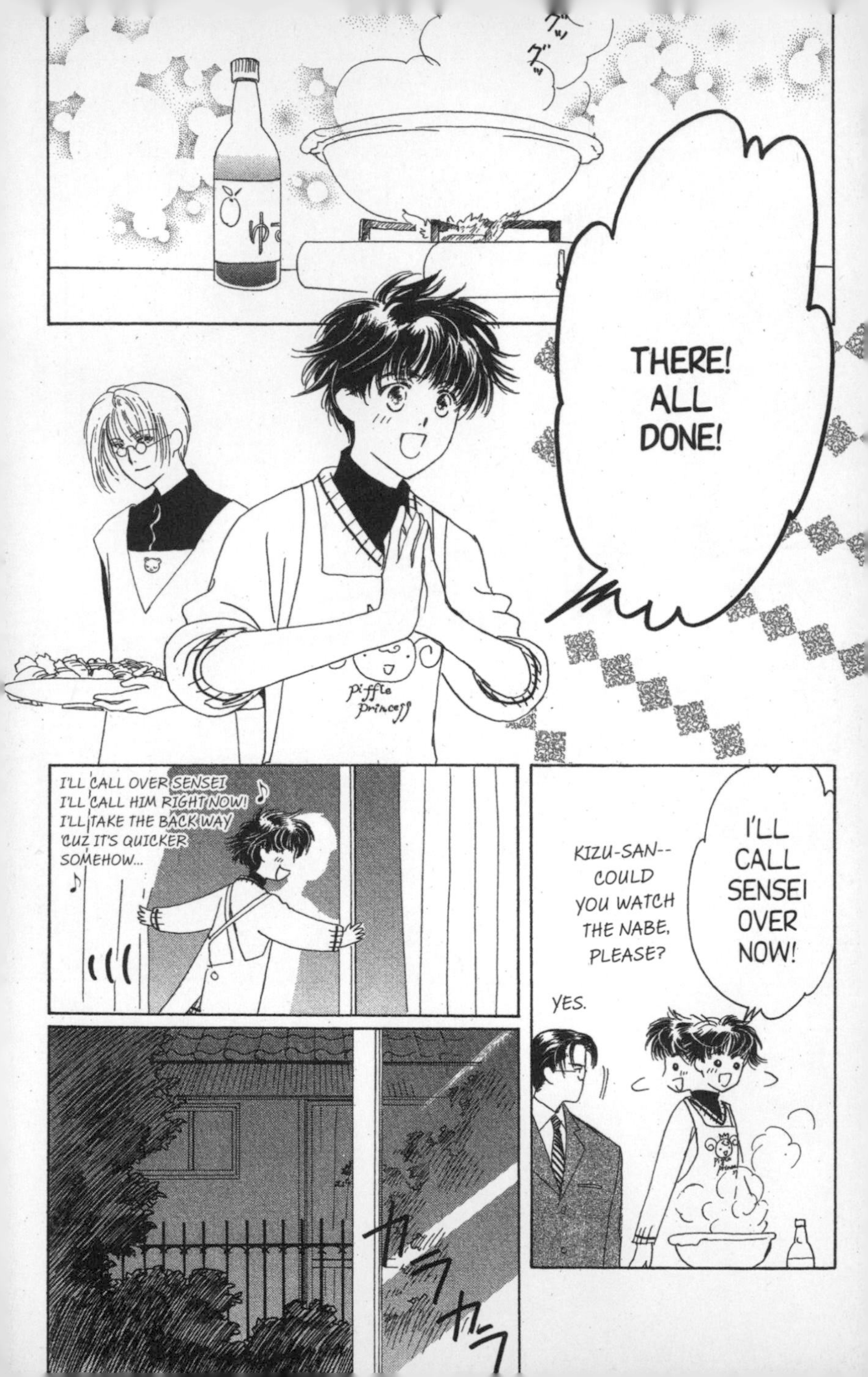
THERE! ALL DONE!
Piffle Princess
I'LL CALL SENSEI OVER NOW!
KIZU-SAN-- COULD YOU WATCH THE NABE, PLEASE?
YES.
I'LL CALL OVER SENSEI I'LL CALL HIM RIGHT NOW! I'LL TAKE THE BACK WAY 'CUZ IT'S QUICKER SOMEHOW... ♪
カラ カラ

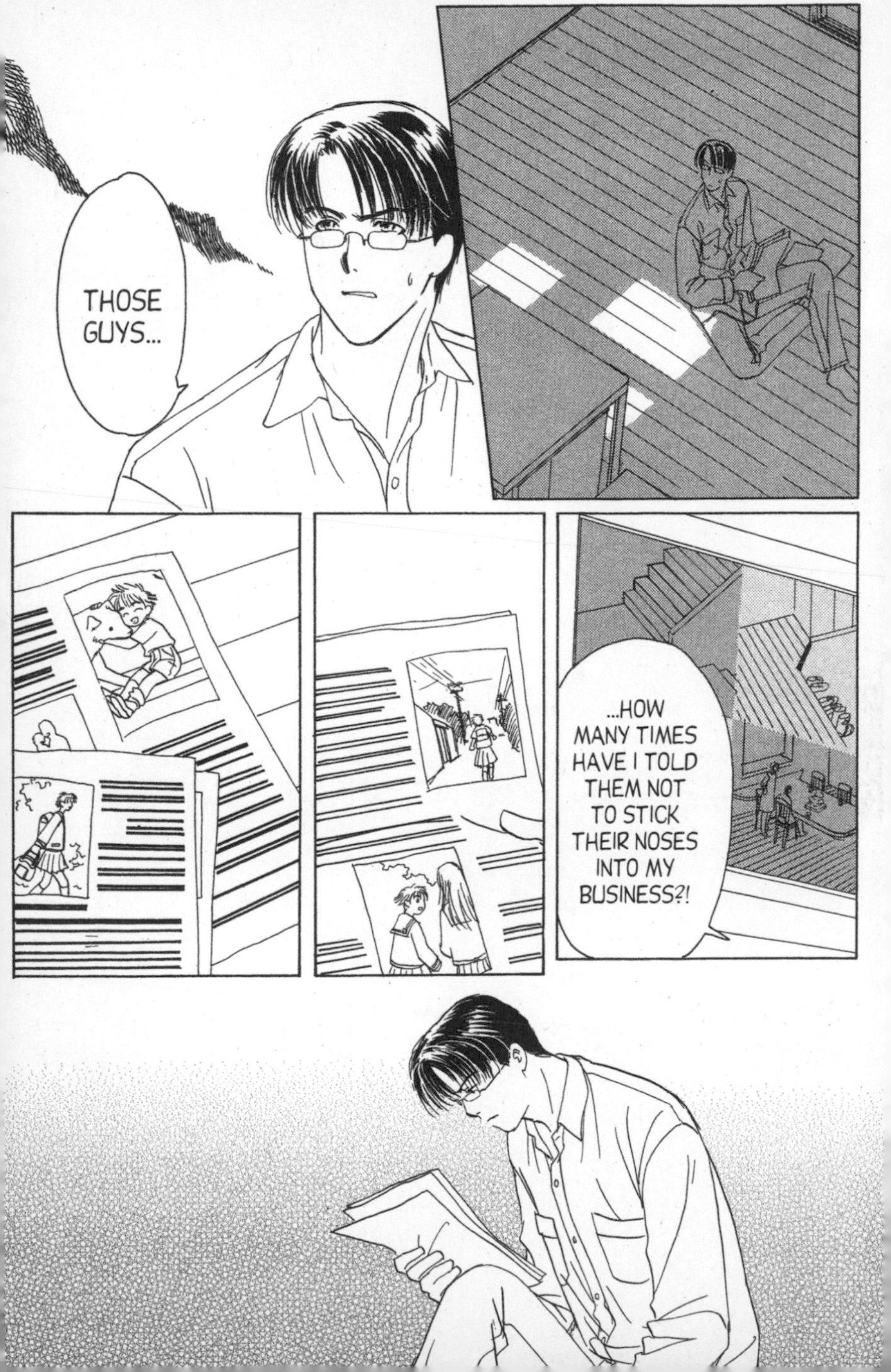
THOSE GUYS...
...HOW MANY TIMES HAVE I TOLD THEM NOT TO STICK THEIR NOSES INTO MY BUSINESS?!

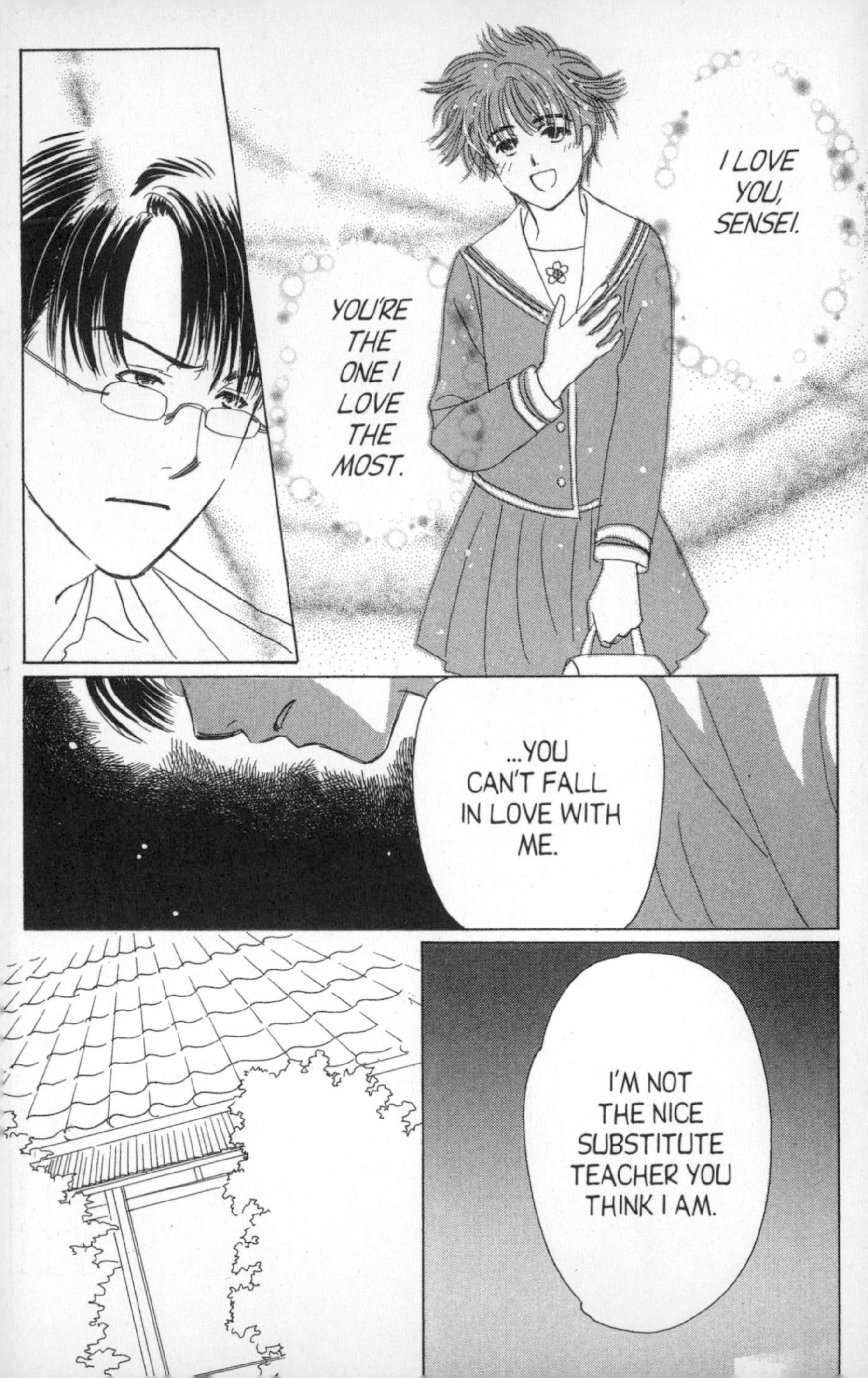
I LOVE YOU, SENSEI.
YOU'RE THE ONE I LOVE THE MOST.
...YOU CAN'T FALL IN LOVE WITH ME.
I'M NOT THE NICE SUBSTITUTE TEACHER YOU THINK I AM.

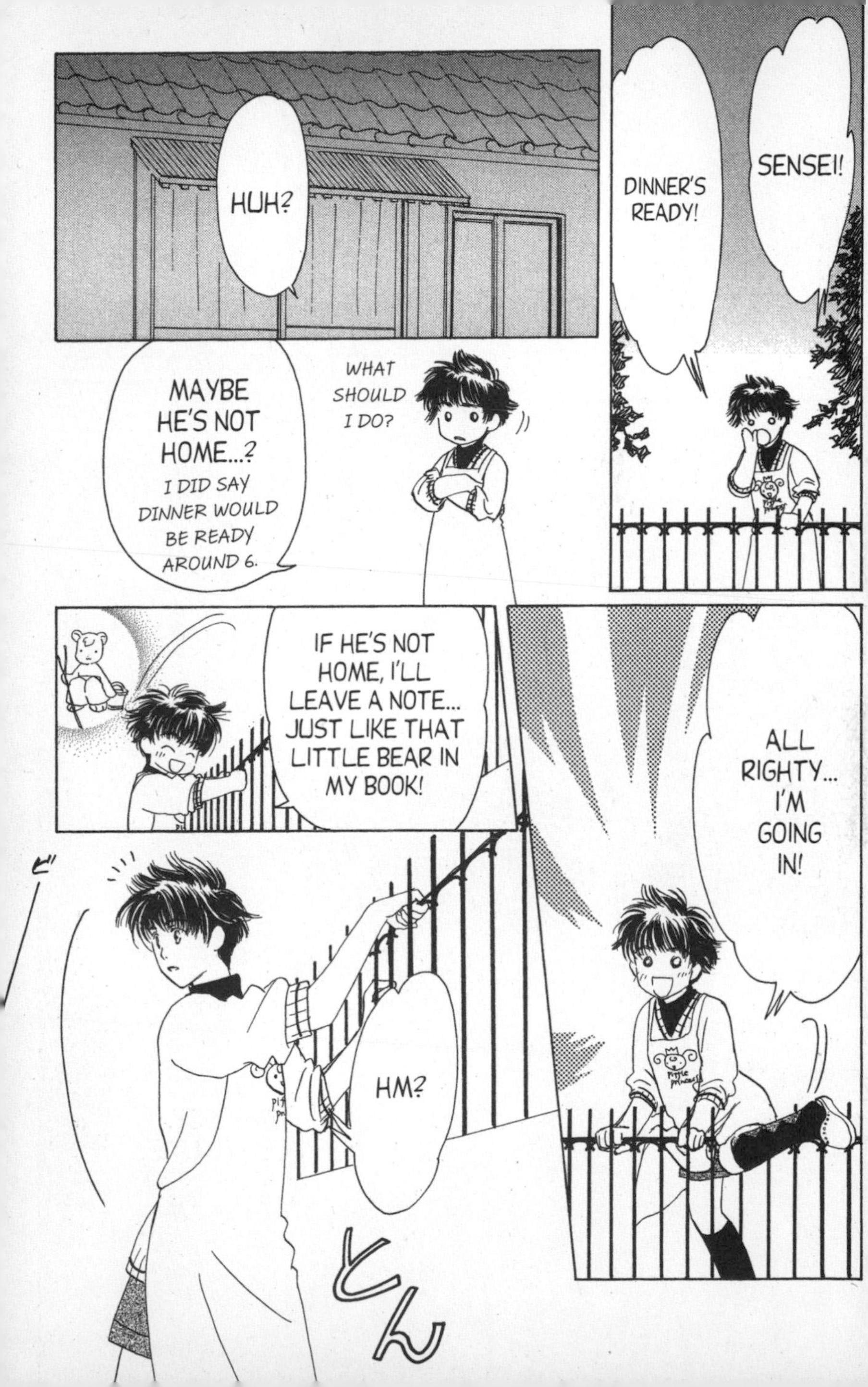
SENSEI!
DINNER'S READY!
HUH?
MAYBE HE'S NOT HOME...? I DID SAY DINNER WOULD BE READY AROUND 6.
WHAT SHOULD I DO?
ALL RIGHTY... I'M GOING IN!
IF HE'S NOT HOME, I'LL LEAVE A NOTE... JUST LIKE THAT LITTLE BEAR IN MY BOOK!
HM?
とん

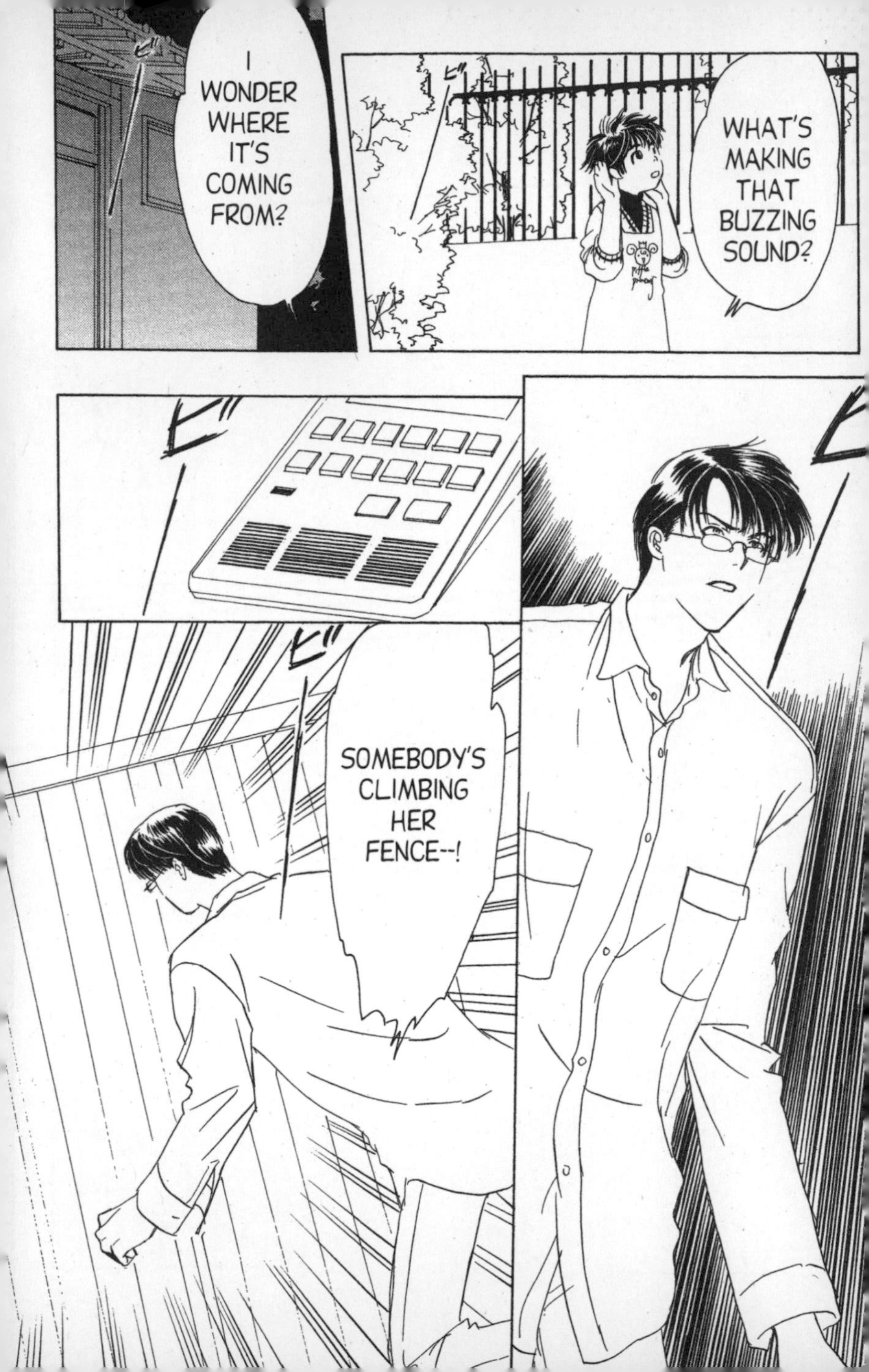
ビ
WHAT'S MAKING THAT BUZZING SOUND?
ビ
I WONDER WHERE IT'S COMING FROM?
ビ
ビ
ビ
SOMEBODY'S CLIMBING HER FENCE--!

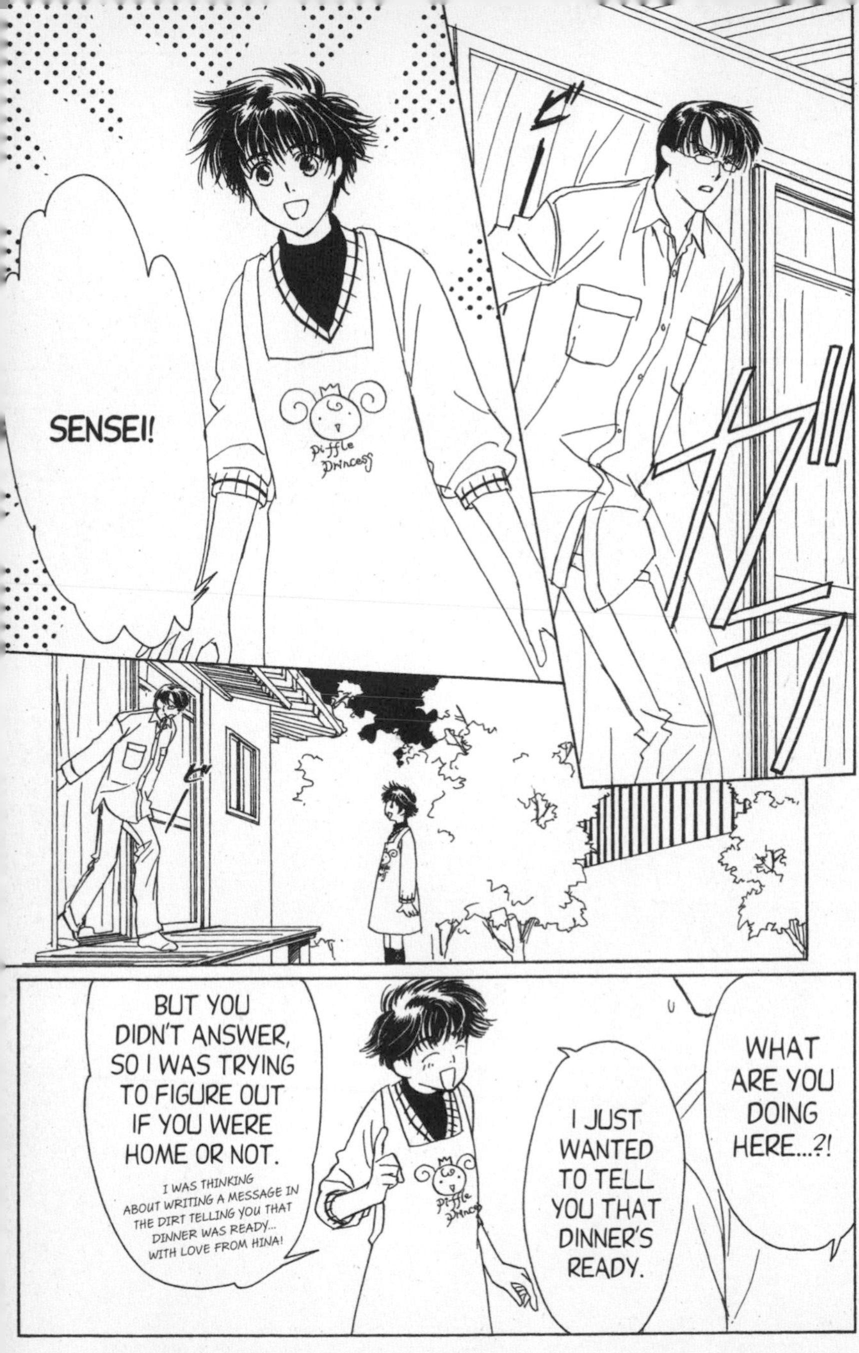
SENSEI!
WHAT ARE YOU DOING HERE...?!
I JUST WANTED TO TELL YOU THAT DINNER'S READY.
BUT YOU DIDN'T ANSWER, SO I WAS TRYING TO FIGURE OUT IF YOU WERE HOME OR NOT.
I WAS THINKING ABOUT WRITING A MESSAGE IN THE DIRT TELLING YOU THAT DINNER WAS READY... WITH LOVE FROM HINA!

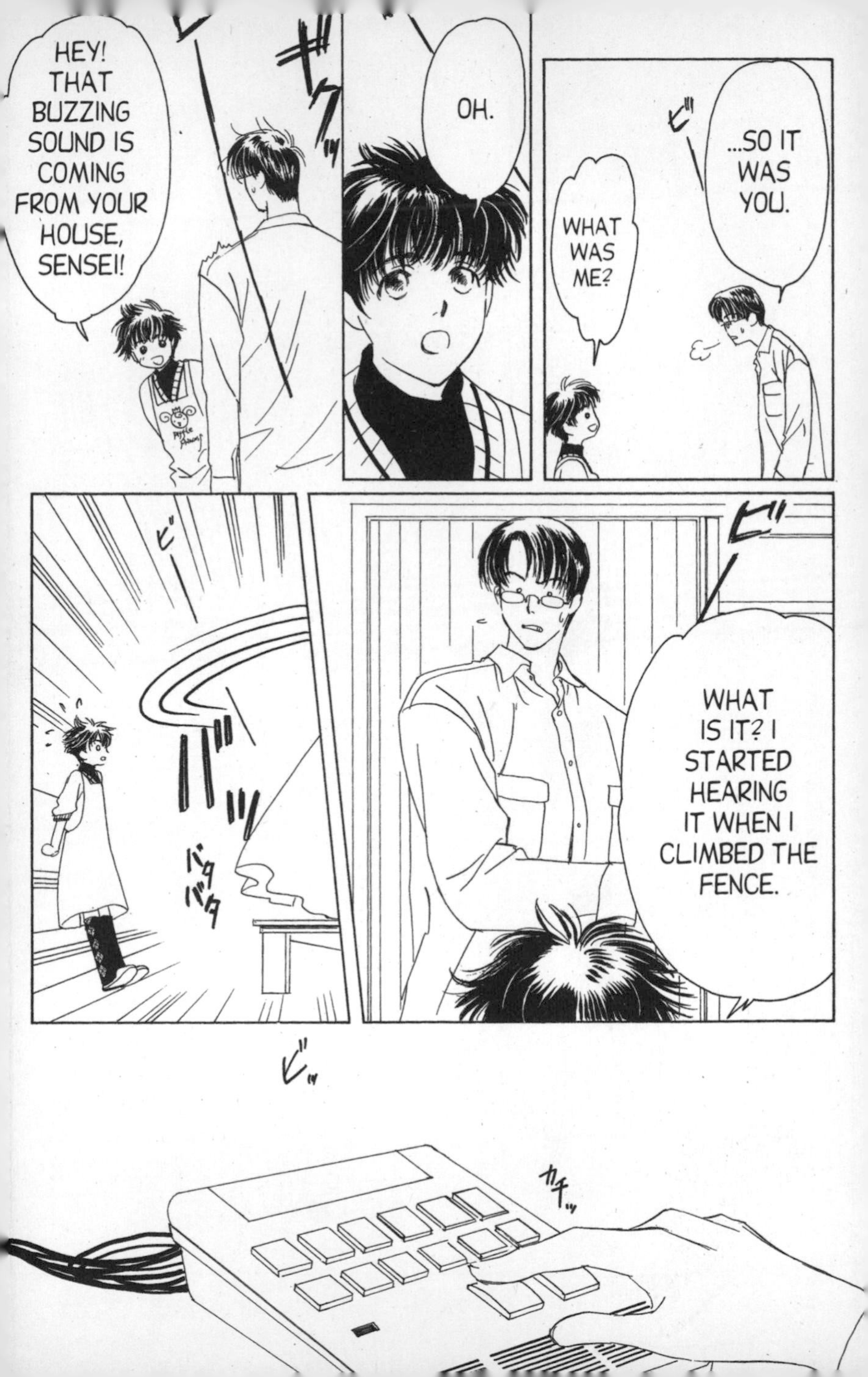
...SO IT WAS YOU.
WHAT WAS ME?
OH.
HEY! THAT BUZZING SOUND IS COMING FROM YOUR HOUSE, SENSEI!
WHAT IS IT? I STARTED HEARING IT WHEN I CLIMBED THE FENCE.
バタバタ
カチッ

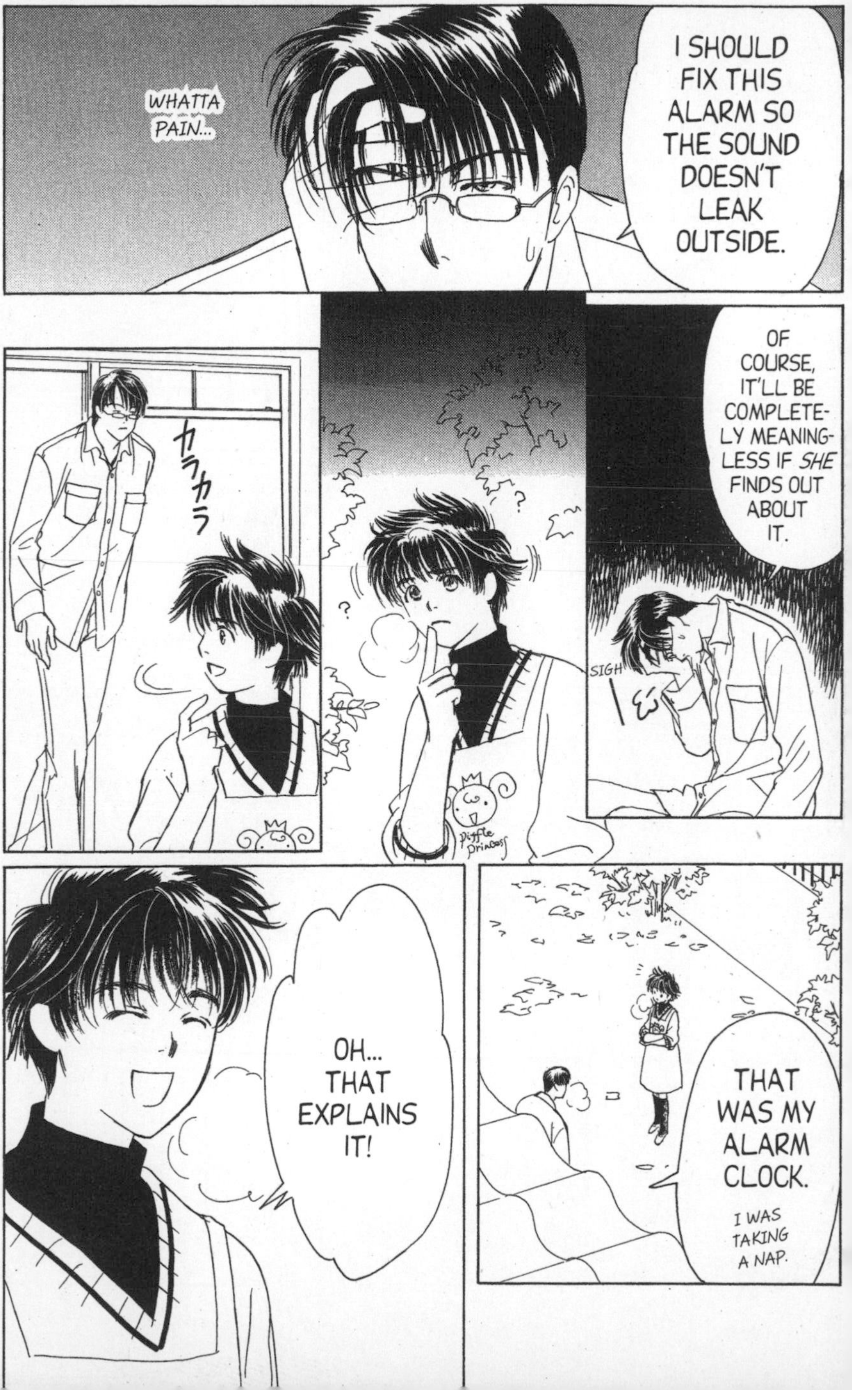
I SHOULD FIX THIS ALARM SO THE SOUND DOESN'T LEAK OUTSIDE.
WHATTA PAIN...
OF COURSE, IT'LL BE COMPLETELY MEANINGLESS IF *SHE* FINDS OUT ABOUT IT.
SIGH
?
?
Piffle Princess
カラカラ
THAT WAS MY ALARM CLOCK.
I WAS TAKING A NAP.
OH... THAT EXPLAINS IT!

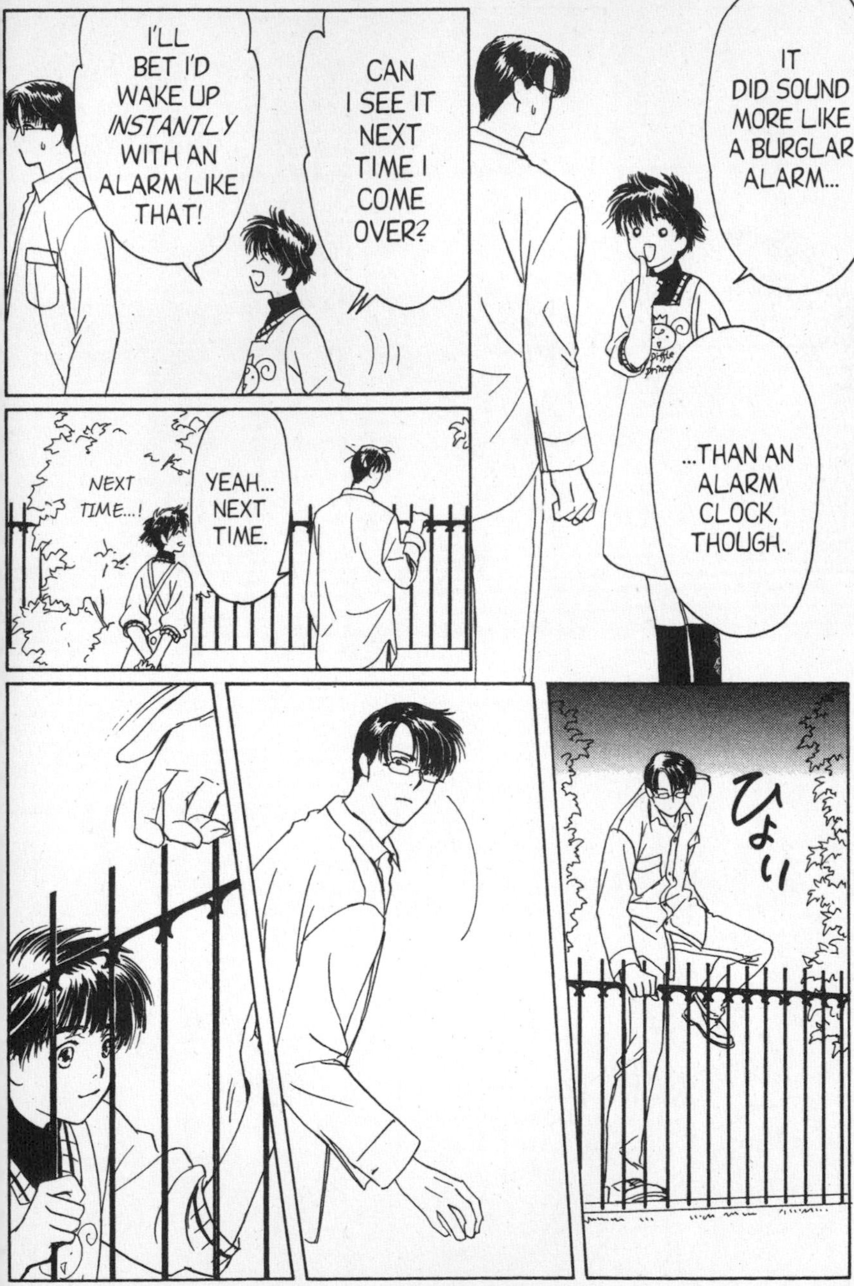
IT DID SOUND MORE LIKE A BURGLAR ALARM...
...THAN AN ALARM CLOCK, THOUGH.
CAN I SEE IT NEXT TIME I COME OVER?
I'LL BET I'D WAKE UP *INSTANTLY* WITH AN ALARM LIKE THAT!
YEAH... NEXT TIME.
NEXT TIME...!
ひょい

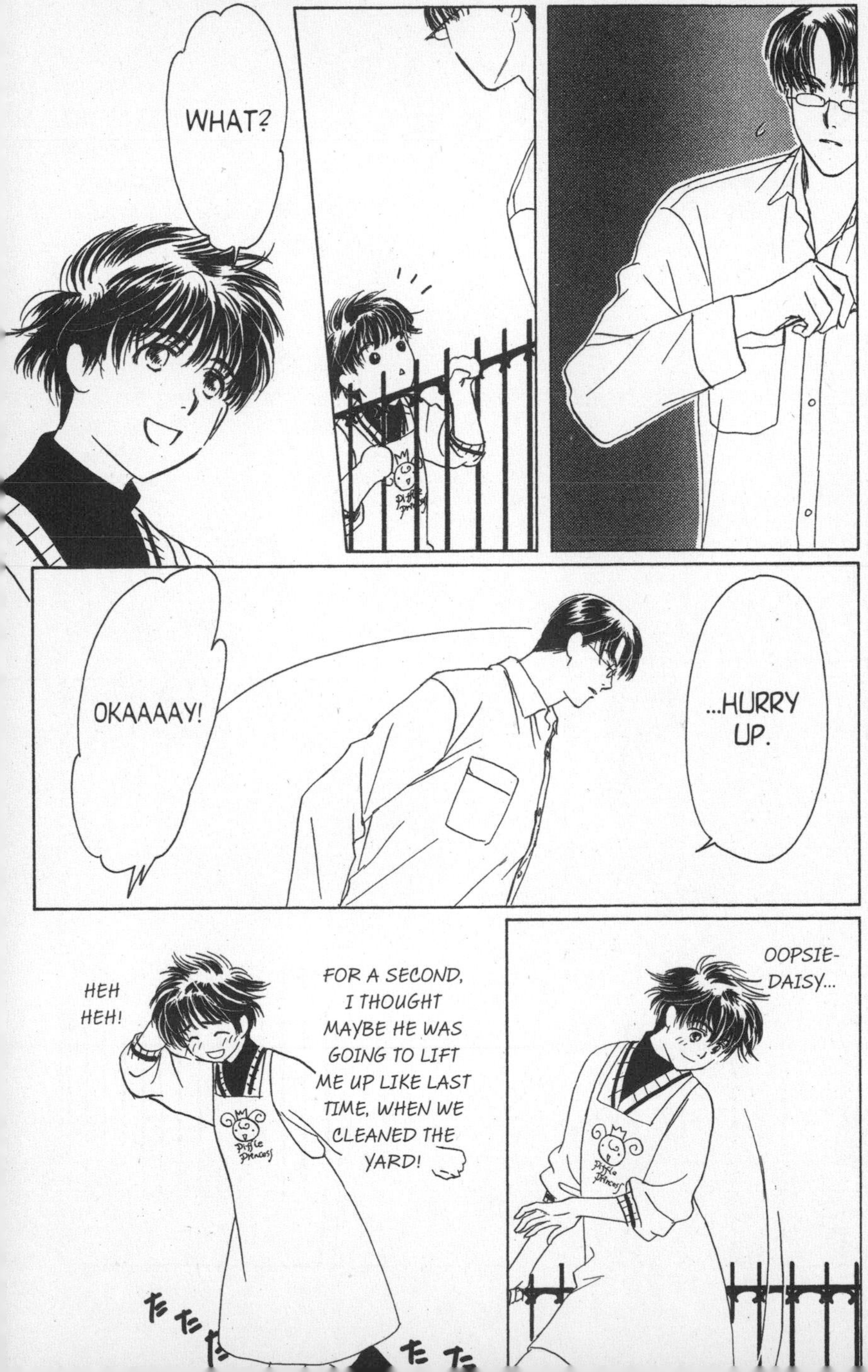
WHAT?
...HURRY UP.
OKAAAAY!
OOPSIE-DAISY...
FOR A SECOND, I THOUGHT MAYBE HE WAS GOING TO LIFT ME UP LIKE LAST TIME, WHEN WE CLEANED THE YARD!
HEH HEH!
たたた
たた

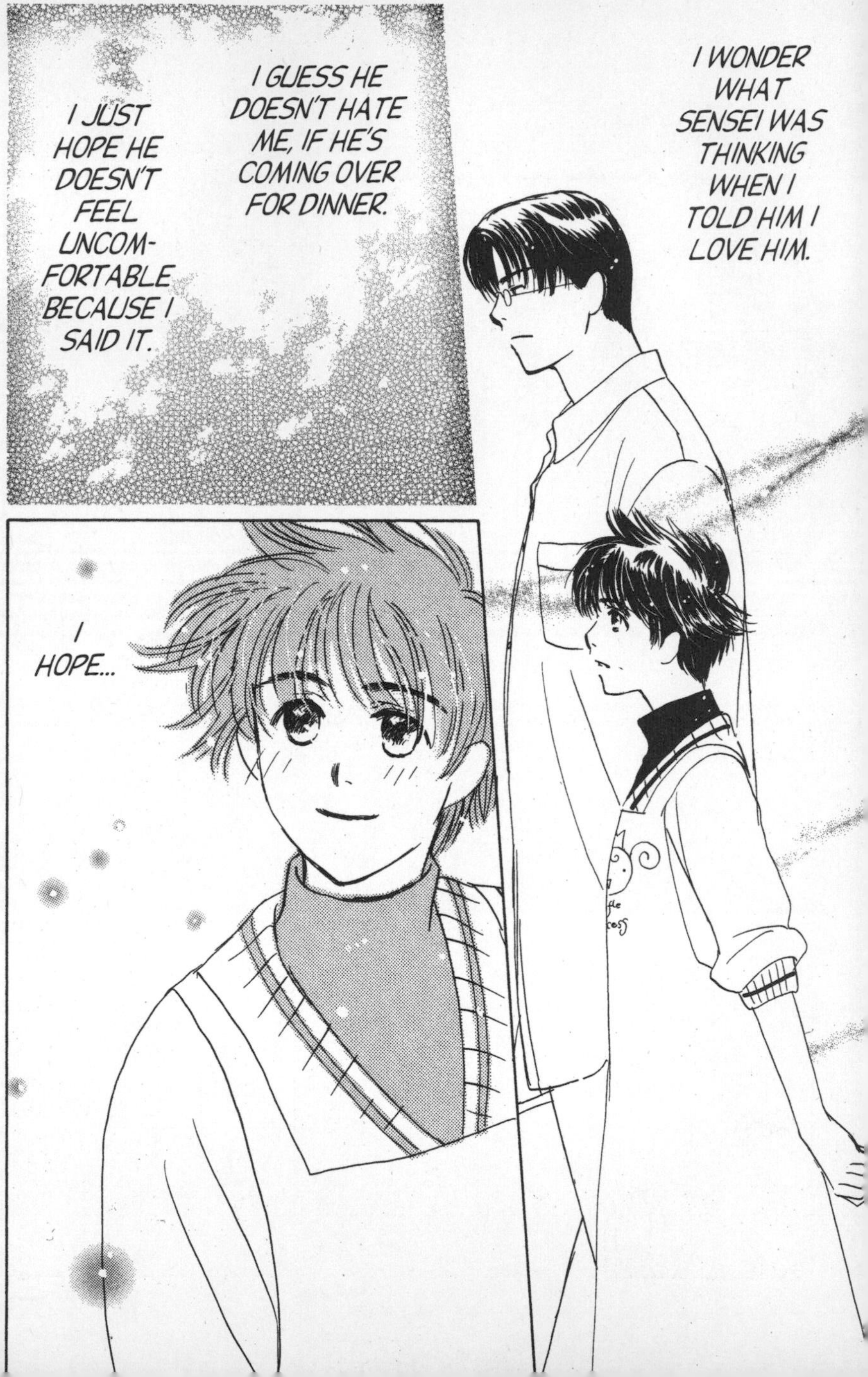
I WONDER WHAT SENSEI WAS THINKING WHEN I TOLD HIM I LOVE HIM.
I GUESS HE DOESN'T HATE ME, IF HE'S COMING OVER FOR DINNER.
I JUST HOPE HE DOESN'T FEEL UNCOM-FORTABLE BECAUSE I SAID IT.
I HOPE...

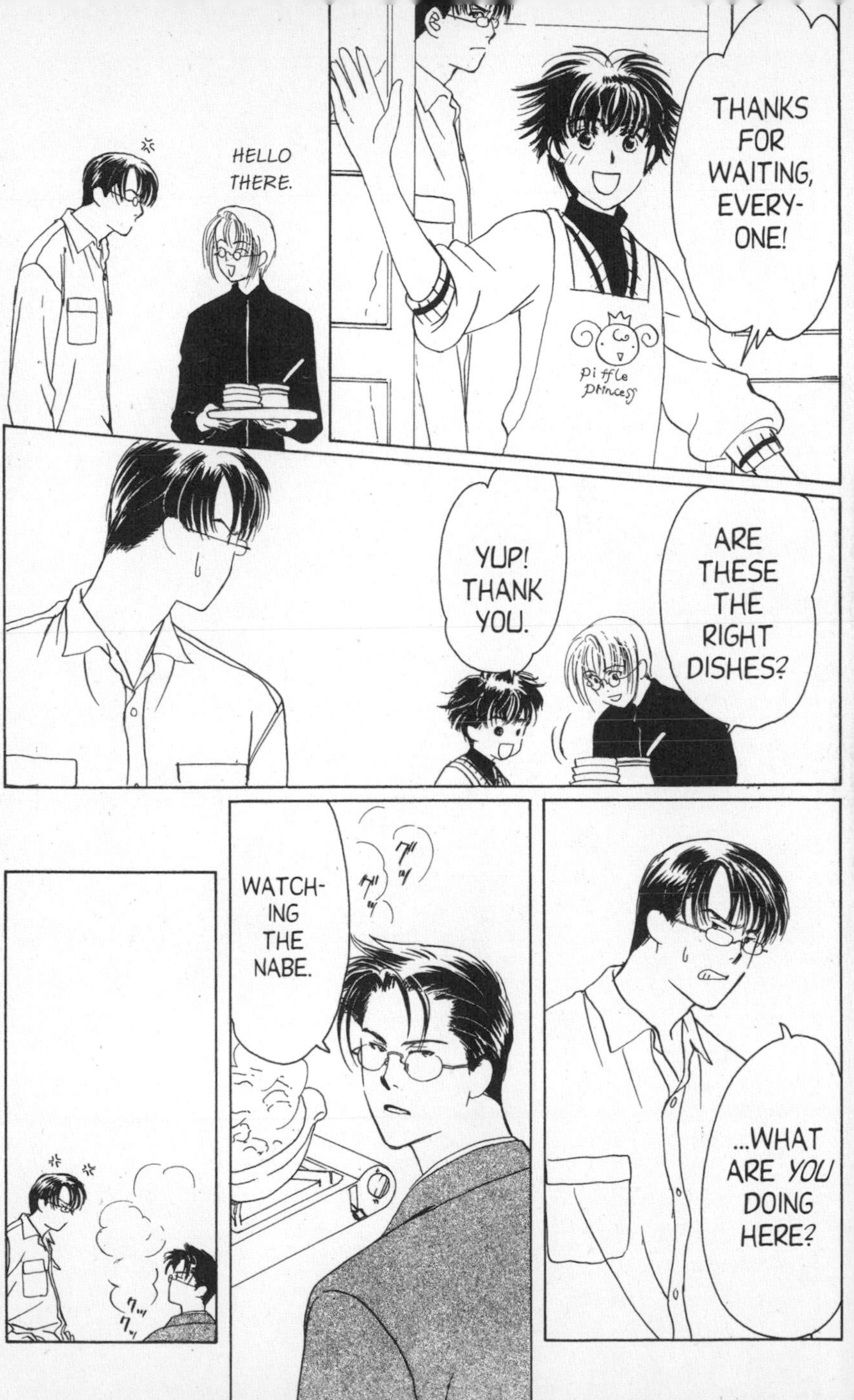
THANKS FOR WAITING, EVERY-ONE!
piffle princess
HELLO THERE.
ARE THESE THE RIGHT DISHES?
YUP! THANK YOU.
...WHAT ARE YOU DOING HERE?
WATCHING THE NABE.

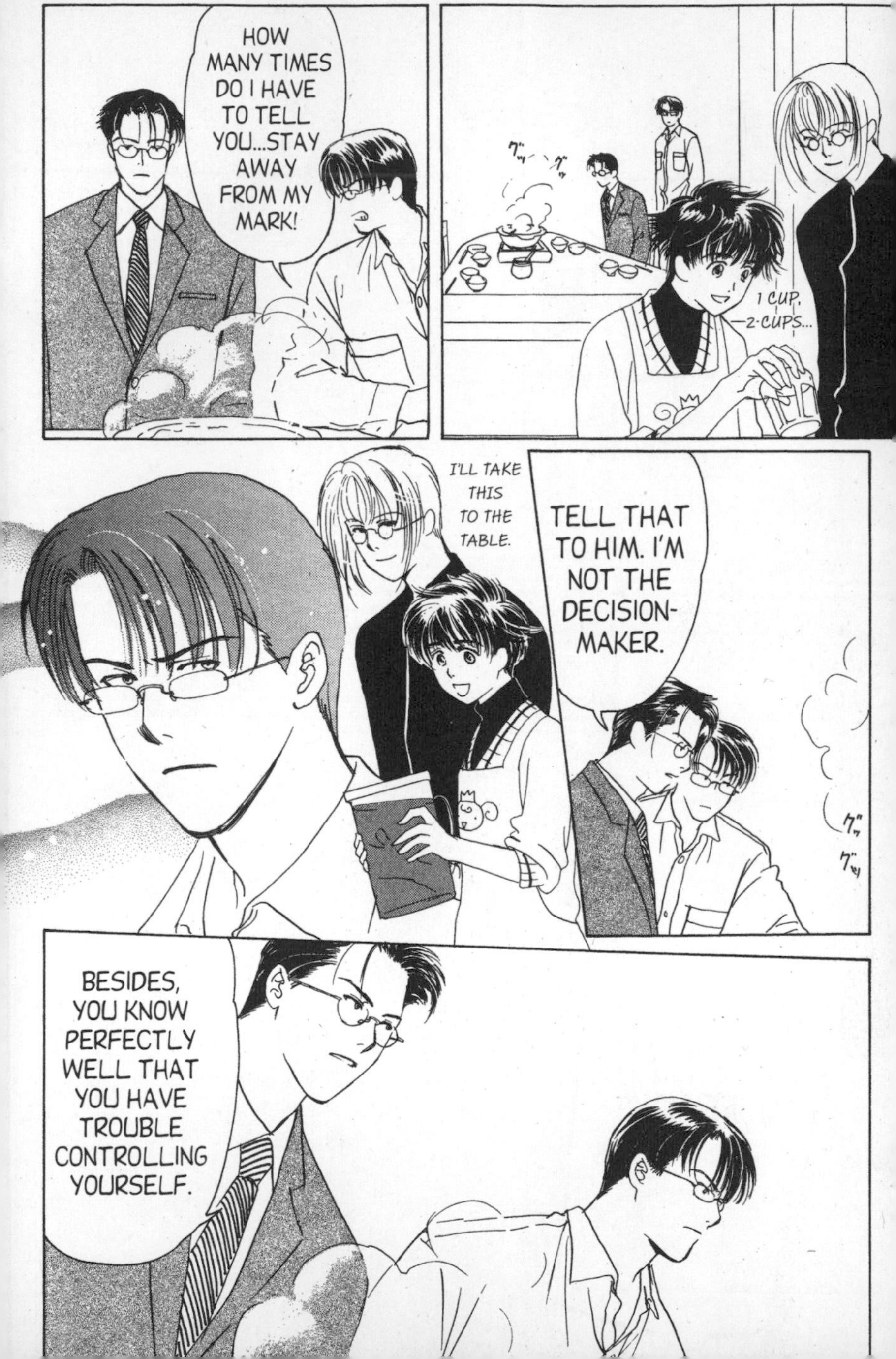
グッ グッ
1 CUP, 2-CUPS...
HOW MANY TIMES DO I HAVE TO TELL YOU...STAY AWAY FROM MY MARK!
グッ グッ
TELL THAT TO HIM. I'M NOT THE DECISION-MAKER.
I'LL TAKE THIS TO THE TABLE.
BESIDES, YOU KNOW PERFECTLY WELL THAT YOU HAVE TROUBLE CONTROLLING YOURSELF.

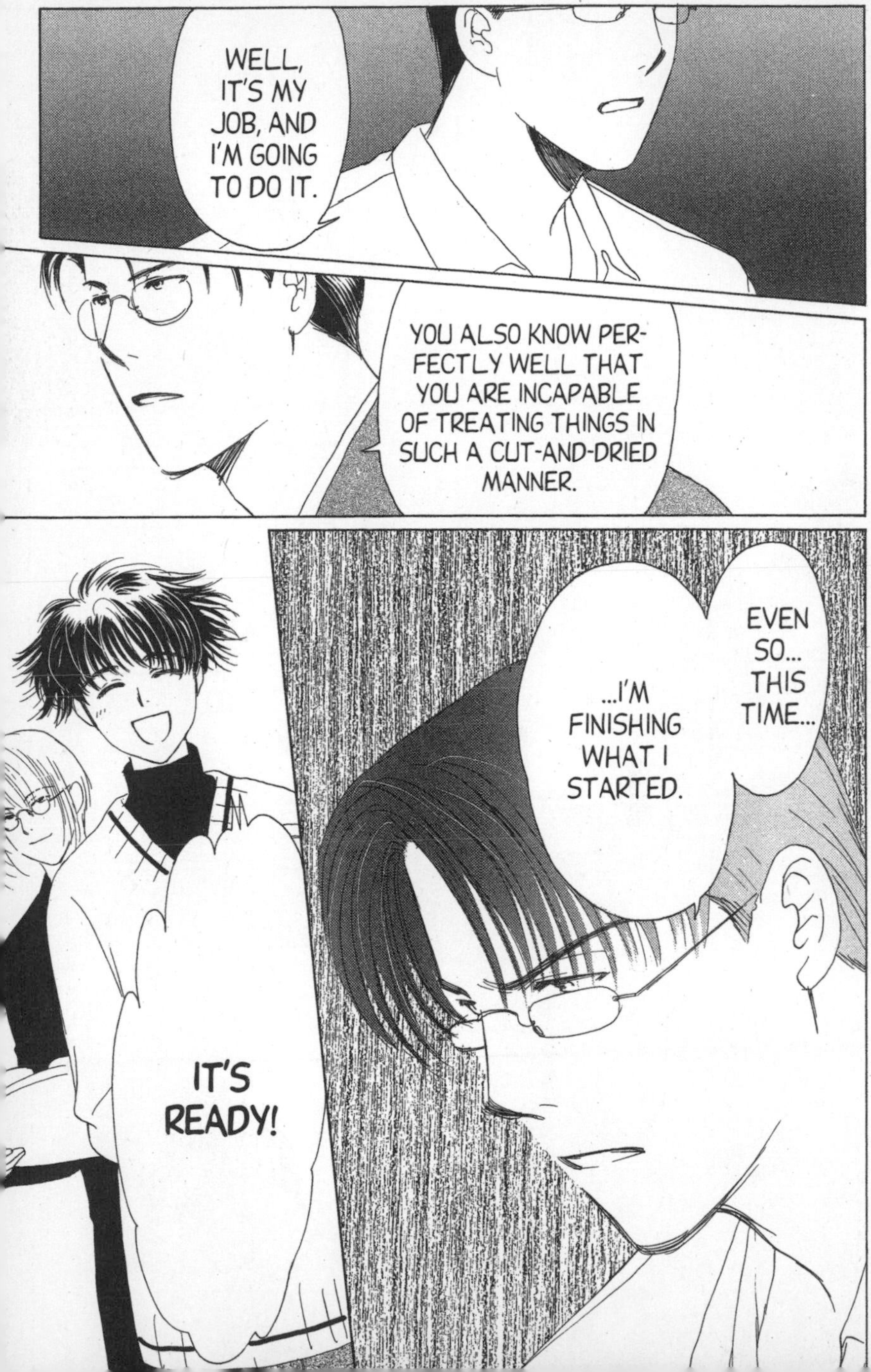
WELL, IT'S MY JOB, AND I'M GOING TO DO IT.
YOU ALSO KNOW PERFECTLY WELL THAT YOU ARE INCAPABLE OF TREATING THINGS IN SUCH A CUT-AND-DRIED MANNER.
EVEN SO... THIS TIME...
...I'M FINISHING WHAT I STARTED.
IT'S READY!

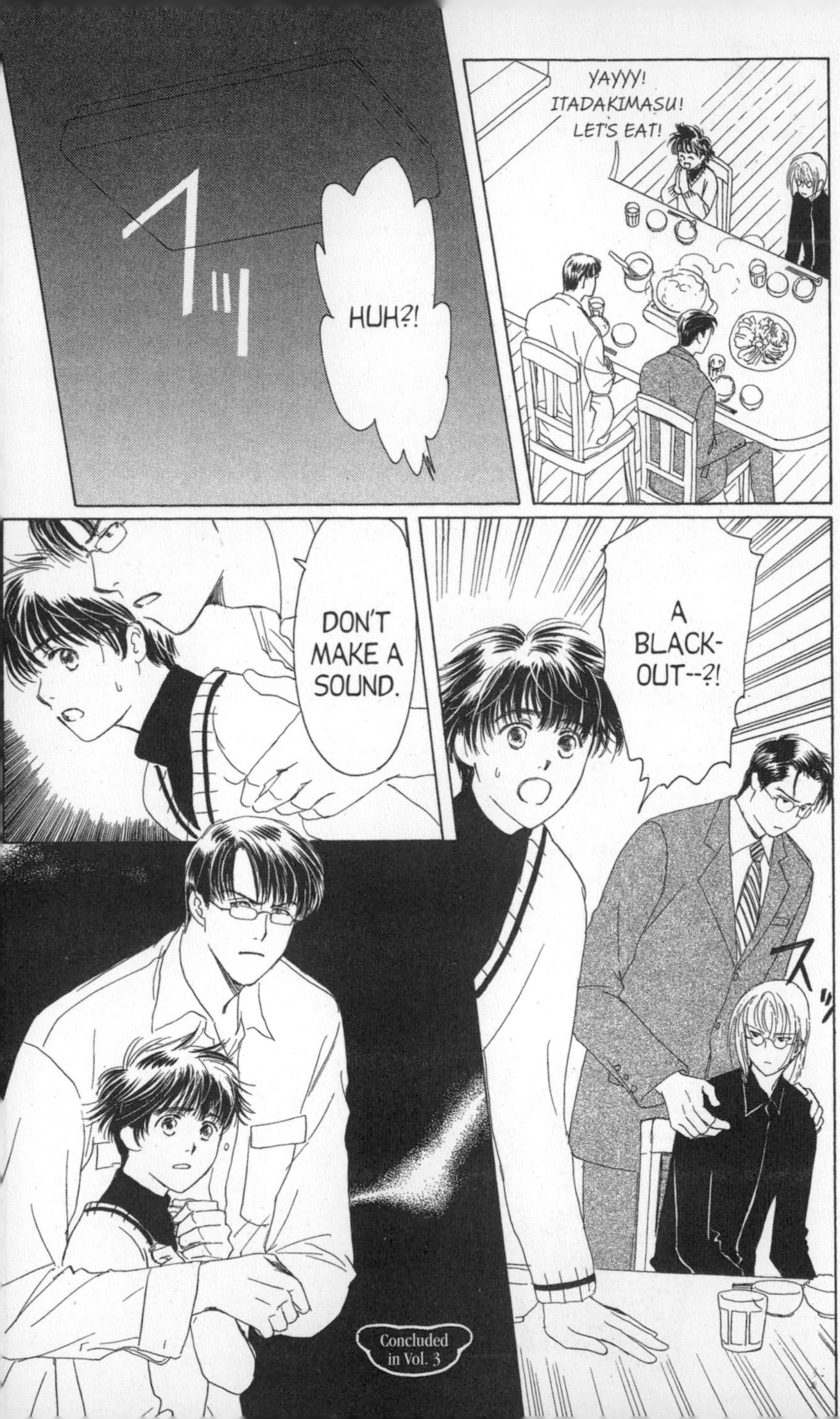
YAYYY! ITADAKIMASU! LET'S EAT!
HUH?!
A BLACK-OUT--?!
DON'T MAKE A SOUND.
Concluded in Vol. 3

HISTORY REPEATING

AS THE DAUGHTER
OF A WEALTHY BUSINESSMAN,
YOUNG HINA'S NO STRANGER
TO KIDNAPPING. WHILE HINA SEES
ONLY THE GOOD IN LIFE, THAT
DOESN'T MEAN BAD PEOPLE ARE
HIDING RIGHT UNDER HER NOSE.
WILL HINA'S NAIVETÉ LEAD
HER INTO DANGER?

SUKI VOL. 3 AVAILABLE JUNE 2004.

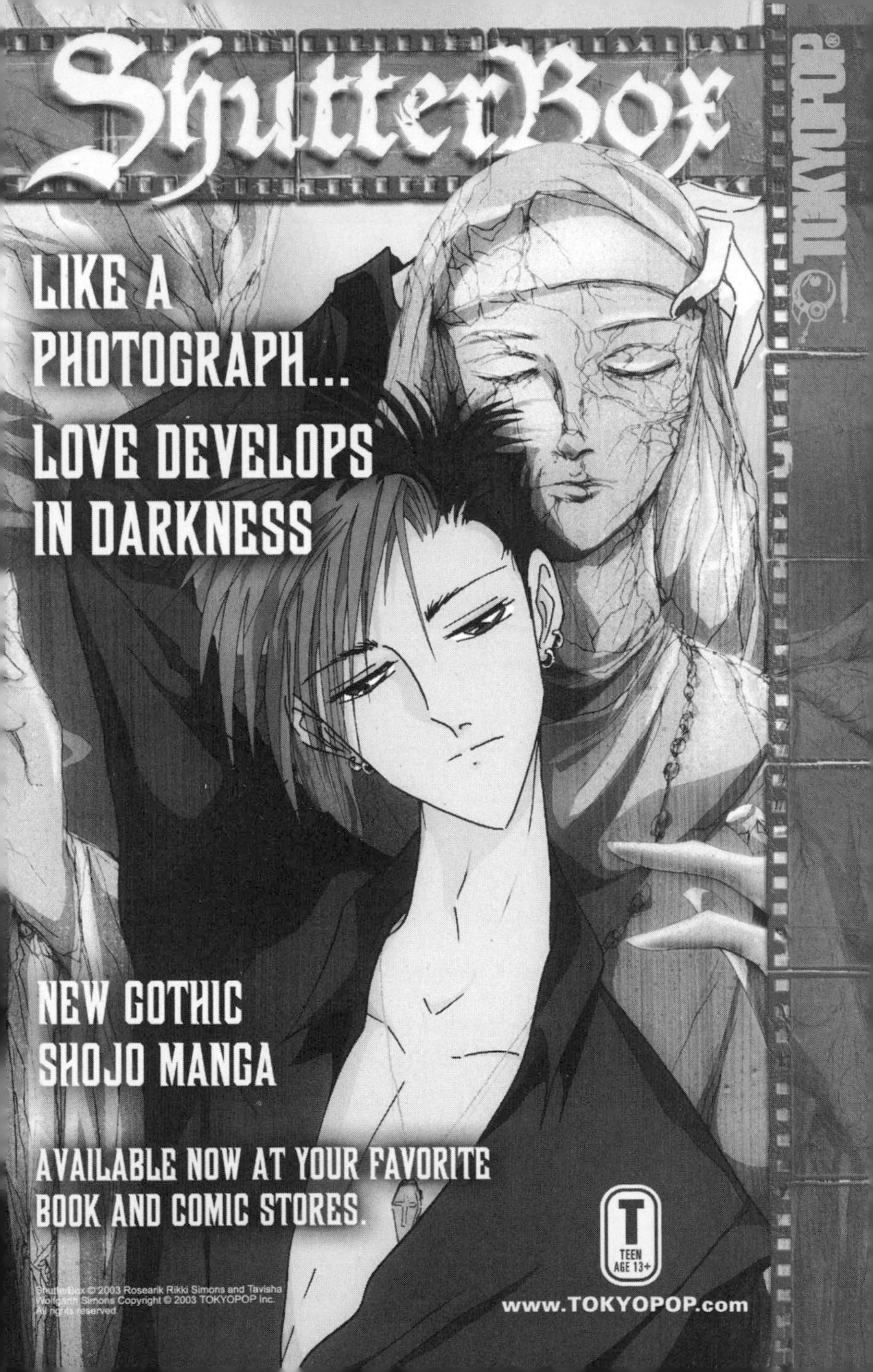
ShutterBox
TOKYOPOP
LIKE A PHOTOGRAPH...
LOVE DEVELOPS IN DARKNESS
NEW GOTHIC SHOJO MANGA
AVAILABLE NOW AT YOUR FAVORITE BOOK AND COMIC STORES.
T TEEN AGE 13+
ShutterBox © 2003 Rosearik Rikki Simons and Tavisha Wolfgarth Simons Copyright © 2003 TOKYOPOP Inc. All rights reserved
www.TOKYOPOP.com

forbidden Dance

by Hinako Ashihara

Dancing was her life...

Her dance partner might be her future...

Available Now

When darkness is in your genes,
only love can steal it away.

TOKYOPOP®

D·N·ANGEL·

STOP!

This is the back of the book.
You wouldn't want to spoil a great ending!

This book is printed "manga-style," in the authentic Japanese right-to-left format. Since none of the artwork has been flipped or altered, readers get to experience the story just as the creator intended. You've been asking for it, so TOKYOPOP® delivered: authentic, hot-off-the-press, and far more fun!

DIRECTIONS

If this is your first time reading manga-style, here's a quick guide to help you understand how it works.

It's easy... just start in the top right panel and follow the numbers. Have fun, and look for more 100% authentic manga from TOKYOPOP®!